WRITER: **BRIAN MICHAEL BENDIS**

ISSUE #15
ARTIST: **SARA PICHELLI**
COLORIST: **JUSTIN PONSOR**
COVER: **DAVID LAFUENTE**
JUSTIN PONSOR

ISSUES #151-154
ARTISTS: **SARA PICHELLI**
WITH **DAVID LAFUENTE** (ISSUES #152-154),
LAN MEDINA & ED TADEO (ISSUE #153)
AND **ELENA CASAGRANDE** (ISSUE #154)
COLORIST: **JUSTIN PONSOR**
COVER ART: **DAVID LAFUENTE** &
JUSTIN PONSOR (ISSUE #151),
J. SCOTT CAMPBELL & JUSTIN PONSOR
(ISSUE #152), **ED MCGUINNESS** &
MORRY HOLLOWELL (ISSUE #153)
AND **STEVE MCNIVEN**
& **DEAN WHITE** (ISSUE #154)

ISSUE #...
SPID...THE RINGER:
DAV...LAFUENTE & JUSTIN PONSOR
CAR...VERS & THE ULTIMATES:
SARA...PICHELLI & JUSTIN PONSOR
SPID...ION MAN: **JOËLLE JONES,**
SUN...HO & SAKTI YUWONO OF IFS
SPID...APTAIN AMERICA:
JAM...MCKELVIE & MATTHEW WILSON
SPID...THOR: **SKOTTIE YOUNG**
& J...FRANCOIS BEAULIEU
COV...ART: **DAVID LAFUENTE**
& J...N PONSOR

ISSUE #155
ARTIST: **CHRIS SAMNEE**
COLORIST: **JUSTIN PONSOR**
COVER ART: **OLIVIER COIPEL,**
MARK MORALES & LAURA MARTIN

LETT...RTUAL CALLIGRAPHY'S CORY PETIT
COV...DAVID LAFUENTE & JUSTIN PONSOR
ASS...ANT EDITOR: **SANA AMANAT**   SENIOR EDITOR: **MARK PANICCIA**

COLLECTION EDITOR: **JENNIFER GRÜNWALD**
EDITORIAL ASSISTANTS: **JAMES EMMETT & JOE HOCHSTEIN**
ASSISTANT EDITORS: **ALEX STARBUCK & NELSON RIBEIRO**
EDITOR, SPECIAL PROJECTS: **MARK D. BEAZLEY**
SENIOR EDITOR, SPECIAL PROJECTS: **JEFF YOUNGQUIST**
SENIOR VICE PRESIDENT OF SALES: **DAVID GABRIEL**
SVP OF BRAND PLANNING & COMMUNICATIONS: **MICHAEL PASCIULLO**
BOOK DESIGNER: **RODOLFO MURAGUCHI**

EDITOR IN CHIEF: **AXEL ALONSO** CHIEF CREATIVE OFFICER: **JOE QUESADA**
PUBLISHER: **DAN BUCKLEY** EXECUTIVE PRODUCER: **ALAN FINE**

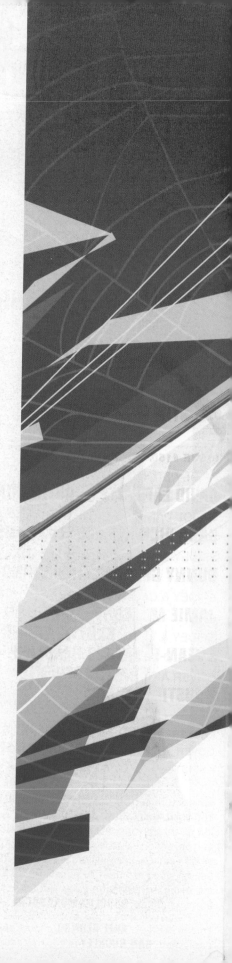

The bite of a genetically altered spider granted high
school student Peter Parker incredible arachnid-
like powers. When a burglar killed his beloved
Uncle Ben, a grief-stricken Peter vowed to use
his amazing abilities to protect his fellow man.
He learned the invaluable lesson that with great
power there must also come great responsibility.

Now the fledgling super hero tries to balance
a full high school curriculum, a part-time job, a
relationship with Gwen Stacy and swing time as
the misunderstood, web-slinging Spider-Man!

PREVIOUSLY IN ULTIMATE SPIDER-MAN:

Spider-Man is now living with Johnny Storm,
a.k.a. the Human Torch, and Bobby Drake, a.k.a.
Iceman. Both have disguised themselves as his
cousins and are going to school like normal kids.

A chameleon-like imposter overpowers Peter and takes
his place in Peter's life. The phony Peter wreaks havoc
on Peter's personal life, playing with the emotions
of both Gwen Stacy and MJ. Fake Peter finally finds
out who Peter Parker really is and uses his identity as
Spider-Man to carry on a crime wave through the city.

The Human Torch and Iceman eventually rescue Peter
but the damage is done.

ULTIMATE COMICS SPIDER-MAN VOL. 3: DEATH OF SPIDER-MAN PRELUDE. Contains material originally published in magazine form as ULTIMATE COMICS SPIDER-MAN #15 and #150-155. First printing 2011. ISBN# 978-0-7851-4640-7. Published by MARVEL WORLDWIDE, INC., a subsidiary of MARVEL ENTERTAINMENT, LLC. OFFICE OF PUBLICATION: 135 West 50th Street, New York, NY 10020. Copyright © 2010 and 2011 Marvel Characters, Inc. All rights reserved. $19.99 per copy in the U.S. and $21.99 in Canada (GST #R127032852); Canadian Agreement #40668537. All characters featured in this issue and the distinctive names and likenesses thereof, and all related indicia are trademarks of Marvel Characters, Inc. No similarity between any of the names, characters, persons, and/or institutions in this magazine with those of any living or dead person or institution is intended, and any such similarity which may exist is purely coincidental. **Printed in the U.S.A.** ALAN FINE, EVP - Office of the President, Marvel Worldwide, Inc. and EVP & CMO Marvel Characters B.V.; DAN BUCKLEY, Publisher & President - Print, Animation & Digital Divisions; JOE QUESADA, Chief Creative Officer; DAVID BOGART, SVP of Business Affairs & Talent Management; TOM BREVOORT, SVP of Publishing; C.B. CEBULSKI, SVP of Creator & Content Development; DAVID GABRIEL, SVP of Publishing Sales & Circulation; MICHAEL PASCIULLO, SVP of Brand Planning & Communications; JIM O'KEEFE, VP of Operations & Logistics; DAN CARR, Executive Director of Publishing Technology; SUSAN CRESPI, Editorial Operations Manager; ALEX MORALES, Publishing Operations Manager; STAN LEE, Chairman Emeritus. For information regarding advertising in Marvel Comics or on Marvel.com, please contact John Dokes, SVP Integrated Sales and Marketing, at jdokes@marvel.com. For Marvel subscription inquiries, please call 800-217-9158. **Manufactured between 11/9/2011 and 12/5/2011 by R.R. DONNELLEY, INC., SALEM, VA, USA.**

10 9 8 7 6 5 4 3 2 1

15

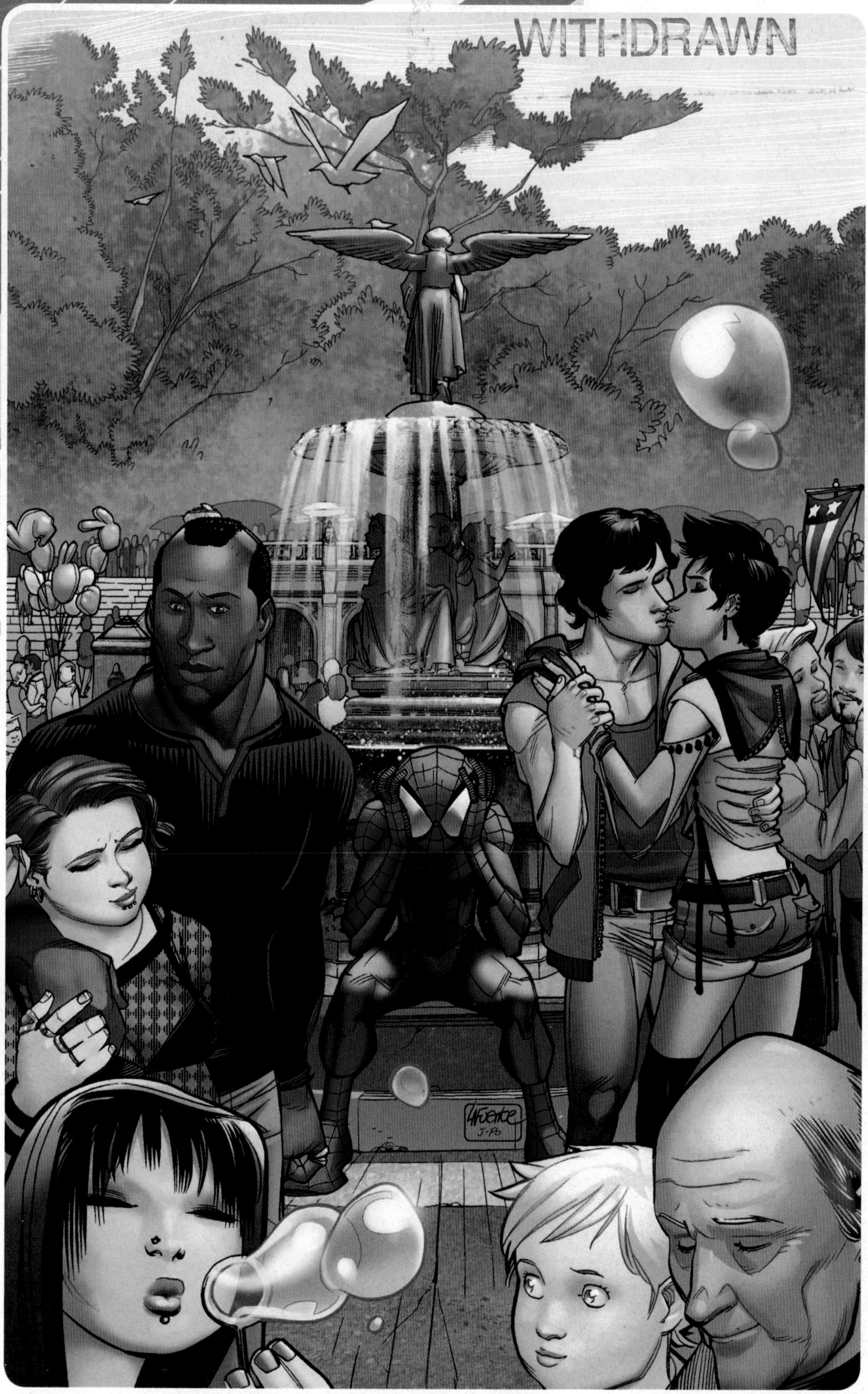
WITHDRAWN

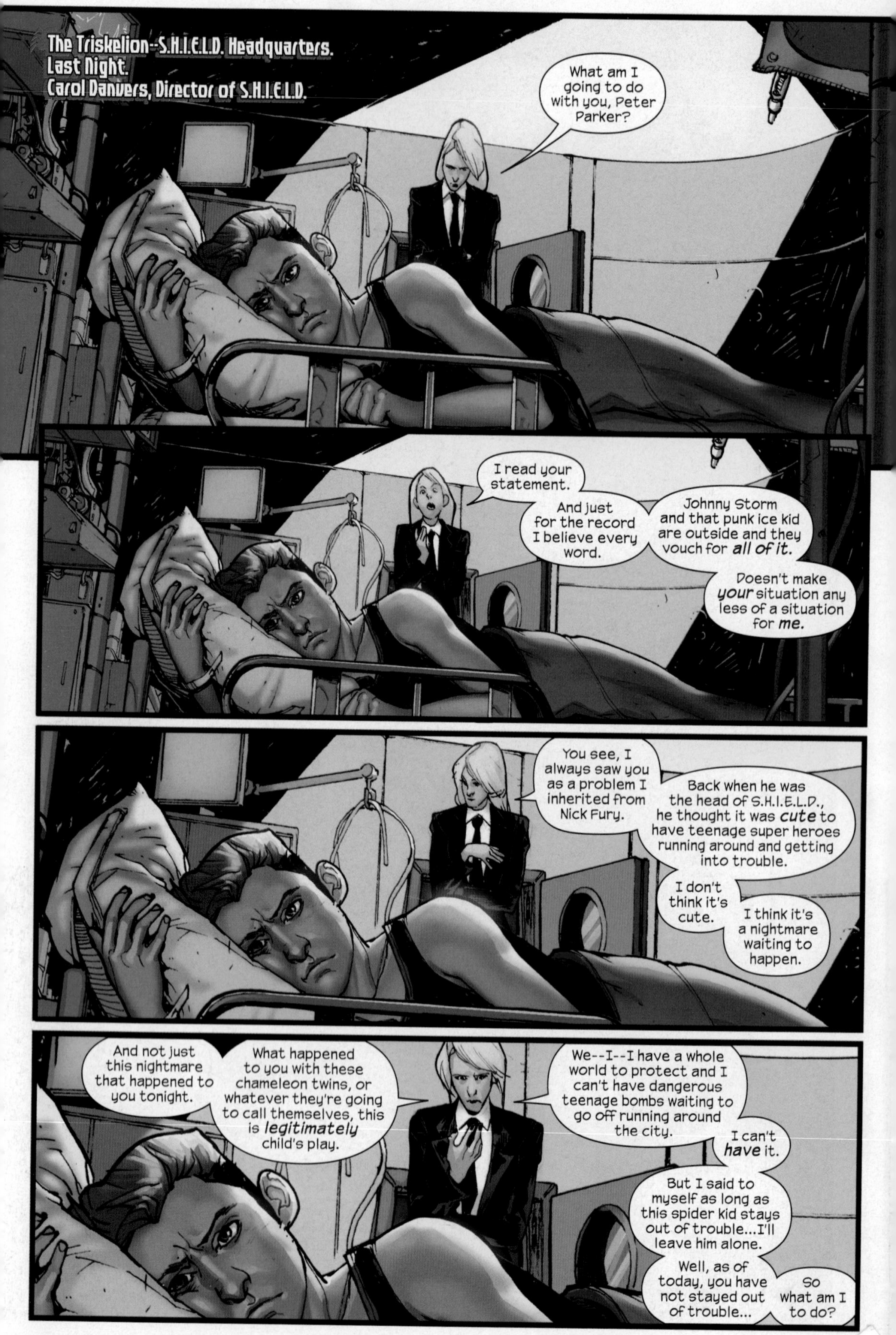
The Triskelion--S.H.I.E.L.D. Headquarters.
Last Night.
Carol Danvers, Director of S.H.I.E.L.D.
What am I going to do with you, Peter Parker?
I read your statement.
And just for the record I believe every word.
Johnny Storm and that punk ice kid are outside and they vouch for all of it.
Doesn't make your situation any less of a situation for me.
You see, I always saw you as a problem I inherited from Nick Fury.
Back when he was the head of S.H.I.E.L.D., he thought it was cute to have teenage super heroes running around and getting into trouble.
I don't think it's cute.
I think it's a nightmare waiting to happen.
And not just this nightmare that happened to you tonight.
What happened to you with these chameleon twins, or whatever they're going to call themselves, this is legitimately child's play.
We--I--I have a whole world to protect and I can't have dangerous teenage bombs waiting to go off running around the city.
I can't have it.
But I said to myself as long as this spider kid stays out of trouble...I'll leave him alone.
Well, as of today, you have not stayed out of trouble...
So what am I to do?

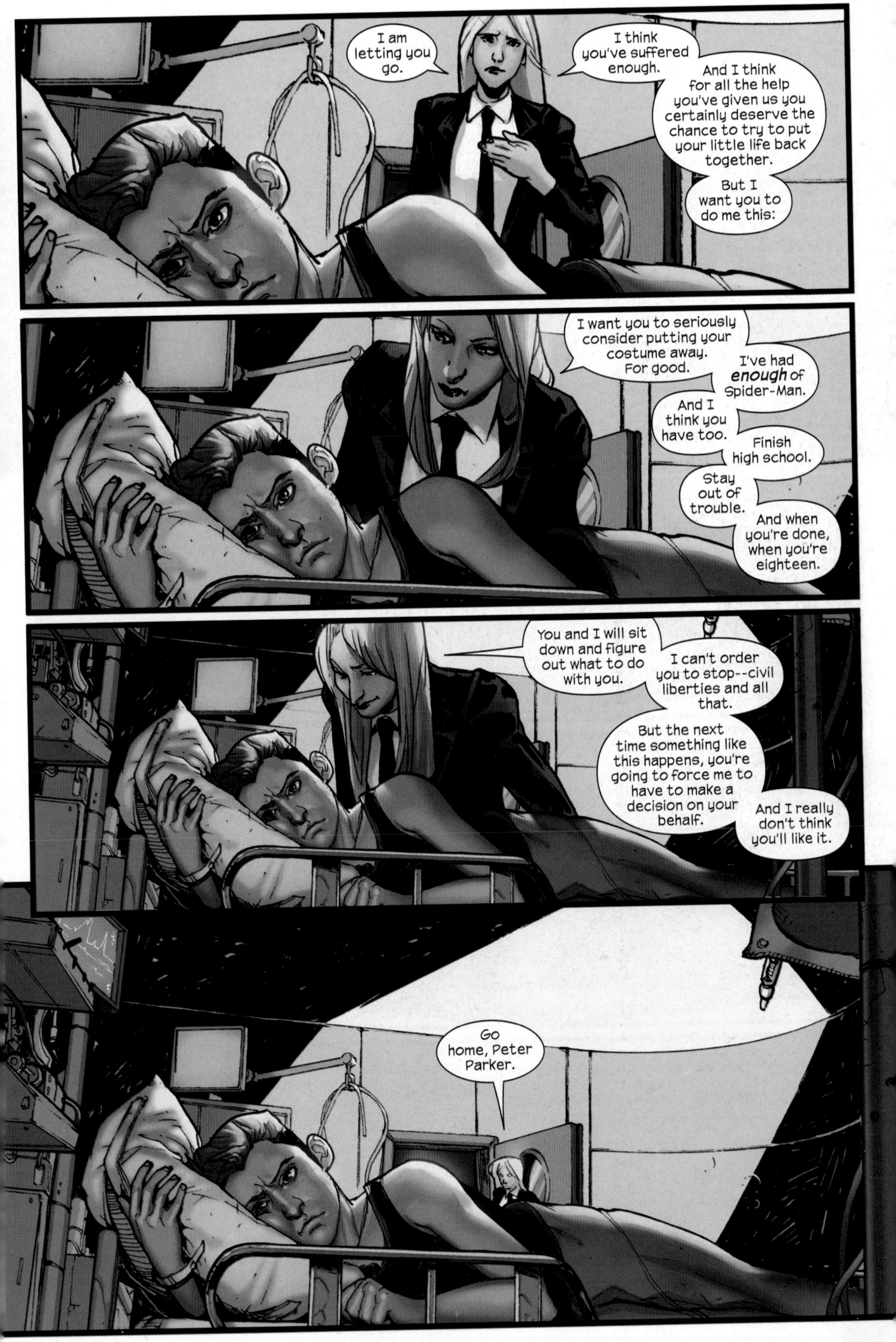

I am letting you go.
I think you've suffered enough.
And I think for all the help you've given us you certainly deserve the chance to try to put your little life back together.
But I want you to do me this:
I want you to seriously consider putting your costume away. For good.
I've had *enough* of Spider-Man.
And I think you have too.
Finish high school.
Stay out of trouble.
And when you're done, when you're eighteen.
You and I will sit down and figure out what to do with you.
I can't order you to stop--civil liberties and all that.
But the next time something like this happens, you're going to force me to have to make a decision on your behalf.
And I really don't think you'll like it.
Go home, Peter Parker.

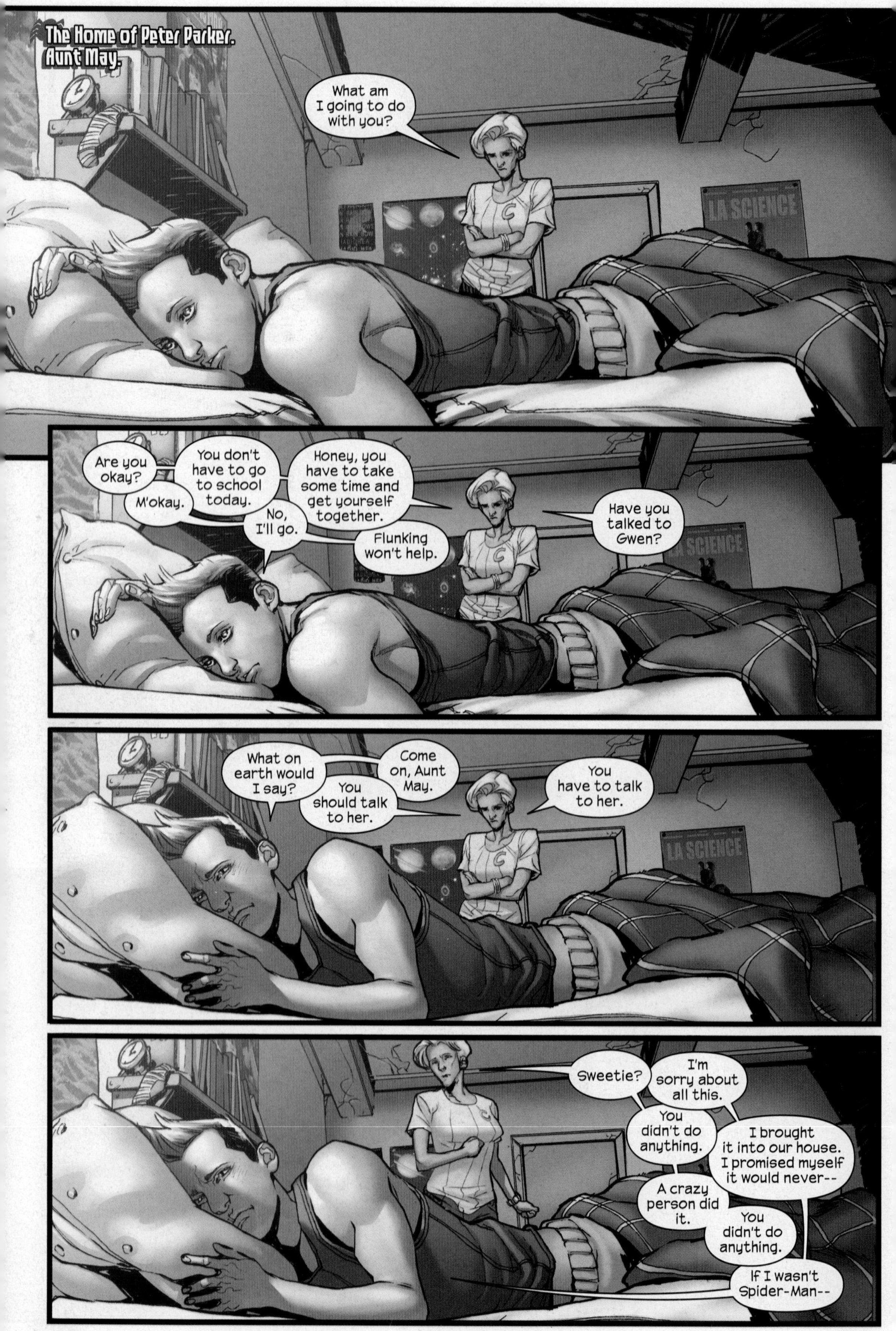

The Home of Peter Parker.
Aunt May.
What am I going to do with you?
Are you okay?
You don't have to go to school today.
Honey, you have to take some time and get yourself together.
M'okay.
No, I'll go.
Flunking won't help.
Have you talked to Gwen?
What on earth would I say?
Come on, Aunt May.
You should talk to her.
You have to talk to her.
Sweetie?
I'm sorry about all this.
You didn't do anything.
I brought it into our house. I promised myself it would never--
A crazy person did it.
You didn't do anything.
If I wasn't Spider-Man--

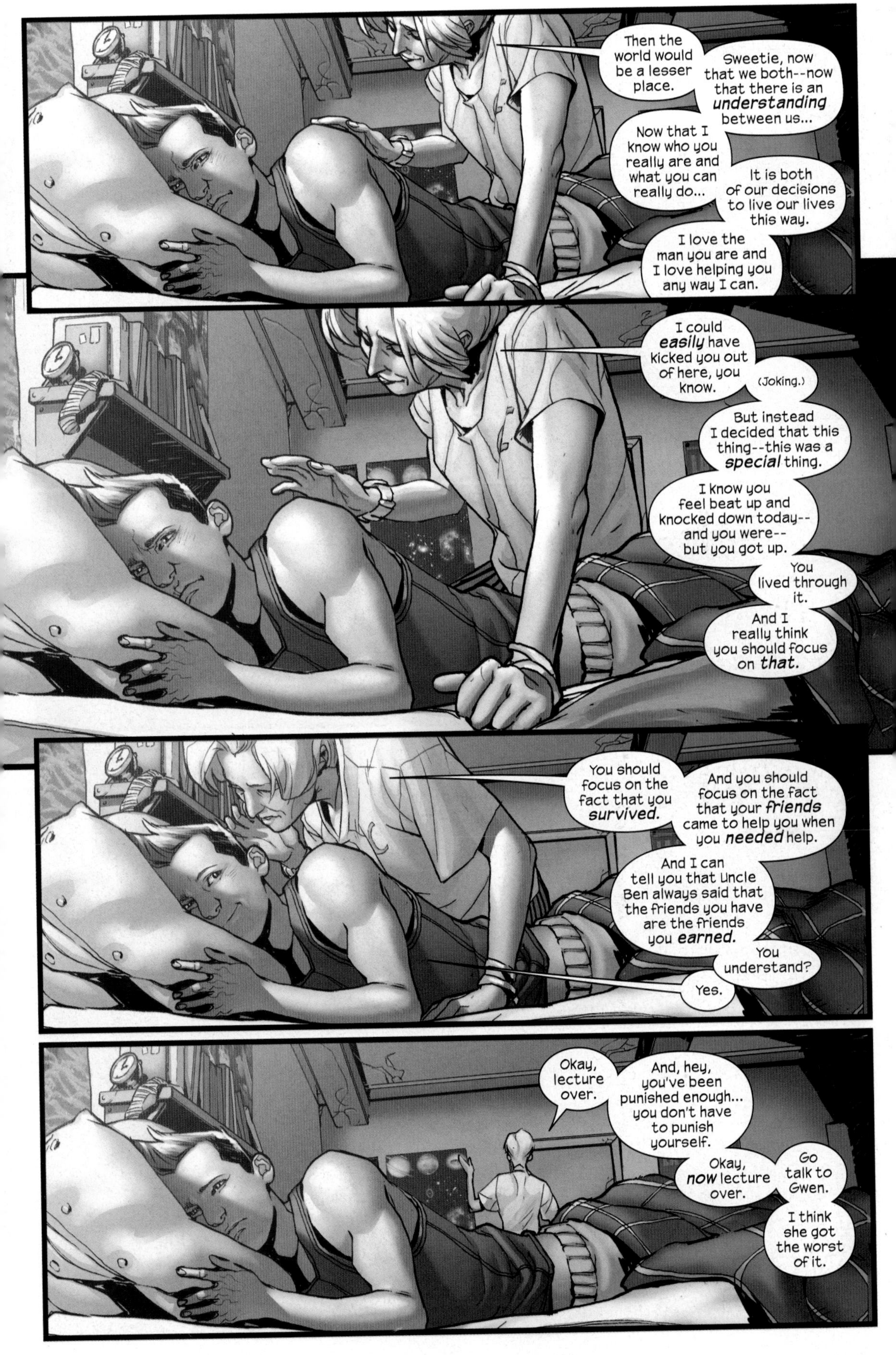
Then the world would be a lesser place.
Sweetie, now that we both--now that there is an *understanding* between us...
Now that I know who you really are and what you can really do...
It is both of our decisions to live our lives this way.
I love the man you are and I love helping you any way I can.
I could *easily* have kicked you out of here, you know.
(Joking.)
But instead I decided that this thing--this was a *special* thing.
I know you feel beat up and knocked down today--and you were--but you got up.
You lived through it.
And I really think you should focus on *that.*
You should focus on the fact that you *survived.*
And you should focus on the fact that your *friends* came to help you when you *needed* help.
And I can tell you that Uncle Ben always said that the friends you have are the friends you *earned.*
You understand?
Yes.
Okay, lecture over.
And, hey, you've been punished enough... you don't have to punish yourself.
Okay, *now* lecture over.
Go talk to Gwen.
I think she got the worst of it.

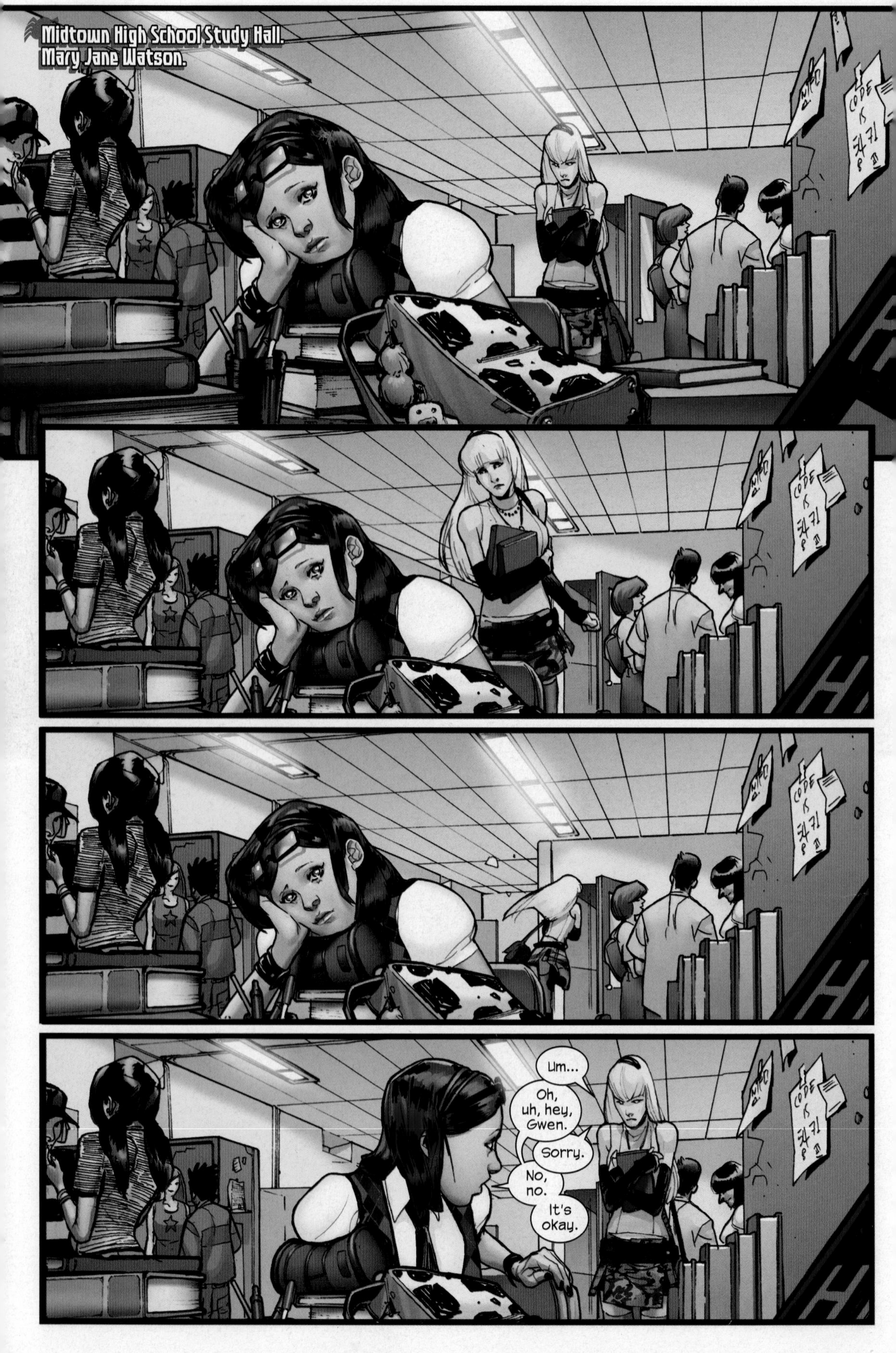
Midtown High School Study Hall.
Mary Jane Watson.
Um...
Oh, uh, hey, Gwen.
Sorry.
No, no.
It's okay.

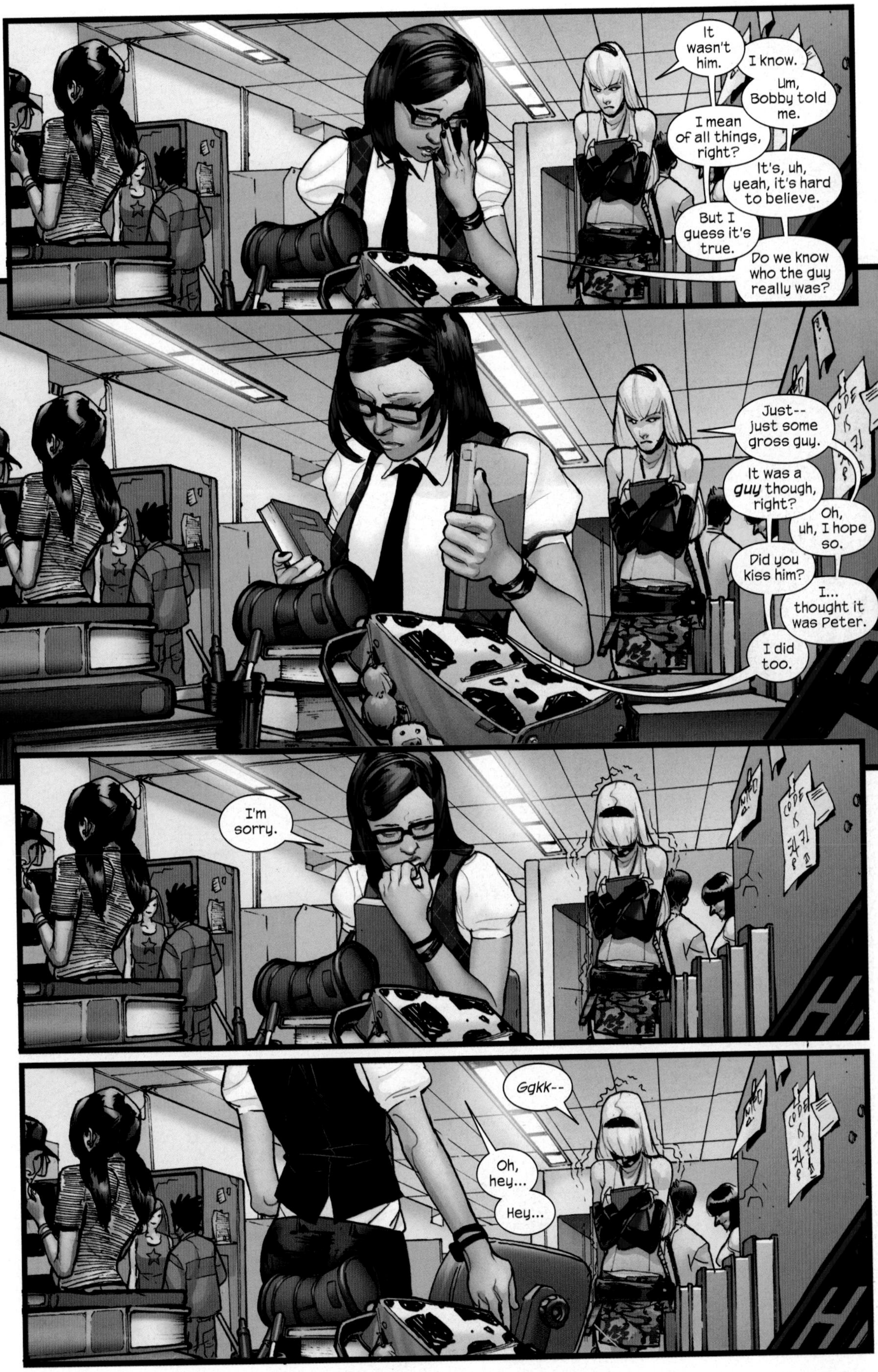
It wasn't him.
I know.
Um, Bobby told me.
I mean of all things, right?
It's, uh, yeah, it's hard to believe.
But I guess it's true.
Do we know who the guy really was?
Just-- just some gross guy.
It was a **guy** though, right?
Oh, uh, I hope so.
Did you kiss him?
I... thought it was Peter.
I did too.
I'm sorry.
Ggkk--
Oh, hey...
Hey...

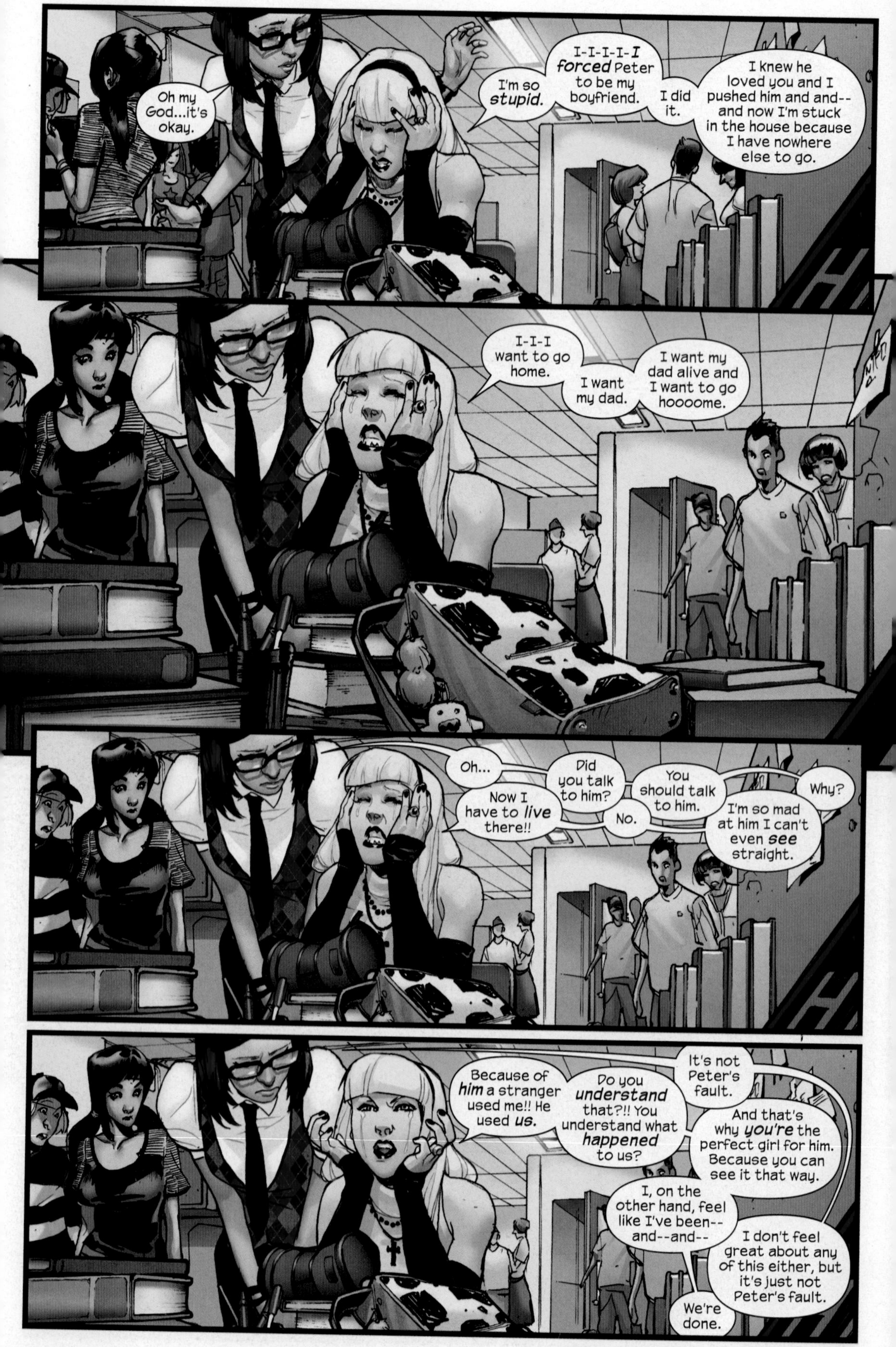
Oh my God...it's okay.
I'm so stupid.
I-I-I-I-I forced Peter to be my boyfriend.
I did it.
I knew he loved you and I pushed him and and-- and now I'm stuck in the house because I have nowhere else to go.
I-I-I want to go home.
I want my dad.
I want my dad alive and I want to go hoooome.
Oh...
Now I have to live there!!
Did you talk to him?
No.
You should talk to him.
Why?
I'm so mad at him I can't even see straight.
Because of him a stranger used me!! He used us.
Do you understand that?!! You understand what happened to us?
It's not Peter's fault.
And that's why you're the perfect girl for him. Because you can see it that way.
I, on the other hand, feel like I've been-- and--and--
I don't feel great about any of this either, but it's just not Peter's fault.
We're done.

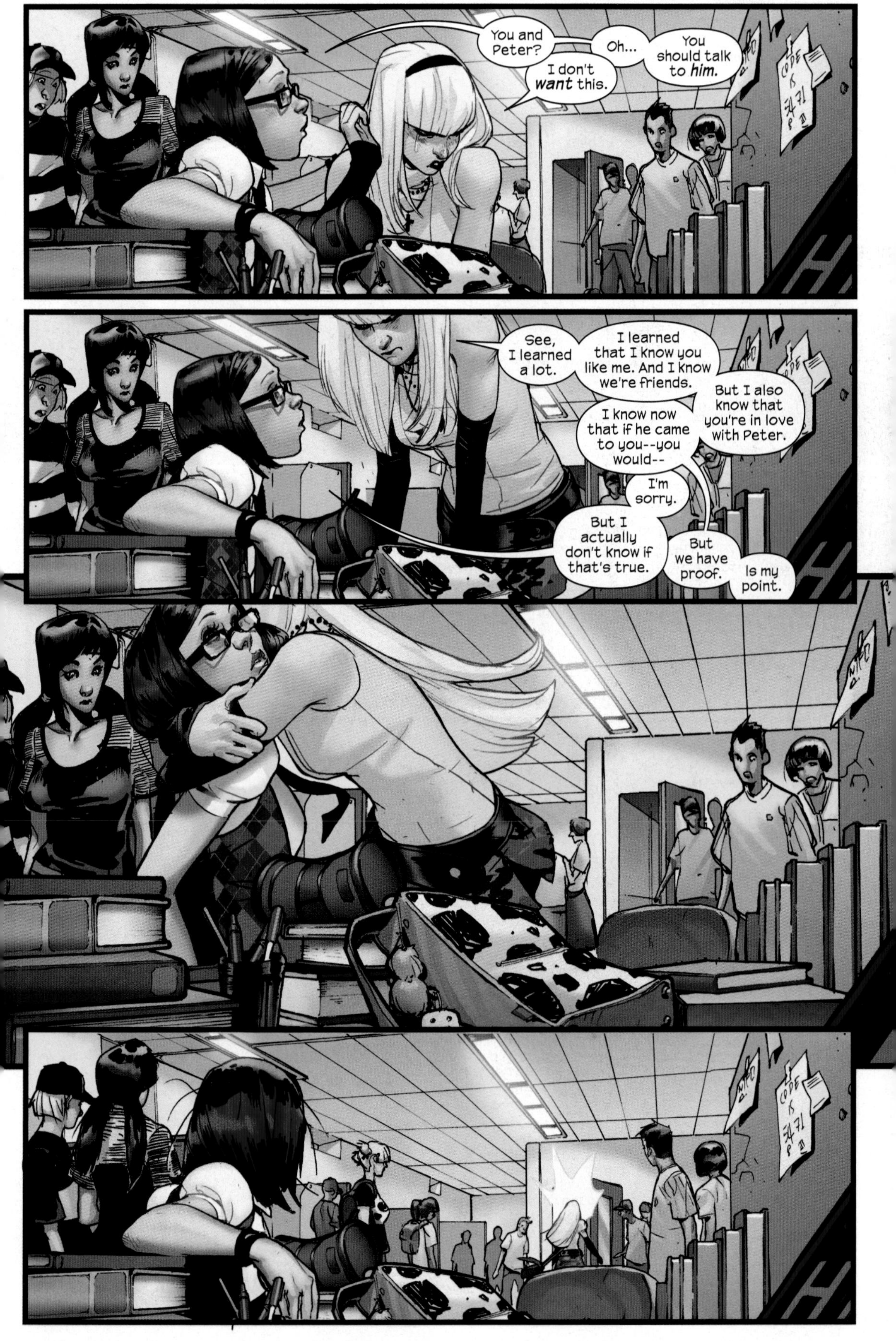
You and Peter?
I don't *want* this.
Oh...
You should talk to *him.*
CODE IS
See, I learned a lot.
I learned that I know you like me. And I know we're friends.
But I also know that you're in love with Peter.
I know now that if he came to you--you would--
I'm sorry.
But I actually don't know if that's true.
But we have proof.
Is my point.

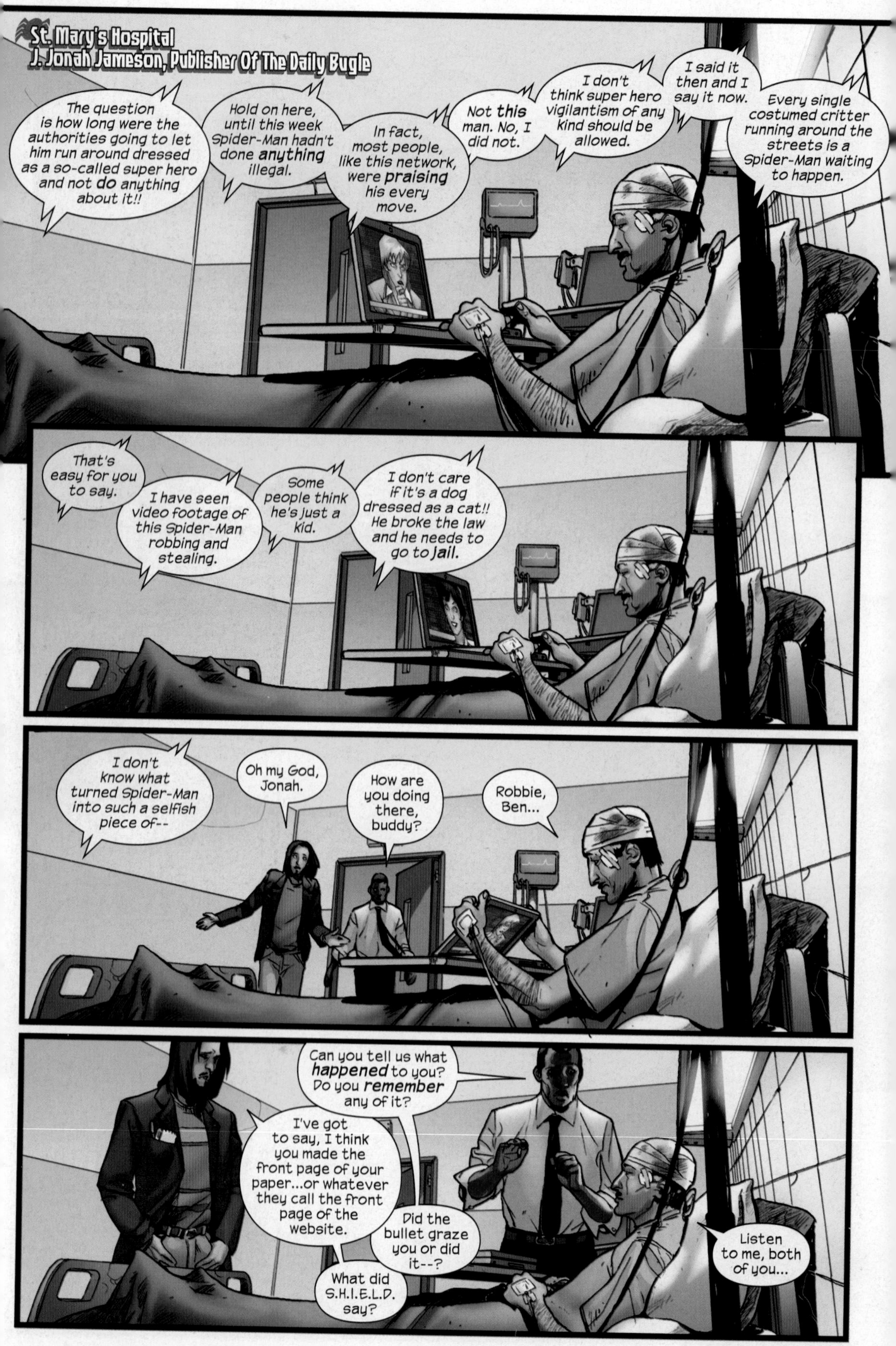
St. Mary's Hospital
J. Jonah Jameson, Publisher Of The Daily Bugle
The question is how long were the authorities going to let him run around dressed as a so-called super hero and not do anything about it!!
Hold on here, until this week Spider-Man hadn't done anything illegal.
In fact, most people, like this network, were praising his every move.
Not this man. No, I did not.
I don't think super hero vigilantism of any kind should be allowed.
I said it then and I say it now.
Every single costumed critter running around the streets is a Spider-Man waiting to happen.
That's easy for you to say.
I have seen video footage of this Spider-Man robbing and stealing.
Some people think he's just a kid.
I don't care if it's a dog dressed as a cat!! He broke the law and he needs to go to jail.
I don't know what turned Spider-Man into such a selfish piece of--
Oh my God, Jonah.
How are you doing there, buddy?
Robbie, Ben...
Can you tell us what happened to you? Do you remember any of it?
I've got to say, I think you made the front page of your paper...or whatever they call the front page of the website.
Did the bullet graze you or did it--?
What did S.H.I.E.L.D. say?
Listen to me, both of you...

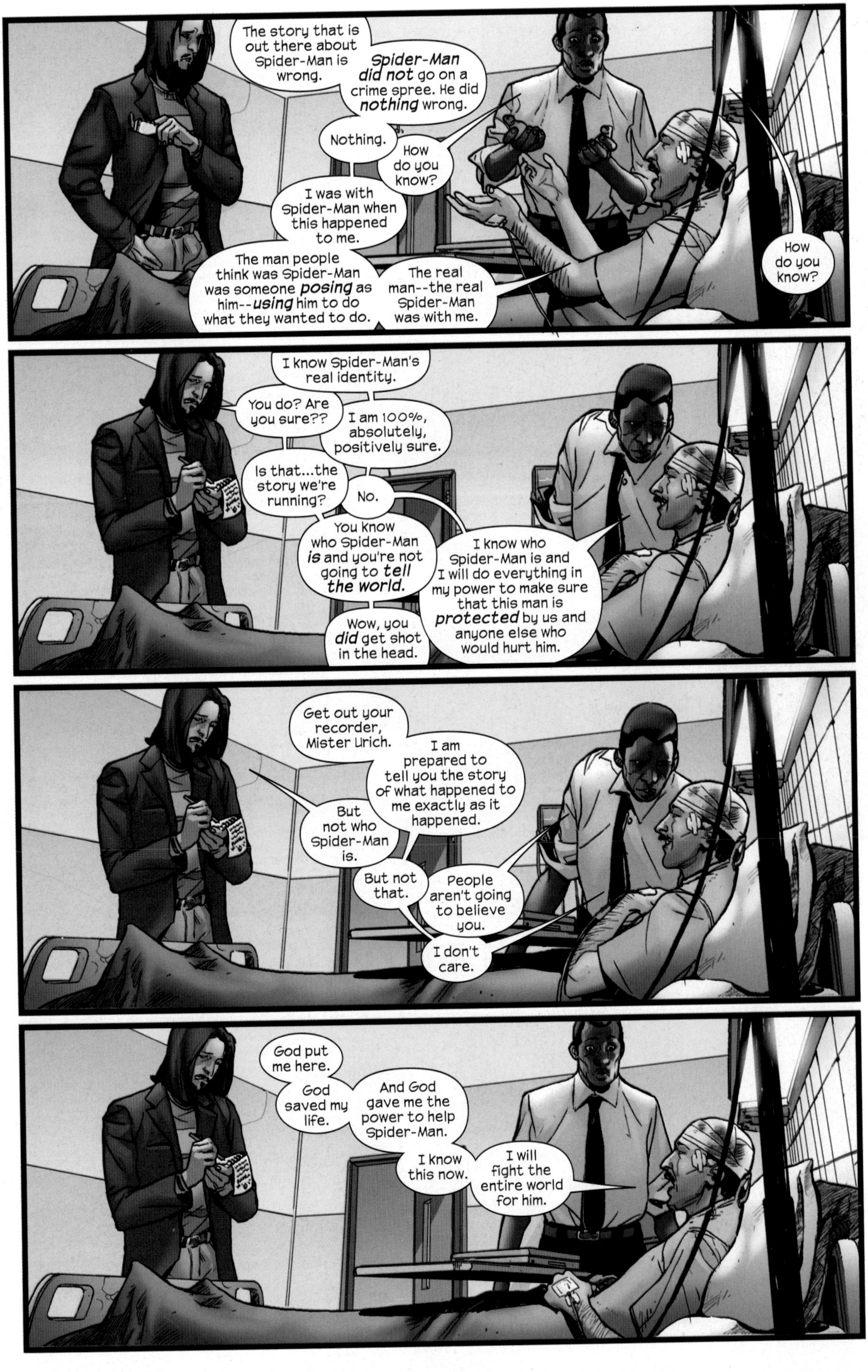

The story that is out there about Spider-Man is wrong.
Spider-Man did not go on a crime spree. He did nothing wrong.
Nothing.
How do you know?
I was with Spider-Man when this happened to me.
The man people think was Spider-Man was someone posing as him--using him to do what they wanted to do.
The real man--the real Spider-Man was with me.
How do you know?
I know Spider-Man's real identity.
You do? Are you sure??
I am 100%, absolutely, positively sure.
Is that...the story we're running?
No.
You know who Spider-Man is and you're not going to tell the world.
I know who Spider-Man is and I will do everything in my power to make sure that this man is protected by us and anyone else who would hurt him.
Wow, you did get shot in the head.
Get out your recorder, Mister Urich.
I am prepared to tell you the story of what happened to me exactly as it happened.
But not who Spider-Man is.
But not that.
People aren't going to believe you.
I don't care.
God put me here.
God saved my life.
And God gave me the power to help Spider-Man.
I know this now.
I will fight the entire world for him.

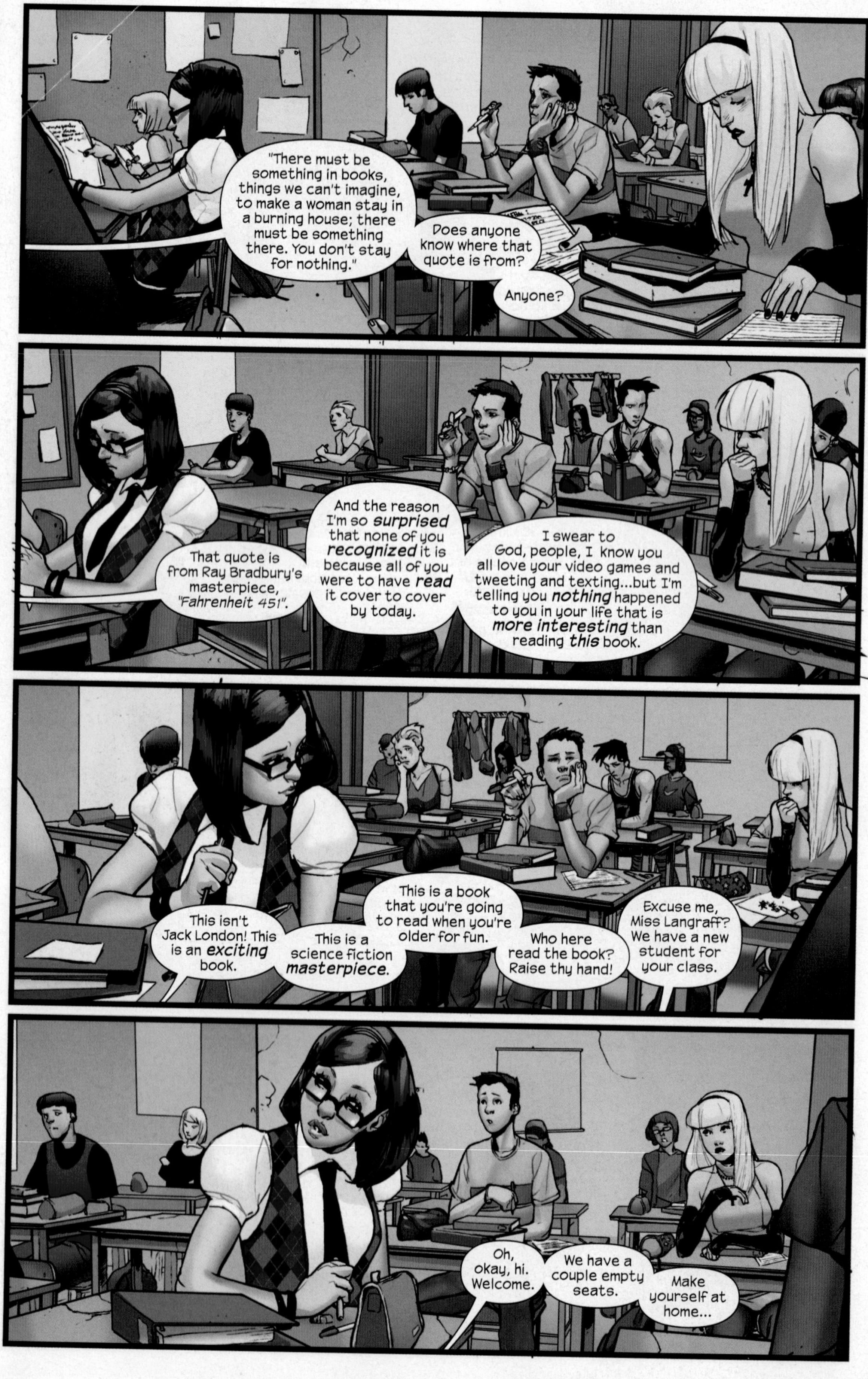
"There must be something in books, things we can't imagine, to make a woman stay in a burning house; there must be something there. You don't stay for nothing."
Does anyone know where that quote is from?
Anyone?
That quote is from Ray Bradbury's masterpiece, "Fahrenheit 451".
And the reason I'm so surprised that none of you recognized it is because all of you were to have read it cover to cover by today.
I swear to God, people, I know you all love your video games and tweeting and texting...but I'm telling you nothing happened to you in your life that is more interesting than reading this book.
This isn't Jack London! This is an exciting book.
This is a science fiction masterpiece.
This is a book that you're going to read when you're older for fun.
Who here read the book? Raise thy hand!
Excuse me, Miss Langraff? We have a new student for your class.
Oh, okay, hi. Welcome.
We have a couple empty seats.
Make yourself at home...

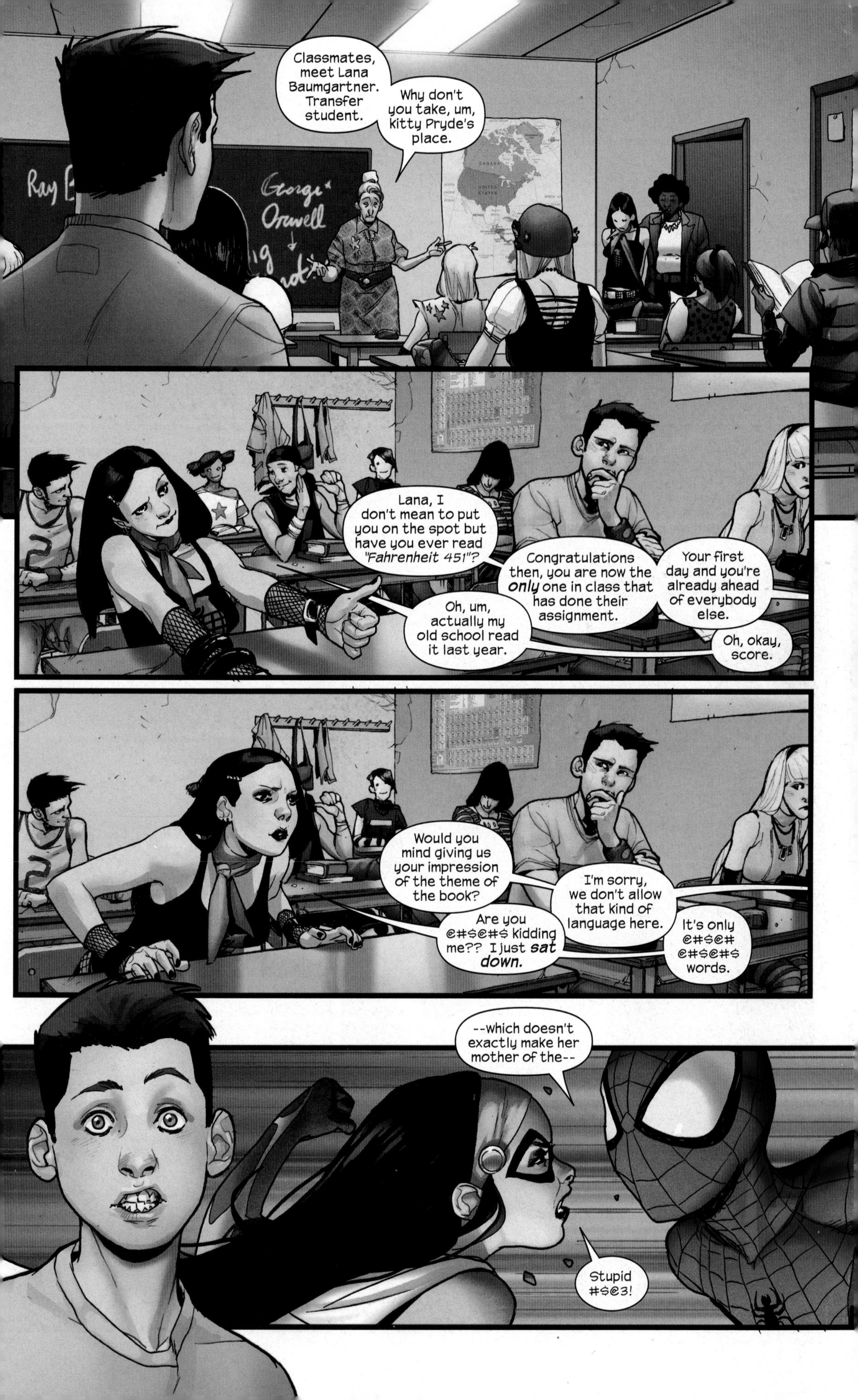
Classmates, meet Lana Baumgartner. Transfer student.
Why don't you take, um, kitty Pryde's place.
Georgi Orwell
Lana, I don't mean to put you on the spot but have you ever read "Fahrenheit 451"?
Oh, um, actually my old school read it last year.
Congratulations then, you are now the *only* one in class that has done their assignment.
Your first day and you're already ahead of everybody else.
Oh, okay, score.
Would you mind giving us your impression of the theme of the book?
Are you @#$@#$ kidding me?? I just **sat down.**
I'm sorry, we don't allow that kind of language here.
It's only @#$@# @#$@#$ words.
--which doesn't exactly make her mother of the--
Stupid #$@3!

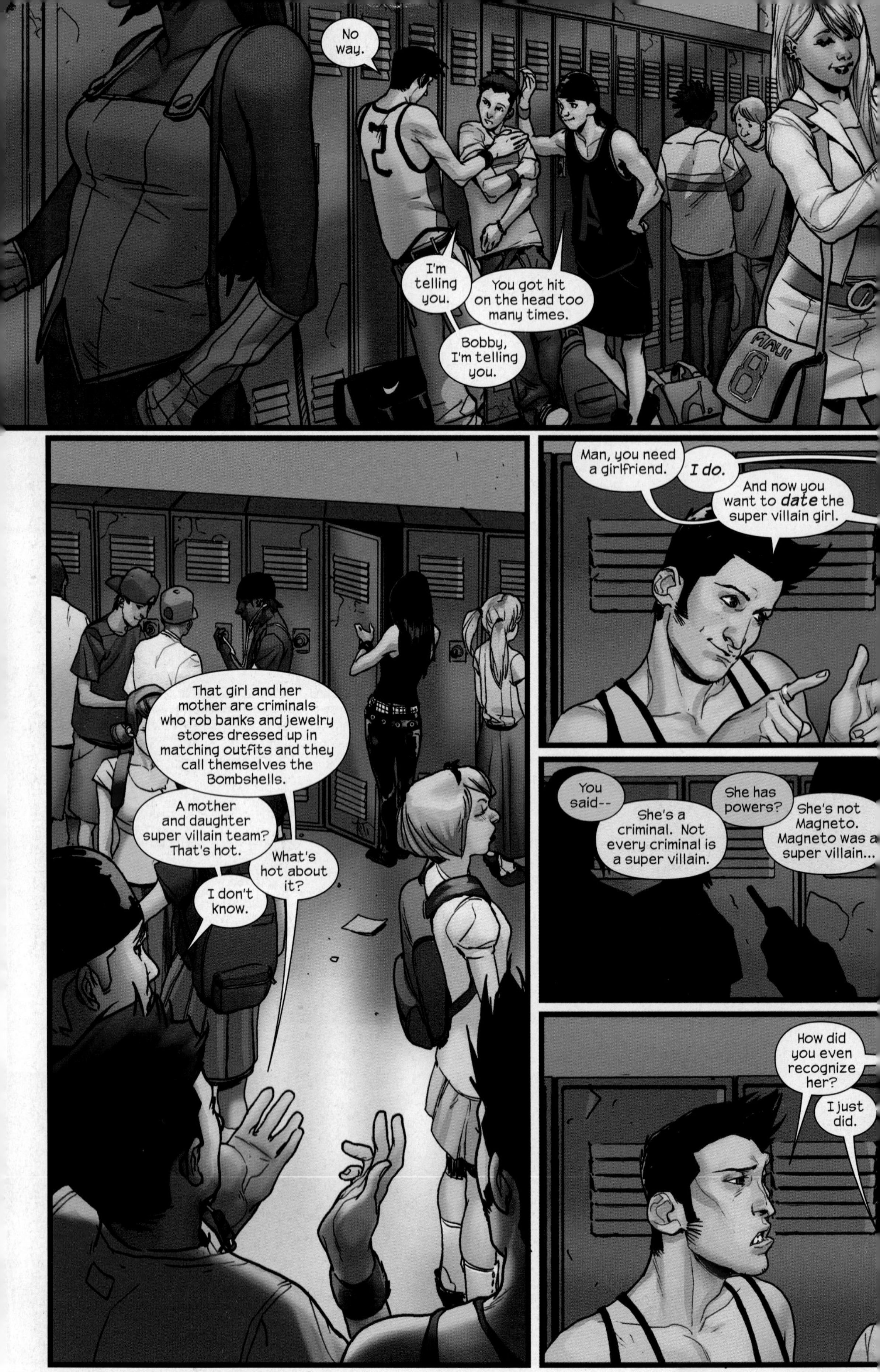
No way.
I'm telling you.
You got hit on the head too many times.
Bobby, I'm telling you.
That girl and her mother are criminals who rob banks and jewelry stores dressed up in matching outfits and they call themselves the Bombshells.
A mother and daughter super villain team? That's hot.
What's hot about it?
I don't know.
Man, you need a girlfriend.
I do.
And now you want to date the super villain girl.
You said--
She's a criminal. Not every criminal is a super villain.
She has powers?
She's not Magneto. Magneto was a super villain...
How did you even recognize her?
I just did.

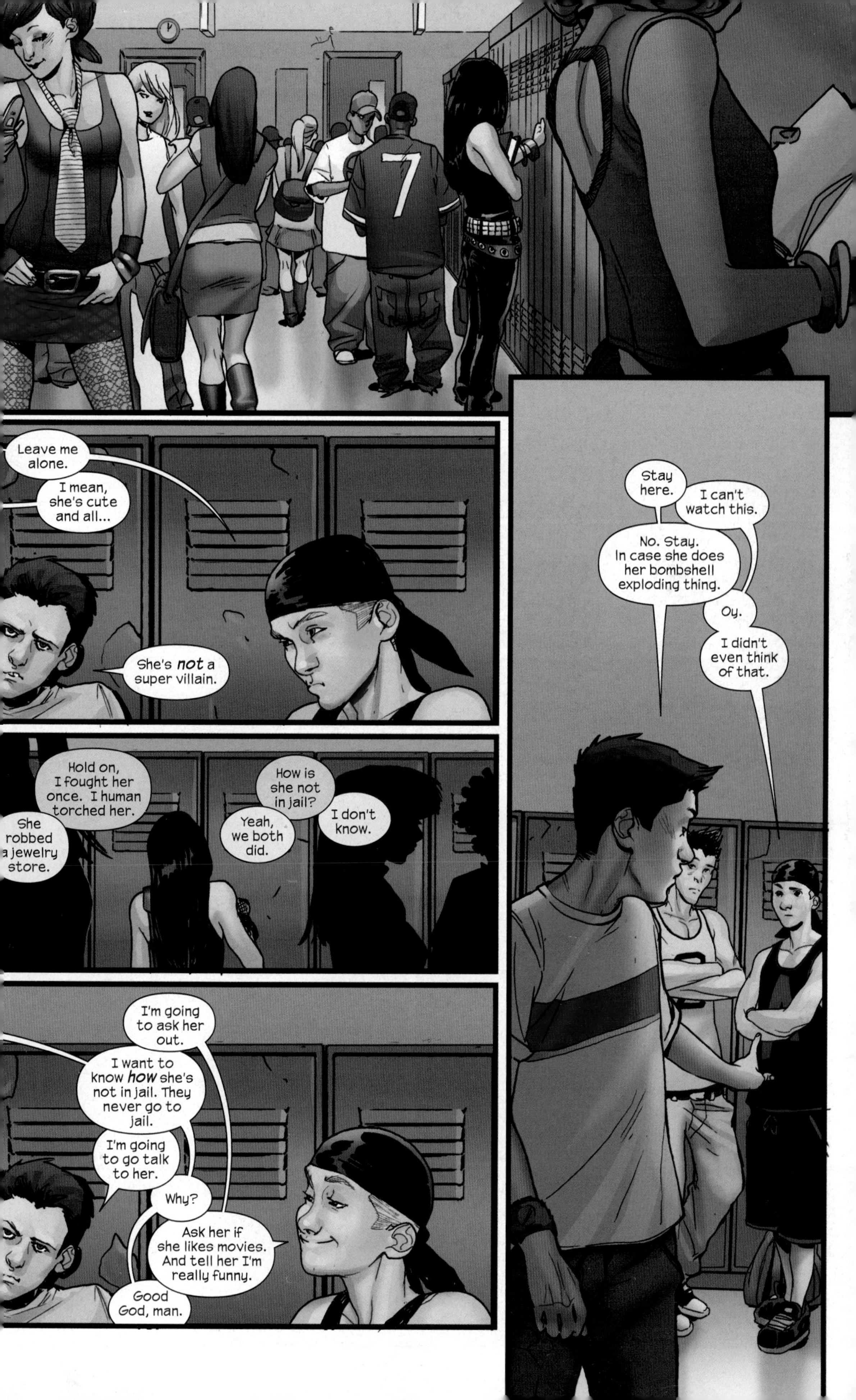
Leave me alone.
I mean, she's cute and all...
She's not a super villain.
Hold on, I fought her once. I human torched her.
She robbed a jewelry store.
How is she not in jail?
Yeah, we both did.
I don't know.
I'm going to ask her out.
I want to know how she's not in jail. They never go to jail.
I'm going to go talk to her.
Why?
Ask her if she likes movies. And tell her I'm really funny.
Good God, man.
Stay here.
I can't watch this.
No. Stay. In case she does her bombshell exploding thing.
Oy.
I didn't even think of that.

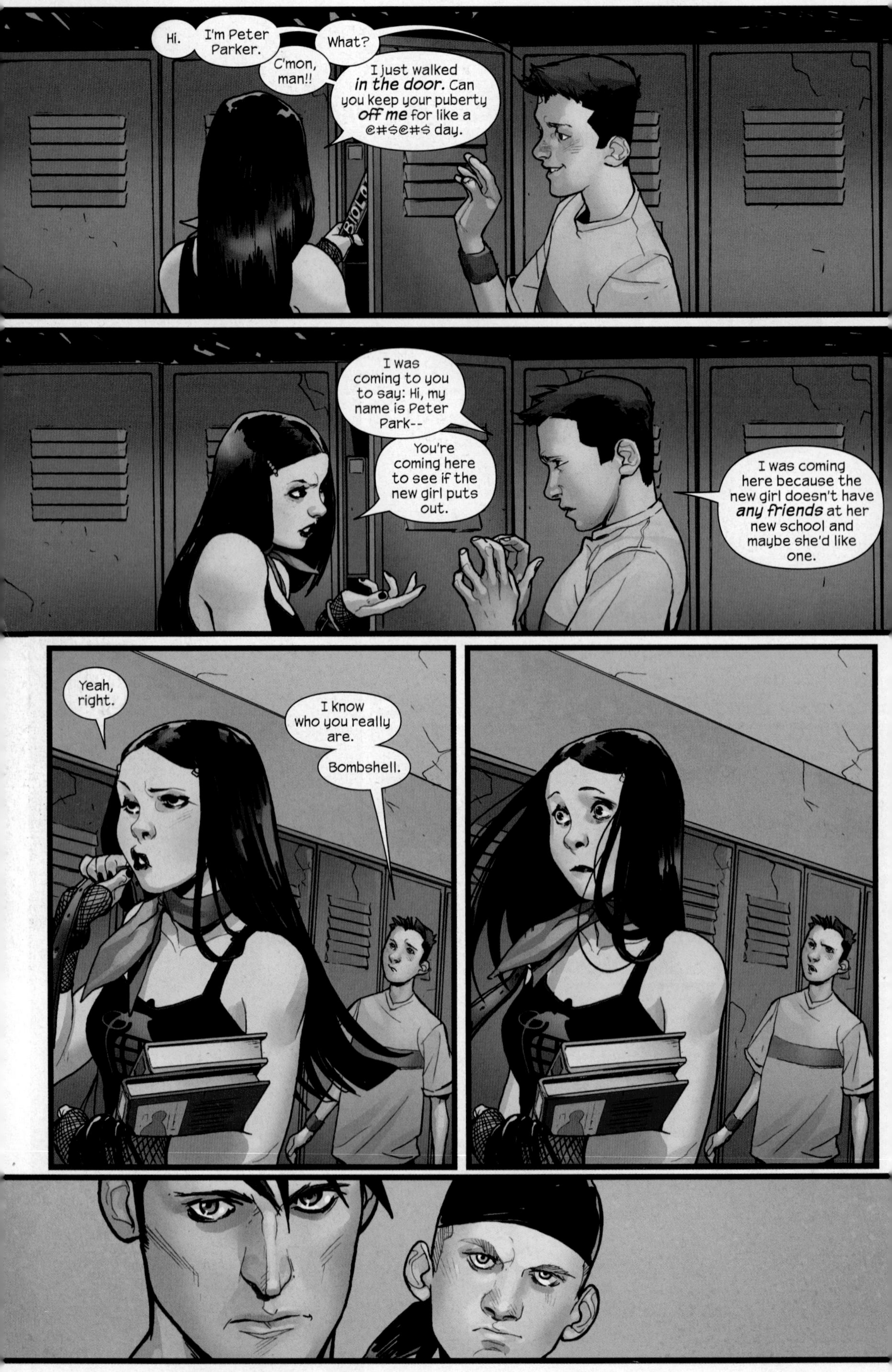
Hi.
I'm Peter Parker.
What?
C'mon, man!!
I just walked in the door. Can you keep your puberty off me for like a @#$@#$ day.
I was coming to you to say: Hi, my name is Peter Park--
You're coming here to see if the new girl puts out.
I was coming here because the new girl doesn't have any friends at her new school and maybe she'd like one.
Yeah, right.
I know who you really are.
Bombshell.

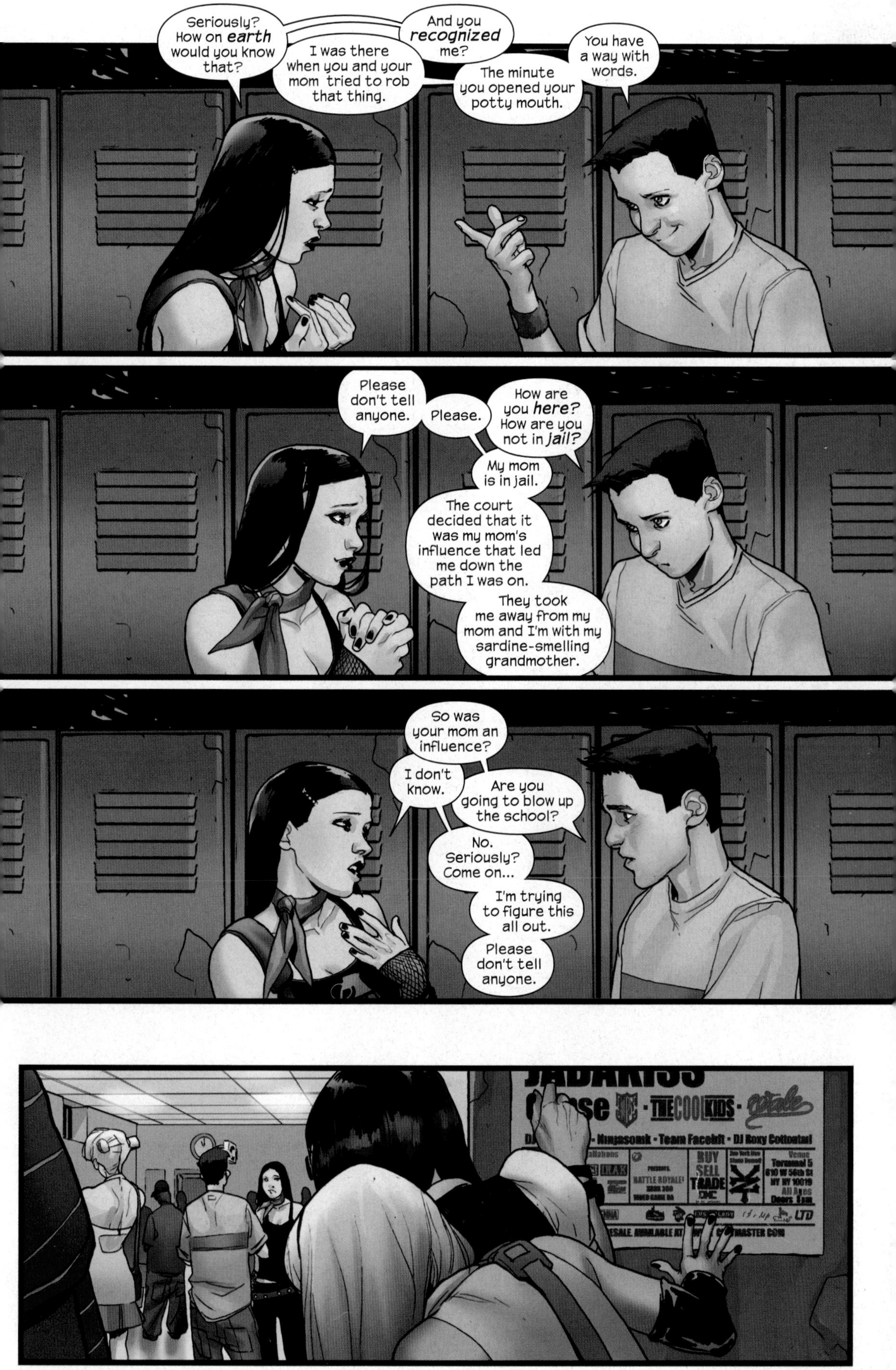
Seriously? How on earth would you know that?
I was there when you and your mom tried to rob that thing.
And you recognized me?
The minute you opened your potty mouth.
You have a way with words.
Please don't tell anyone.
Please.
How are you here? How are you not in jail?
My mom is in jail.
The court decided that it was my mom's influence that led me down the path I was on.
They took me away from my mom and I'm with my sardine-smelling grandmother.
So was your mom an influence?
I don't know.
Are you going to blow up the school?
No. Seriously? Come on...
I'm trying to figure this all out.
Please don't tell anyone.
THE COOL KIDS
Ninjasonik - Team Facelift - DJ Roxy Cottontail
BUY SELL TRADE
Terminal 5
610 W 56th St
NY NY 10019
All Ages

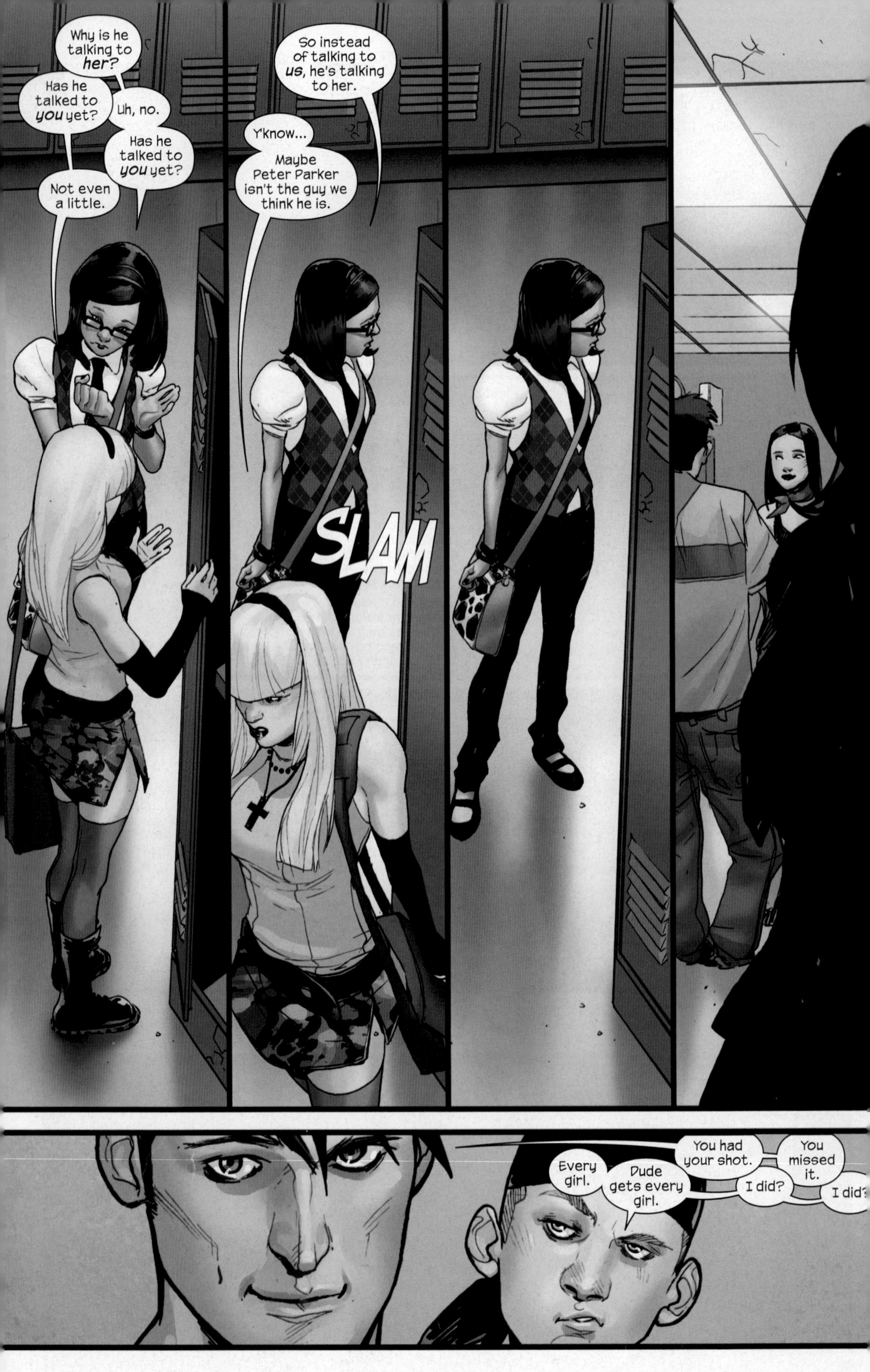
Why is he talking to *her*?
Has he talked to *you* yet?
Uh, no.
Has he talked to *you* yet?
Not even a little.
So instead of talking to *us*, he's talking to her.
Y'know...
Maybe Peter Parker isn't the guy we think he is.
SLAM
Every girl.
Dude gets every girl.
You had your shot.
You missed it.
I did?
I did?

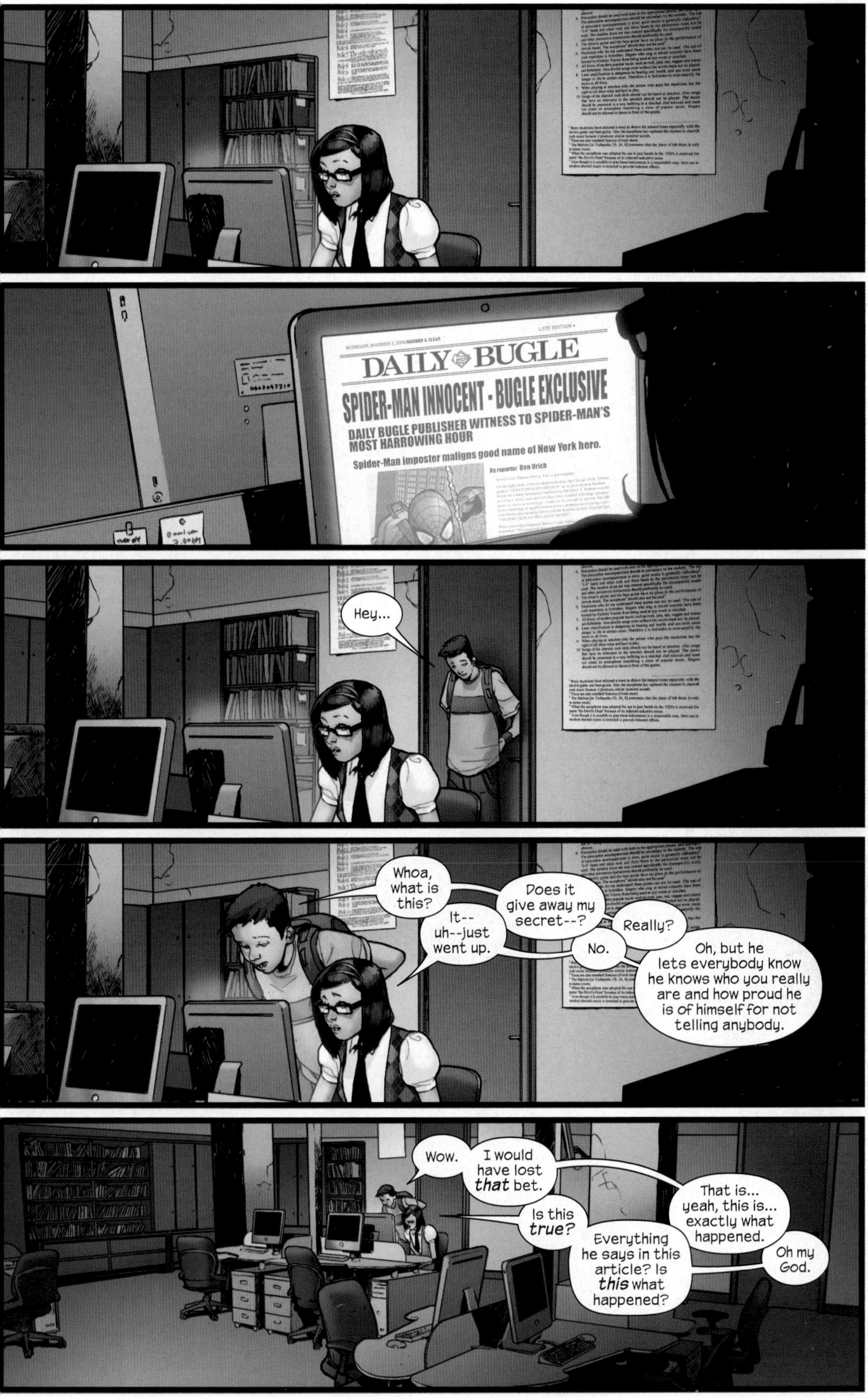

LATE EDITION
DAILY BUGLE
SPIDER-MAN INNOCENT - BUGLE EXCLUSIVE
DAILY BUGLE PUBLISHER WITNESS TO SPIDER-MAN'S MOST HARROWING HOUR
Spider-Man imposter maligns good name of New York hero.
By reporter Ben Urich
Hey...
Whoa, what is this?
It-- uh--just went up.
Does it give away my secret--?
No.
Really?
Oh, but he lets everybody know he knows who you really are and how proud he is of himself for not telling anybody.
Wow.
I would have lost *that* bet.
Is this *true*?
Everything he says in this article? Is *this* what happened?
That is... yeah, this is... exactly what happened.
Oh my God.

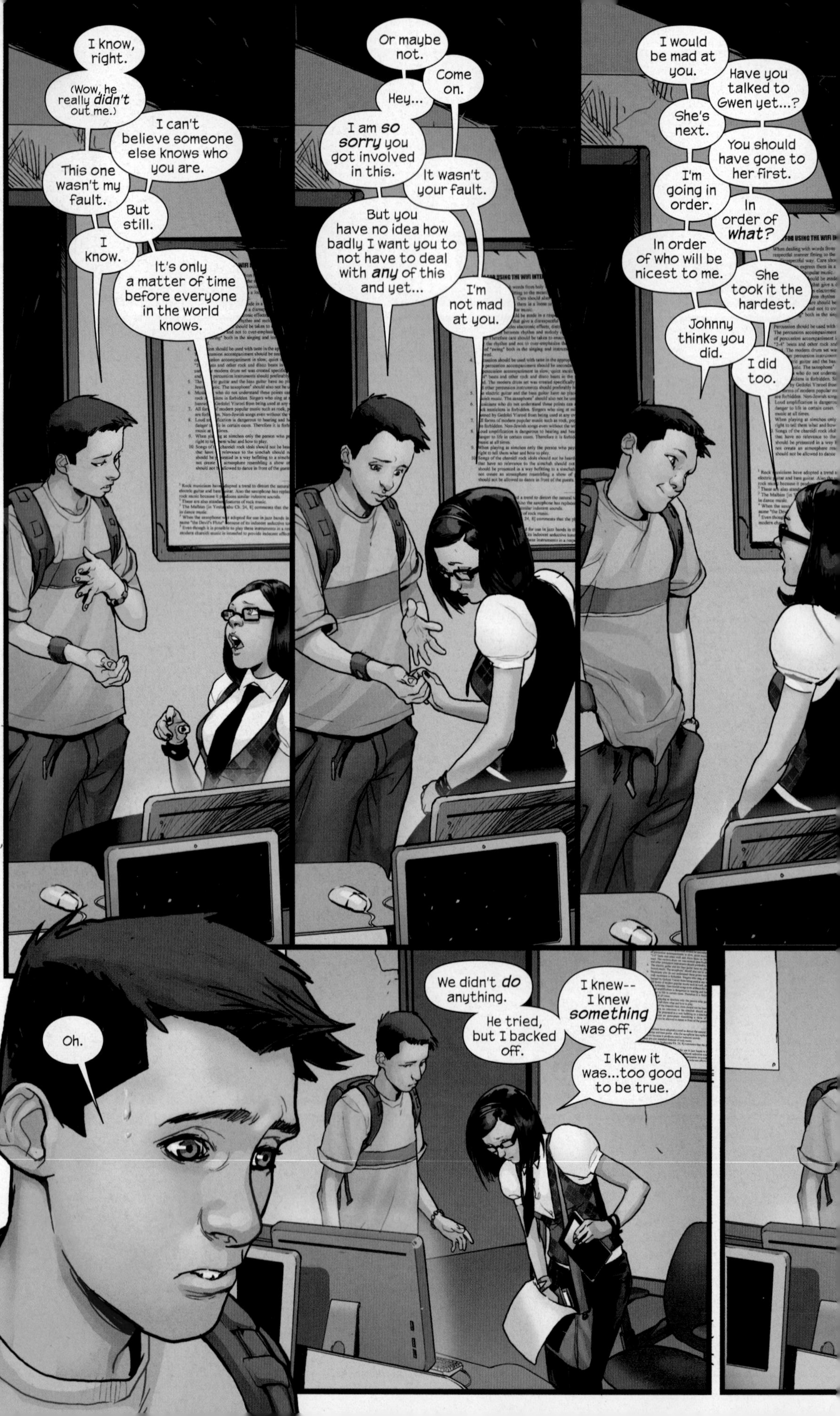

I know, right.
(Wow, he really *didn't* out me.)
I can't believe someone else knows who you are.
This one wasn't my fault.
But still.
I know.
It's only a matter of time before everyone in the world knows.
Or maybe not.
Come on.
Hey...
I am *so sorry* you got involved in this.
It wasn't your fault.
But you have no idea how badly I want you to not have to deal with *any* of this and yet...
I'm not mad at you.
I would be mad at you.
Have you talked to Gwen yet...?
She's next.
You should have gone to her first.
I'm going in order.
In order of *what?*
In order of who will be nicest to me.
She took it the hardest.
Johnny thinks you did.
I did too.
Oh.
We didn't *do* anything.
He tried, but I backed off.
I knew-- I knew *something* was off.
I knew it was...too good to be true.

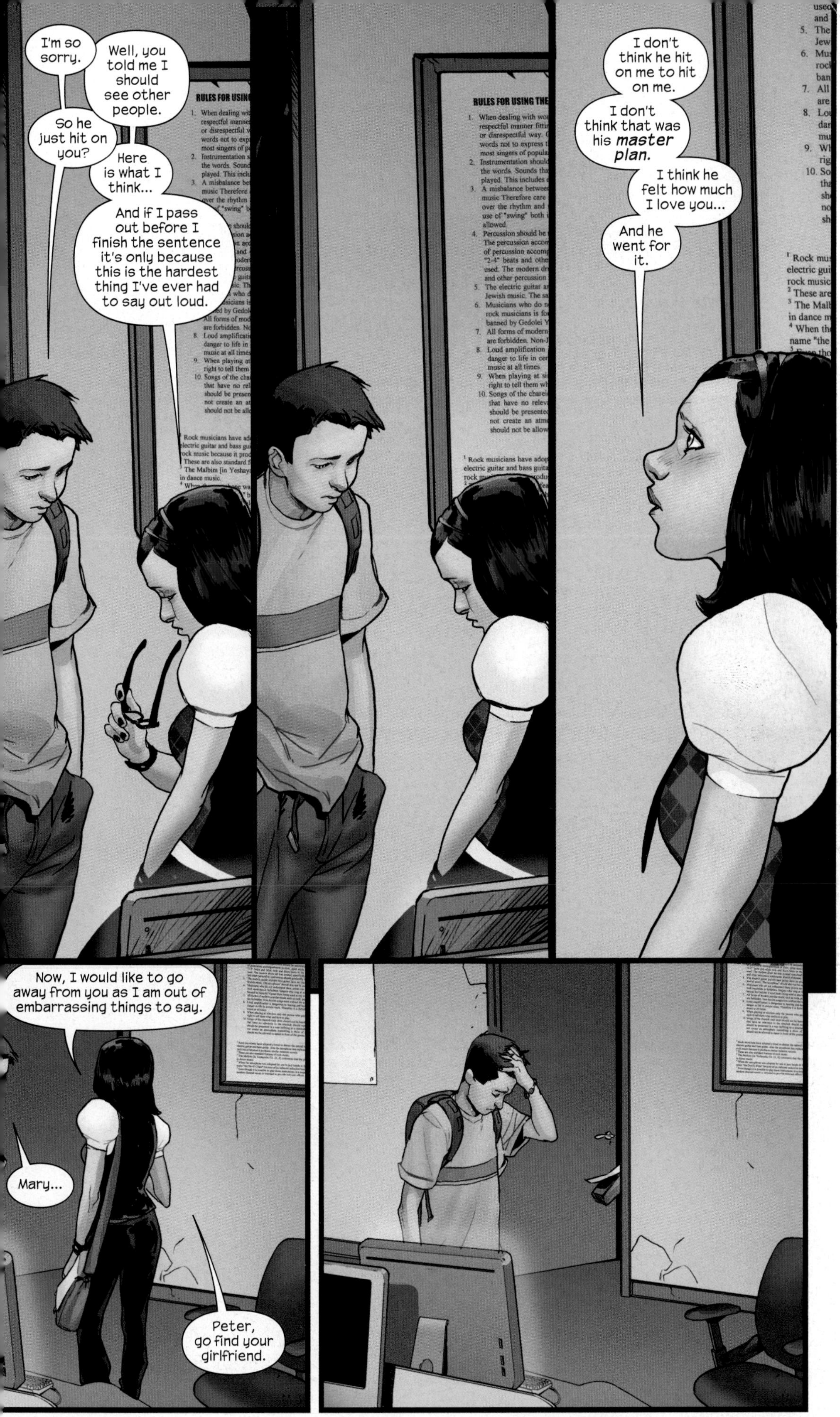
I'm so sorry.
So he just hit on you?
Well, you told me I should see other people.
Here is what I think...
And if I pass out before I finish the sentence it's only because this is the hardest thing I've ever had to say out loud.
I don't think he hit on me to hit on me.
I don't think that was his *master plan.*
I think he felt how much I love you...
And he went for it.
Now, I would like to go away from you as I am out of embarrassing things to say.
Mary...
Peter, go find your girlfriend.

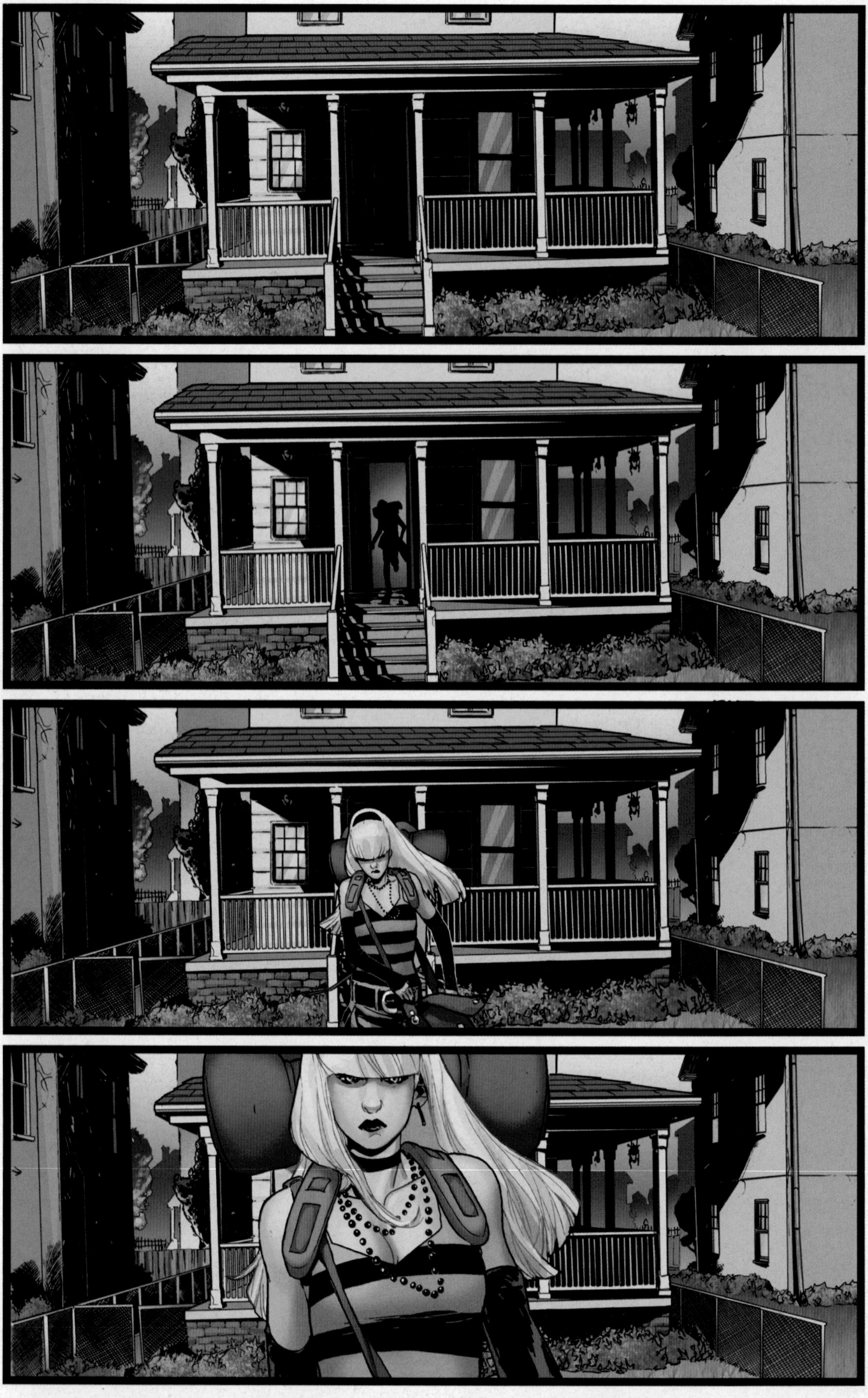

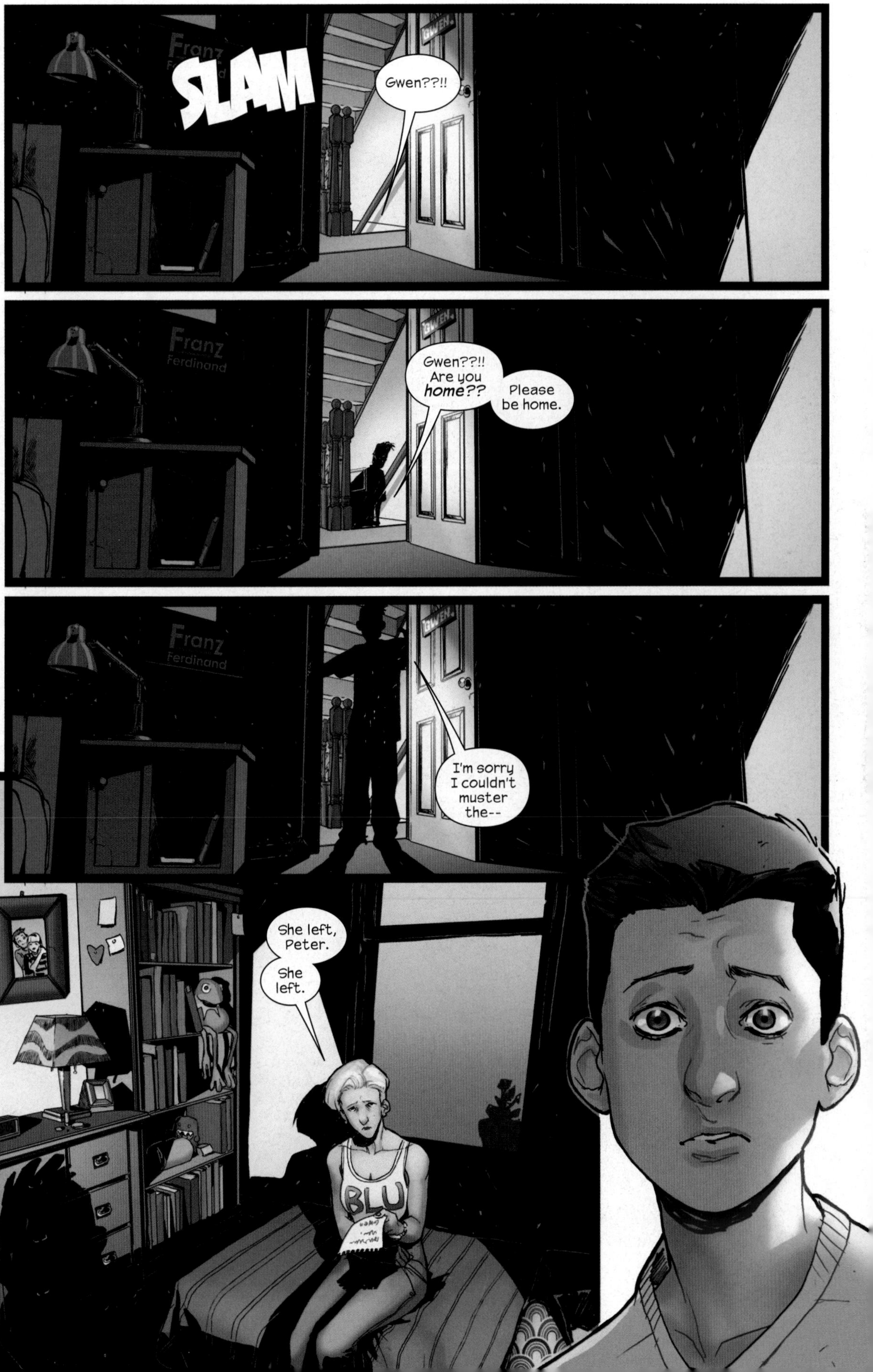
SLAM
Gwen??!!
Gwen??!! Are you *home*??
Please be home.
I'm sorry I couldn't muster the--
She left, Peter.
She left.

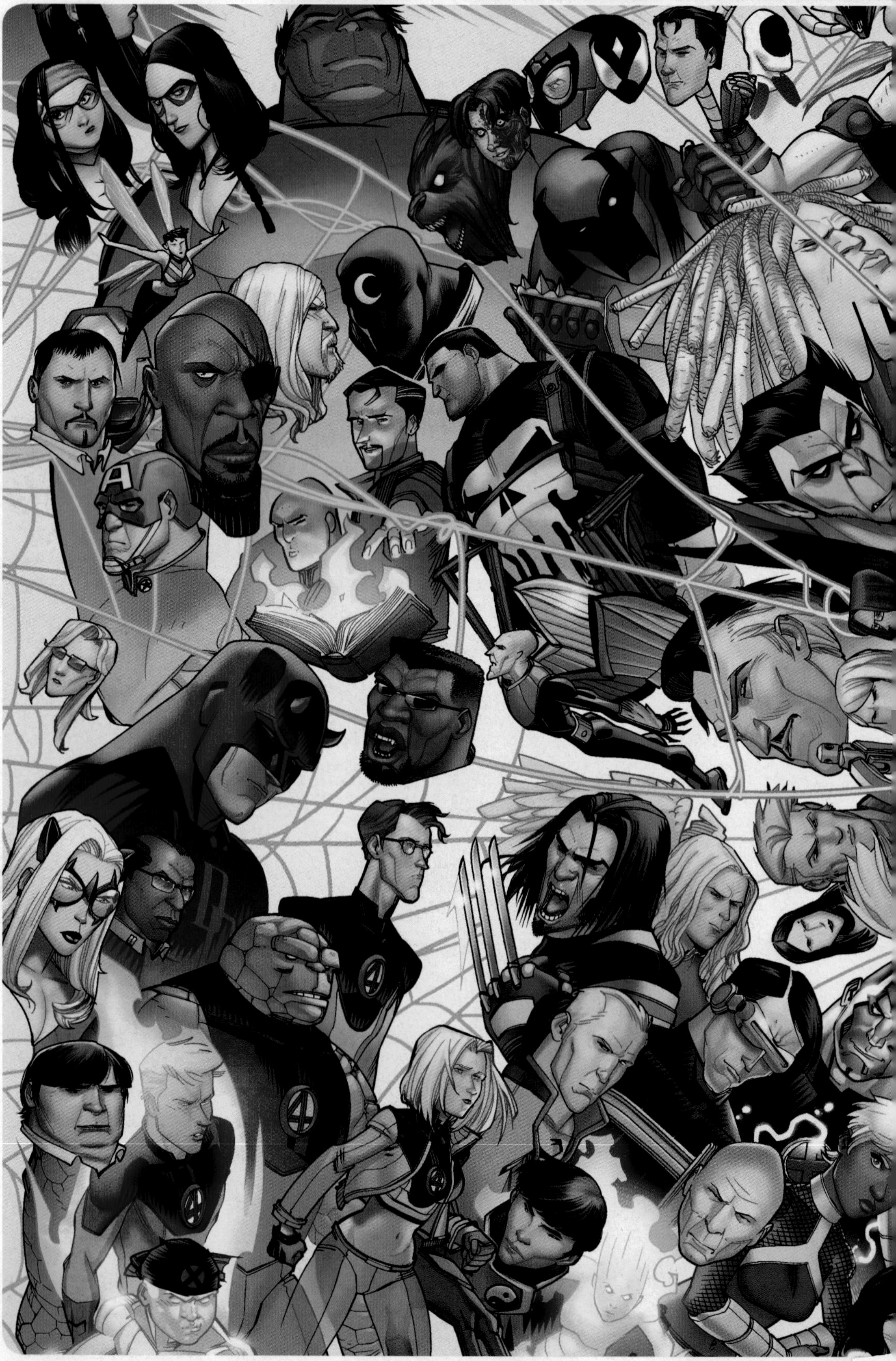

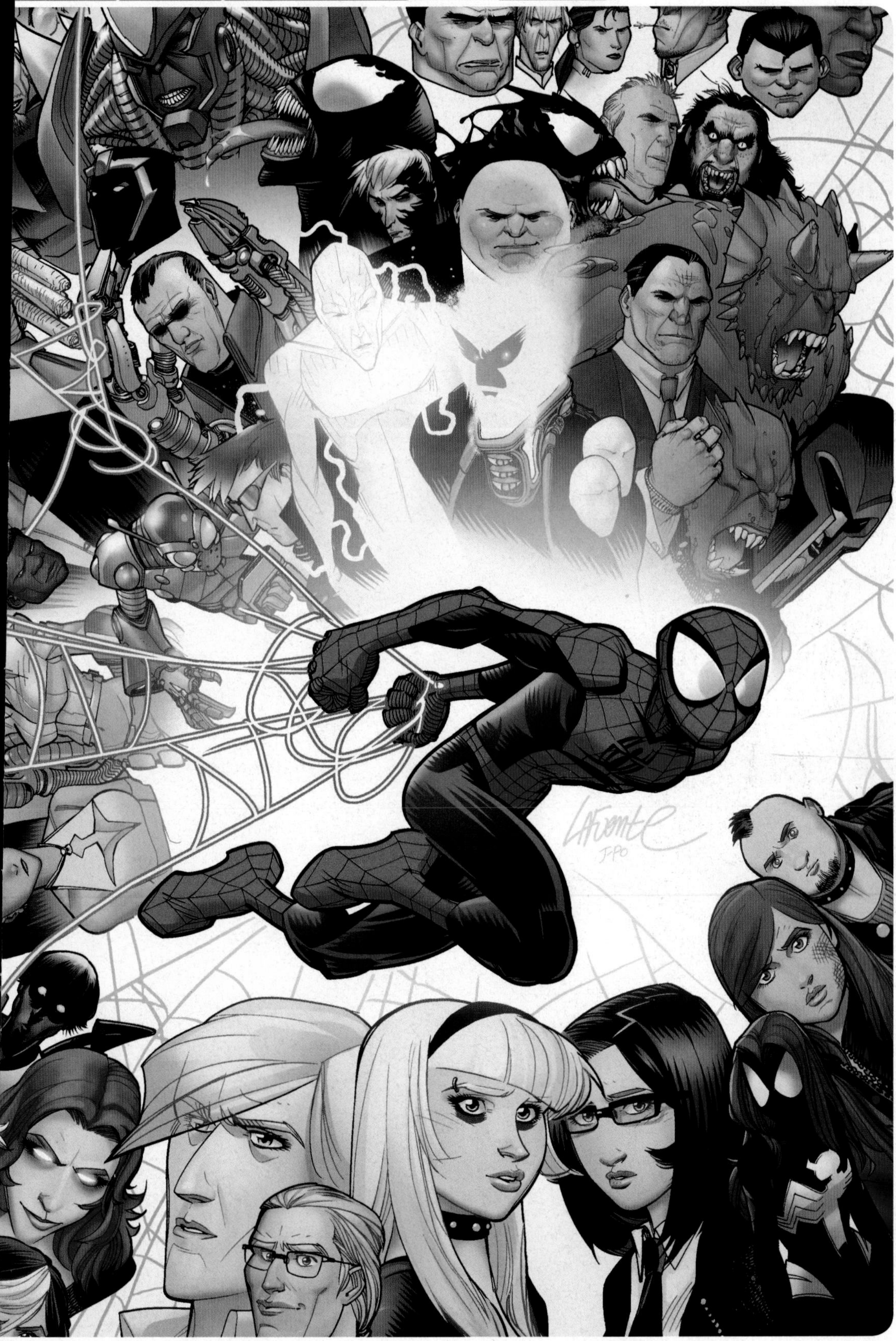
LaFuente
J-PO

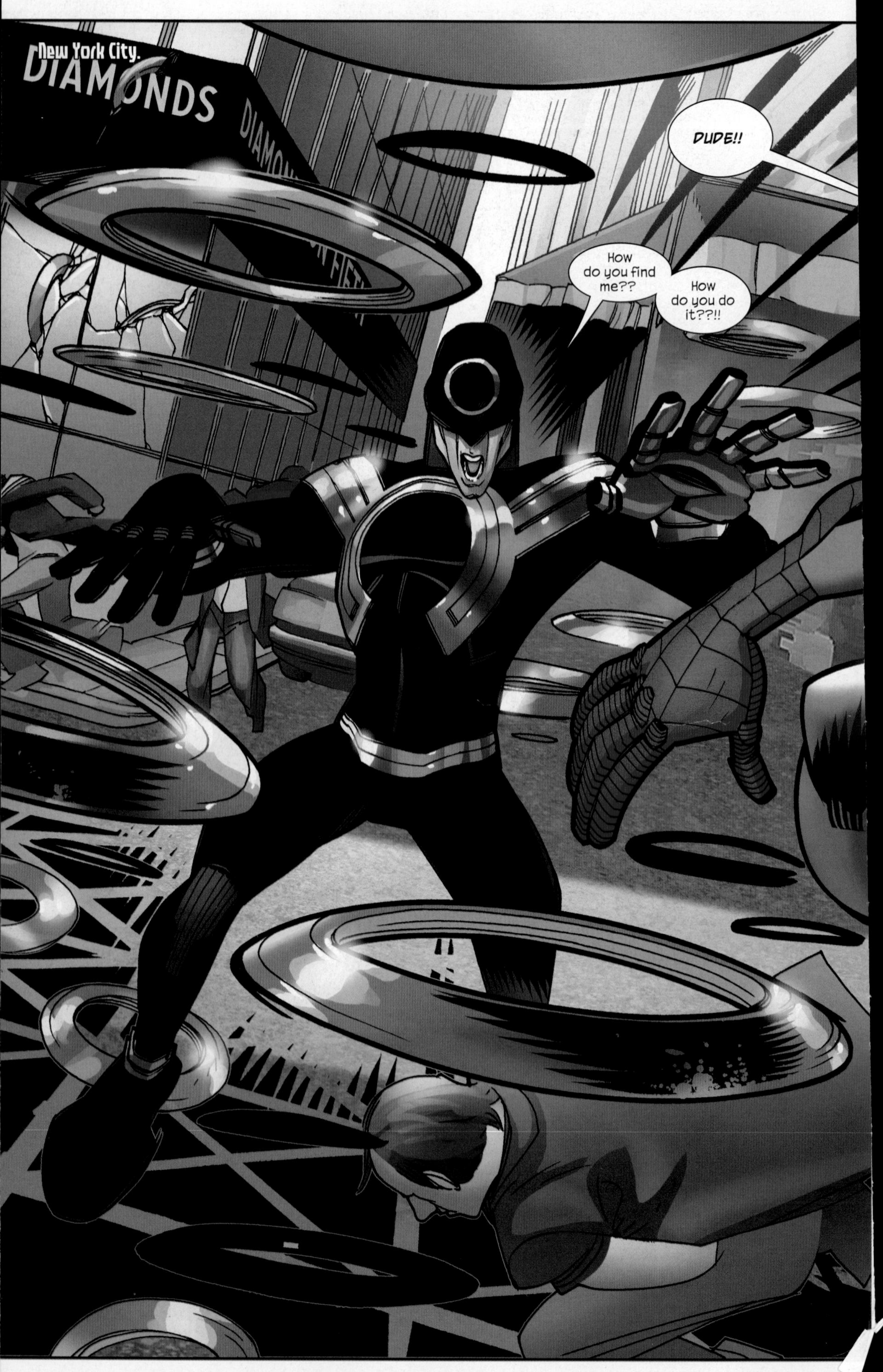
New York City.
DIAMONDS
DIAMONDS
DUDE!!
How do you find me??
How do you do it??!!

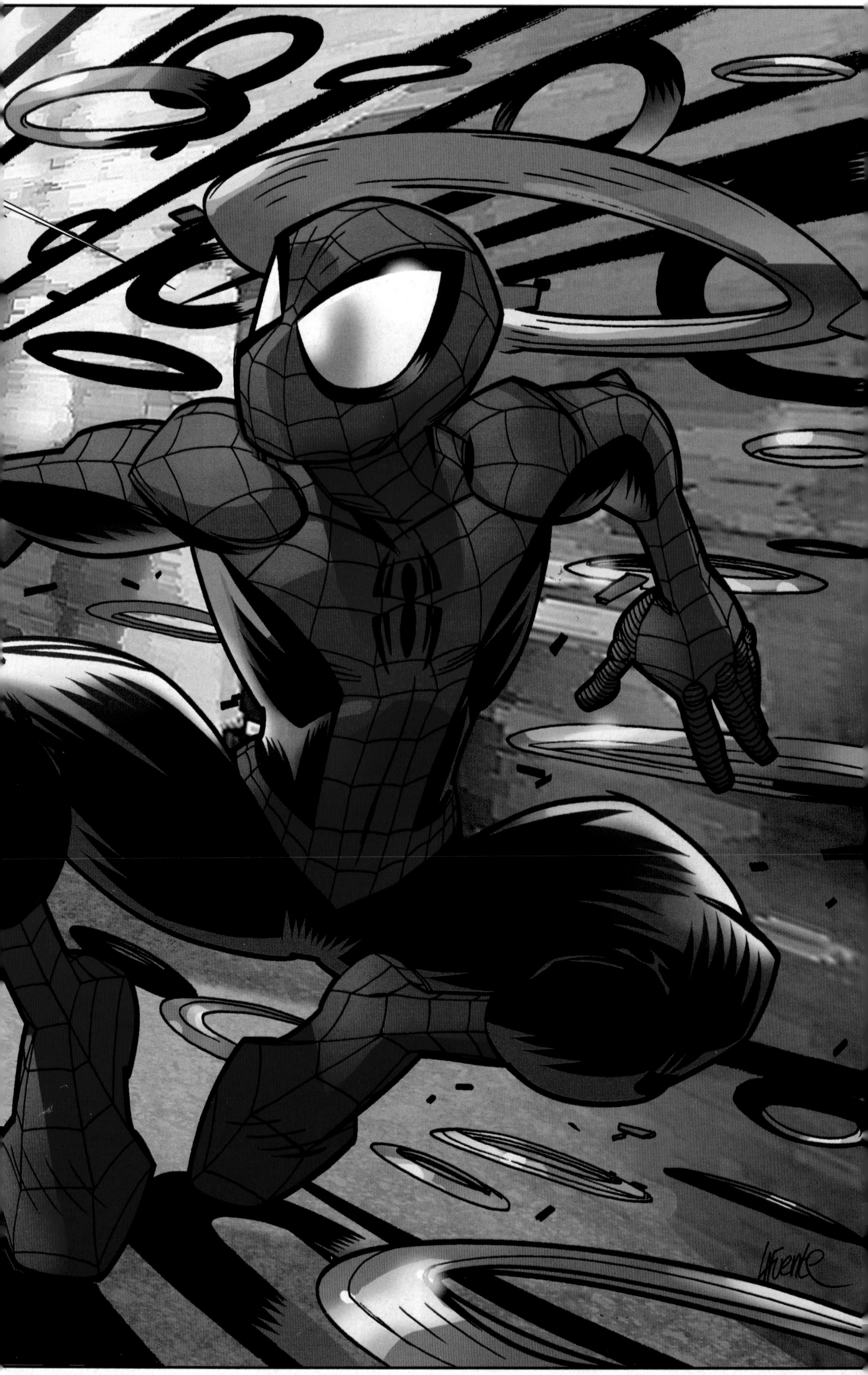

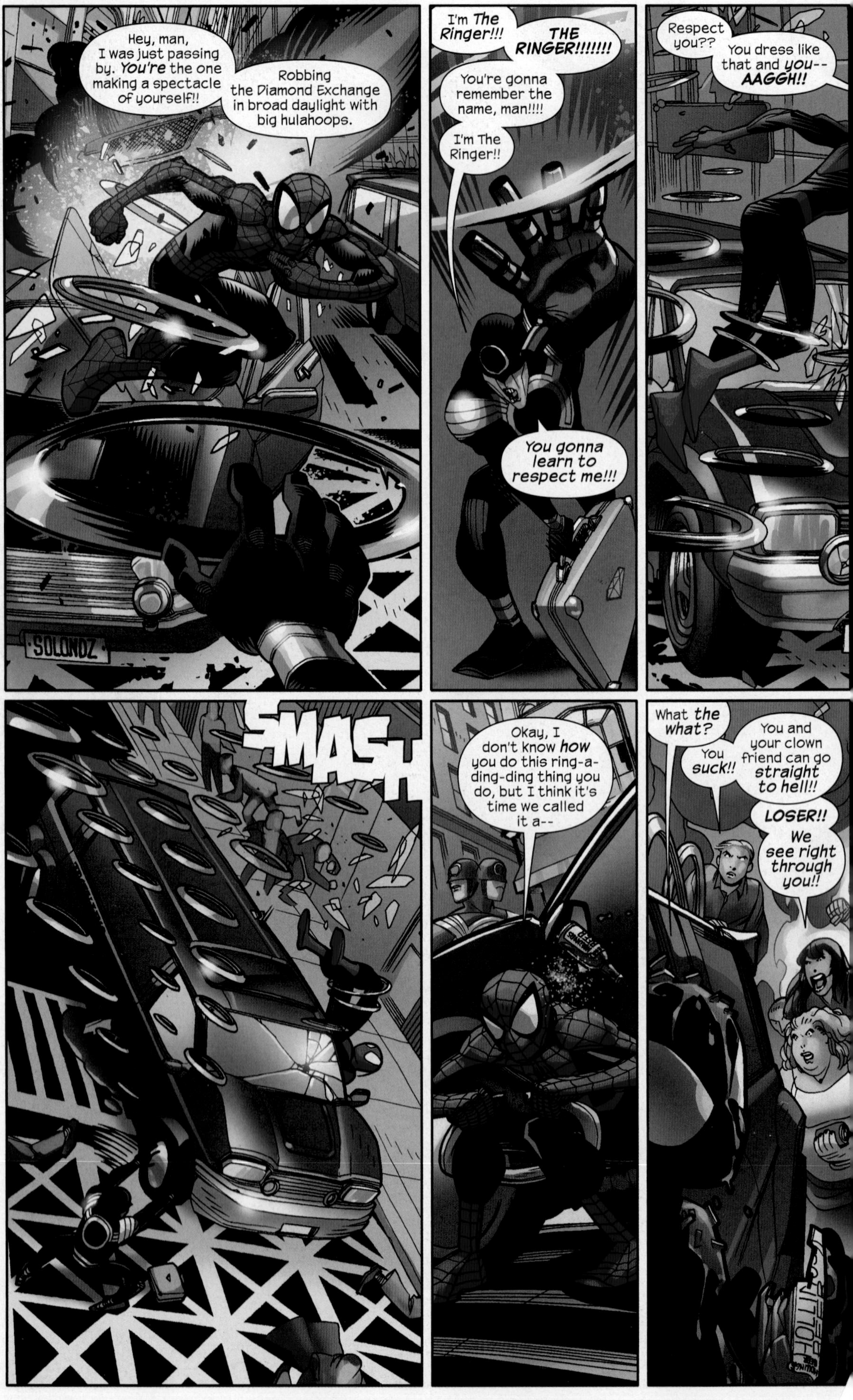
Hey, man, I was just passing by. You're the one making a spectacle of yourself!!
Robbing the Diamond Exchange in broad daylight with big hulahoops.
SOLONDZ
I'm The Ringer!!!
THE RINGER!!!!!!!
You're gonna remember the name, man!!!!
I'm The Ringer!!
You gonna learn to respect me!!!
Respect you??
You dress like that and you-- AAGGH!!
SMASH
Okay, I don't know how you do this ring-a-ding-ding thing you do, but I think it's time we called it a--
What the what?
You suck!!
You and your clown friend can go straight to hell!!
LOSER!!
We see right through you!!

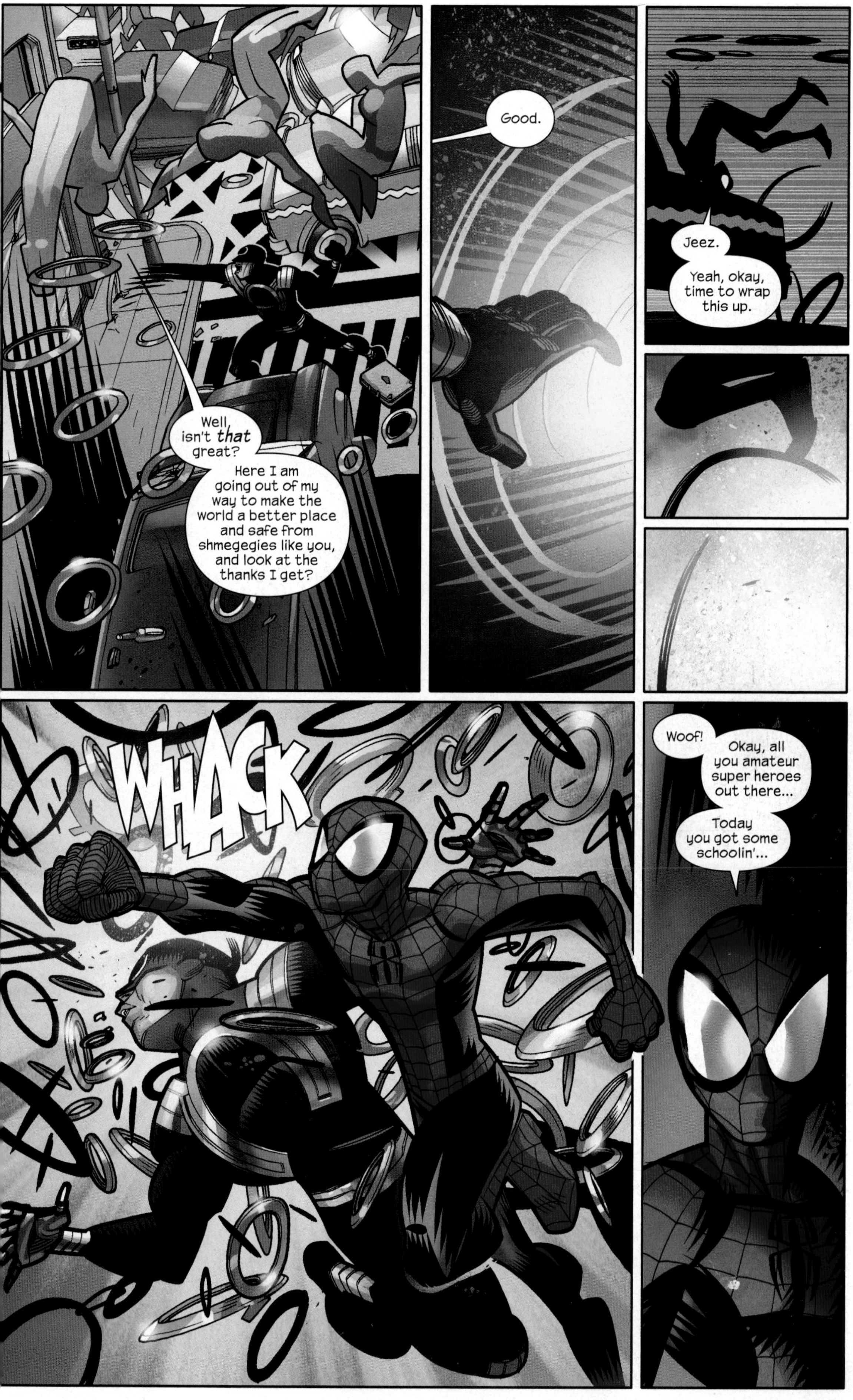
Well, isn't *that* great?
Here I am going out of my way to make the world a better place and safe from shmegegies like you, and look at the thanks I get?
Good.
Jeez.
Yeah, okay, time to wrap this up.
WHACK
Woof!
Okay, all you amateur super heroes out there...
Today you got some schoolin'...

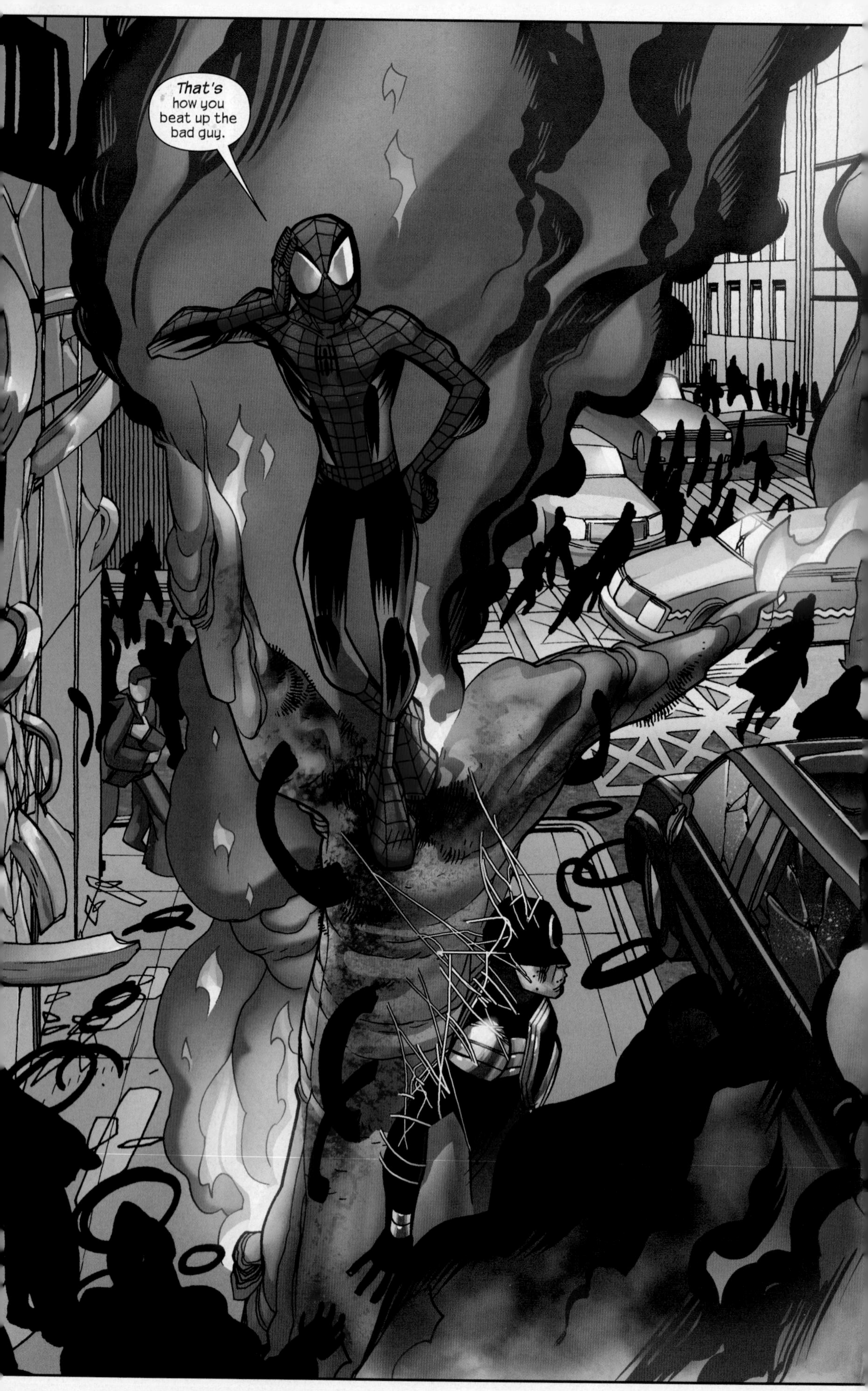
That's how you beat up the bad guy.

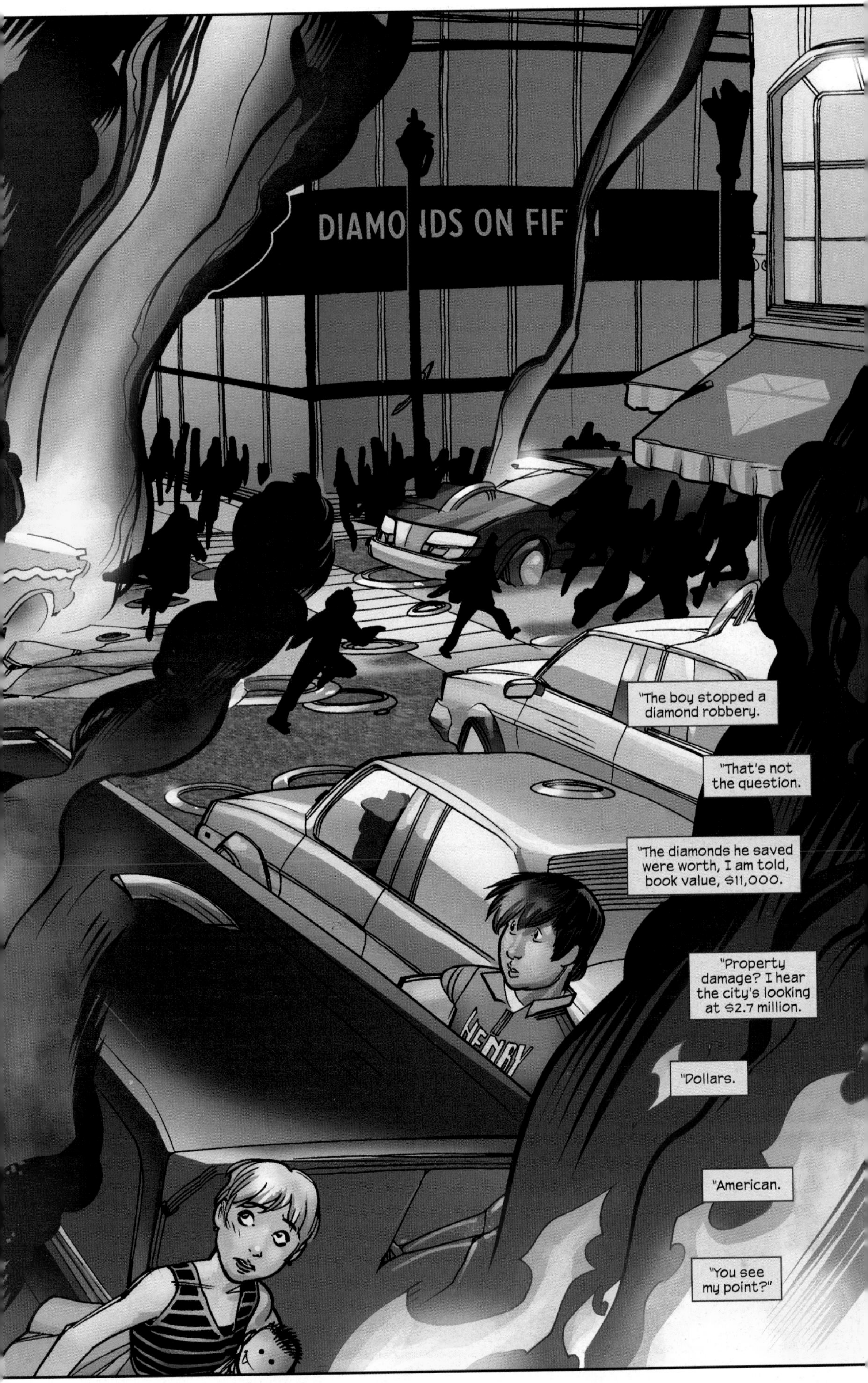

DIAMONDS ON FIFTH
"The boy stopped a diamond robbery.
"That's not the question.
"The diamonds he saved were worth, I am told, book value, $11,000.
"Property damage? I hear the city's looking at $2.7 million.
"Dollars.
"American.
"You see my point?"
HENRY

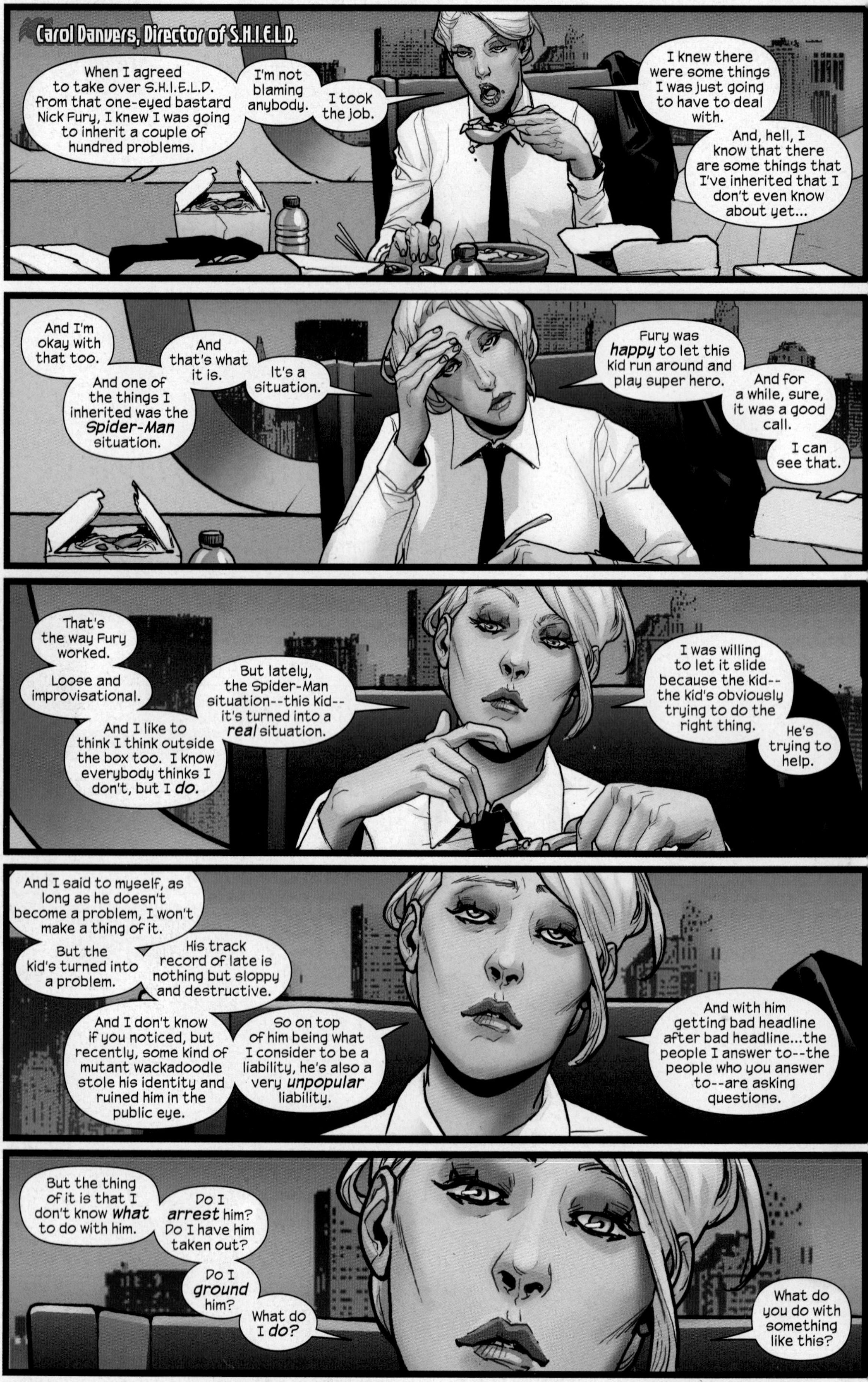
Carol Danvers, Director of S.H.I.E.L.D.
When I agreed to take over S.H.I.E.L.D. from that one-eyed bastard Nick Fury, I knew I was going to inherit a couple of hundred problems.
I'm not blaming anybody.
I took the job.
I knew there were some things I was just going to have to deal with.
And, hell, I know that there are some things that I've inherited that I don't even know about yet...
And I'm okay with that too.
And one of the things I inherited was the Spider-Man situation.
And that's what it is.
It's a situation.
Fury was happy to let this kid run around and play super hero.
And for a while, sure, it was a good call.
I can see that.
That's the way Fury worked.
Loose and improvisational.
And I like to think I think outside the box too. I know everybody thinks I don't, but I do.
But lately, the Spider-Man situation--this kid--it's turned into a real situation.
I was willing to let it slide because the kid--the kid's obviously trying to do the right thing.
He's trying to help.
And I said to myself, as long as he doesn't become a problem, I won't make a thing of it.
But the kid's turned into a problem.
His track record of late is nothing but sloppy and destructive.
And I don't know if you noticed, but recently, some kind of mutant wackadoodle stole his identity and ruined him in the public eye.
So on top of him being what I consider to be a liability, he's also a very unpopular liability.
And with him getting bad headline after bad headline...the people I answer to--the people who you answer to--are asking questions.
But the thing of it is that I don't know what to do with him.
Do I arrest him? Do I have him taken out?
Do I ground him?
What do I do?
What do you do with something like this?

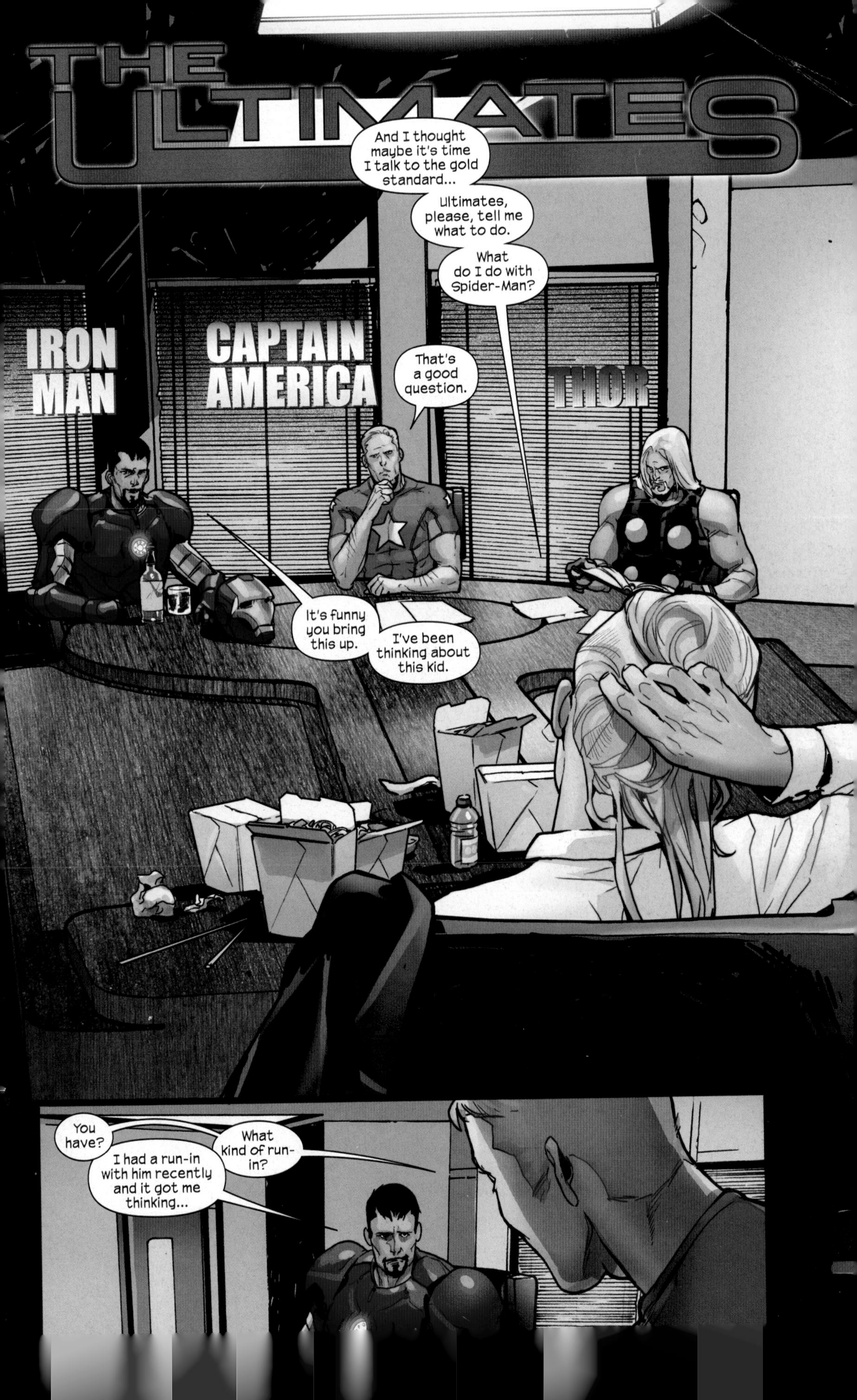

THE ULTIMATES
And I thought maybe it's time I talk to the gold standard...
Ultimates, please, tell me what to do.
What do I do with Spider-Man?
IRON MAN
CAPTAIN AMERICA
THOR
That's a good question.
It's funny you bring this up.
I've been thinking about this kid.
You have?
I had a run-in with him recently and it got me thinking...
What kind of run-in?

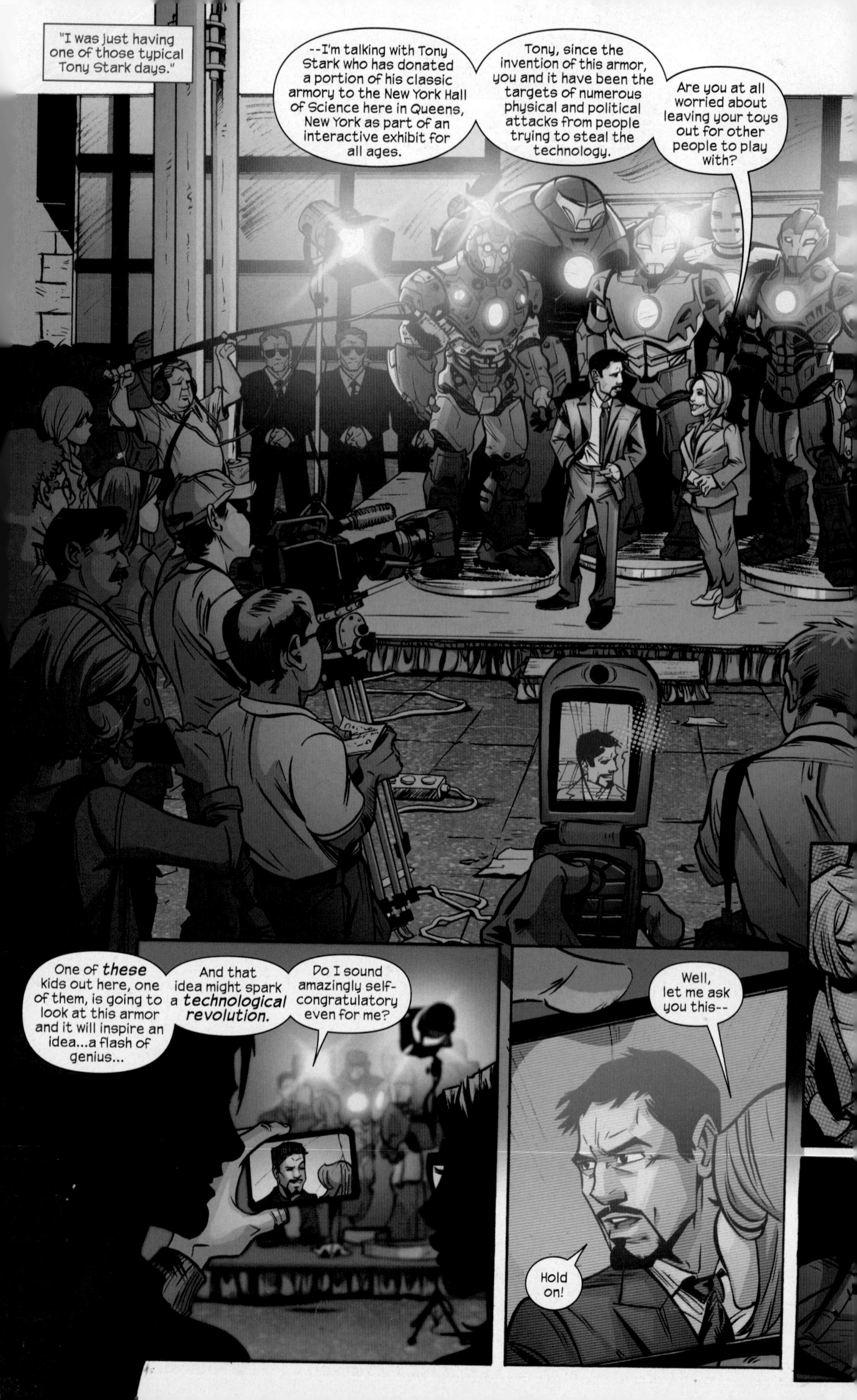
"I was just having one of those typical Tony Stark days."
--I'm talking with Tony Stark who has donated a portion of his classic armory to the New York Hall of Science here in Queens, New York as part of an interactive exhibit for all ages.
Tony, since the invention of this armor, you and it have been the targets of numerous physical and political attacks from people trying to steal the technology.
Are you at all worried about leaving your toys out for other people to play with?
One of *these* kids out here, one of them, is going to look at this armor and it will inspire an idea...a flash of genius...
And that idea might spark a *technological revolution.*
Do I sound amazingly self-congratulatory even for me?
Well, let me ask you this--
Hold on!

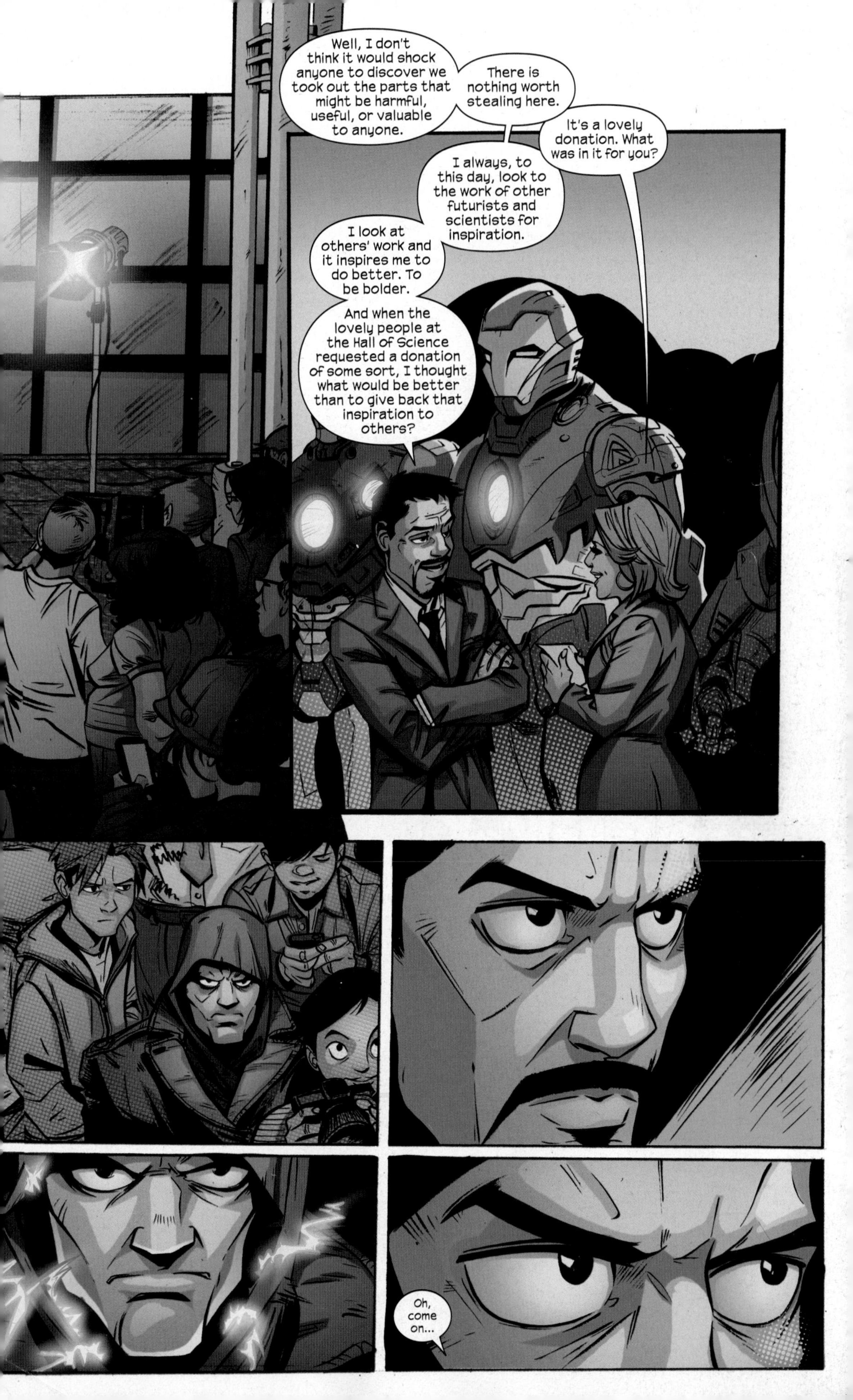
Well, I don't think it would shock anyone to discover we took out the parts that might be harmful, useful, or valuable to anyone.
There is nothing worth stealing here.
It's a lovely donation. What was in it for you?
I always, to this day, look to the work of other futurists and scientists for inspiration.
I look at others' work and it inspires me to do better. To be bolder.
And when the lovely people at the Hall of Science requested a donation of some sort, I thought what would be better than to give back that inspiration to others?
Oh, come on...

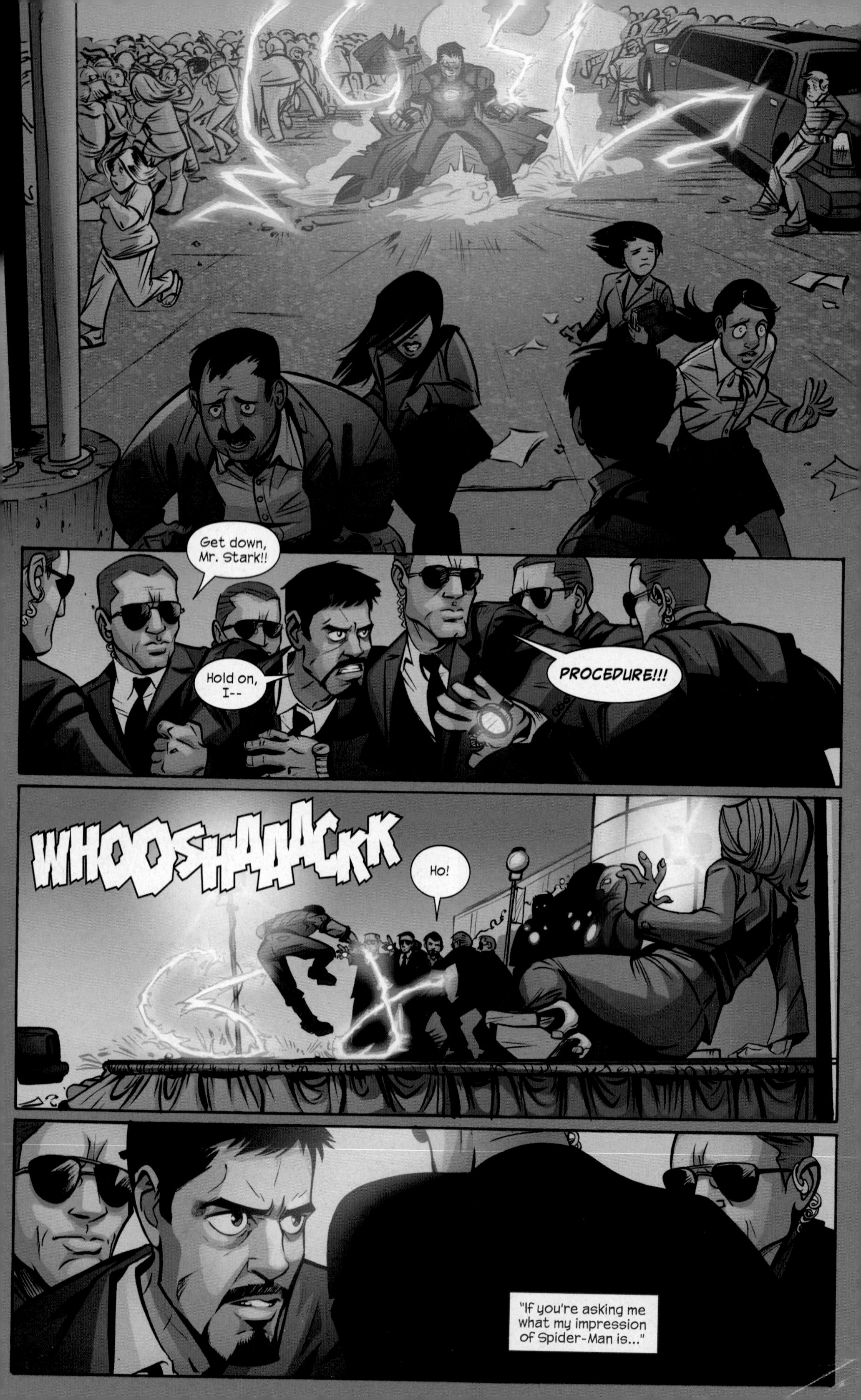
Get down, Mr. Stark!!
Hold on, I--
PROCEDURE!!!
WHOOSHAAACKK
Ho!
"If you're asking me what my impression of Spider-Man is..."

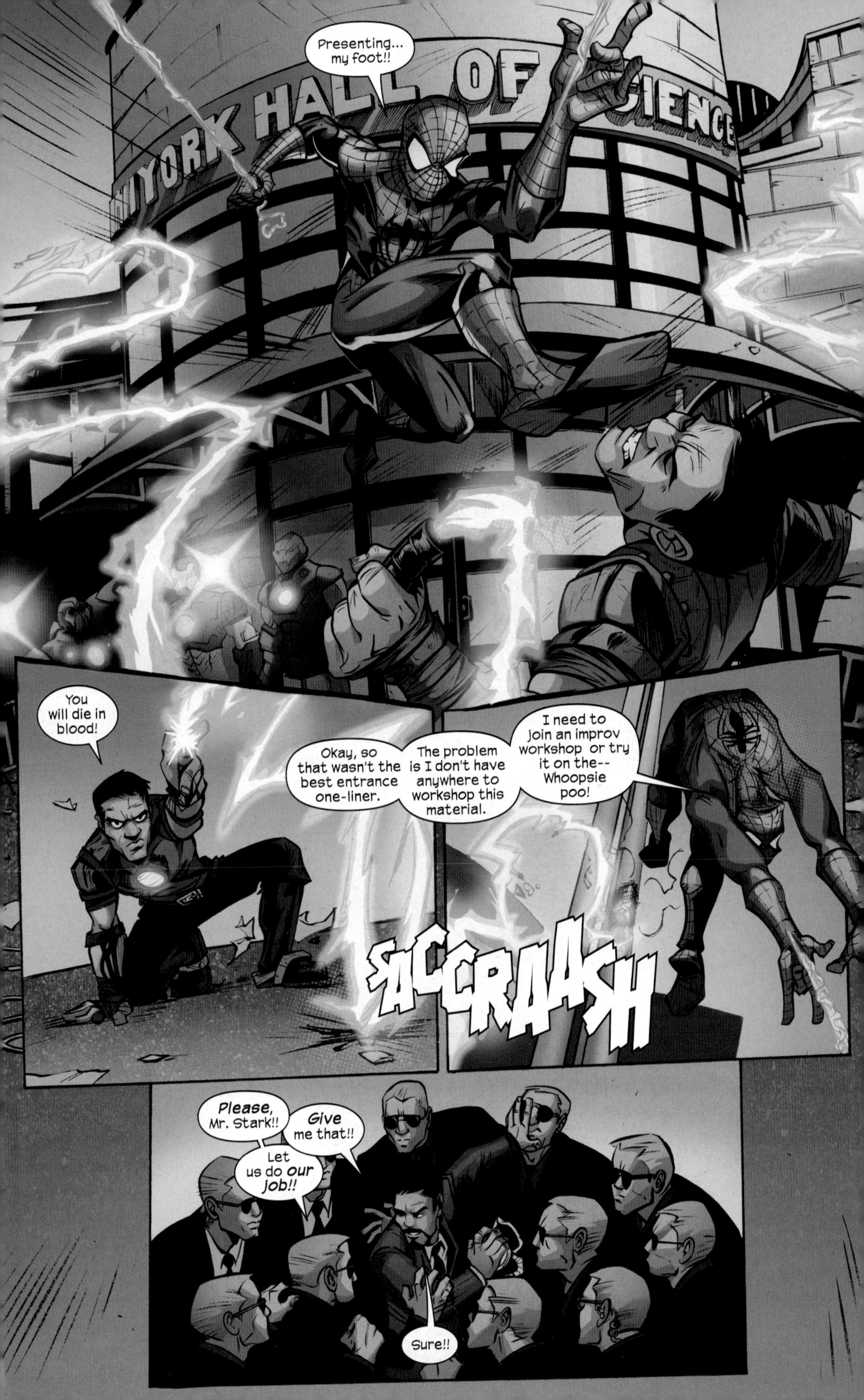
Presenting... my foot!!
NEW YORK HALL OF SCIENCE
You will die in blood!
Okay, so that wasn't the best entrance one-liner.
The problem is I don't have anywhere to workshop this material.
I need to join an improv workshop or try it on the-- Whoopsie poo!
SACCRAASH
Please, Mr. Stark!!
Give me that!!
Let us do our job!!
Sure!!

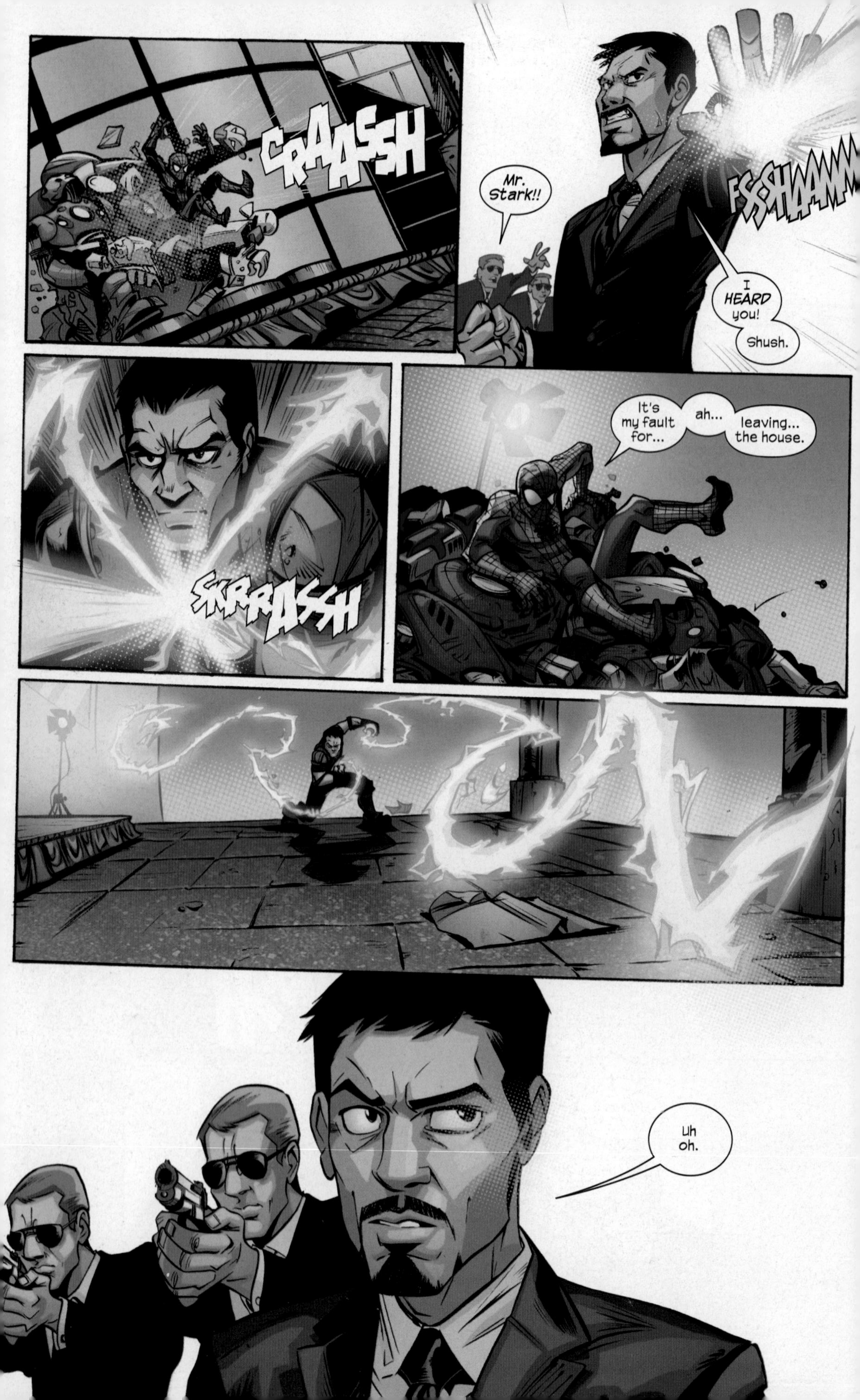
CRAAASSH
Mr. Stark!!
FSSSHAAMM
I HEARD you!
Shush.
SKRRASSH
It's my fault for...
ah...
leaving... the house.
Uh oh.

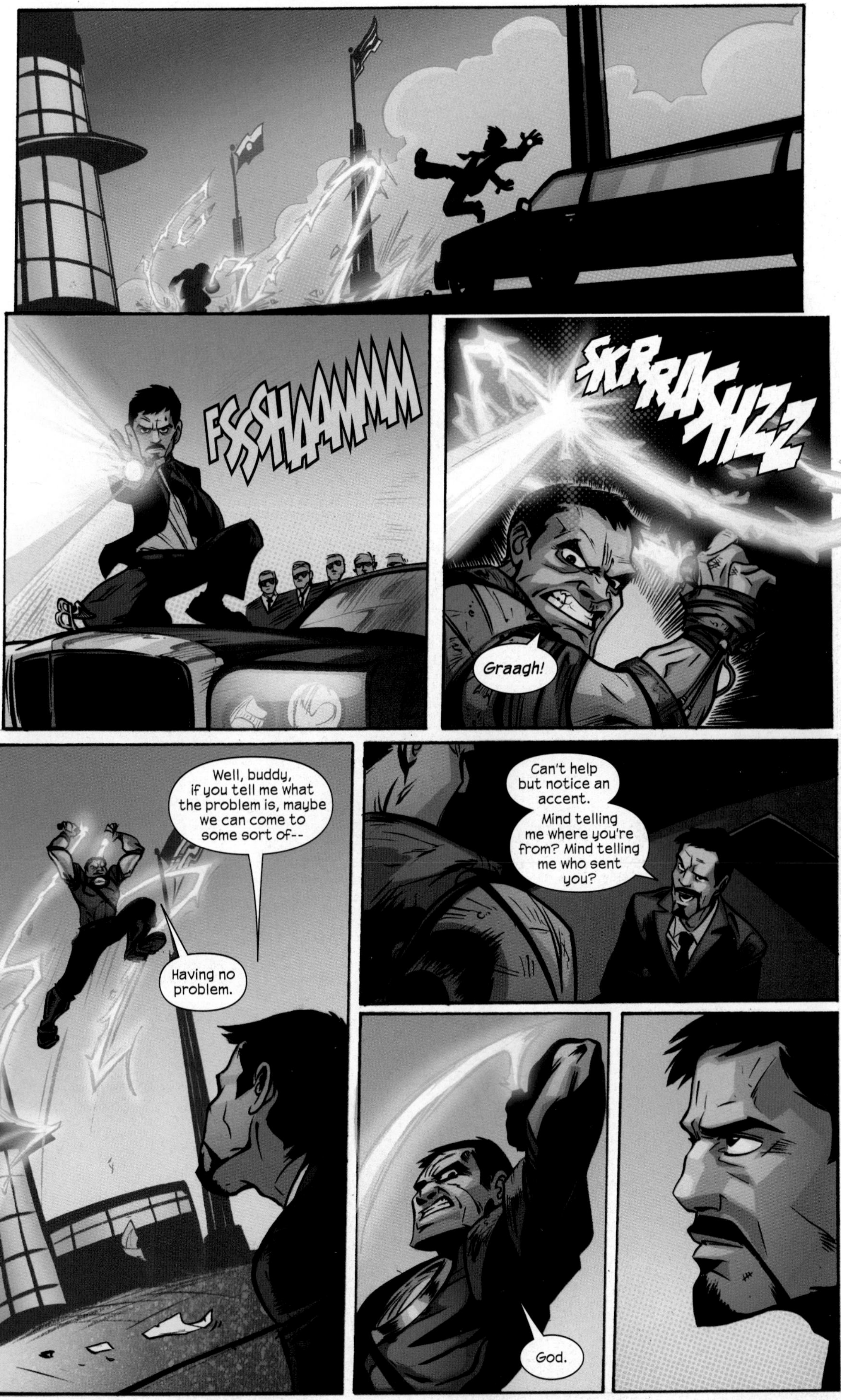
FSSHAAMMM
SKRRASHZZ
Graagh!
Well, buddy, if you tell me what the problem is, maybe we can come to some sort of--
Having no problem.
Can't help but notice an accent.
Mind telling me where you're from? Mind telling me who sent you?
God.

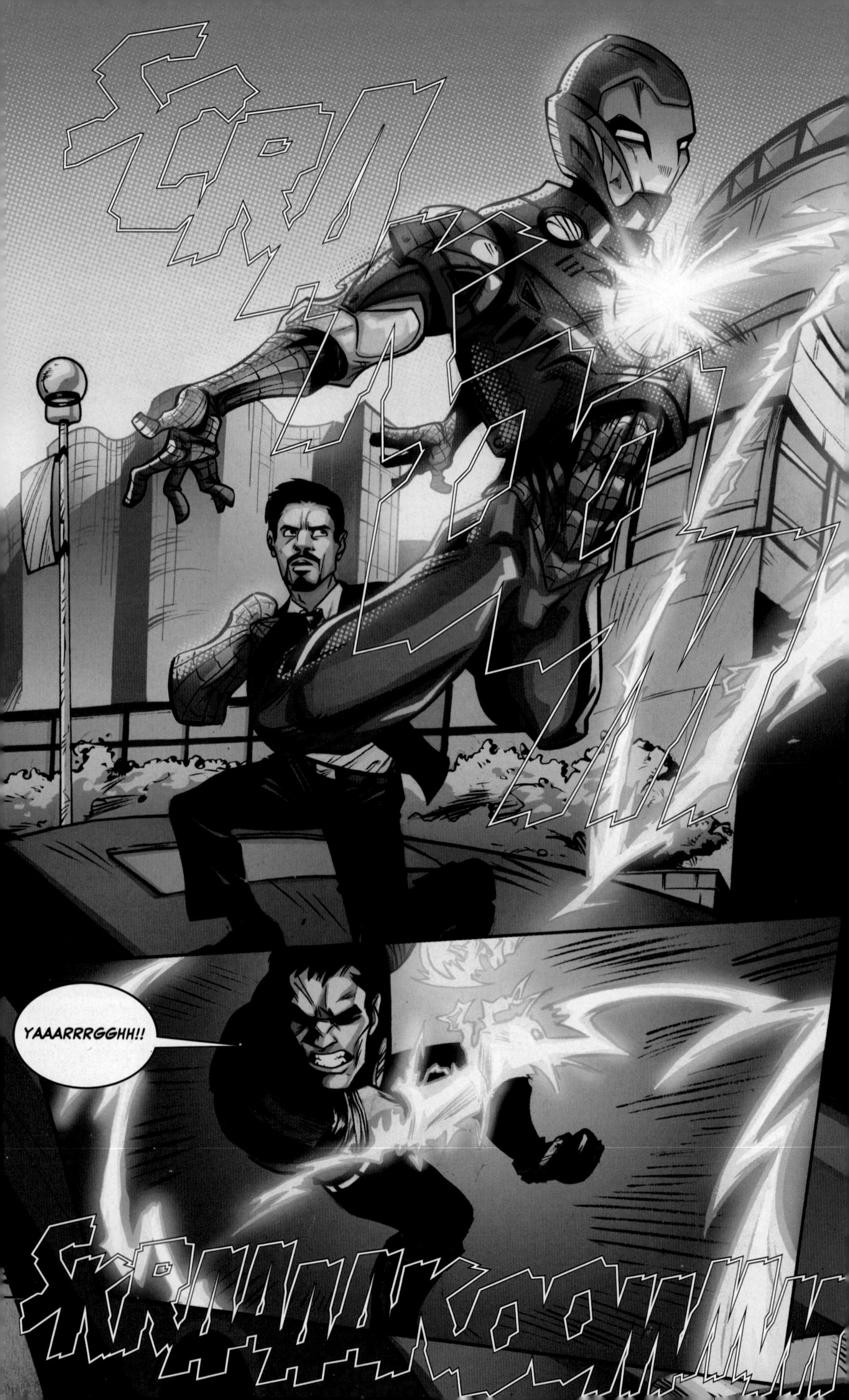
YAAARRRGGHH!!

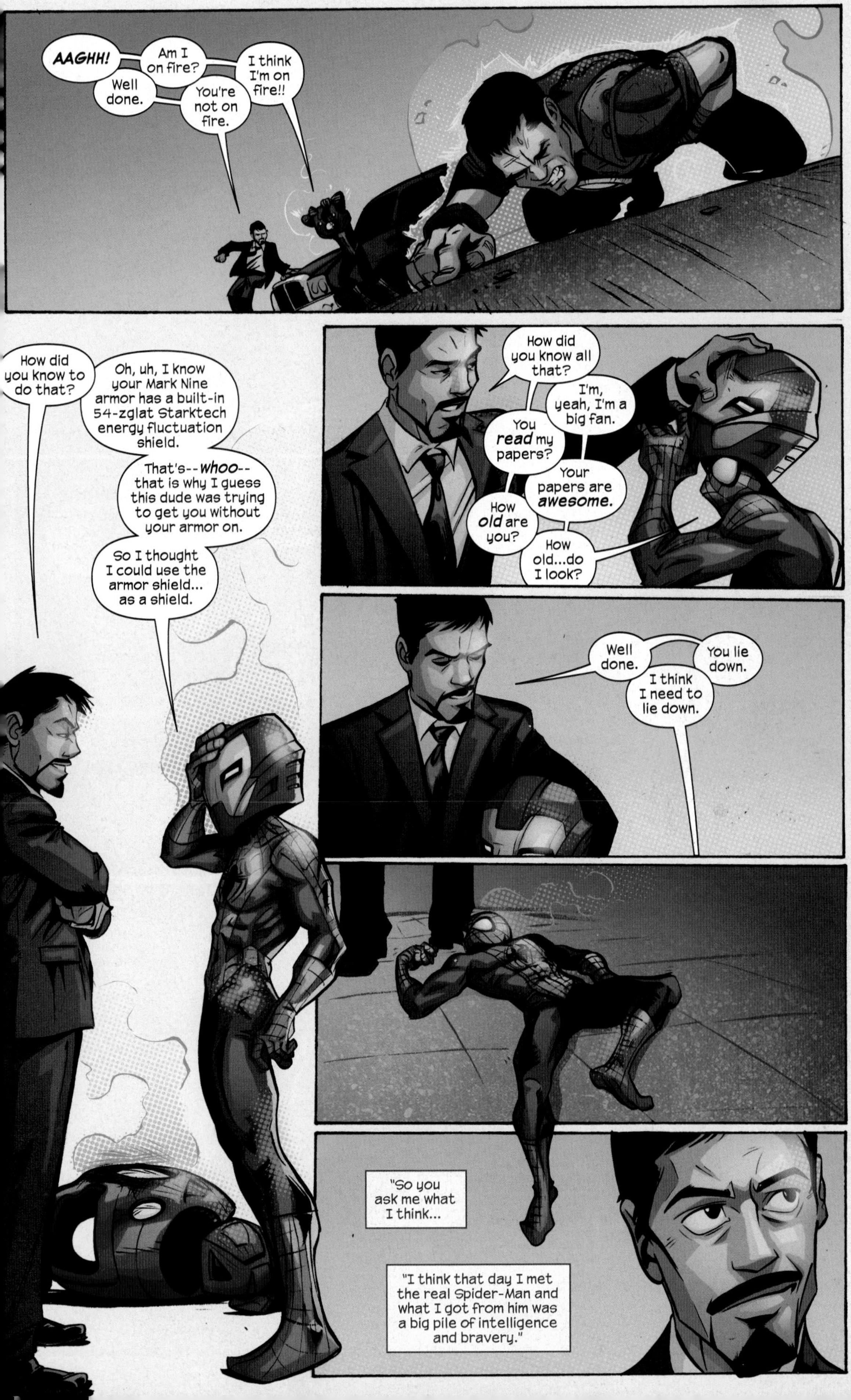
AAGHH!
Am I on fire?
I think I'm on fire!!
Well done.
You're not on fire.
How did you know to do that?
Oh, uh, I know your Mark Nine armor has a built-in 54-zglat Starktech energy fluctuation shield.
That's--*whoo*--that is why I guess this dude was trying to get you without your armor on.
So I thought I could use the armor shield... as a shield.
How did you know all that?
I'm, yeah, I'm a big fan.
You *read* my papers?
Your papers are *awesome.*
How *old* are you?
How old...do I look?
Well done.
You lie down.
I think I need to lie down.
"So you ask me what I think...
"I think that day I met the real Spider-Man and what I got from him was a big pile of intelligence and bravery."

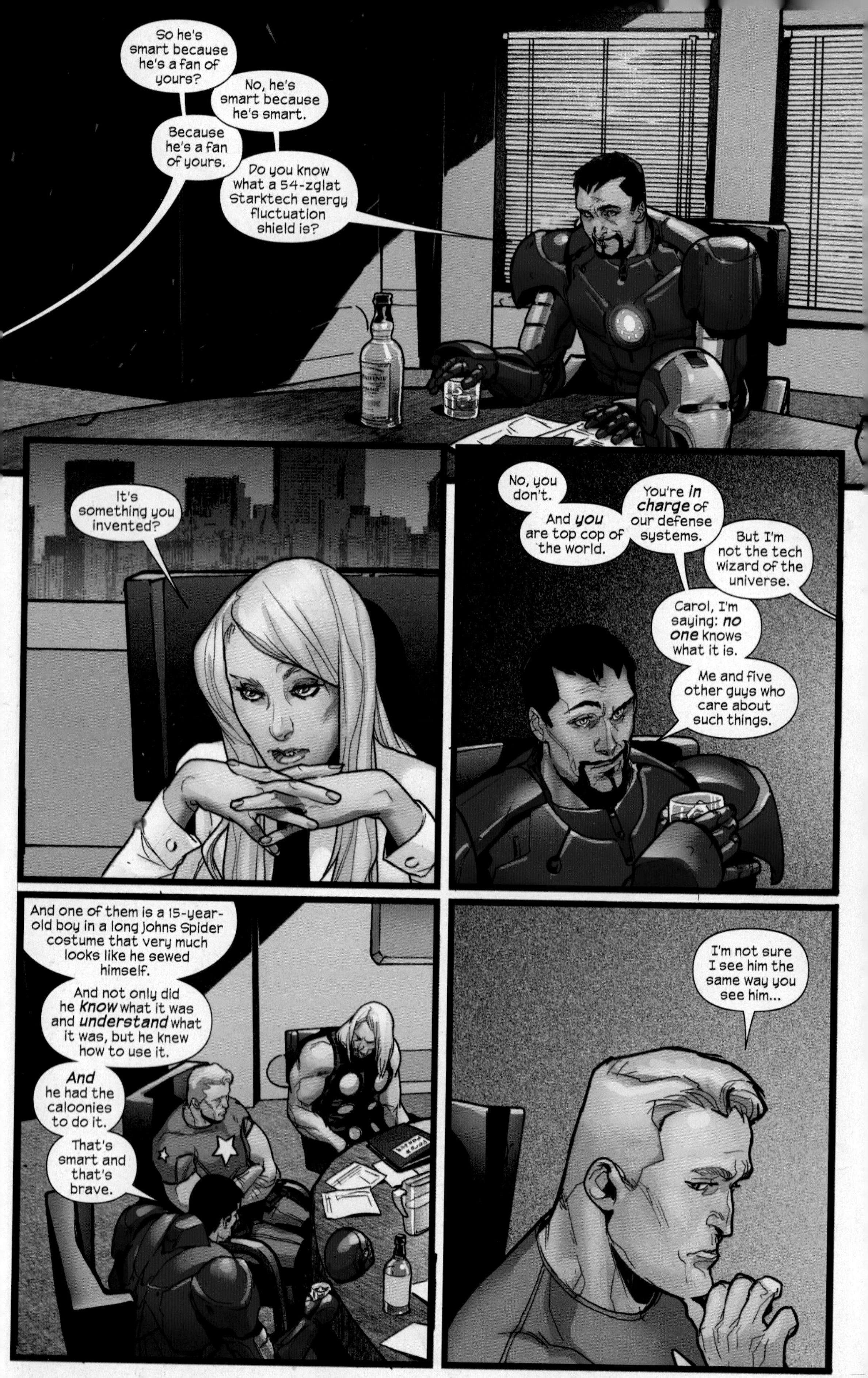
So he's smart because he's a fan of yours?
No, he's smart because he's smart.
Because he's a fan of yours.
Do you know what a 54-zglat Starktech energy fluctuation shield is?
It's something you invented?
No, you don't.
And you are top cop of the world.
You're in charge of our defense systems.
But I'm not the tech wizard of the universe.
Carol, I'm saying: no one knows what it is.
Me and five other guys who care about such things.
And one of them is a 15-year-old boy in a long johns Spider costume that very much looks like he sewed himself.
And not only did he know what it was and understand what it was, but he knew how to use it.
And he had the caloonies to do it.
That's smart and that's brave.
I'm not sure I see him the same way you see him...

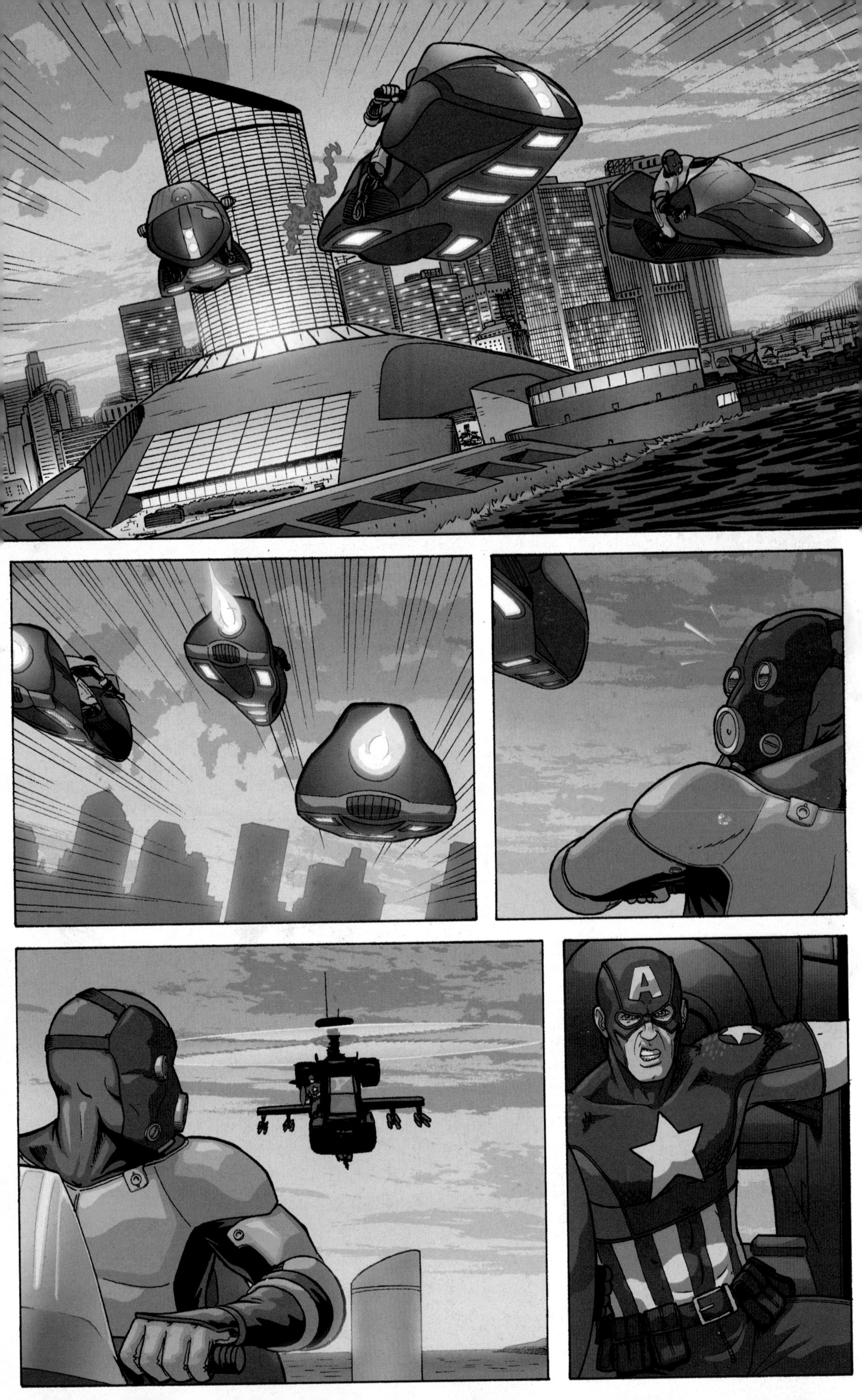

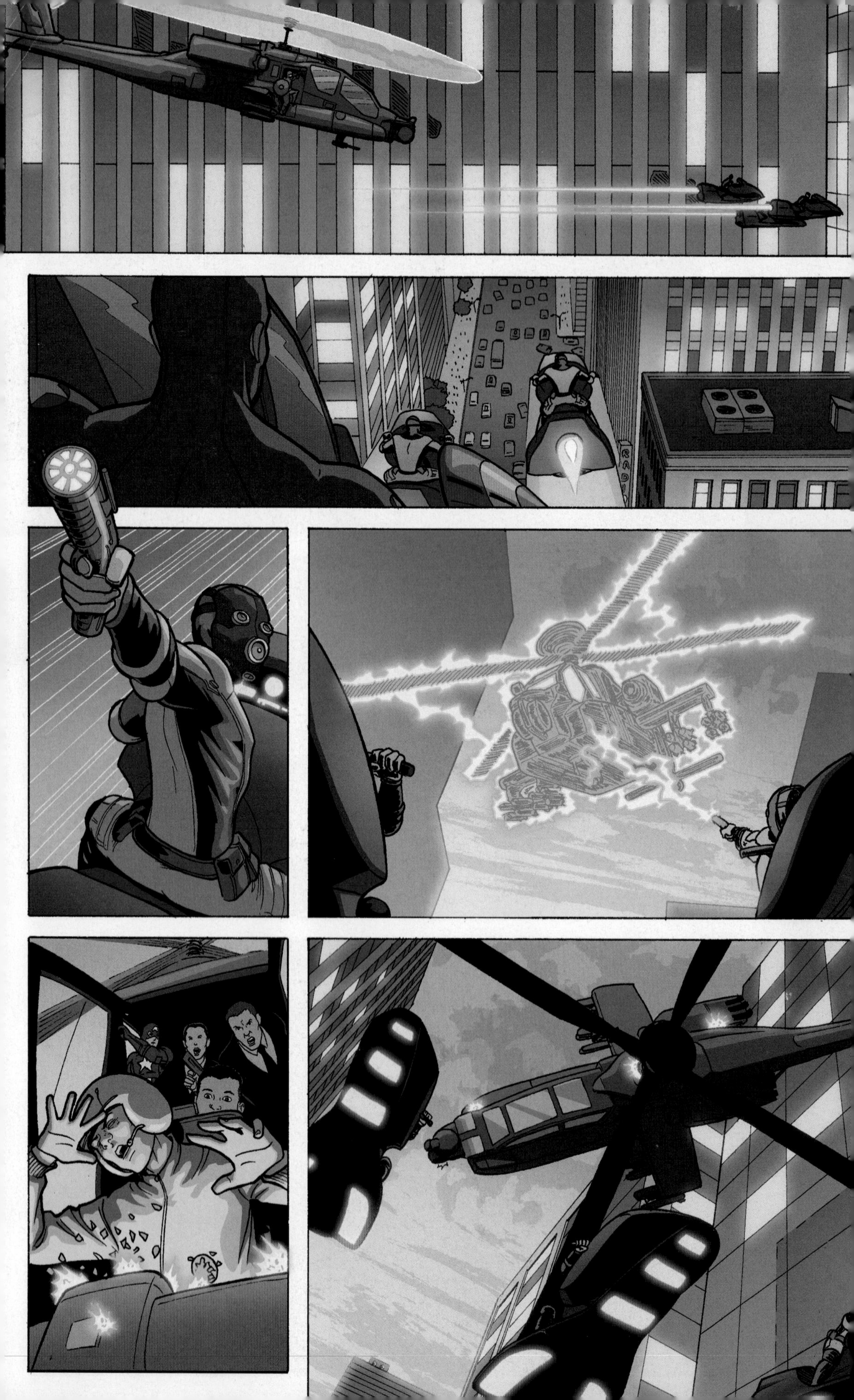

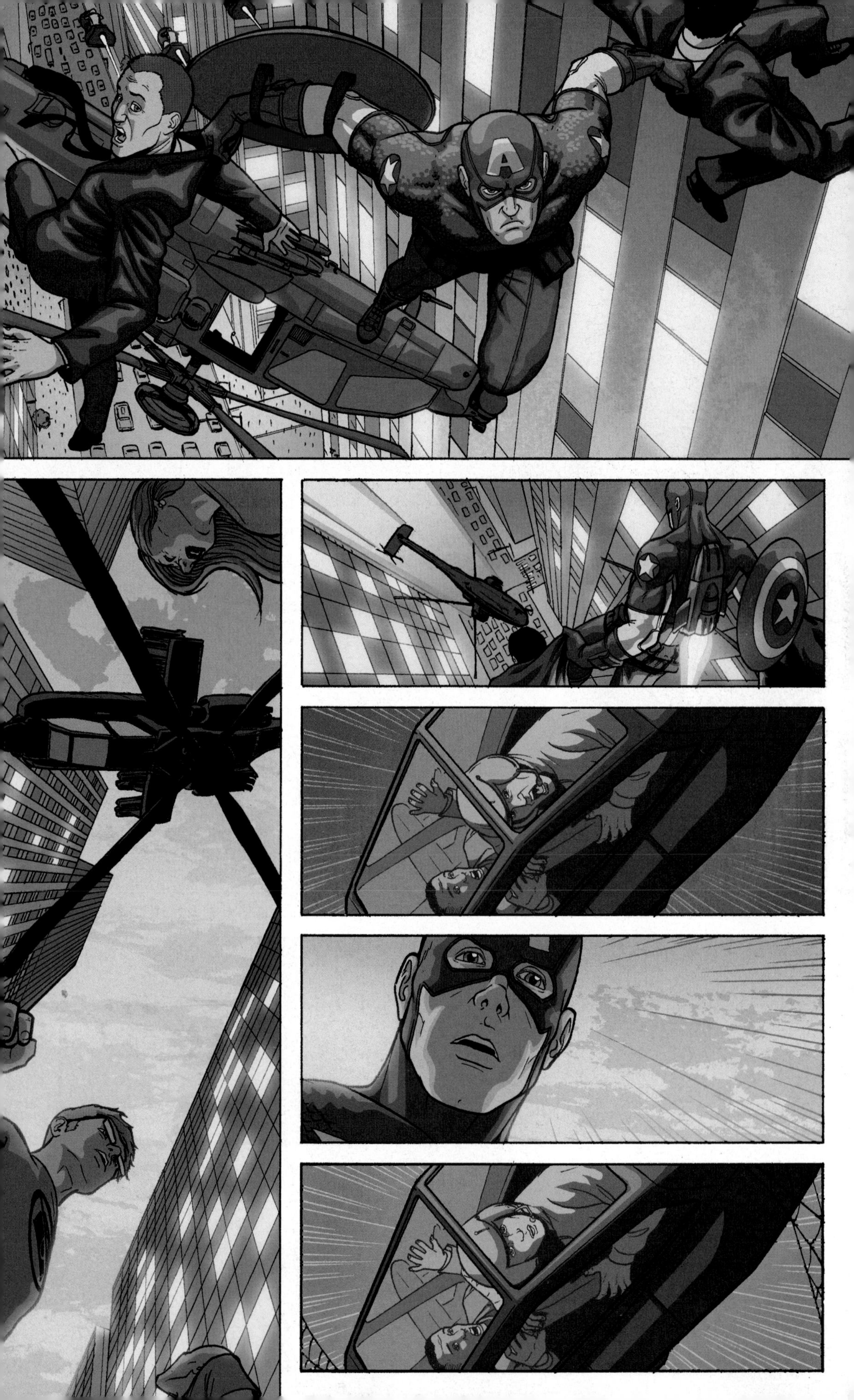

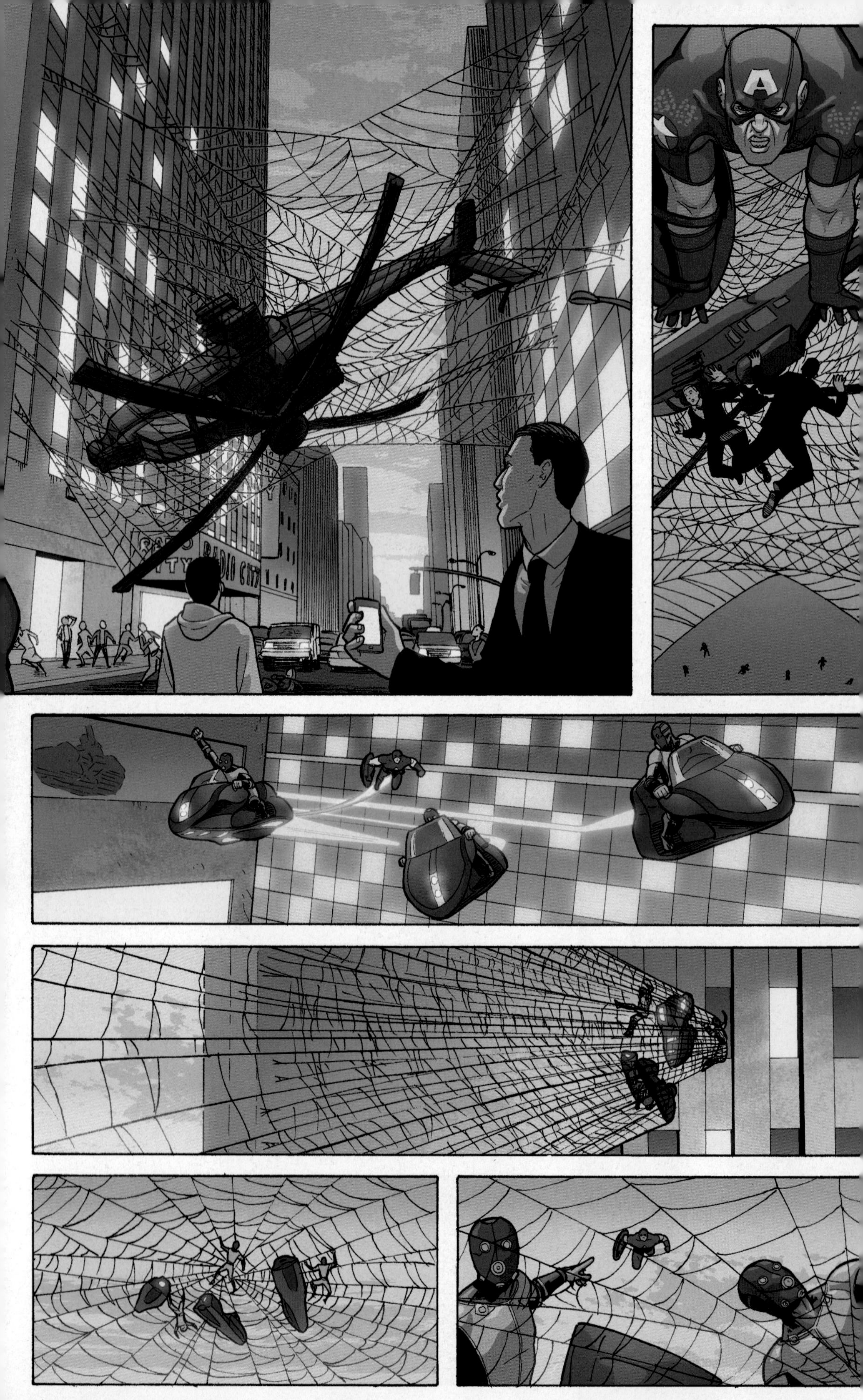
RADIO CITY

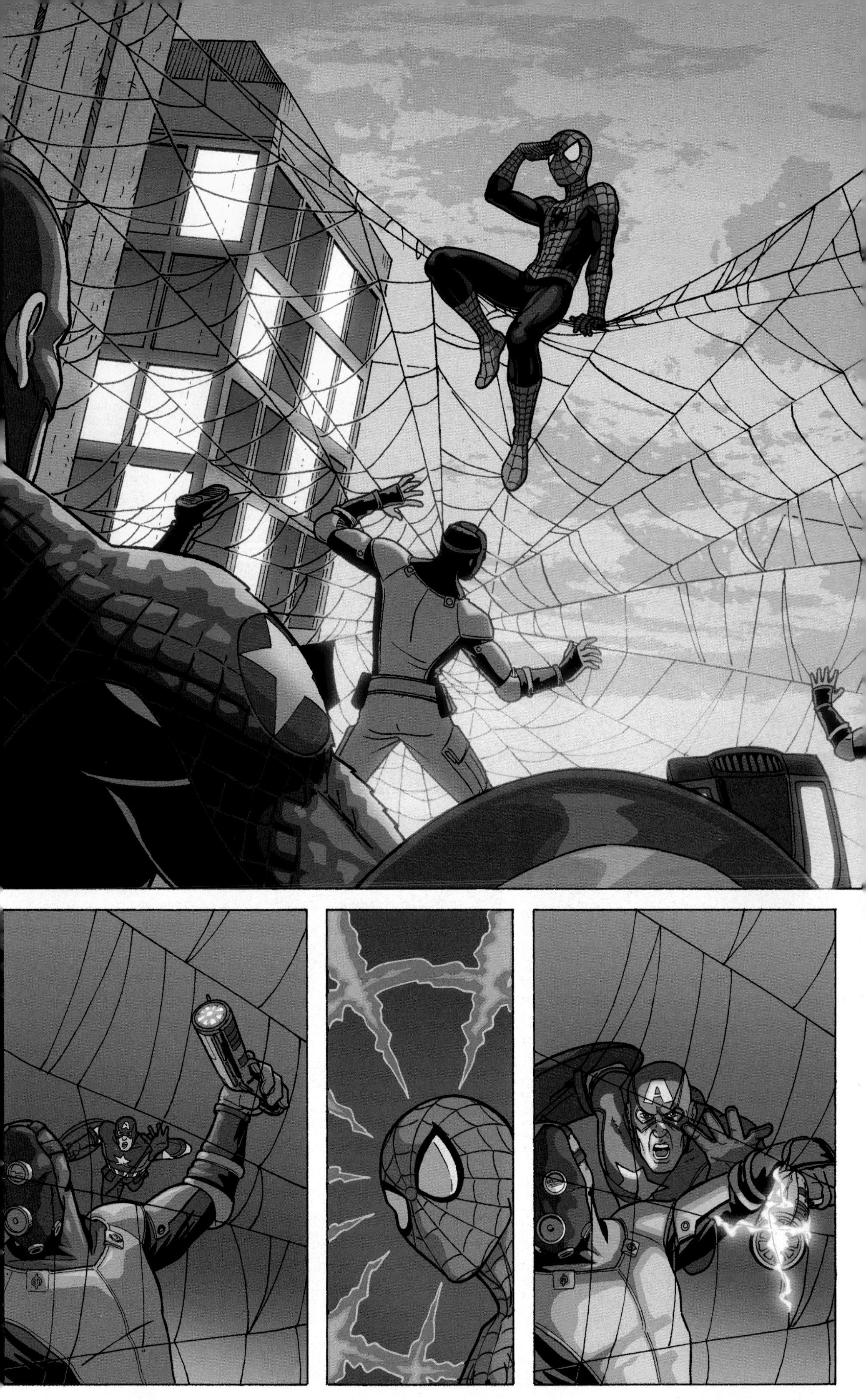

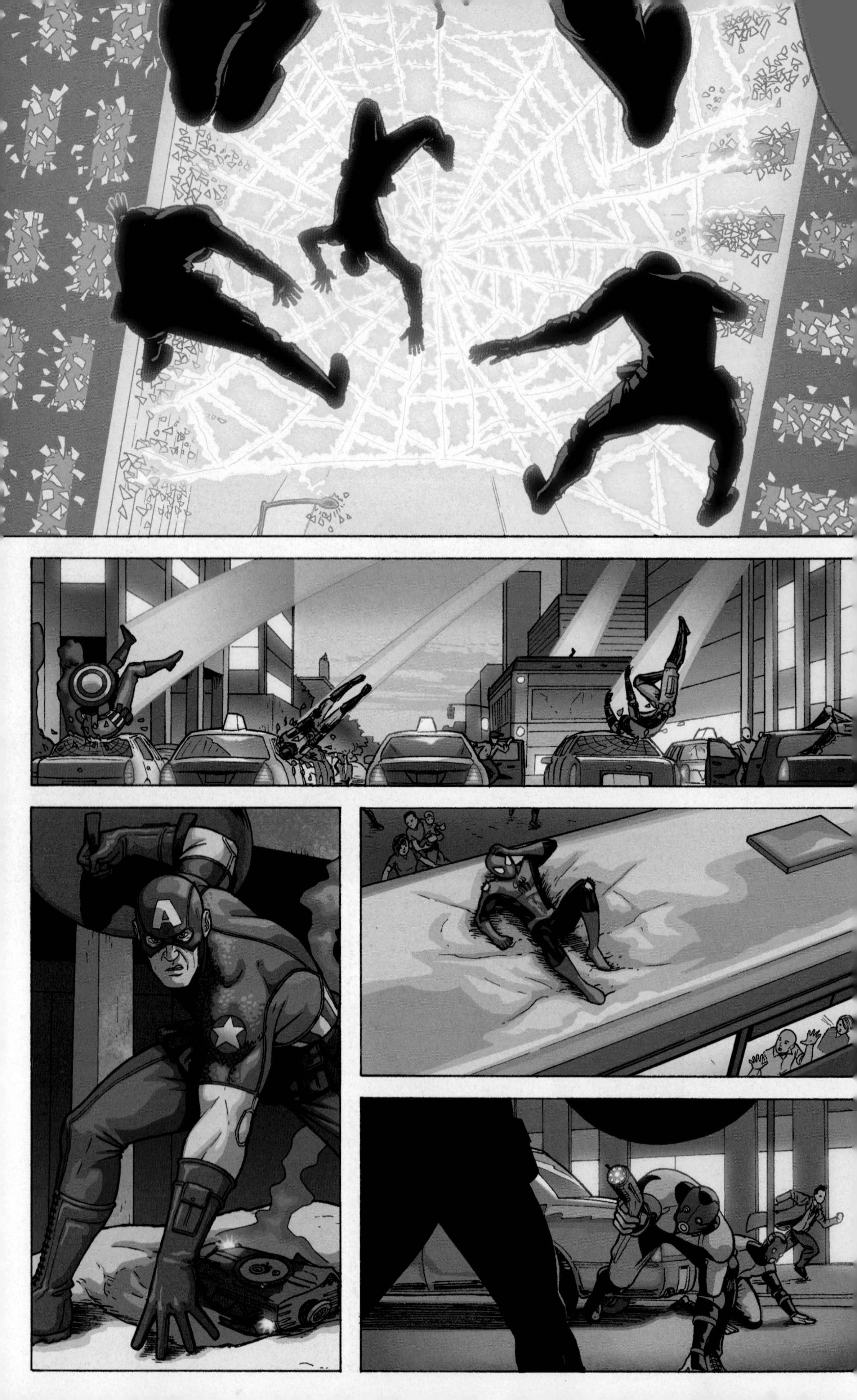

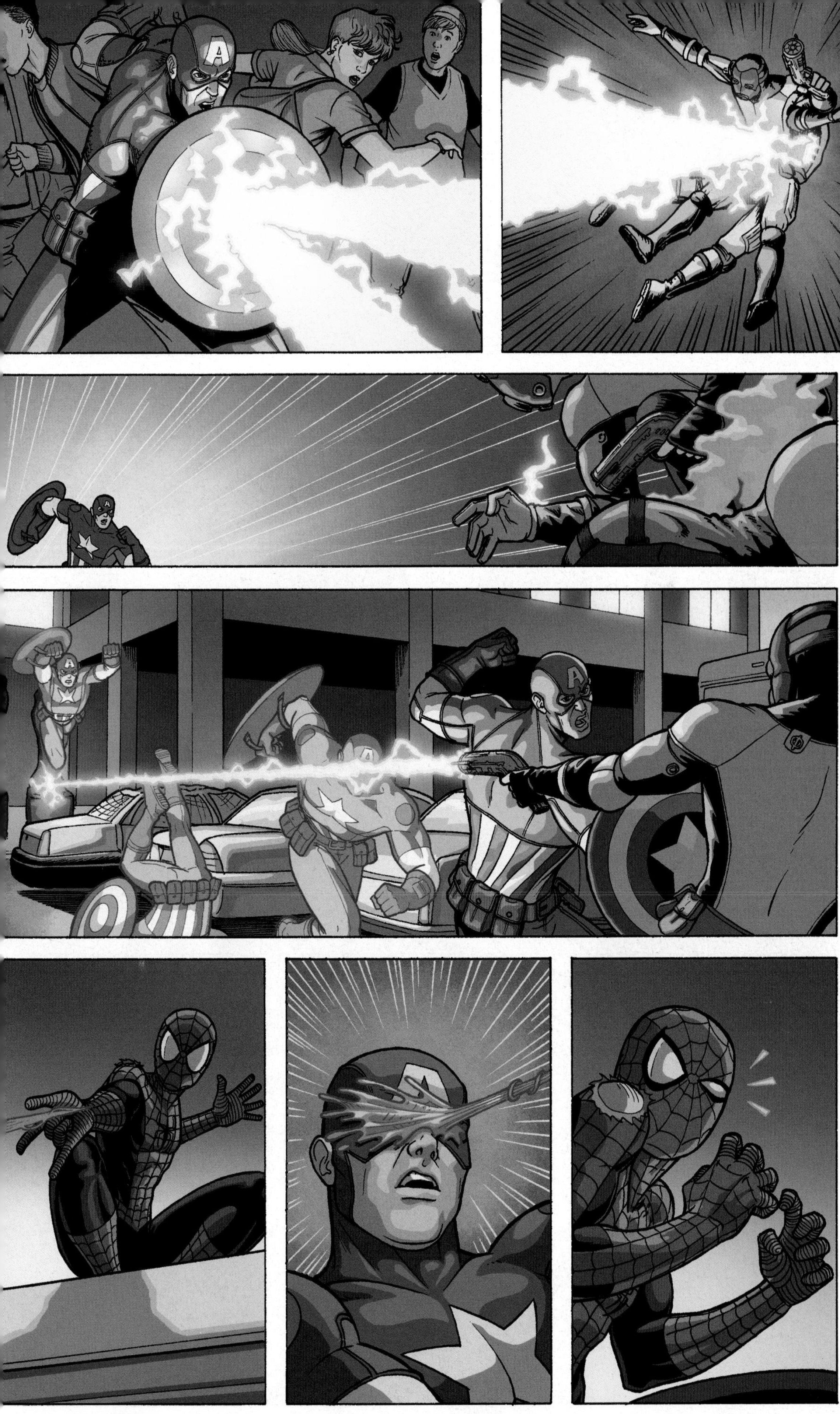

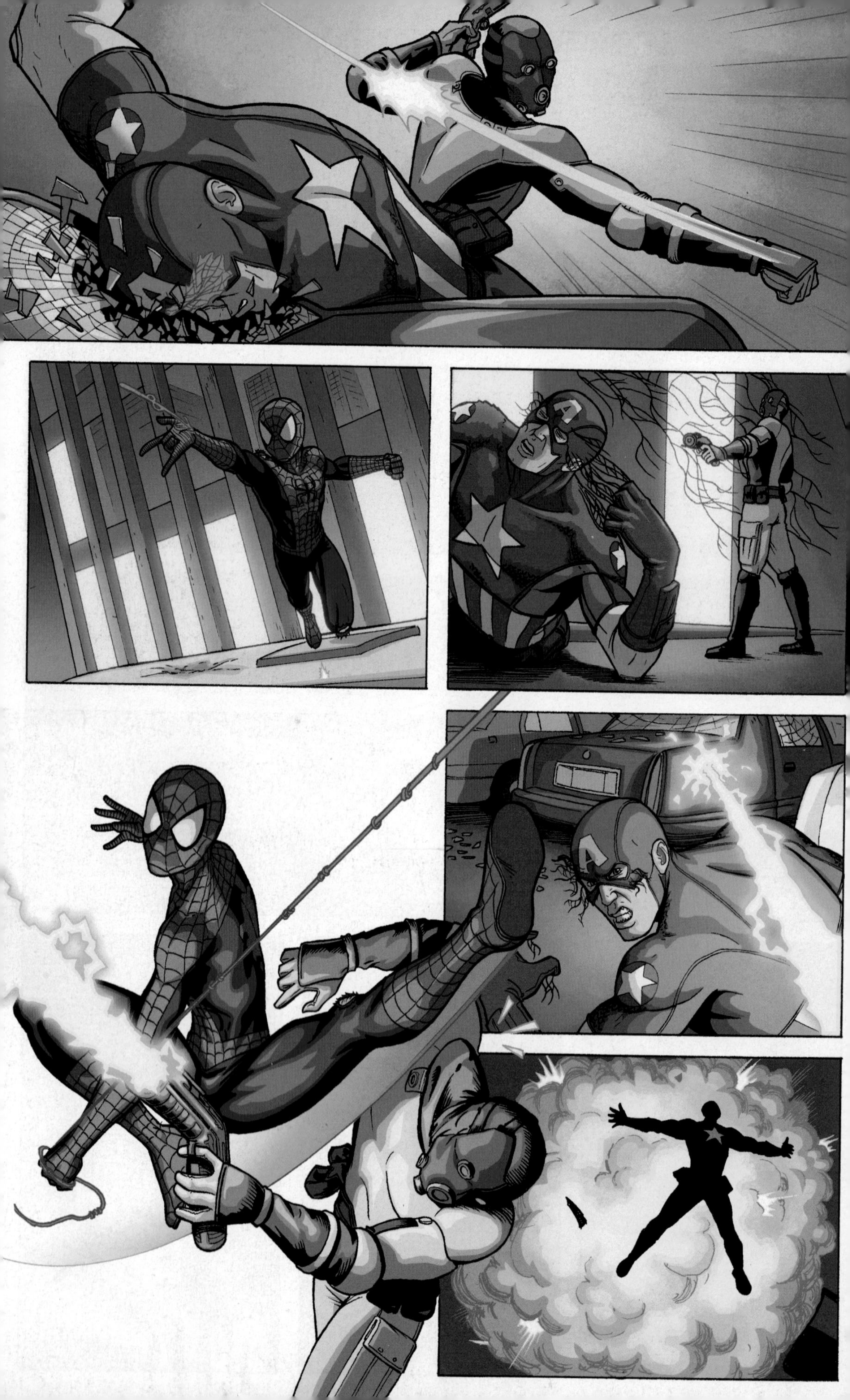

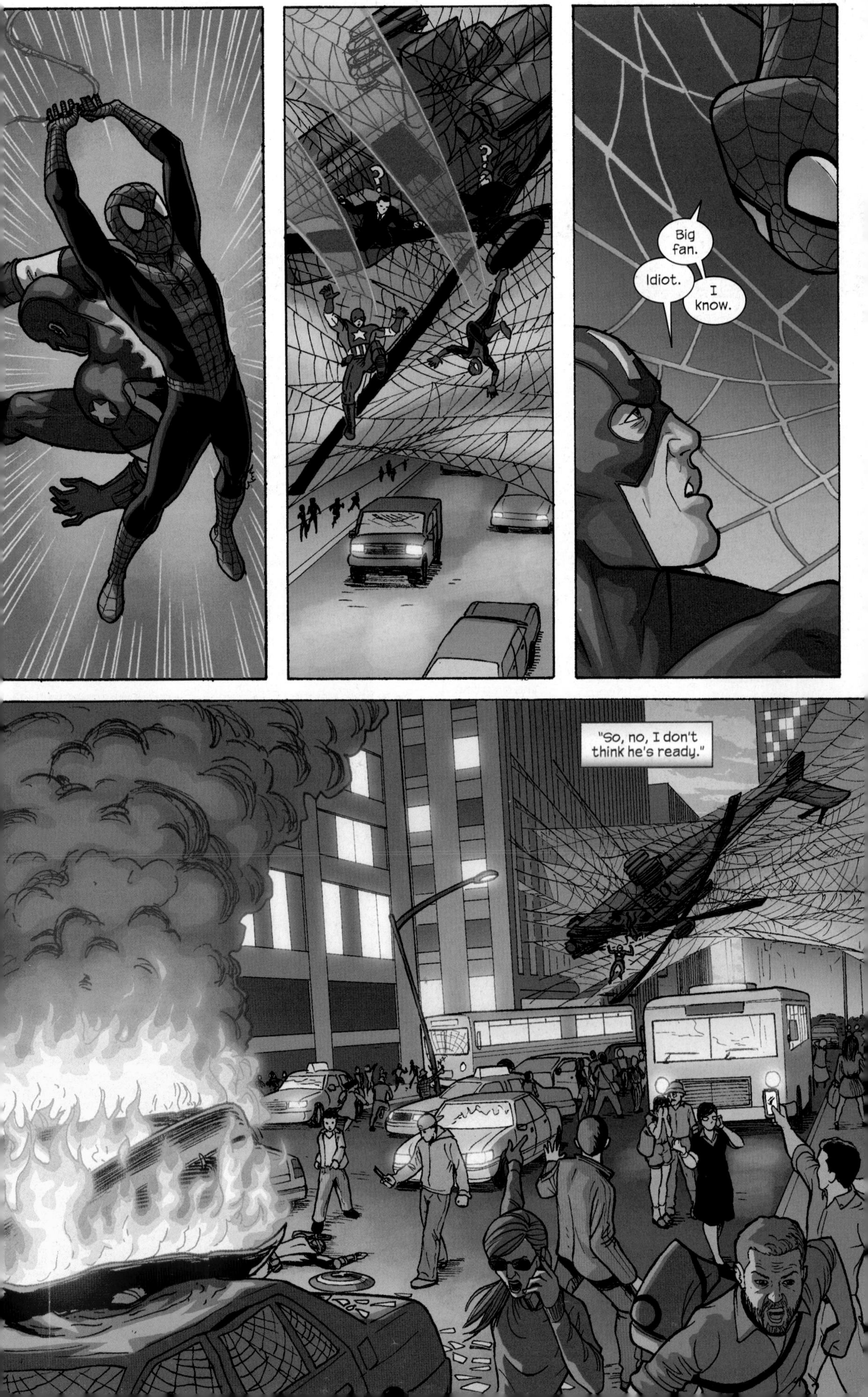
?
?
Big fan.
Idiot.
I know.
"So, no, I don't think he's ready."

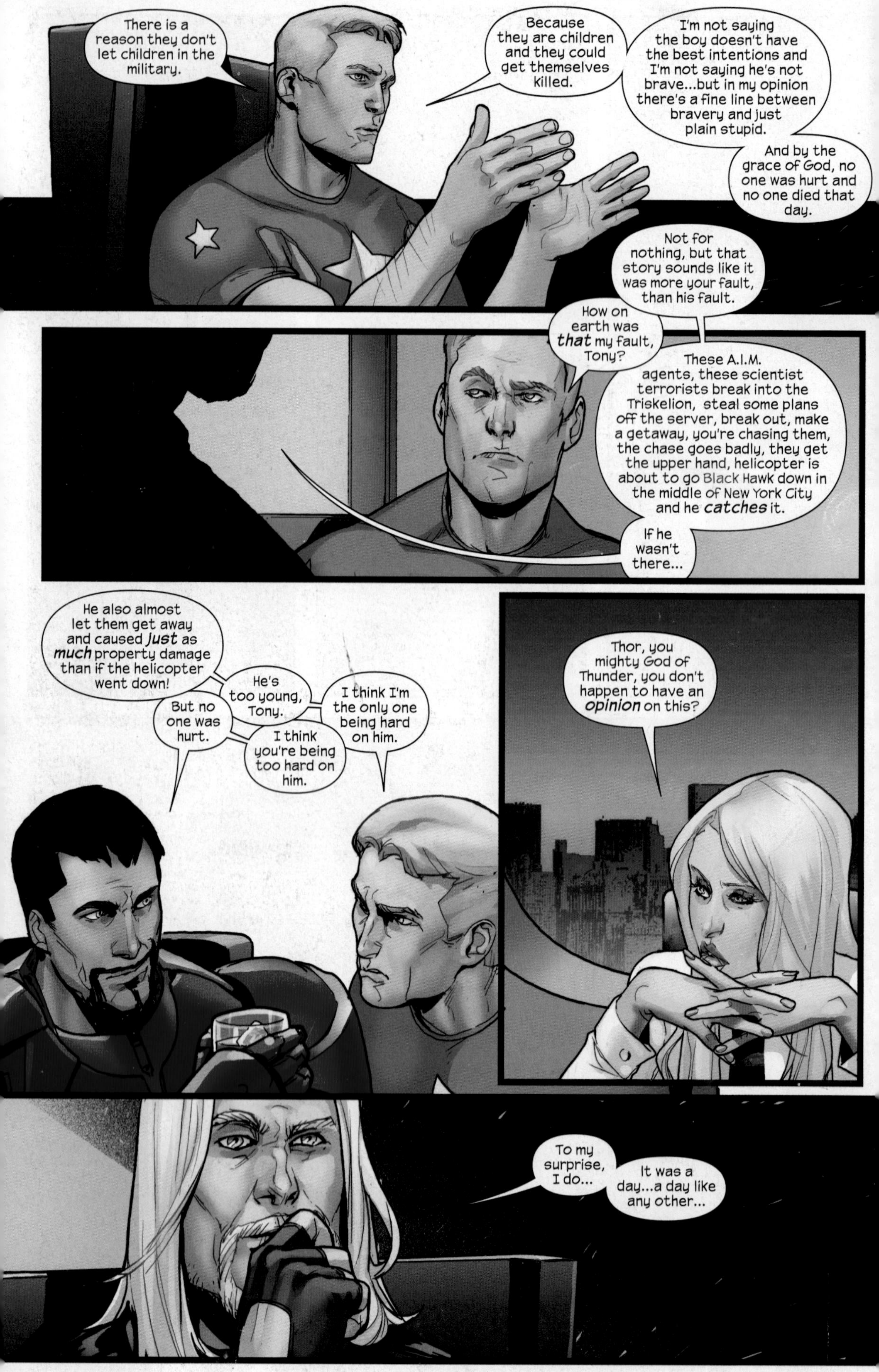
There is a reason they don't let children in the military.
Because they are children and they could get themselves killed.
I'm not saying the boy doesn't have the best intentions and I'm not saying he's not brave...but in my opinion there's a fine line between bravery and just plain stupid.
And by the grace of God, no one was hurt and no one died that day.
Not for nothing, but that story sounds like it was more your fault, than his fault.
How on earth was *that* my fault, Tony?
These A.I.M. agents, these scientist terrorists break into the Triskelion, steal some plans off the server, break out, make a getaway, you're chasing them, the chase goes badly, they get the upper hand, helicopter is about to go Black Hawk down in the middle of New York City and he *catches* it.
If he wasn't there...
He also almost let them get away and caused *just* as *much* property damage than if the helicopter went down!
But no one was hurt.
He's too young, Tony.
I think you're being too hard on him.
I think I'm the only one being hard on him.
Thor, you mighty God of Thunder, you don't happen to have an *opinion* on this?
To my surprise, I do...
It was a day...a day like any other...

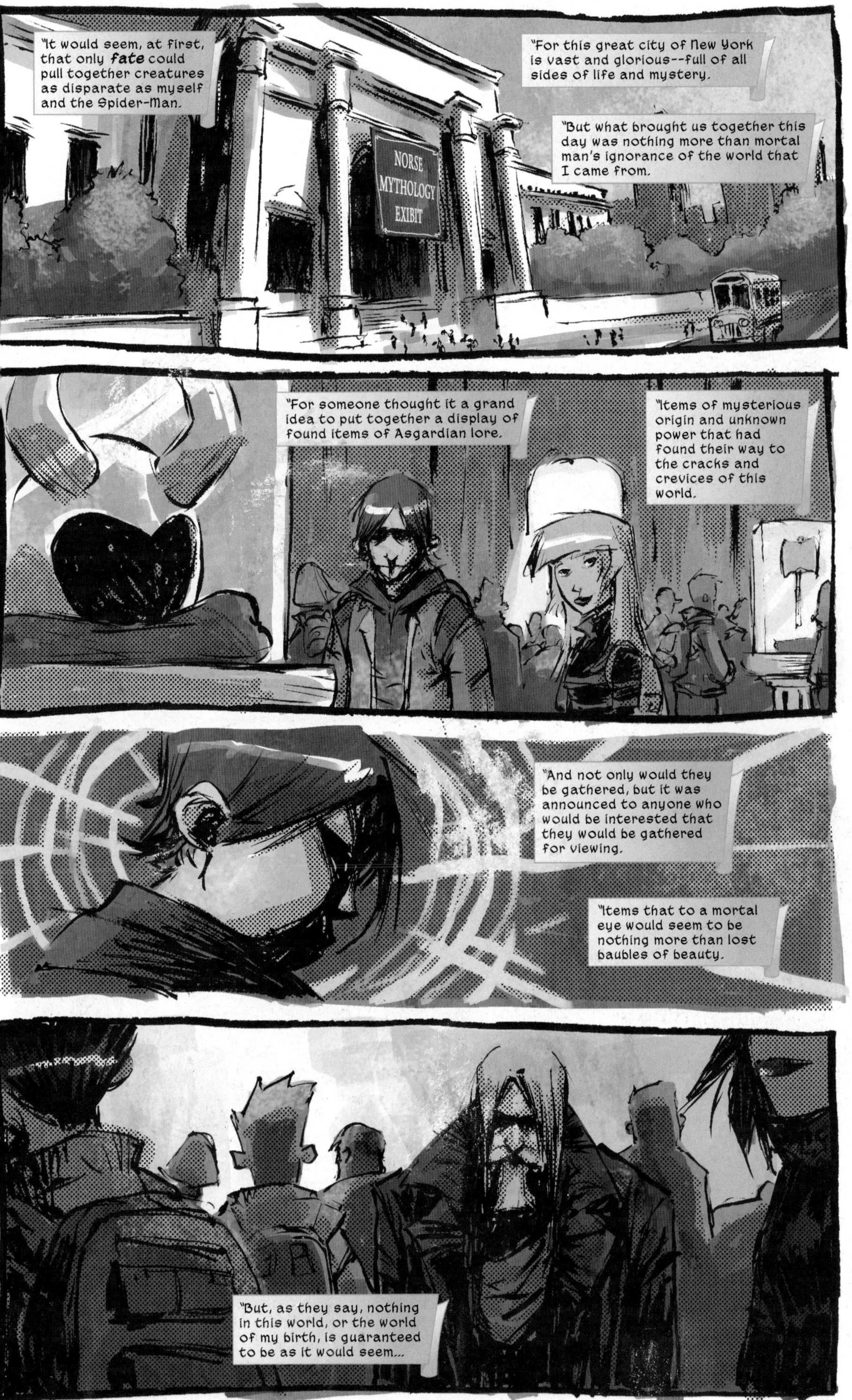
"It would seem, at first, that only *fate* could pull together creatures as disparate as myself and the Spider-Man.
"For this great city of New York is vast and glorious--full of all sides of life and mystery.
"But what brought us together this day was nothing more than mortal man's ignorance of the world that I came from.
NORSE MYTHOLOGY EXIBIT
"For someone thought it a grand idea to put together a display of found items of Asgardian lore.
"Items of mysterious origin and unknown power that had found their way to the cracks and crevices of this world.
"And not only would they be gathered, but it was announced to anyone who would be interested that they would be gathered for viewing.
"Items that to a mortal eye would seem to be nothing more than lost baubles of beauty.
"But, as they say, nothing in this world, or the world of my birth, is guaranteed to be as it would seem...

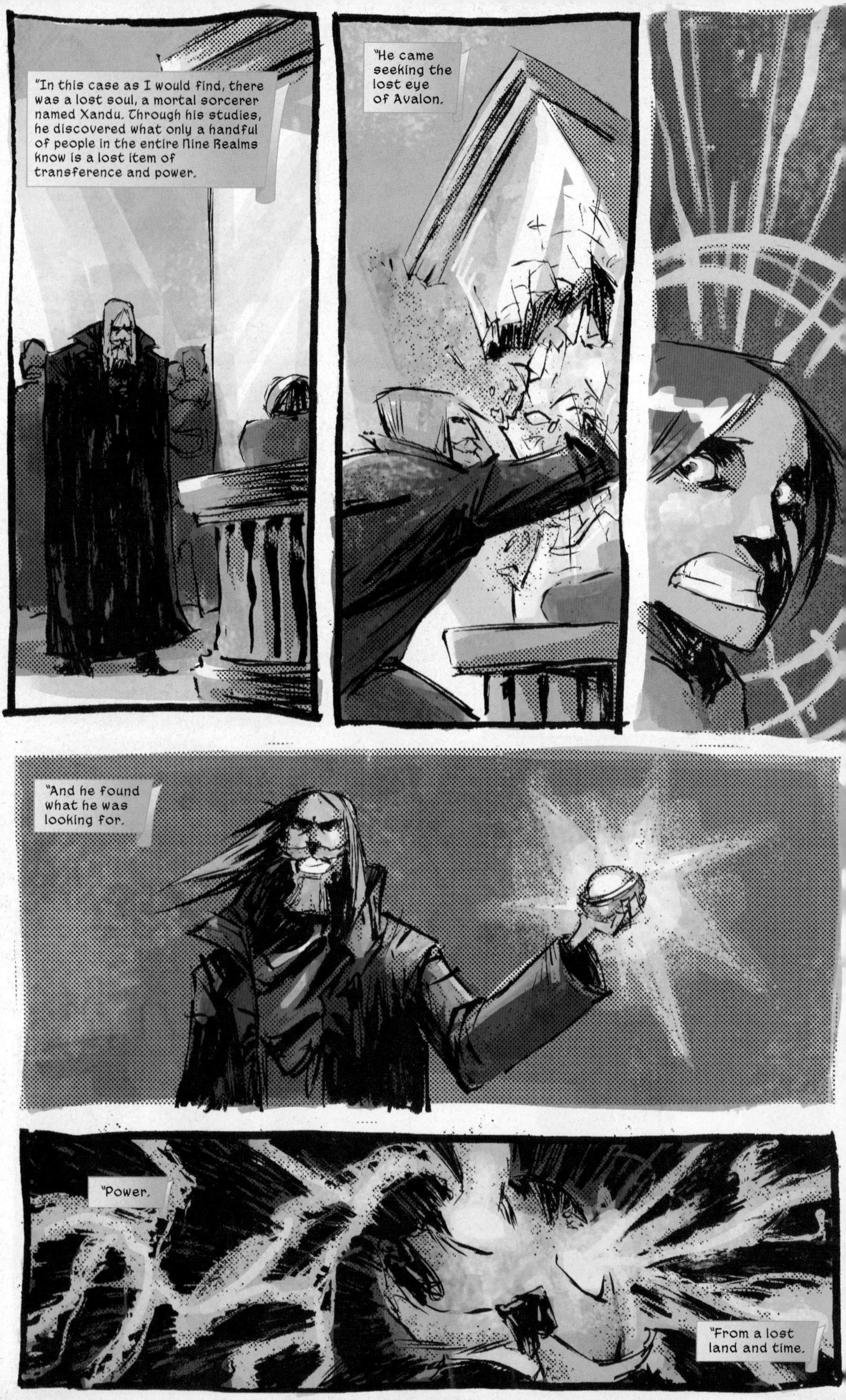
"In this case as I would find, there was a lost soul, a mortal sorcerer named Xandu. Through his studies, he discovered what only a handful of people in the entire Nine Realms know is a lost item of transference and power.
"He came seeking the lost eye of Avalon.
"And he found what he was looking for.
"Power.
"From a lost land and time.

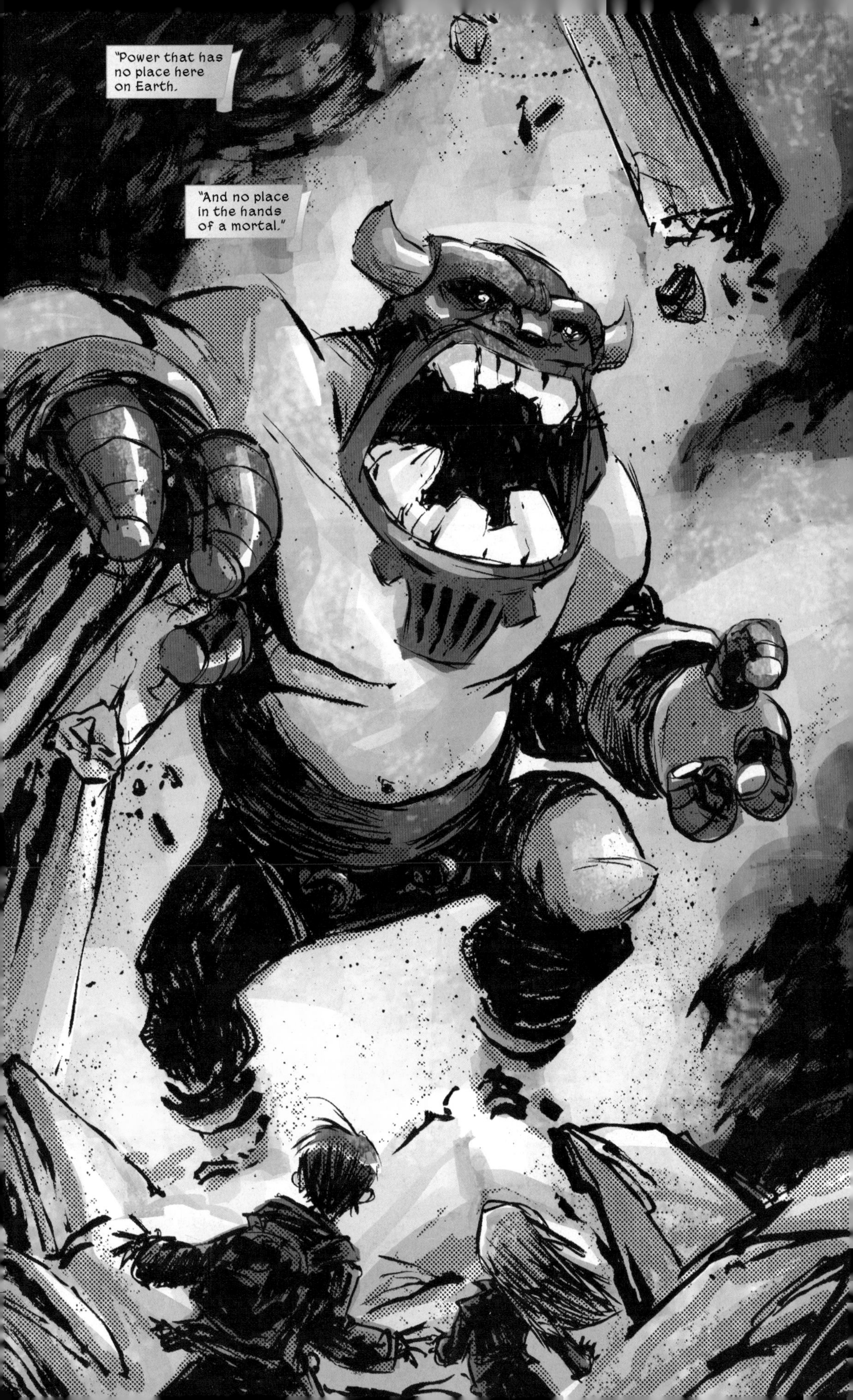
"Power that has no place here on Earth.
"And no place in the hands of a mortal."

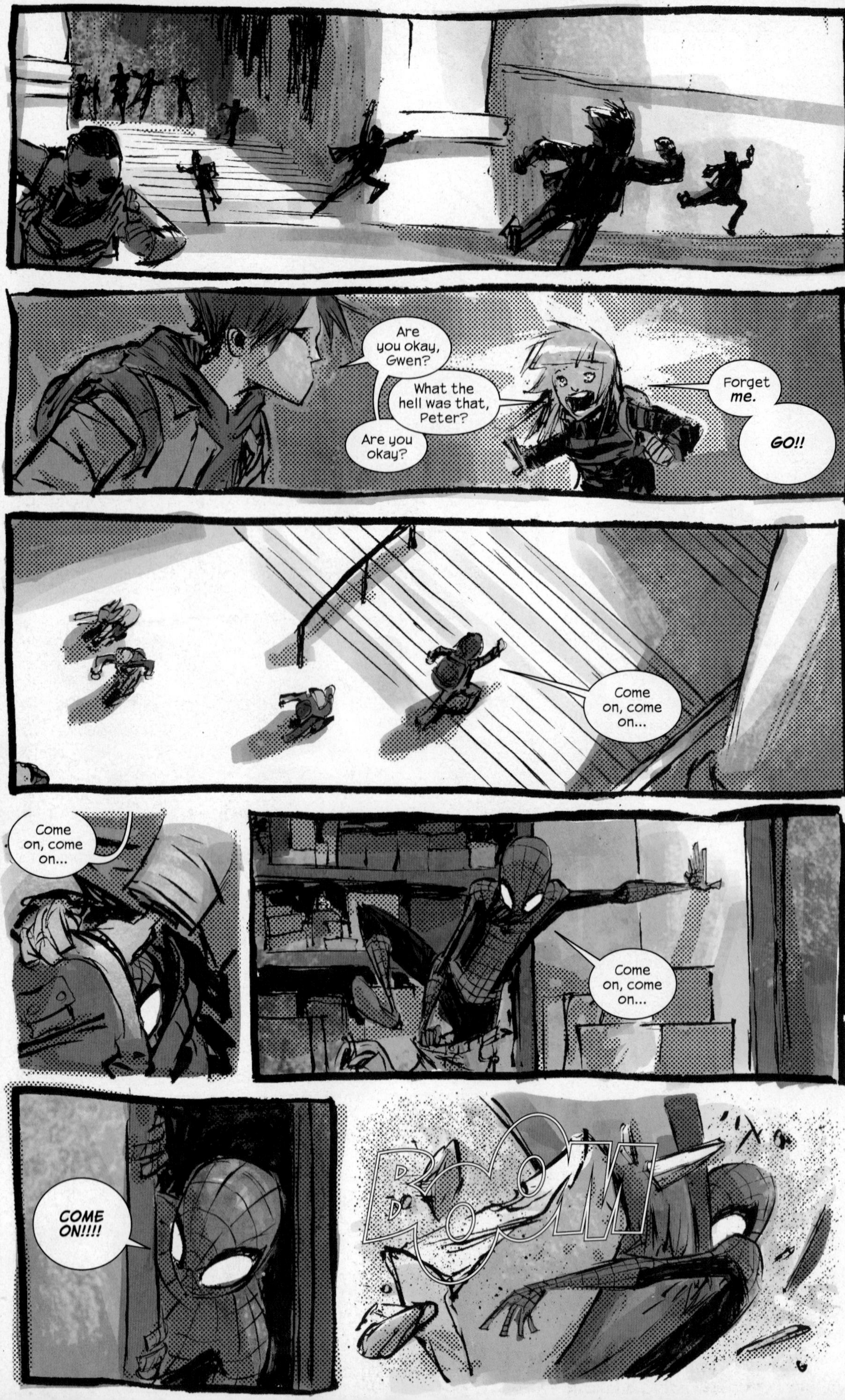
Are you okay, Gwen?
What the hell was that, Peter?
Are you okay?
Forget me.
GO!!
Come on, come on...
Come on, come on...
Come on, come on...
COME ON!!!!
BOOM

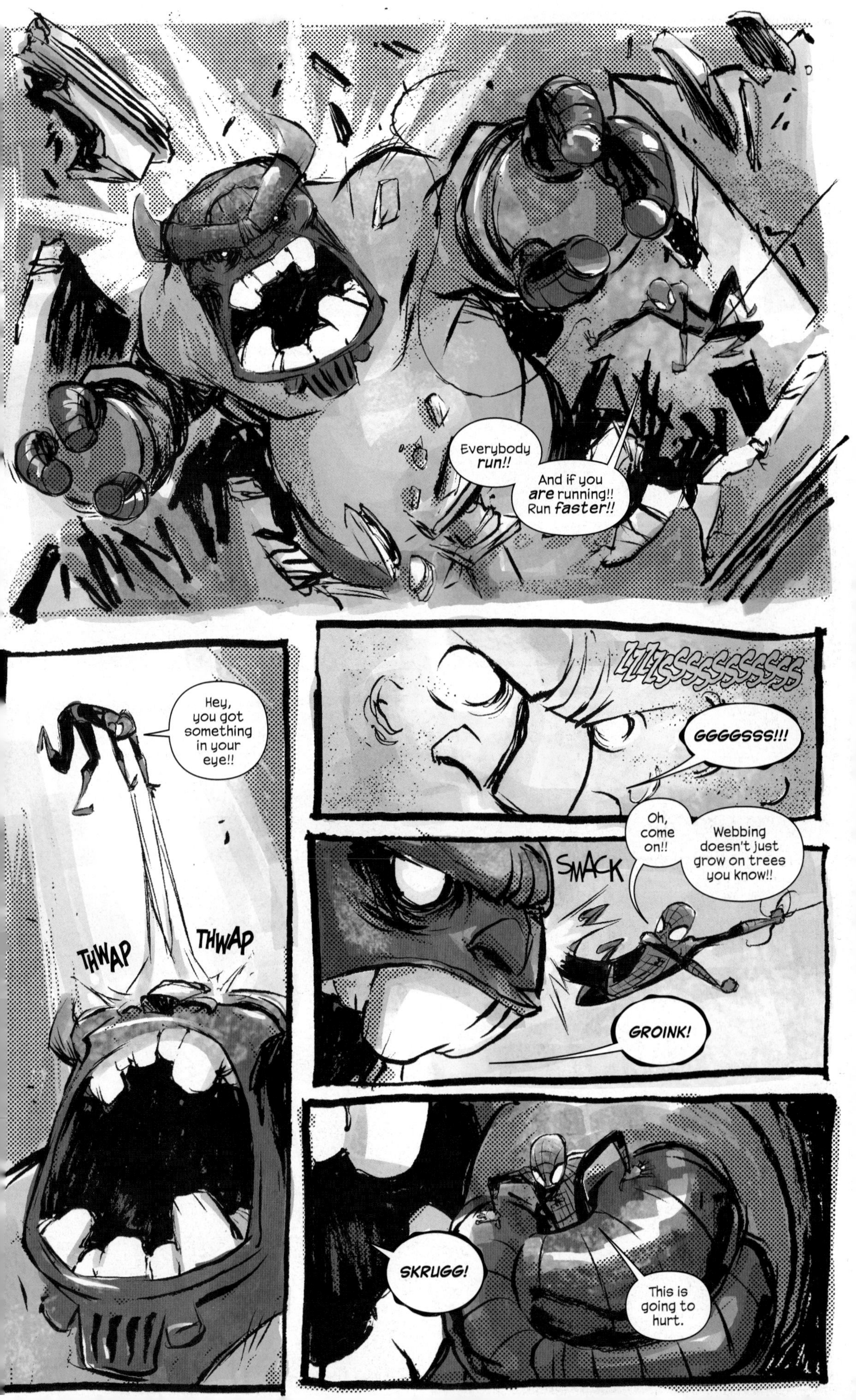
Everybody *run!!*
And if you *are* running!! Run *faster!!*
Hey, you got something in your eye!!
THWAP
THWAP
ZZZZSSSSSSSSSSS
GGGGSSS!!!
SMACK
Oh, come on!!
Webbing doesn't just grow on trees you know!!
GROINK!
SKRUGG!
This is going to hurt.

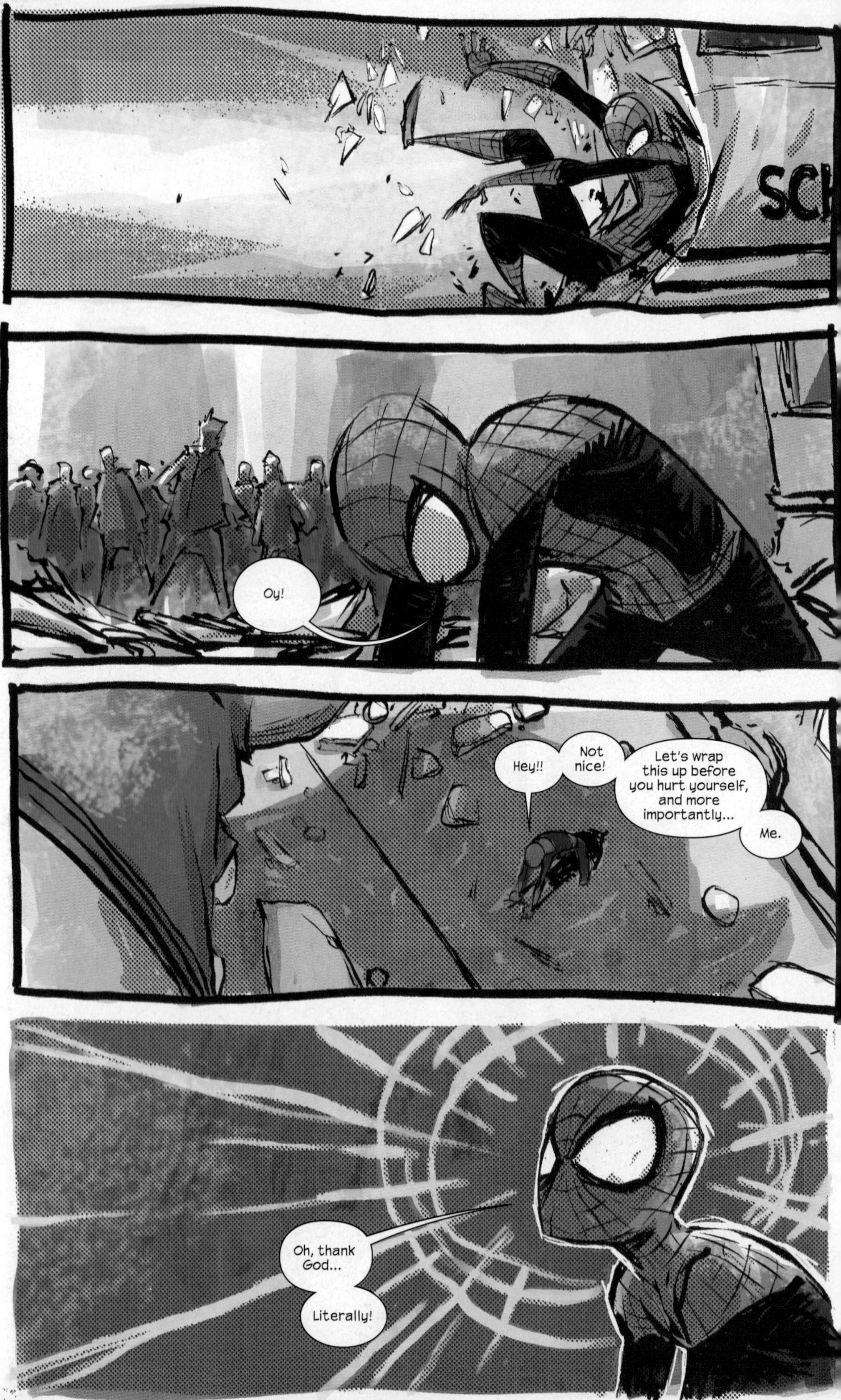
SCH
Oy!
Hey!!
Not nice!
Let's wrap this up before you hurt yourself, and more importantly...
Me.
Oh, thank God...
Literally!

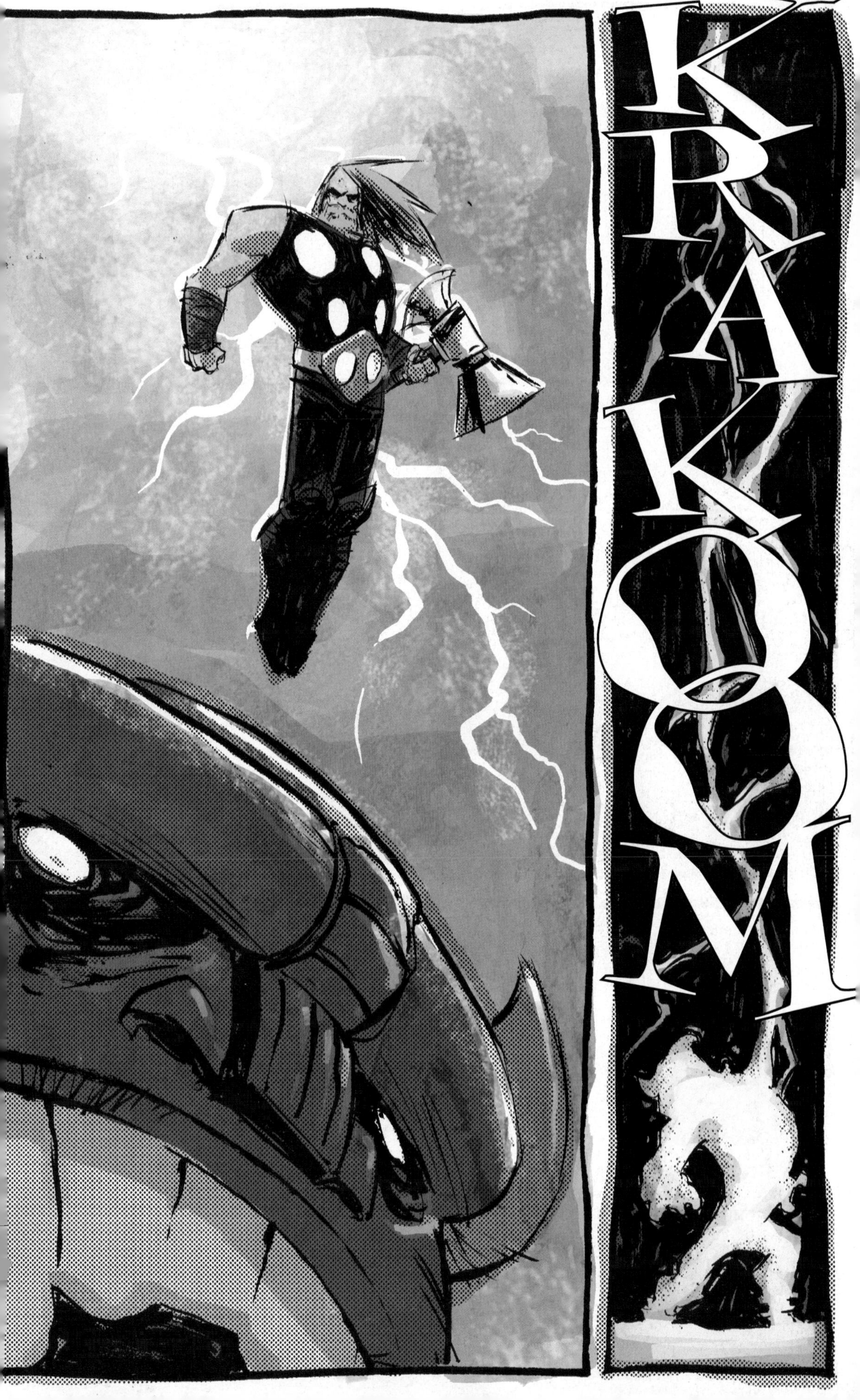
KRAKOOM

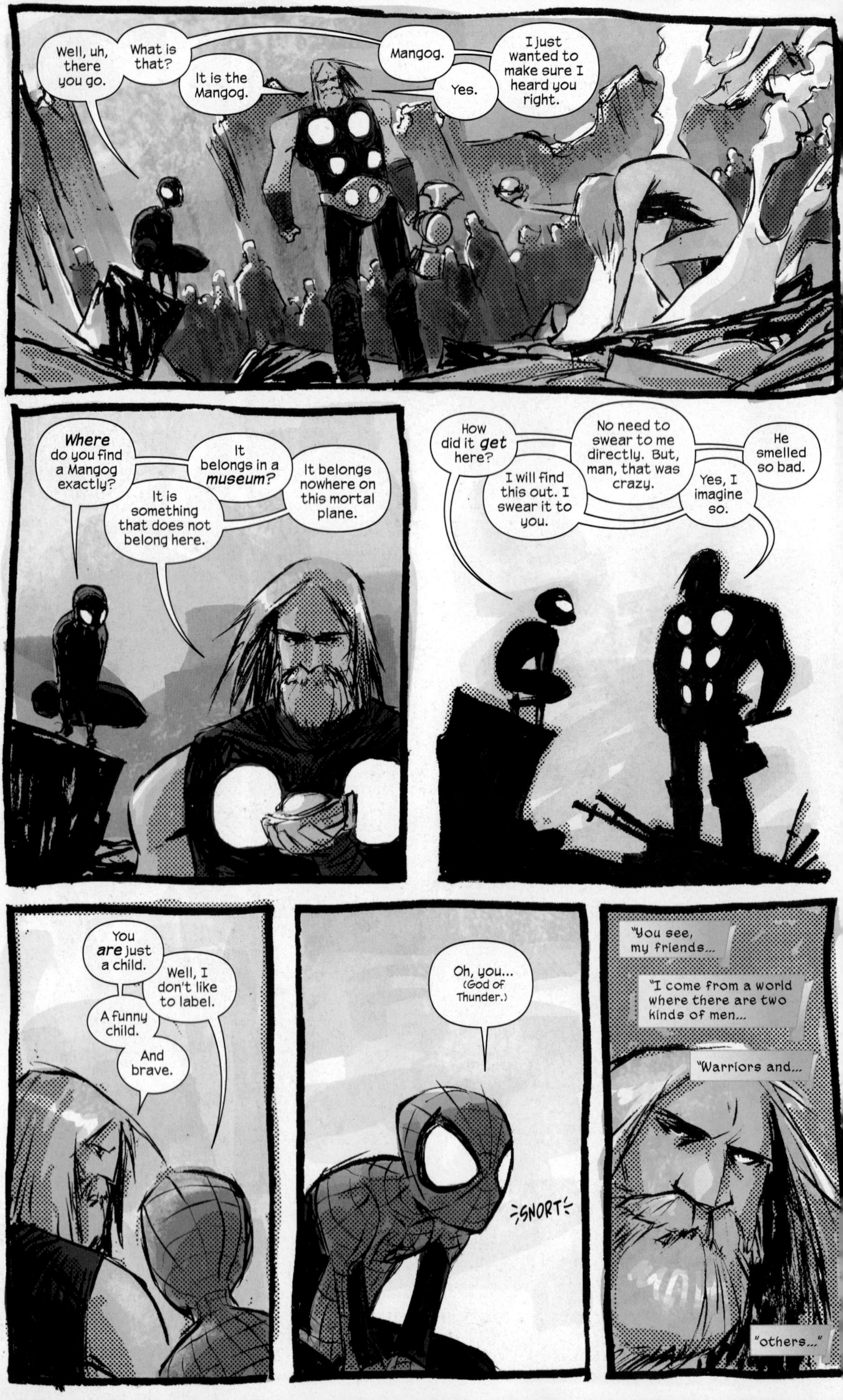
Well, uh, there you go.
What is that?
It is the Mangog.
Mangog.
Yes.
I just wanted to make sure I heard you right.
Where do you find a Mangog exactly?
It is something that does not belong here.
It belongs in a *museum?*
It belongs nowhere on this mortal plane.
How did it *get* here?
I will find this out. I swear it to you.
No need to swear to me directly. But, man, that was crazy.
Yes, I imagine so.
He smelled so bad.
You *are* just a child.
Well, I don't like to label.
A funny child.
And brave.
Oh, you... (God of Thunder.)
SNORT
"You see, my friends...
"I come from a world where there are two kinds of men...
"Warriors and...
"others..."

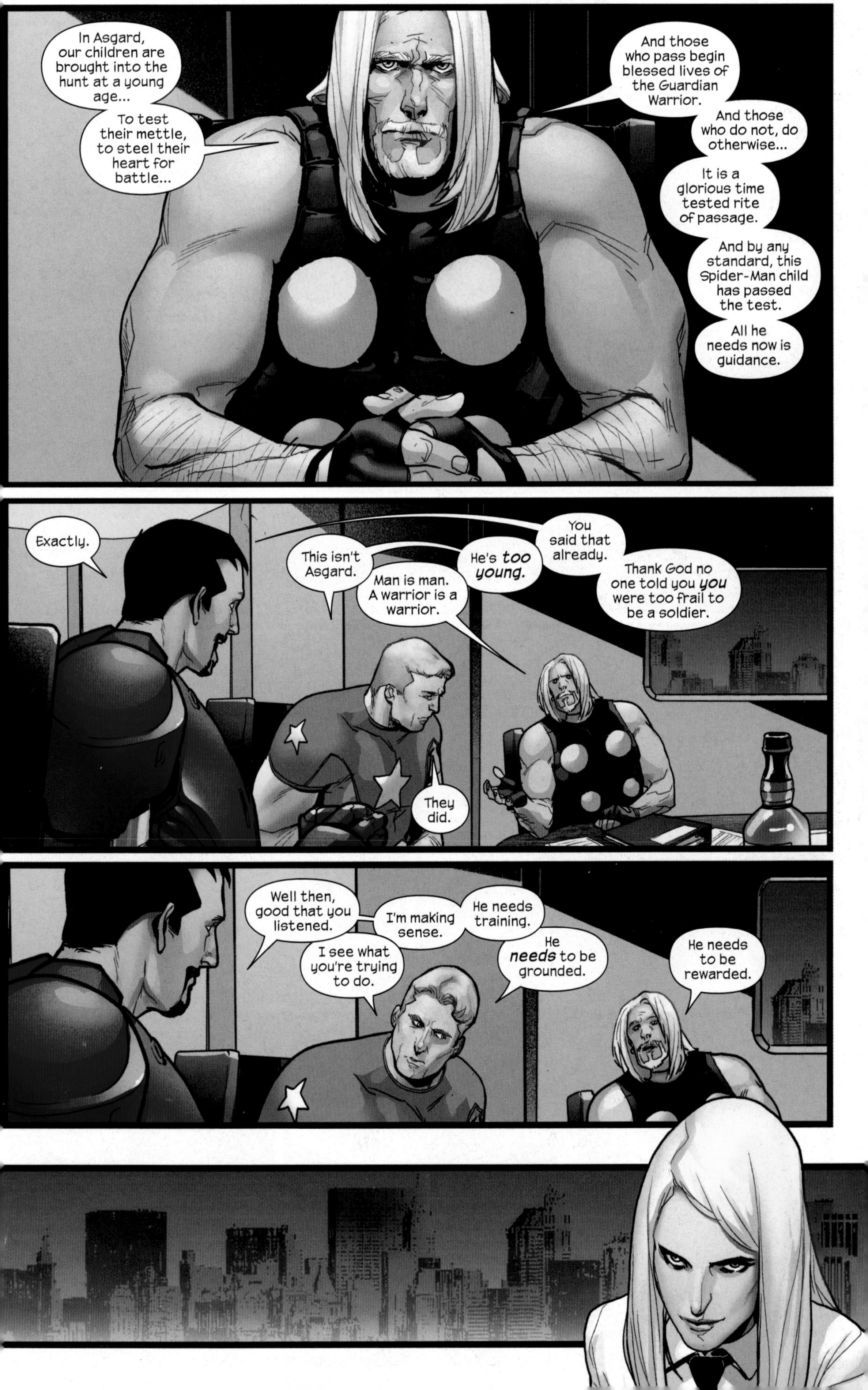
In Asgard, our children are brought into the hunt at a young age...
To test their mettle, to steel their heart for battle...
And those who pass begin blessed lives of the Guardian Warrior.
And those who do not, do otherwise...
It is a glorious time tested rite of passage.
And by any standard, this Spider-Man child has passed the test.
All he needs now is guidance.
Exactly.
This isn't Asgard.
He's *too young.*
You said that already.
Man is man. A warrior is a warrior.
Thank God no one told you *you* were too frail to be a soldier.
They did.
Well then, good that you listened.
I'm making sense.
He needs training.
I see what you're trying to do.
He *needs* to be grounded.
He needs to be rewarded.

Queens.

Dude, the **bald** one.

I never saw her.

Johnny, she's the only smoking hot **bald chick** in our entire school. Shaved head.

What do you want from me?

I want you to stay away from her so I can ask her out.

She's a bald chick?

She's the hottest chick in school.

Uh, guys.

What's going on?

I think someone is here.

You're right.

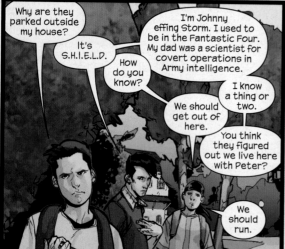

Why are they parked outside my house?

It's S.H.I.E.L.D.

How do you know?

I'm Johnny effing Storm. I used to be in the Fantastic Four. My dad was a scientist for covert operations in Army intelligence. I know a thing or two.

We should get out of here.

You think they figured out we live here with Peter?

We should run.

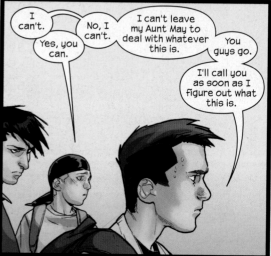

I can't.

Yes, you can.

No, I can't.

I can't leave my Aunt May to deal with whatever this is. You guys go.

I'll call you as soon as I figure out what this is.

Peter...

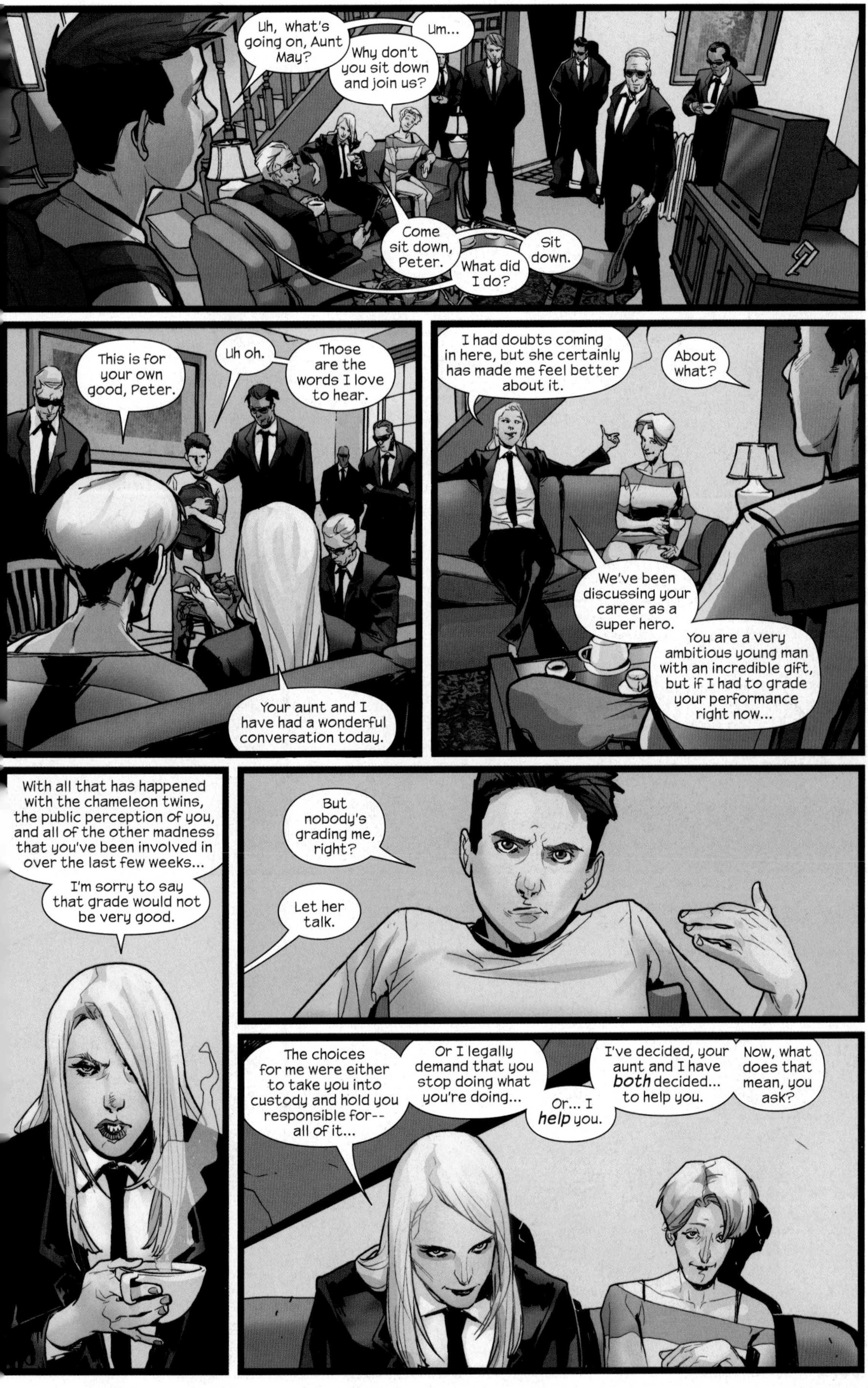

Uh, what's going on, Aunt May?
Um...
Why don't you sit down and join us?
Come sit down, Peter.
Sit down.
What did I do?
This is for your own good, Peter.
Uh oh.
Those are the words I love to hear.
Your aunt and I have had a wonderful conversation today.
I had doubts coming in here, but she certainly has made me feel better about it.
About what?
We've been discussing your career as a super hero.
You are a very ambitious young man with an incredible gift, but if I had to grade your performance right now...
With all that has happened with the chameleon twins, the public perception of you, and all of the other madness that you've been involved in over the last few weeks...
I'm sorry to say that grade would not be very good.
But nobody's grading me, right?
Let her talk.
The choices for me were either to take you into custody and hold you responsible for-- all of it...
Or I legally demand that you stop doing what you're doing...
Or... I *help* you.
I've decided, your aunt and I have *both* decided... to help you.
Now, what does that mean, you ask?

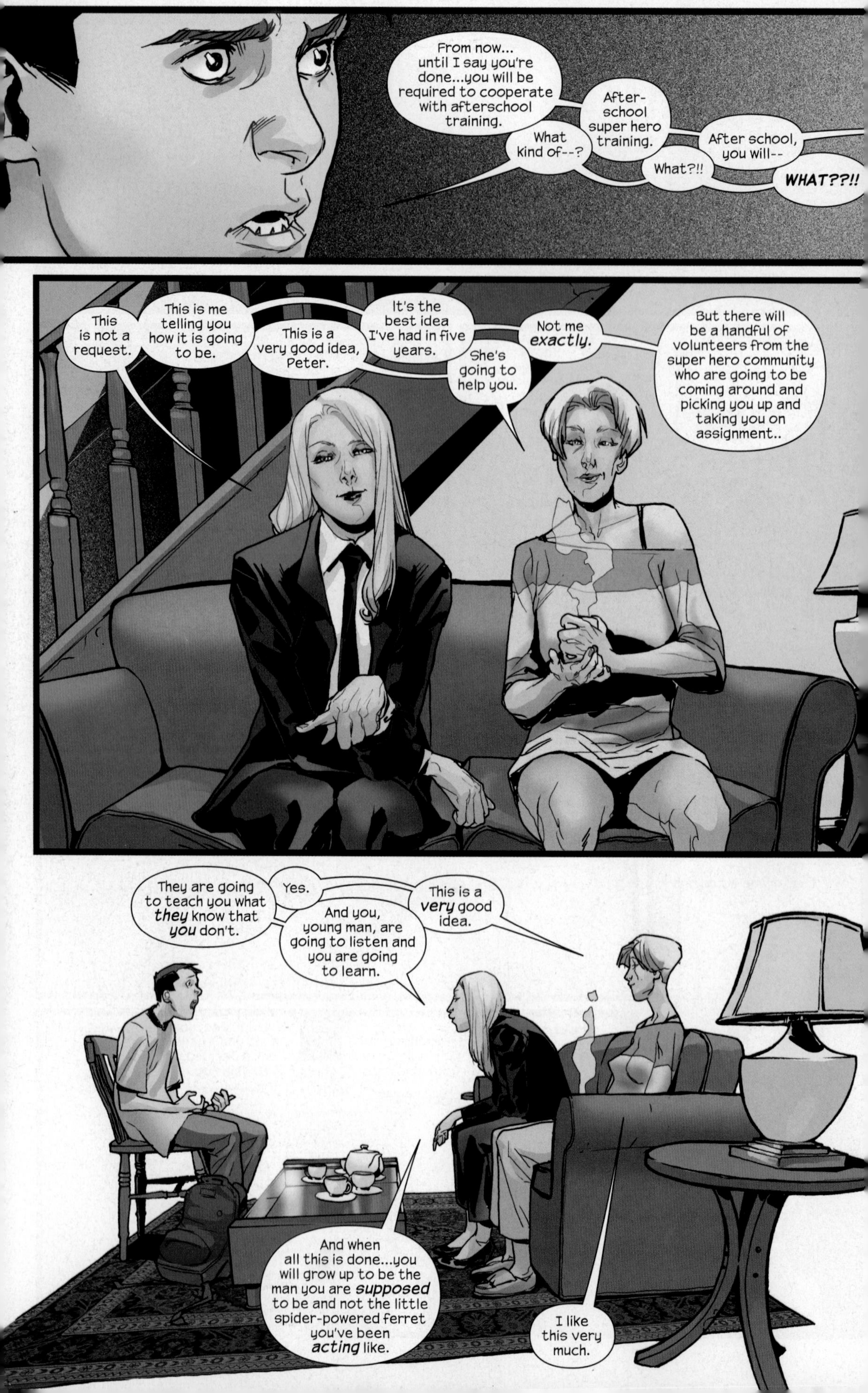
From now... until I say you're done...you will be required to cooperate with afterschool training.
After-school super hero training.
What kind of--?
After school, you will--
What?!!
WHAT??!!
This is not a request.
This is me telling you how it is going to be.
This is a very good idea, Peter.
It's the best idea I've had in five years.
She's going to help you.
Not me exactly.
But there will be a handful of volunteers from the super hero community who are going to be coming around and picking you up and taking you on assignment..
They are going to teach you what they know that you don't.
Yes.
This is a very good idea.
And you, young man, are going to listen and you are going to learn.
And when all this is done...you will grow up to be the man you are supposed to be and not the little spider-powered ferret you've been acting like.
I like this very much.

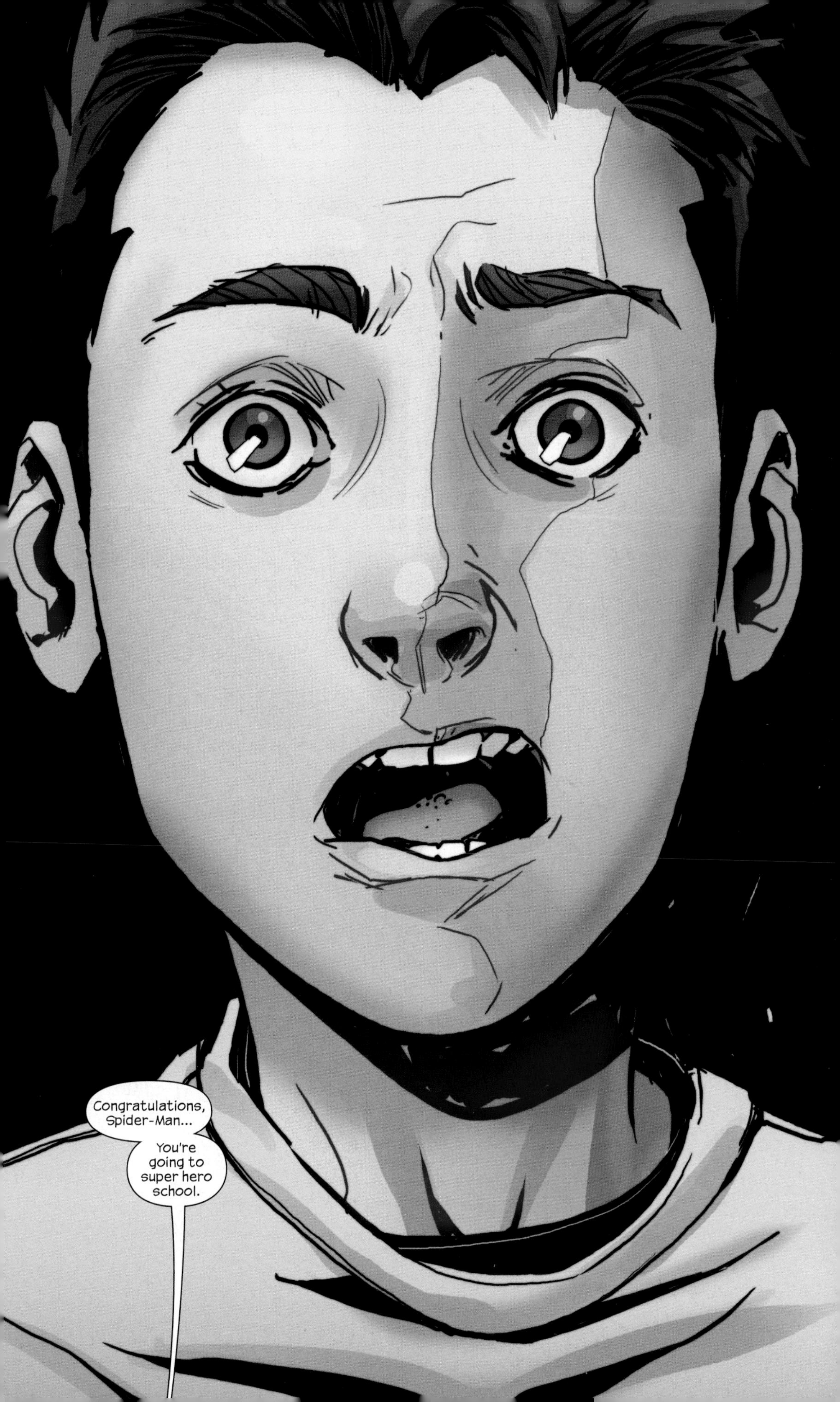

Congratulations, Spider-Man...
You're going to super hero school.

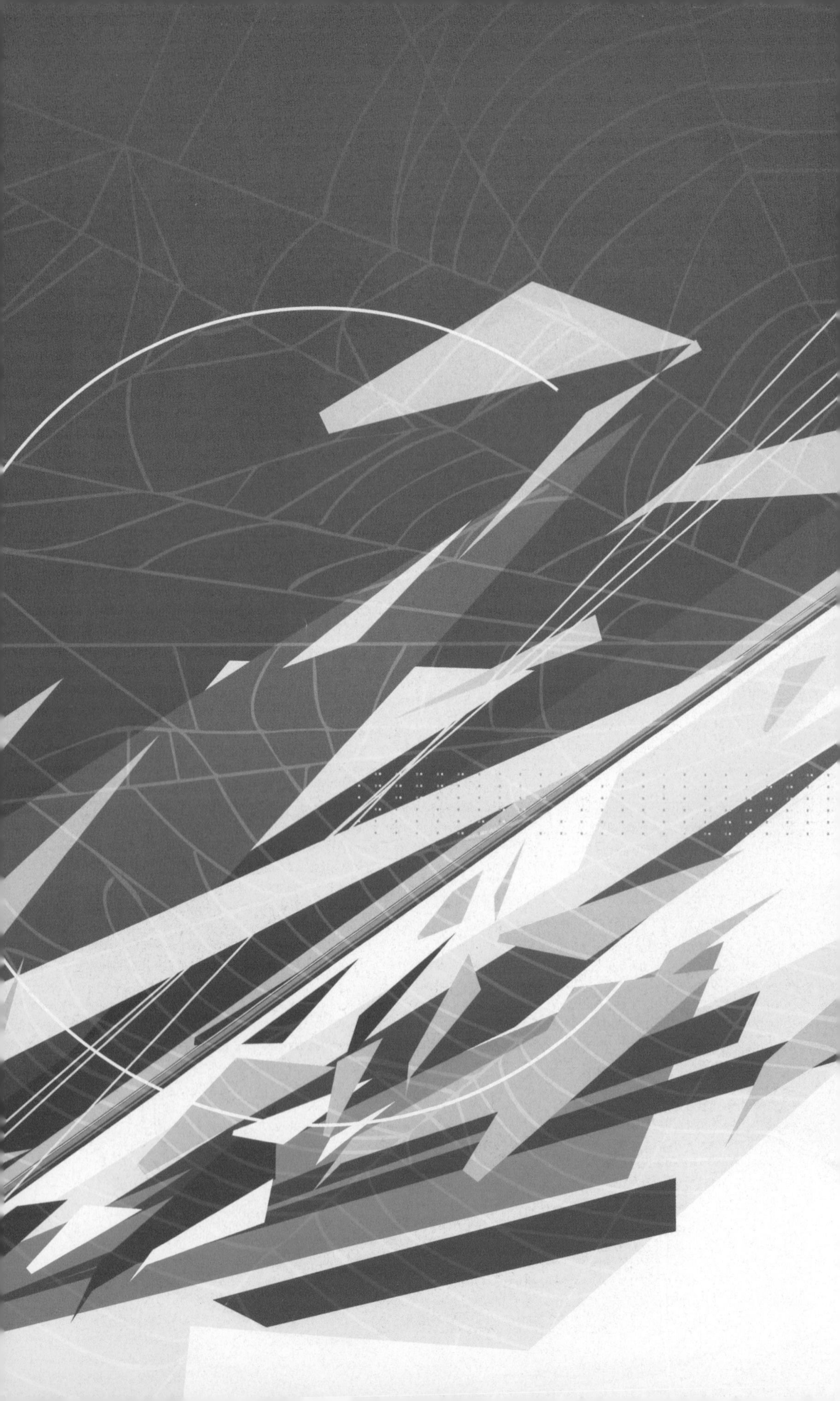

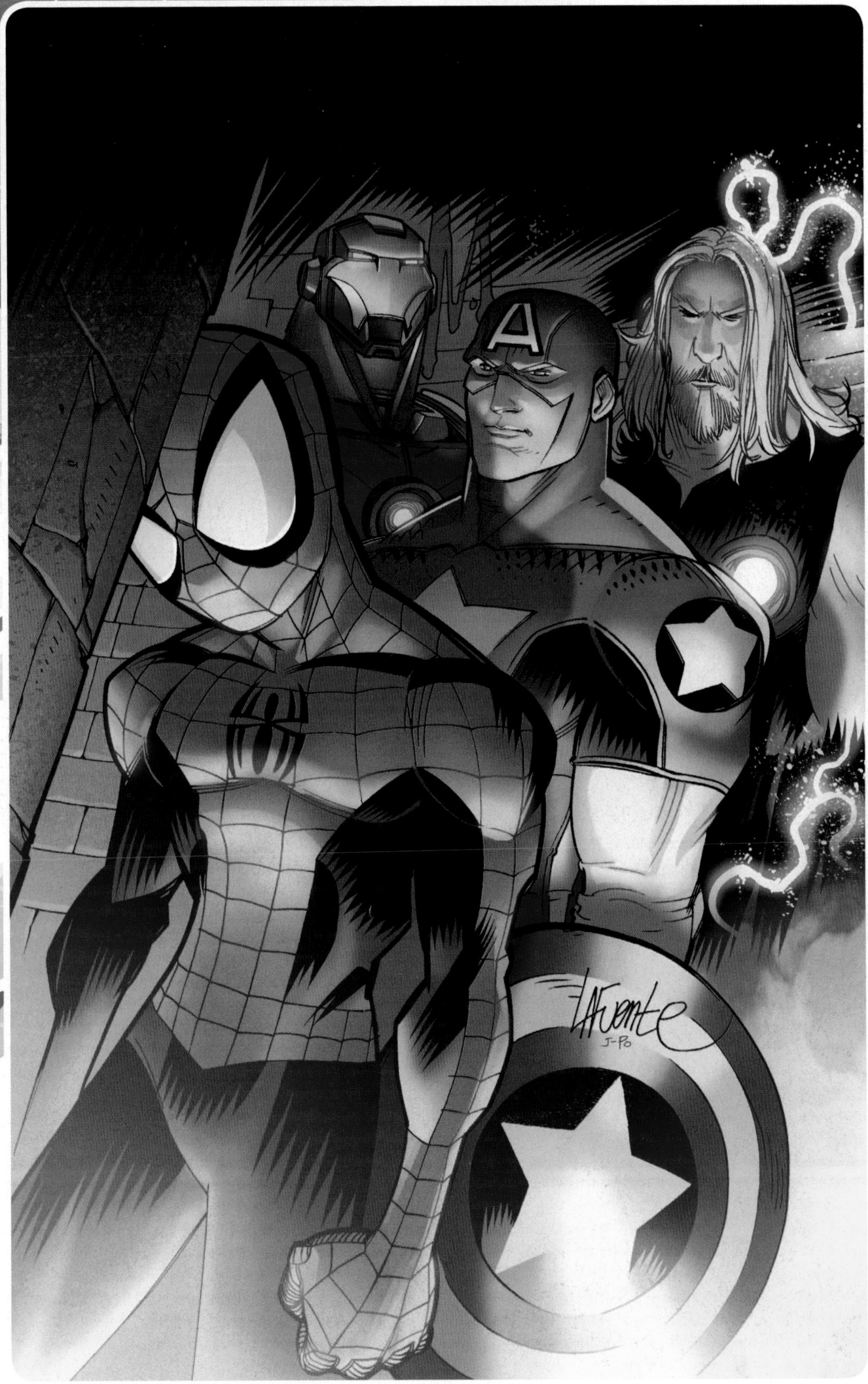
LaFuente
J-Po

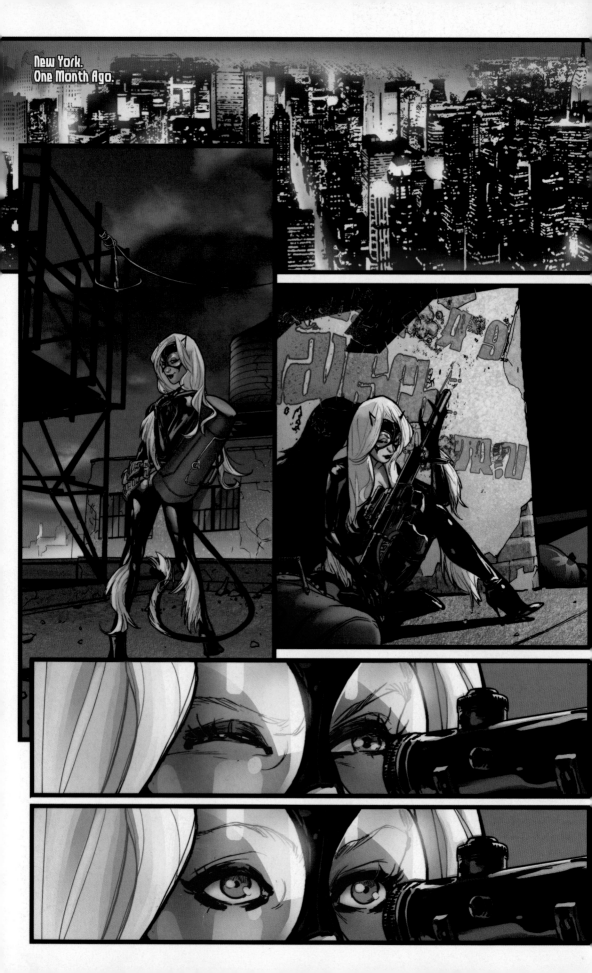

New York.
One Month Ago.

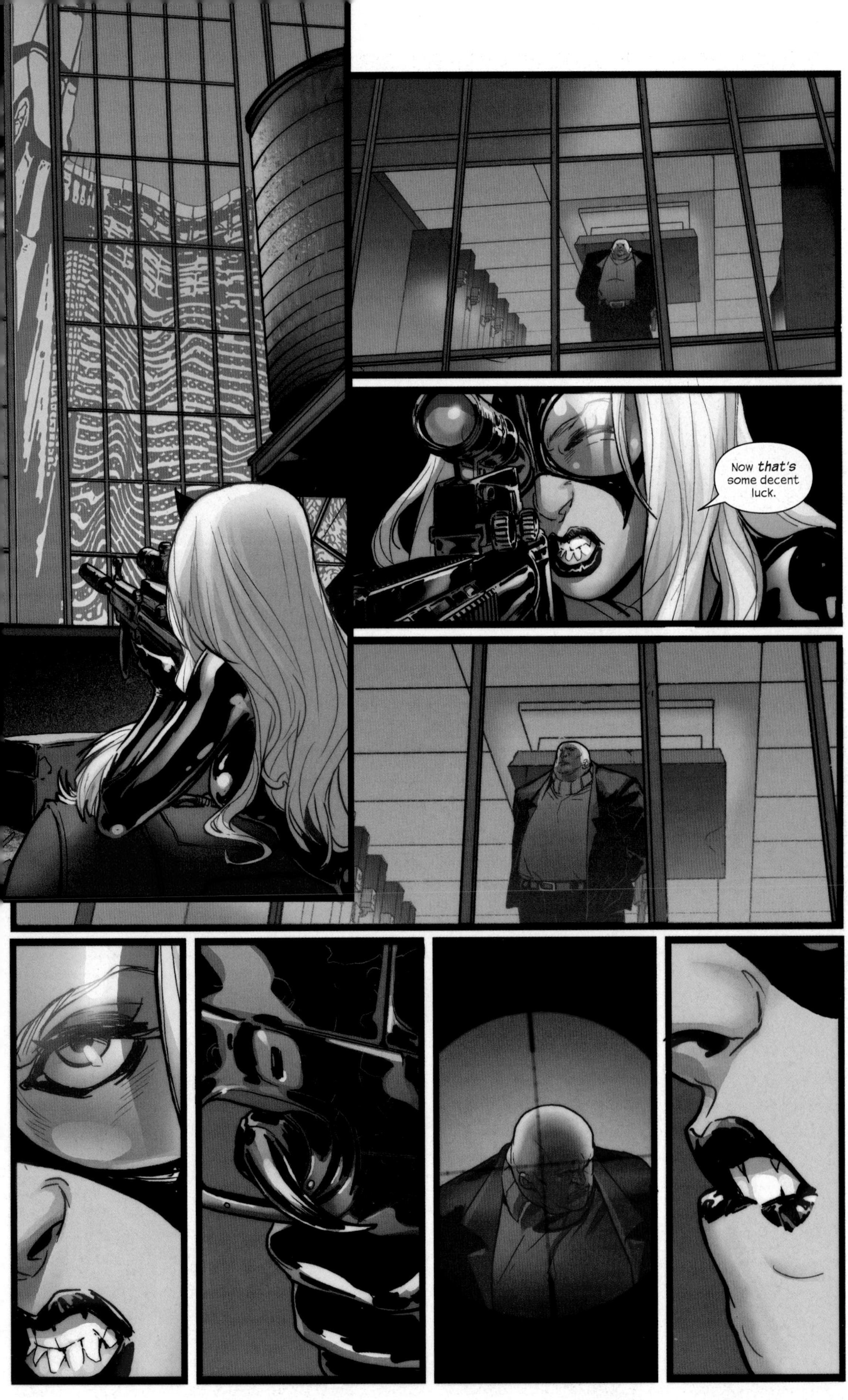
Now *that's* some decent luck.

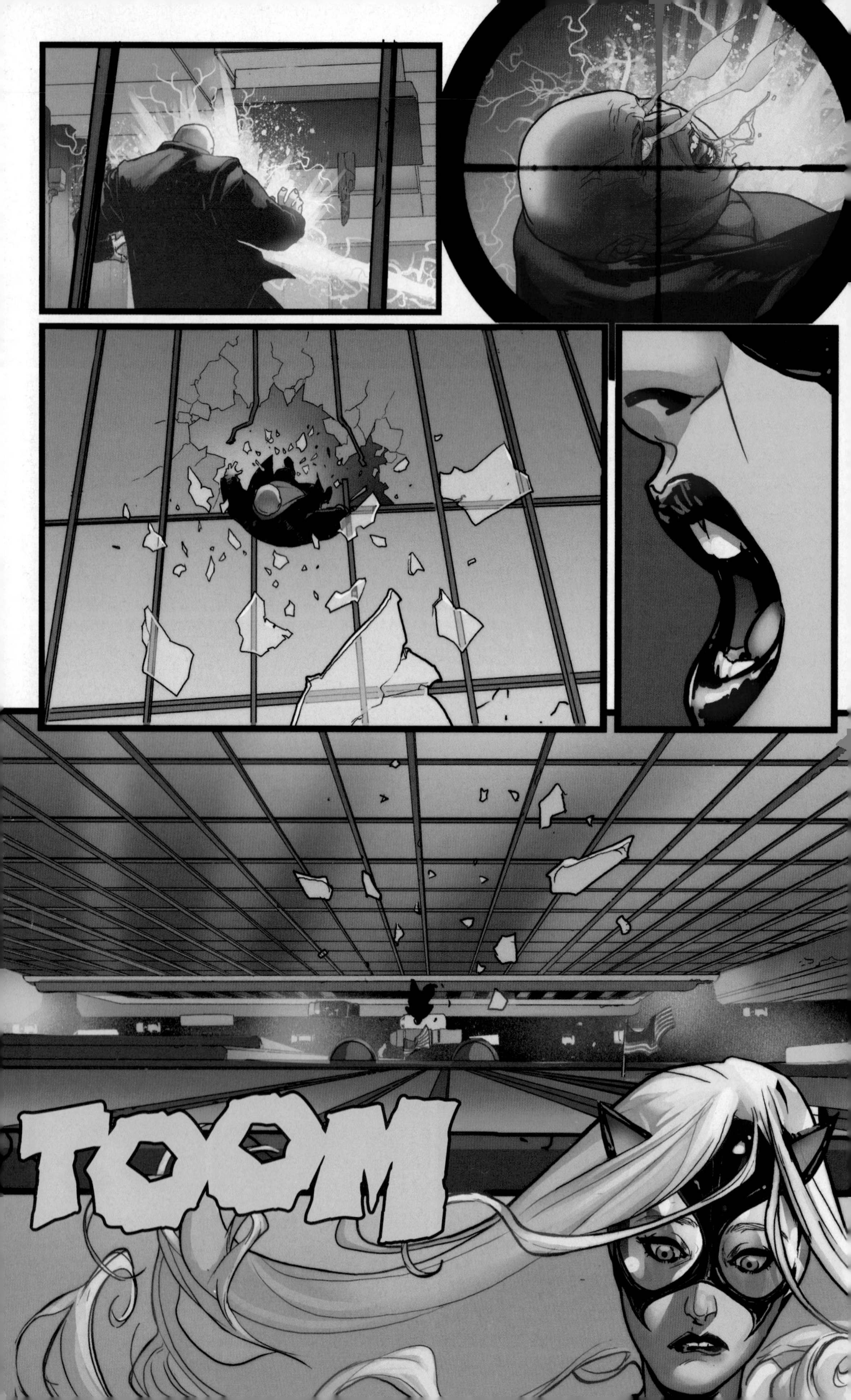
TOOM

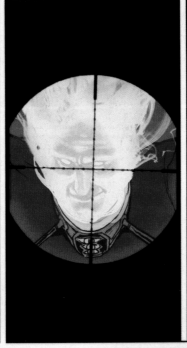

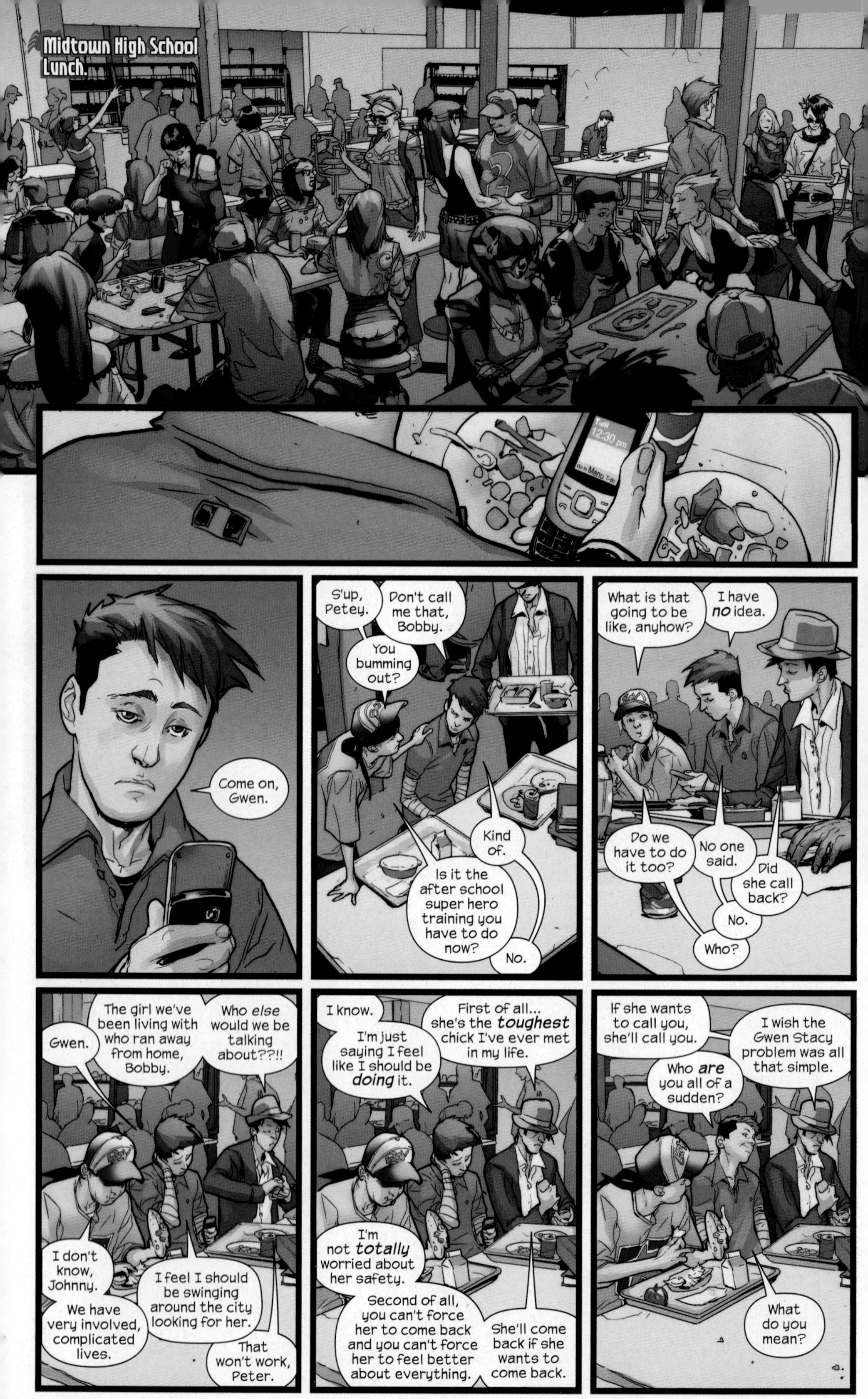
Midtown High School
Lunch.
12:30 pm
Come on, Gwen.
S'up, Petey.
Don't call me that, Bobby.
You bumming out?
Kind of.
Is it the after school super hero training you have to do now?
No.
What is that going to be like, anyhow?
I have *no* idea.
Do we have to do it too?
No one said.
Did she call back?
No.
Who?
Gwen.
The girl we've been living with who ran away from home, Bobby.
Who *else* would we be talking about??!!
I don't know, Johnny.
We have very involved, complicated lives.
I feel I should be swinging around the city looking for her.
That won't work, Peter.
I know.
I'm just saying I feel like I should be *doing* it.
First of all... she's the *toughest* chick I've ever met in my life.
I'm not *totally* worried about her safety.
Second of all, you can't force her to come back and you can't force her to feel better about everything.
She'll come back if she wants to come back.
If she wants to call you, she'll call you.
Who *are* you all of a sudden?
I wish the Gwen Stacy problem was all that simple.
What do you mean?

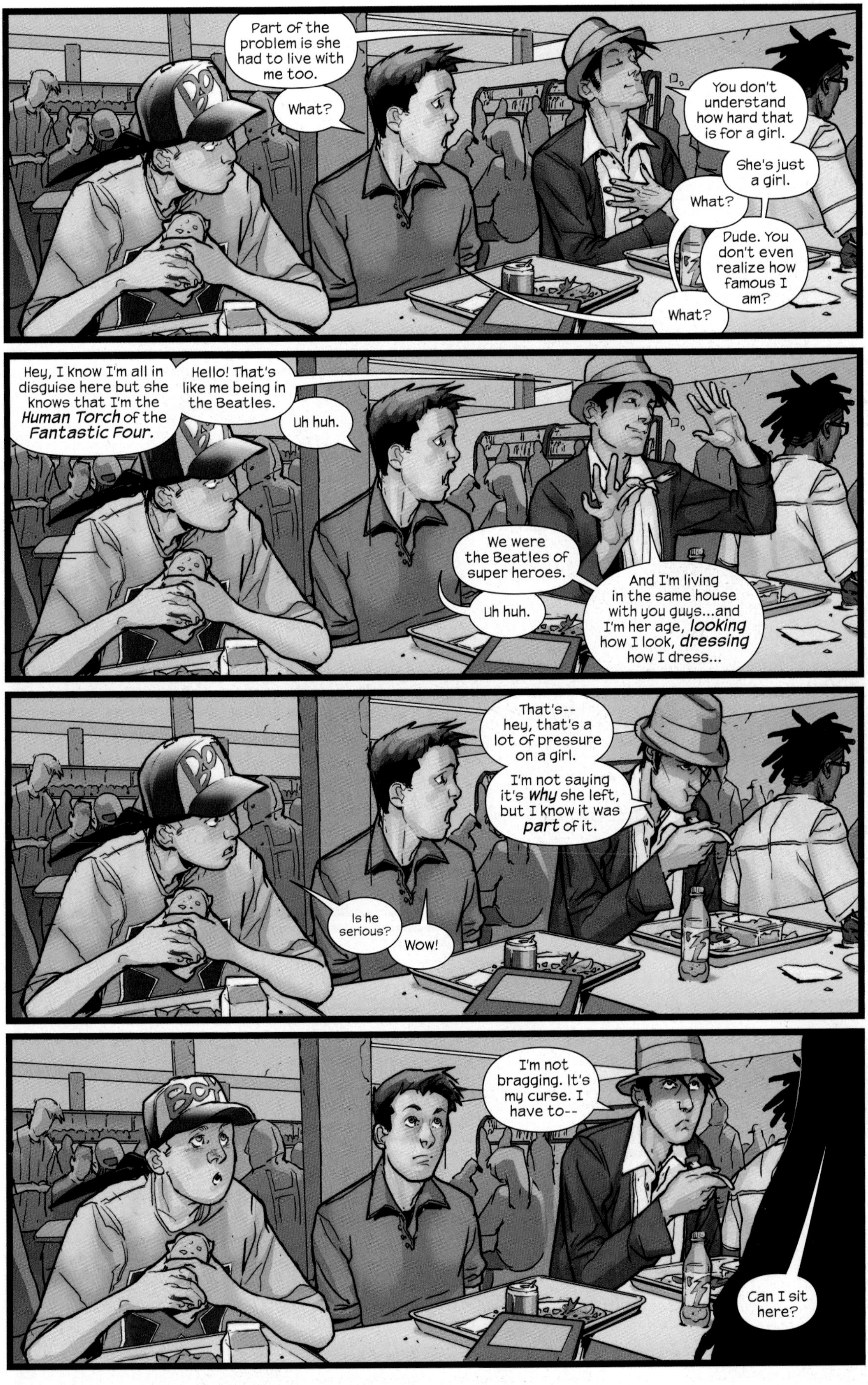
Part of the problem is she had to live with me too.
What?
You don't understand how hard that is for a girl.
She's just a girl.
What?
Dude. You don't even realize how famous I am?
What?
Hey, I know I'm all in disguise here but she knows that I'm the *Human Torch* of the *Fantastic Four.*
Hello! That's like me being in the Beatles.
Uh huh.
We were the Beatles of super heroes.
Uh huh.
And I'm living in the same house with you guys...and I'm her age, *looking* how I look, *dressing* how I dress...
That's-- hey, that's a lot of pressure on a girl.
I'm not saying it's *why* she left, but I know it was *part* of it.
Is he serious?
Wow!
I'm not bragging. It's my curse. I have to--
Can I sit here?

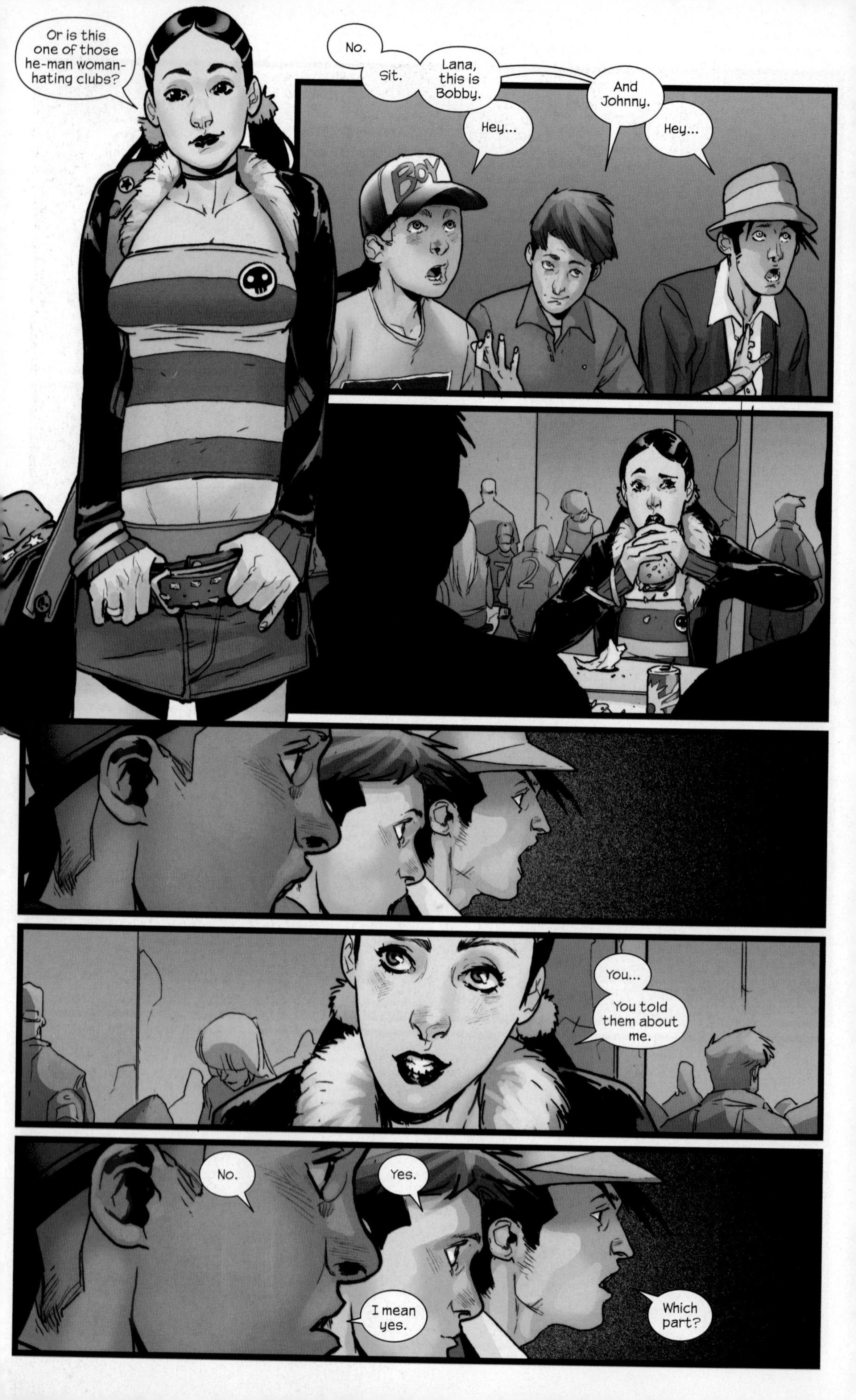
Or is this one of those he-man woman-hating clubs?
No.
Sit.
Lana, this is Bobby.
And Johnny.
Hey...
Hey...
You...
You told them about me.
No.
Yes.
I mean yes.
Which part?

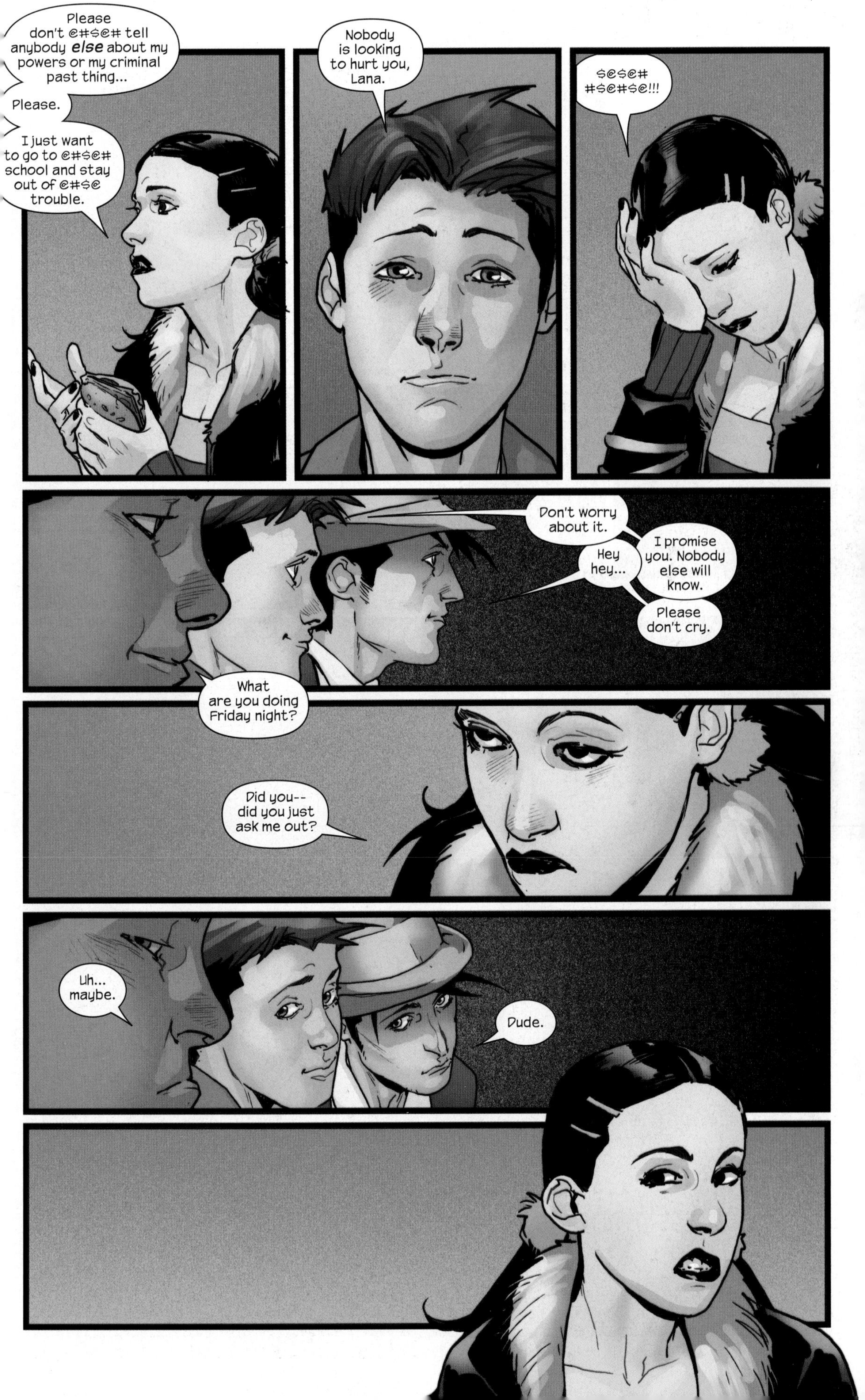

Please don't @#$@# tell anybody *else* about my powers or my criminal past thing...
Please.
I just want to go to @#$@# school and stay out of @#$@ trouble.
Nobody is looking to hurt you, Lana.
$@$@# #$@#$@!!!
Don't worry about it.
I promise you. Nobody else will know.
Hey hey...
Please don't cry.
What are you doing Friday night?
Did you-- did you just ask me out?
Uh... maybe.
Dude.

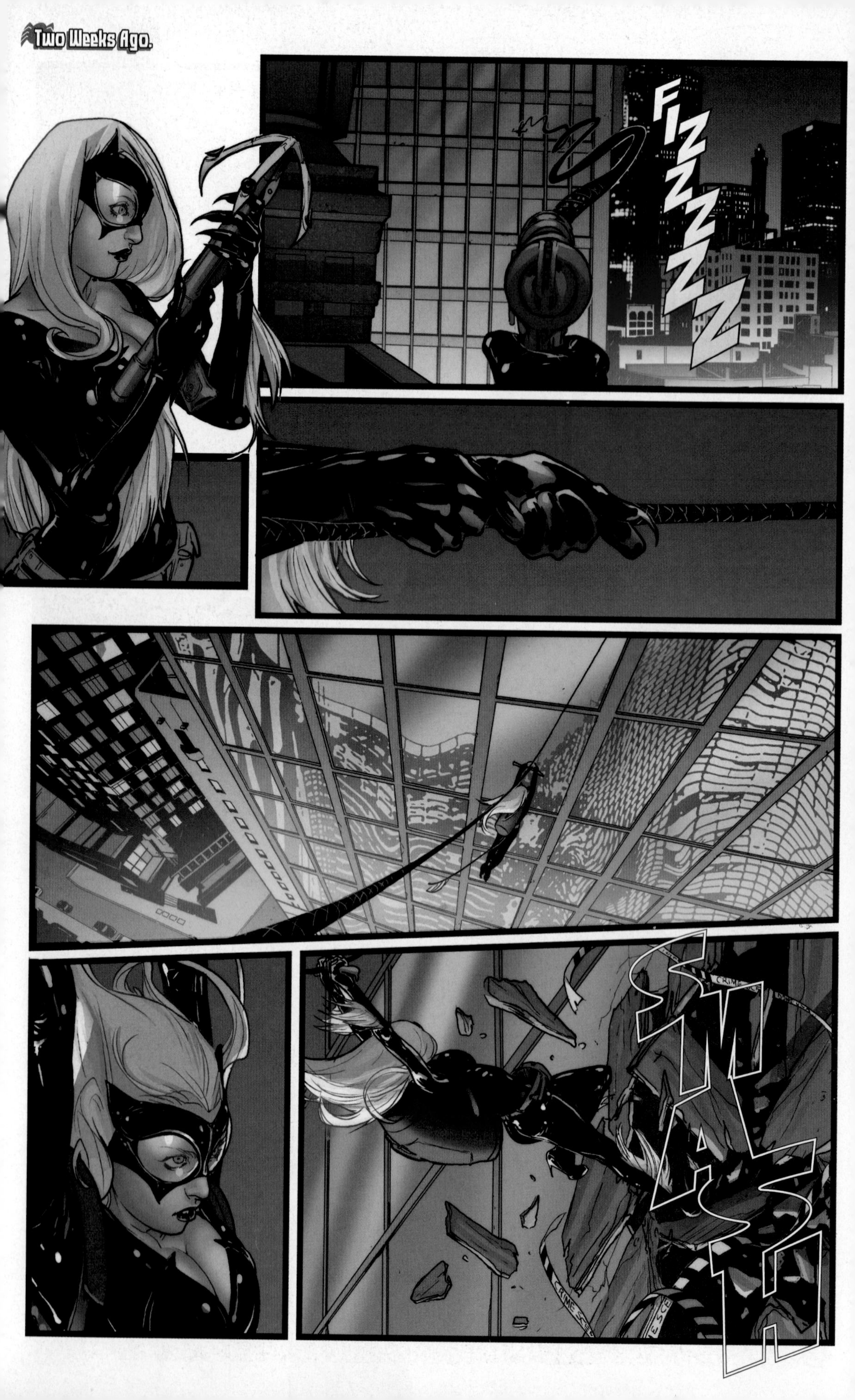
Two Weeks Ago.
FIZZZZ
CRIME SCENE
SMASH

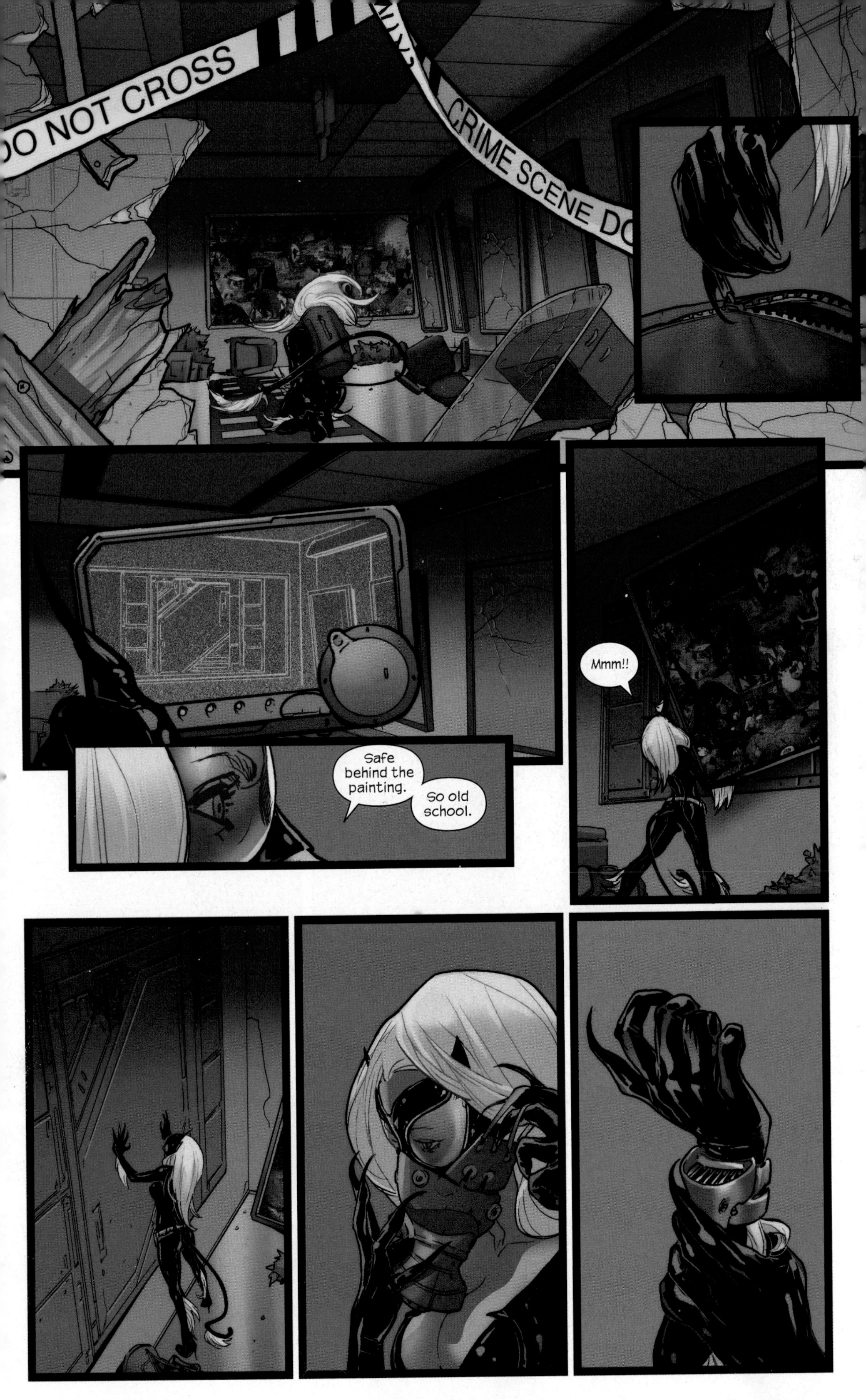
DO NOT CROSS
CRIME SCENE DO
Safe behind the painting.
So old school.
Mmm!!

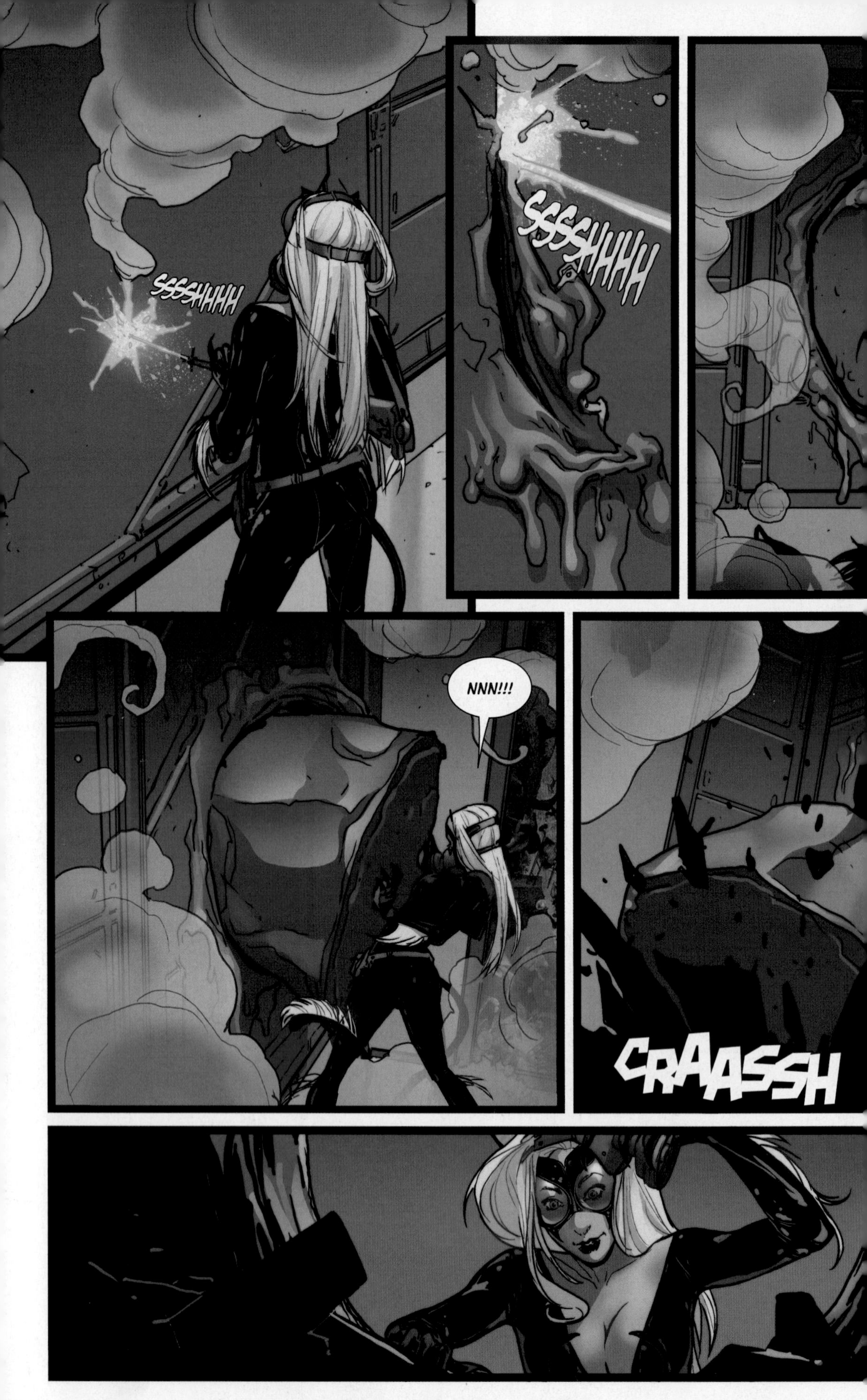
SSSSHHHH
SSSSHHHH
NNN!!!
CRAASSH

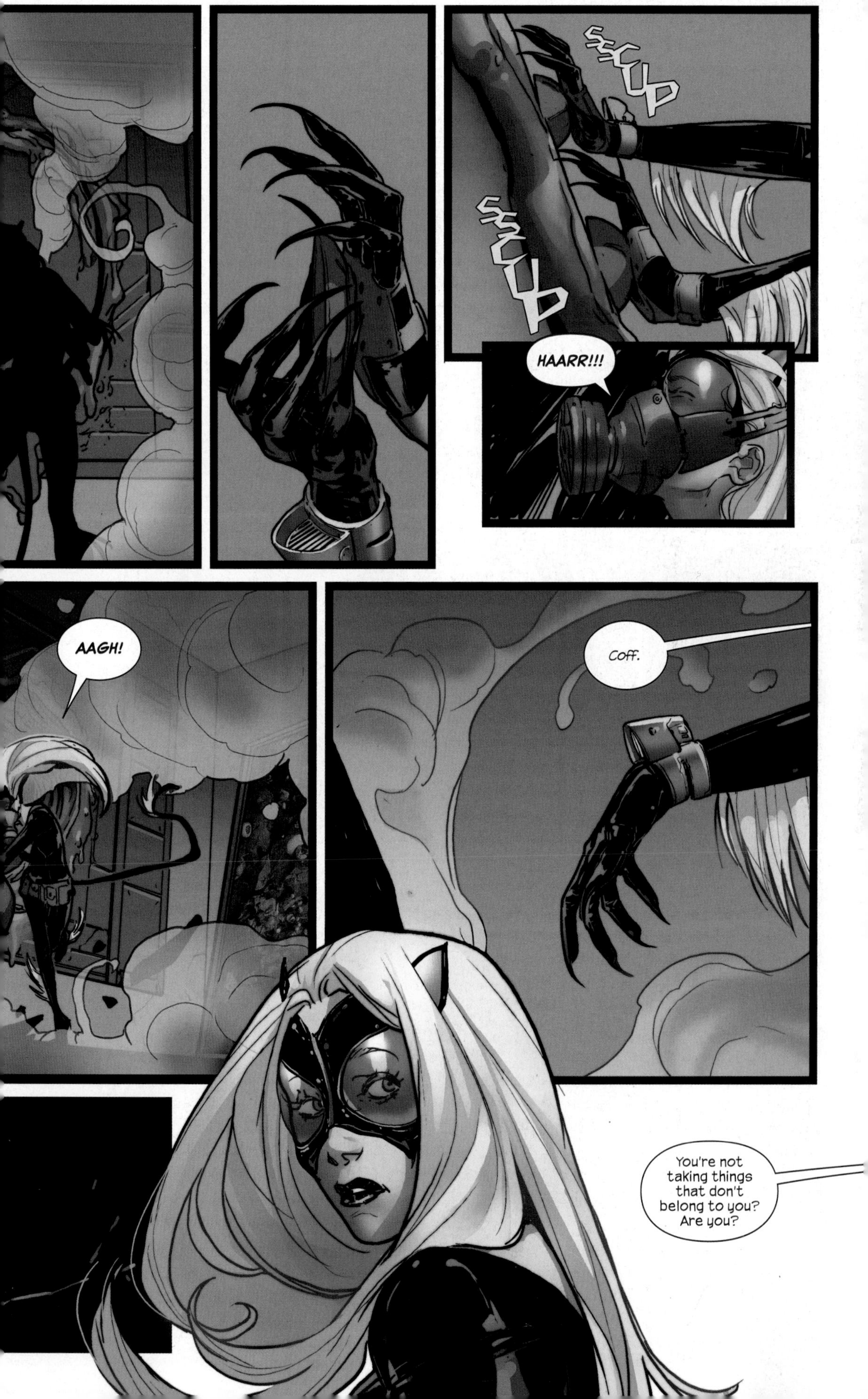
SSSCUP
SSSCUP
HAARR!!!
AAGH!
Coff.
You're not taking things that don't belong to you? Are you?

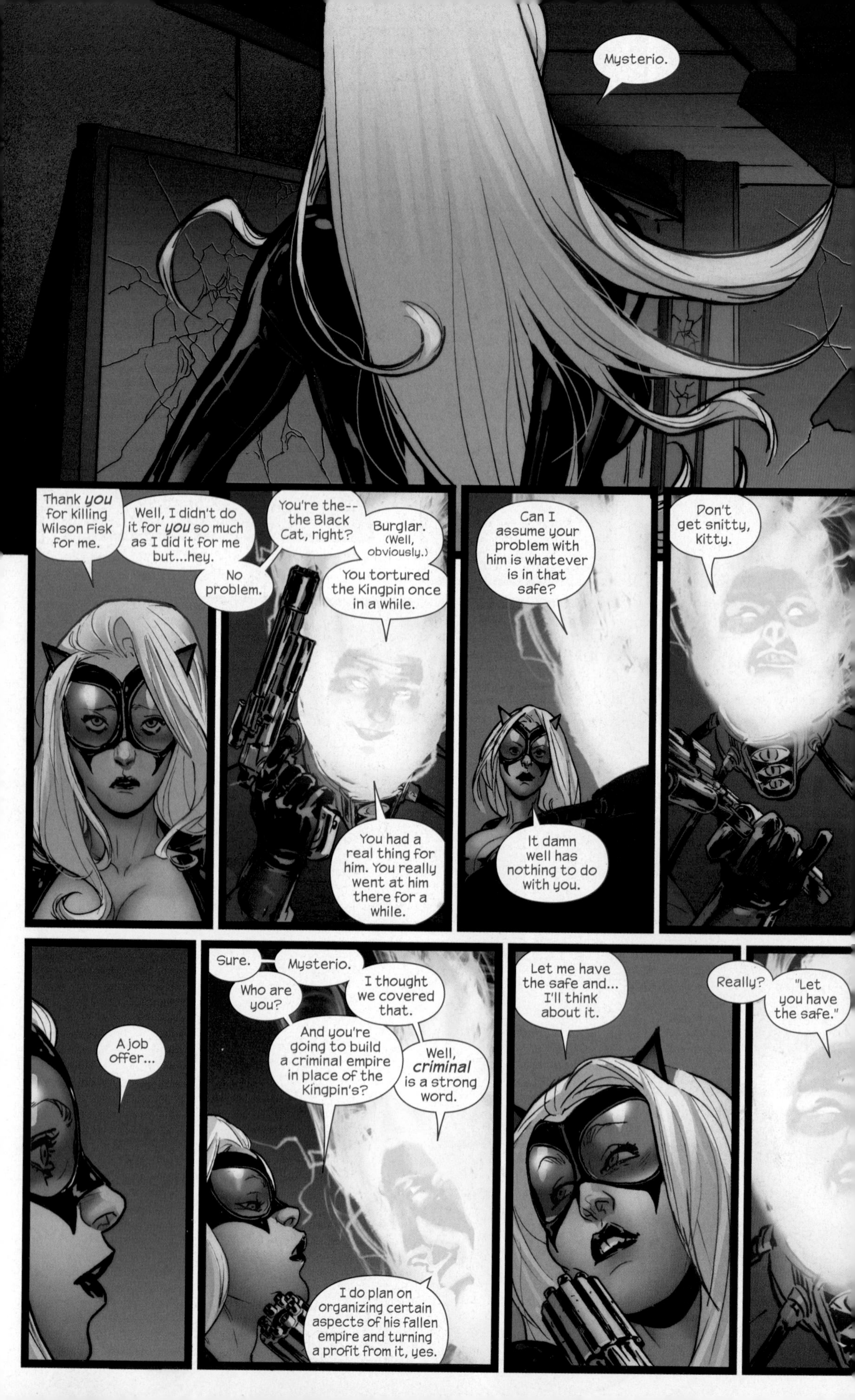
Mysterio.
Thank you for killing Wilson Fisk for me.
Well, I didn't do it for you so much as I did it for me but...hey.
No problem.
You're the-- the Black Cat, right?
Burglar. (Well, obviously.)
You tortured the Kingpin once in a while.
You had a real thing for him. You really went at him there for a while.
Can I assume your problem with him is whatever is in that safe?
It damn well has nothing to do with you.
Don't get snitty, kitty.
A job offer...
Sure.
Mysterio.
Who are you?
I thought we covered that.
And you're going to build a criminal empire in place of the Kingpin's?
Well, criminal is a strong word.
I do plan on organizing certain aspects of his fallen empire and turning a profit from it, yes.
Let me have the safe and... I'll think about it.
Really?
"Let you have the safe."

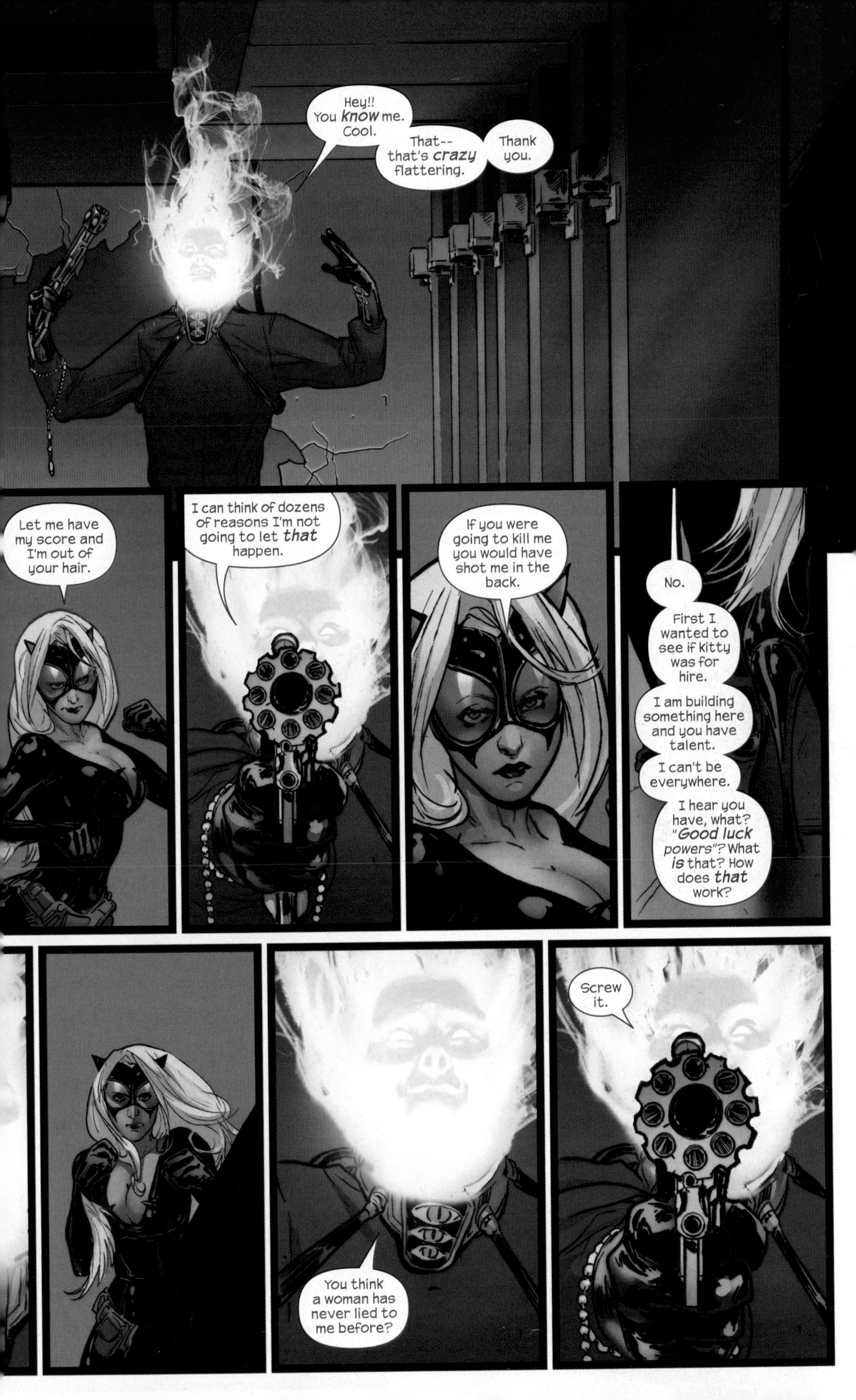
Hey!!
You *know* me.
Cool.
That--
that's *crazy*
flattering.
Thank
you.
Let me have
my score and
I'm out of
your hair.
I can think of dozens
of reasons I'm not
going to let *that*
happen.
If you were
going to kill me
you would have
shot me in the
back.
No.
First I
wanted to
see if kitty
was for
hire.
I am building
something here
and you have
talent.
I can't be
everywhere.
I hear you
have, what?
"*Good luck*
powers"? What
is that? How
does *that*
work?
You think
a woman has
never lied to
me before?
Screw
it.

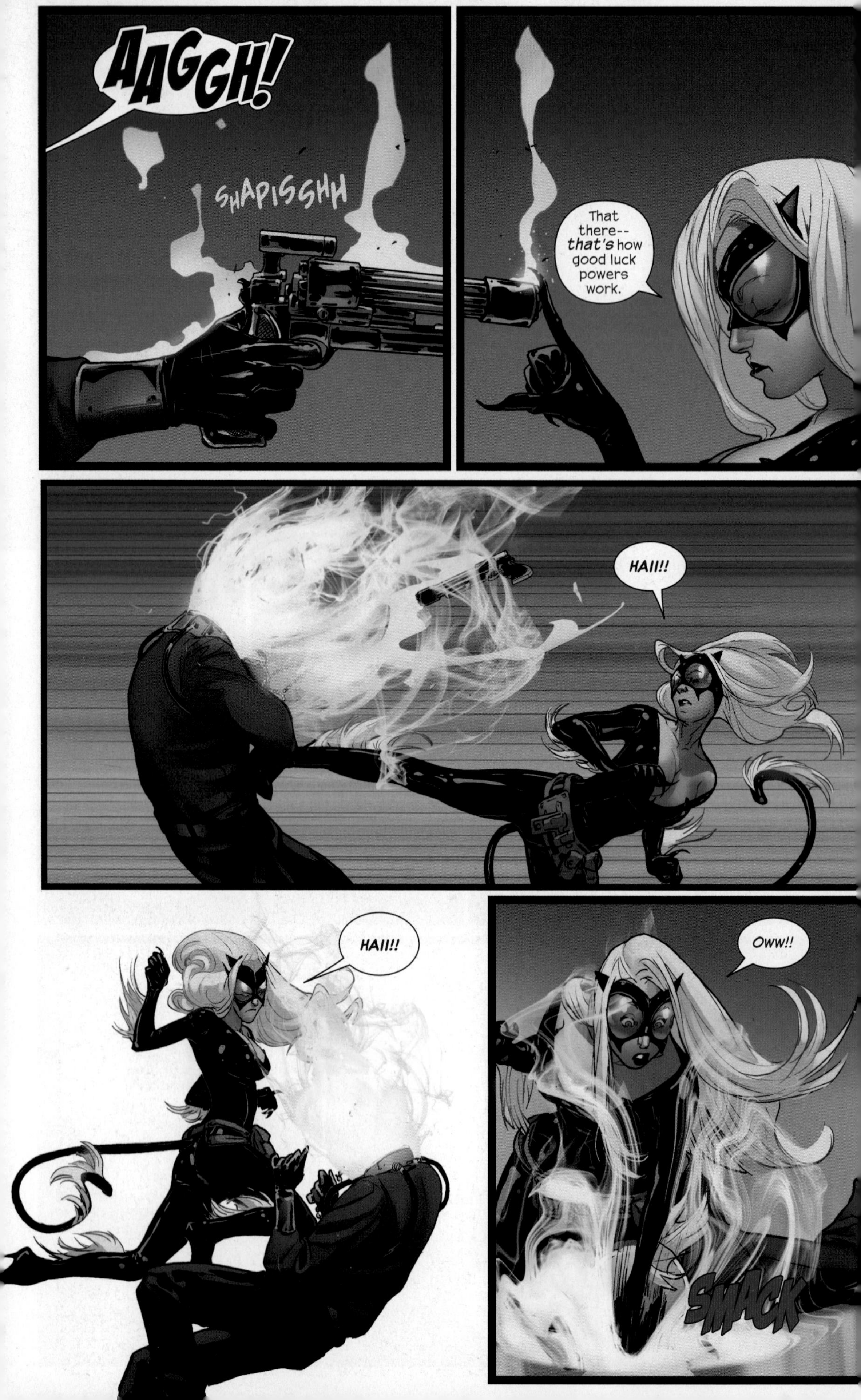
AAGGH!
SHAPISSHH
That there--
that's how good luck powers work.
HAII!!
HAII!!
OWW!!
SMACK

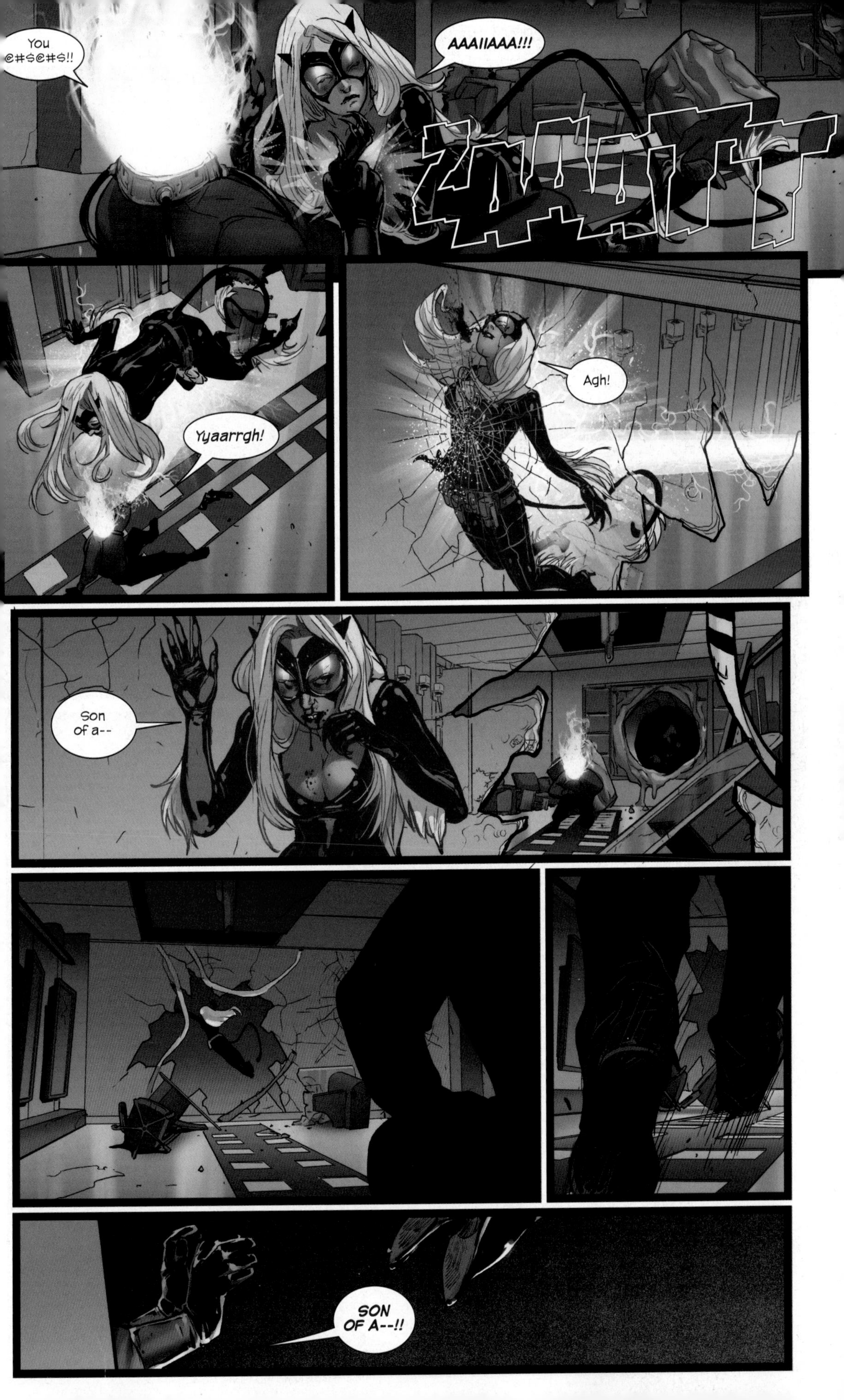
You @#$@#$!!
AAAIIAAA!!!
ZZAAAATT
Yyaarrgh!
Agh!
Son of a--
SON OF A--!!

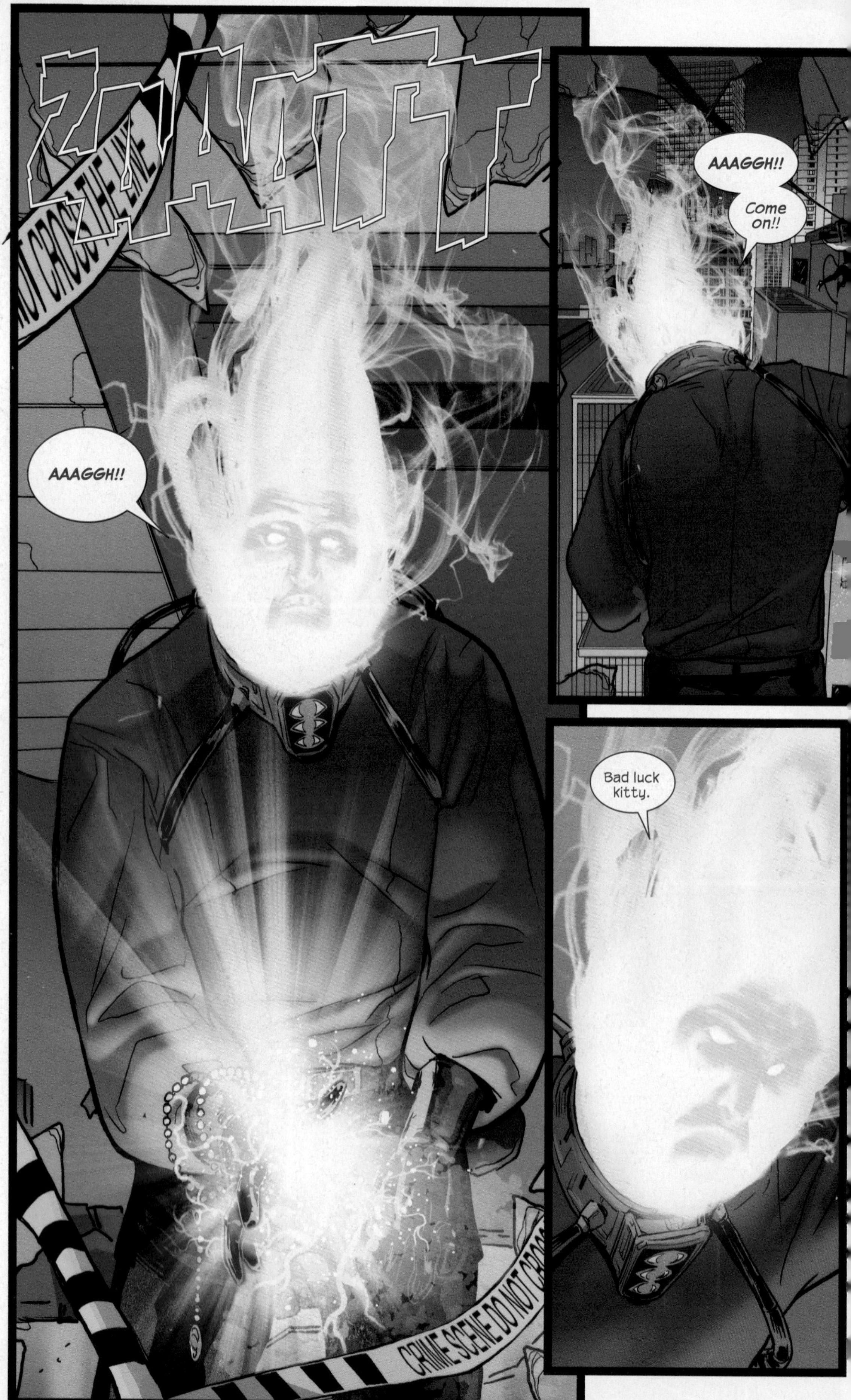

ZZAAAPT
DO NOT CROSS THE LINE
AAAGGH!!
CRIME SCENE DO NOT CROSS
AAAGGH!!
Come on!!
Bad luck kitty.

Let's see what the @#$@ was so important that--

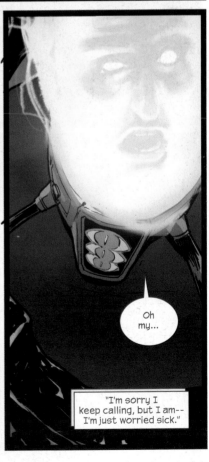

Oh my...

"I'm sorry I keep calling, but I am-- I'm just worried sick."

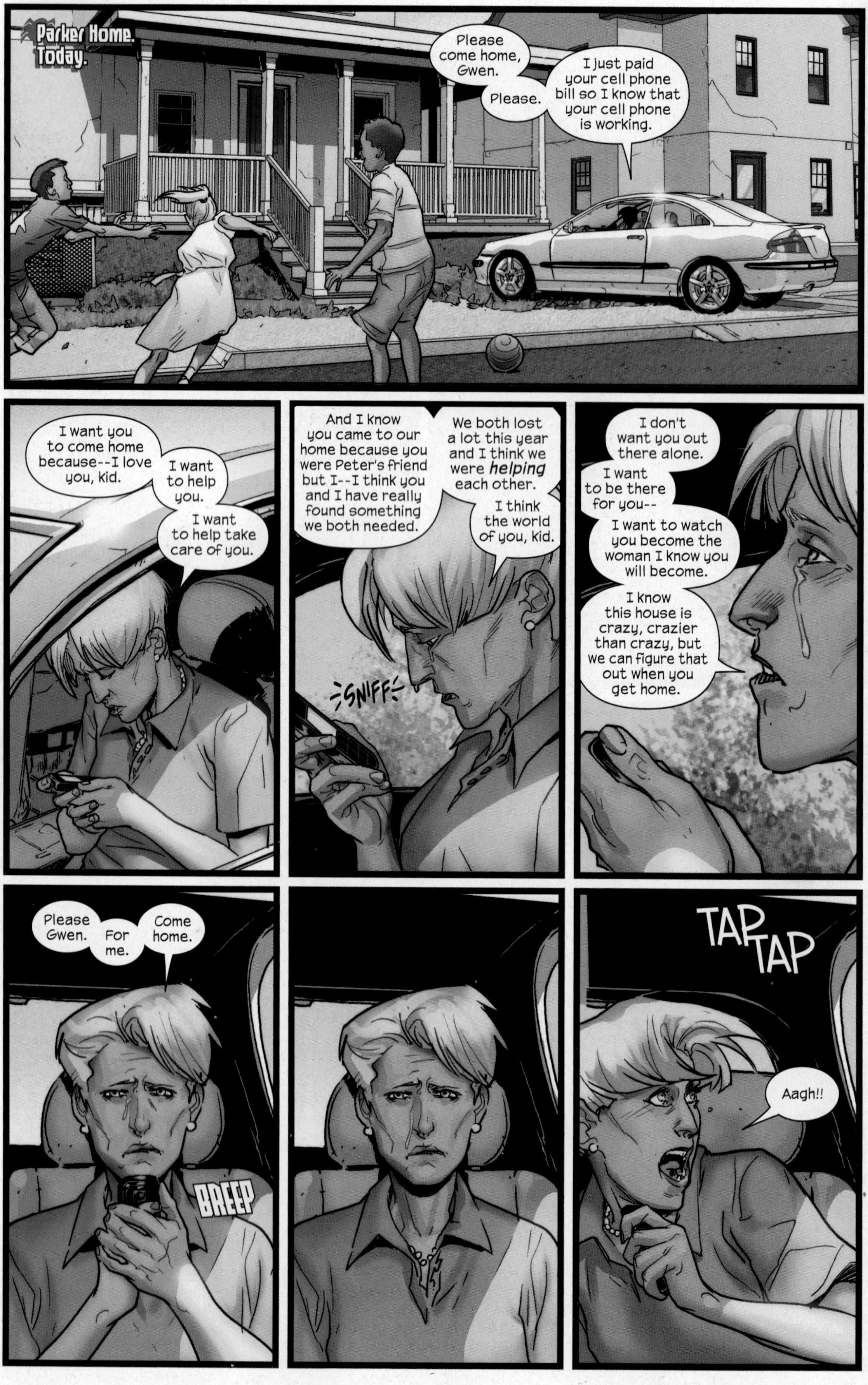
Parker Home.
Today.
Please come home, Gwen.
Please.
I just paid your cell phone bill so I know that your cell phone is working.
I want you to come home because--I love you, kid.
I want to help you.
I want to help take care of you.
And I know you came to our home because you were Peter's friend but I--I think you and I have really found something we both needed.
We both lost a lot this year and I think we were *helping* each other.
I think the world of you, kid.
SNIFF
I don't want you out there alone.
I want to be there for you--
I want to watch you become the woman I know you will become.
I know this house is crazy, crazier than crazy, but we can figure that out when you get home.
Please Gwen.
For me.
Come home.
BREEP
TAP TAP
Aagh!!

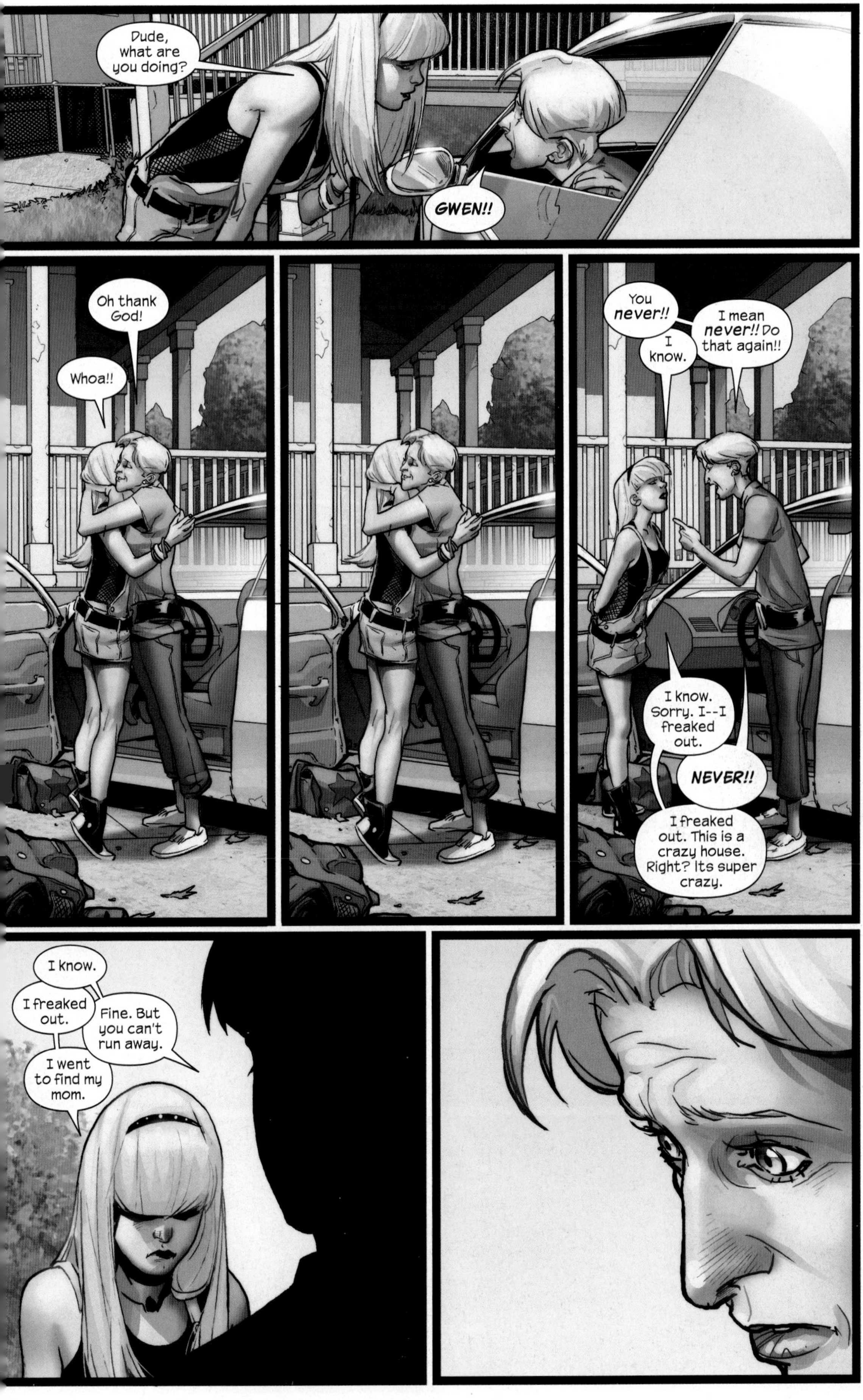
Dude, what are you doing?
GWEN!!
Oh thank God!
Whoa!!
You never!!
I know.
I mean never!! Do that again!!
I know. Sorry. I--I freaked out.
NEVER!!
I freaked out. This is a crazy house. Right? Its super crazy.
I know.
I freaked out.
Fine. But you can't run away.
I went to find my mom.

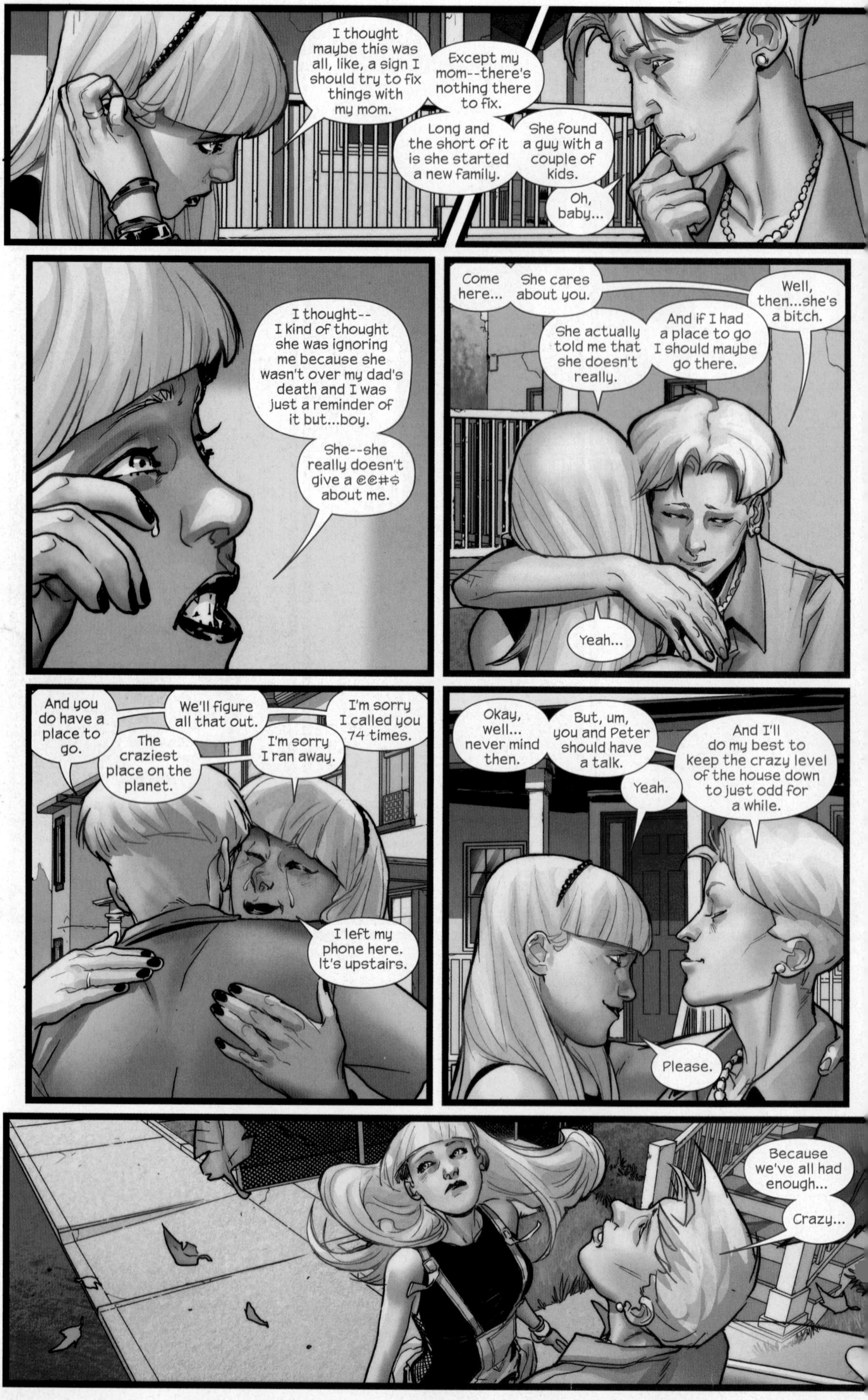
I thought maybe this was all, like, a sign I should try to fix things with my mom.
Except my mom--there's nothing there to fix.
Long and the short of it is she started a new family.
She found a guy with a couple of kids.
Oh, baby...
I thought-- I kind of thought she was ignoring me because she wasn't over my dad's death and I was just a reminder of it but...boy.
She--she really doesn't give a @@#$ about me.
Come here...
She cares about you.
Well, then...she's a bitch.
She actually told me that she doesn't really.
And if I had a place to go I should maybe go there.
Yeah...
And you do have a place to go.
We'll figure all that out.
I'm sorry I called you 74 times.
The craziest place on the planet.
I'm sorry I ran away.
I left my phone here. It's upstairs.
Okay, well... never mind then.
But, um, you and Peter should have a talk.
And I'll do my best to keep the crazy level of the house down to just odd for a while.
Yeah.
Please.
Because we've all had enough...
Crazy...

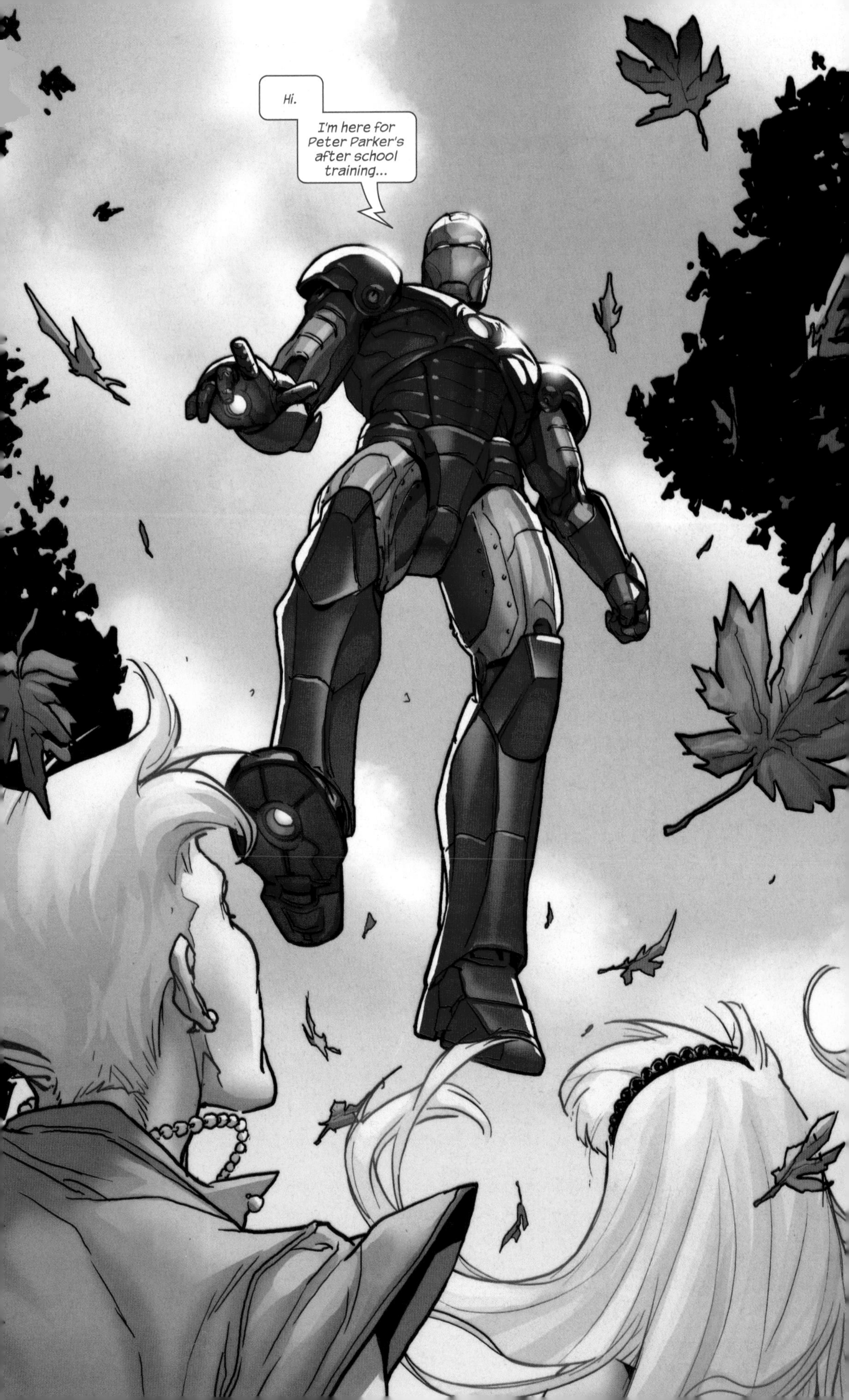
Hi.
I'm here for Peter Parker's after school training...

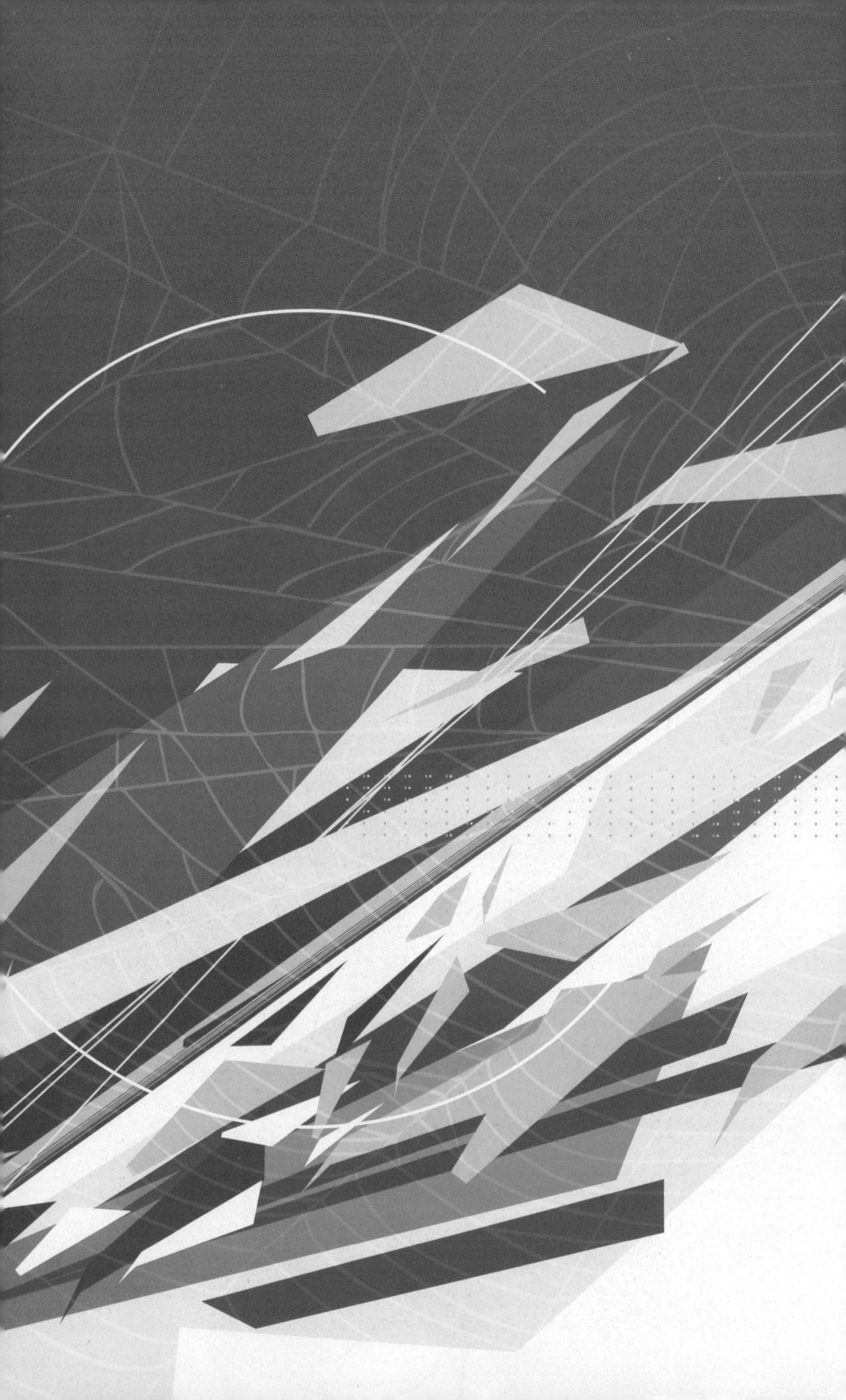

152

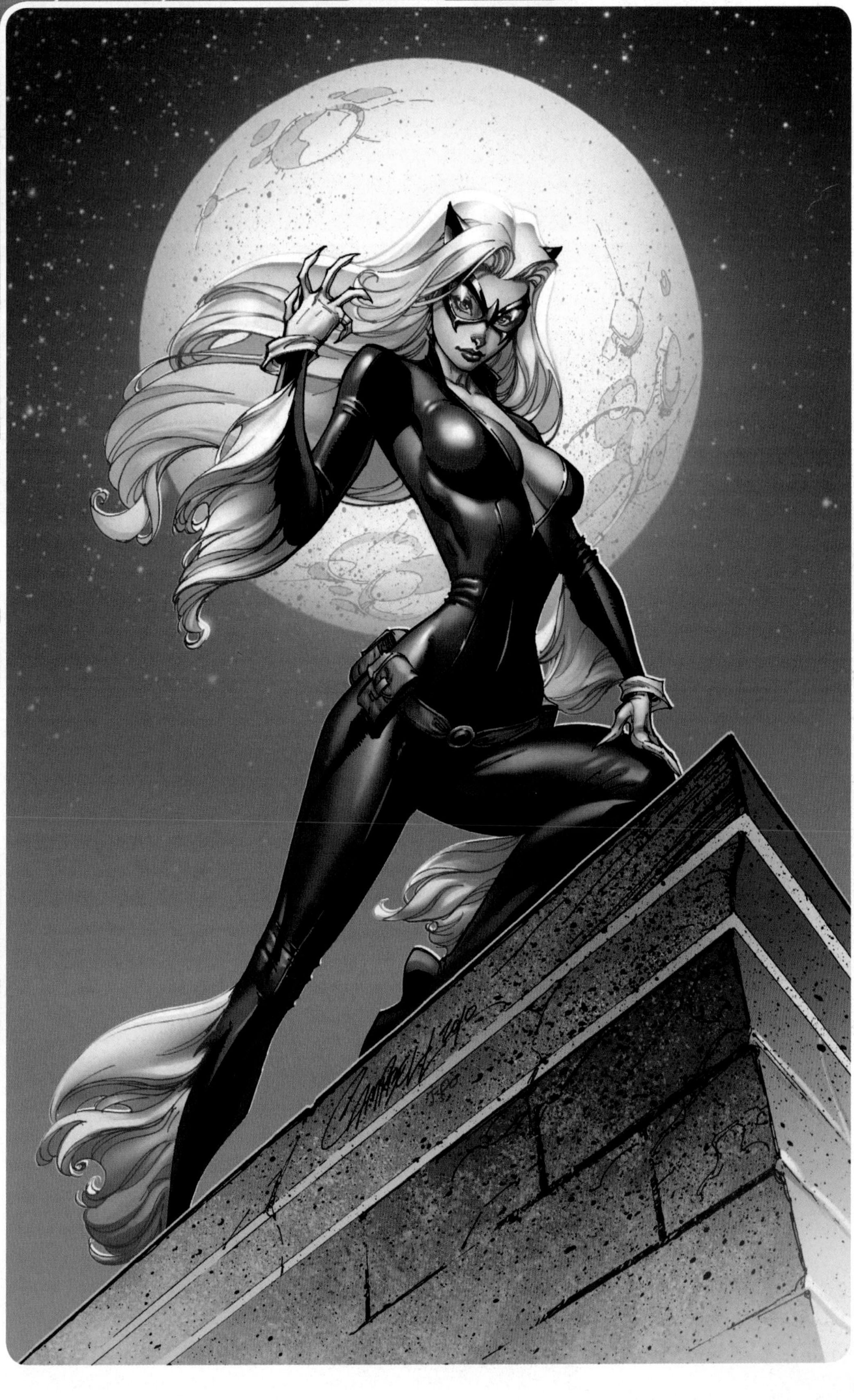

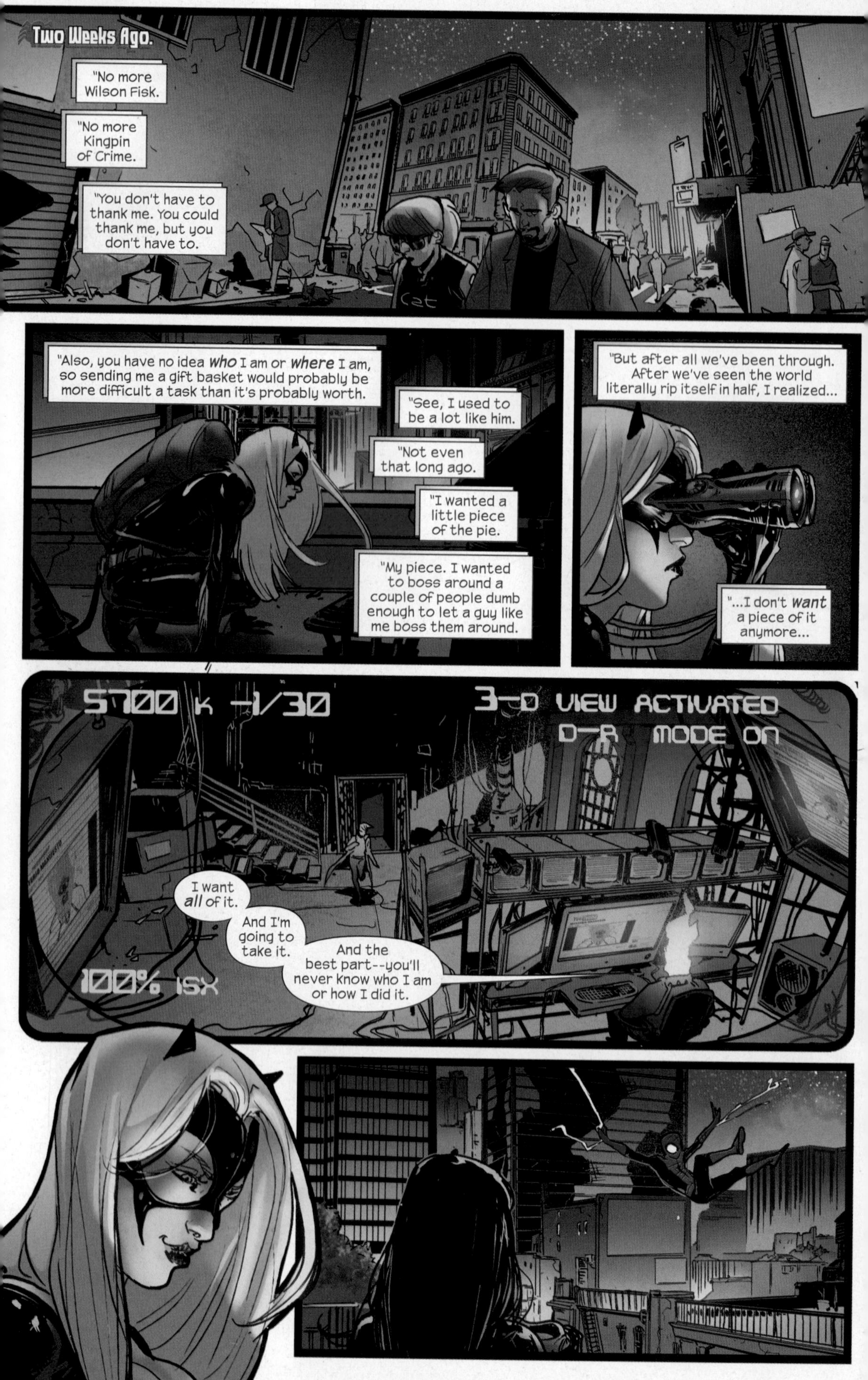
Two Weeks Ago.
"No more Wilson Fisk.
"No more Kingpin of Crime.
"You don't have to thank me. You could thank me, but you don't have to.
Cat
"Also, you have no idea who I am or where I am, so sending me a gift basket would probably be more difficult a task than it's probably worth.
"See, I used to be a lot like him.
"Not even that long ago.
"I wanted a little piece of the pie.
"My piece. I wanted to boss around a couple of people dumb enough to let a guy like me boss them around.
"But after all we've been through. After we've seen the world literally rip itself in half, I realized...
"...I don't want a piece of it anymore...
5700 K -1/30
3-D VIEW ACTIVATED
D-R MODE ON
I want all of it.
And I'm going to take it.
And the best part--you'll never know who I am or how I did it.
100% ISX

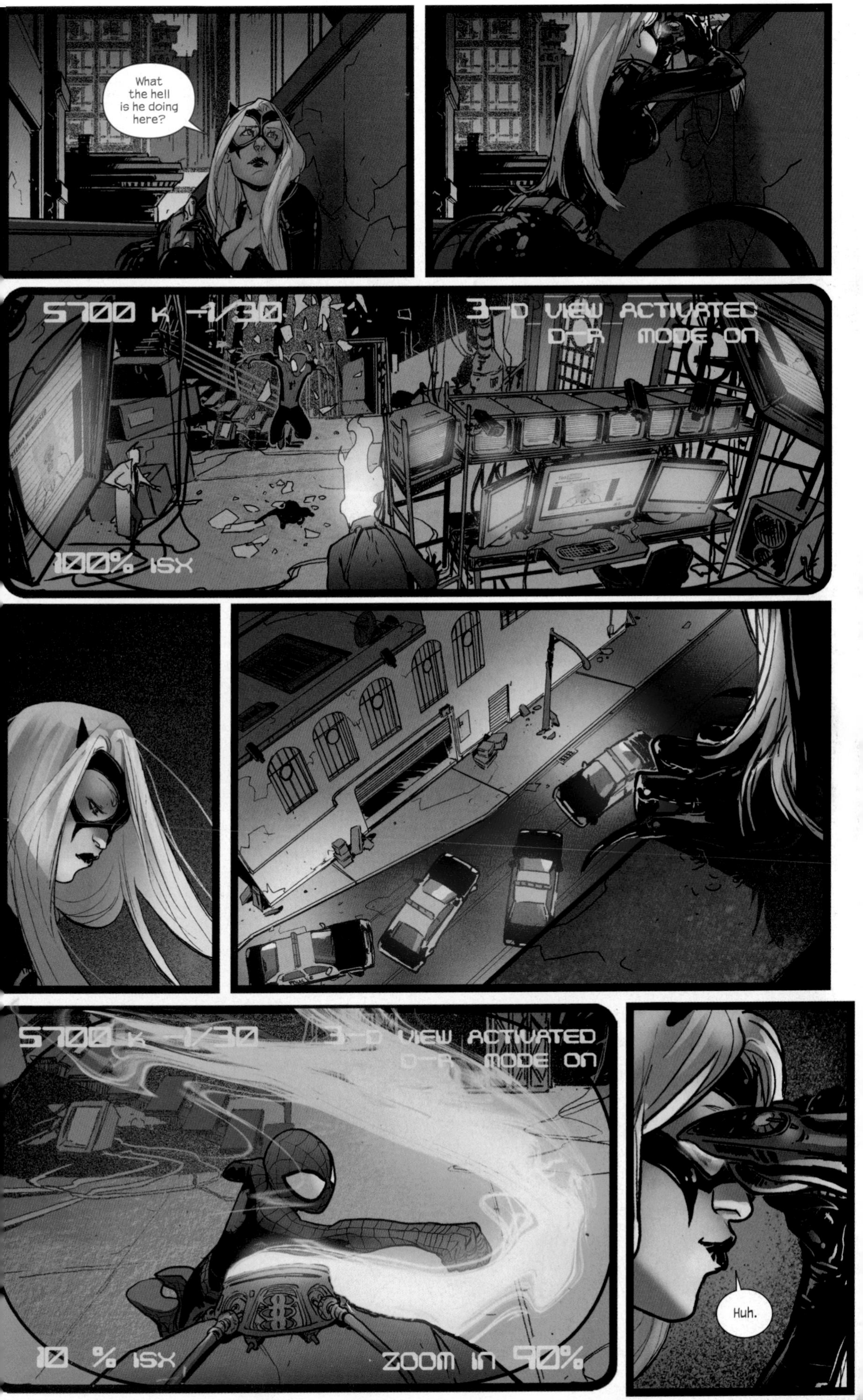
What the hell is he doing here?
5700 K -1/30
3-D VIEW ACTIVATED
D-R MODE ON
100% ISX
5700 K -1/30
3-D VIEW ACTIVATED
D-R MODE ON
10 % ISX
ZOOM IN 90%
Huh.

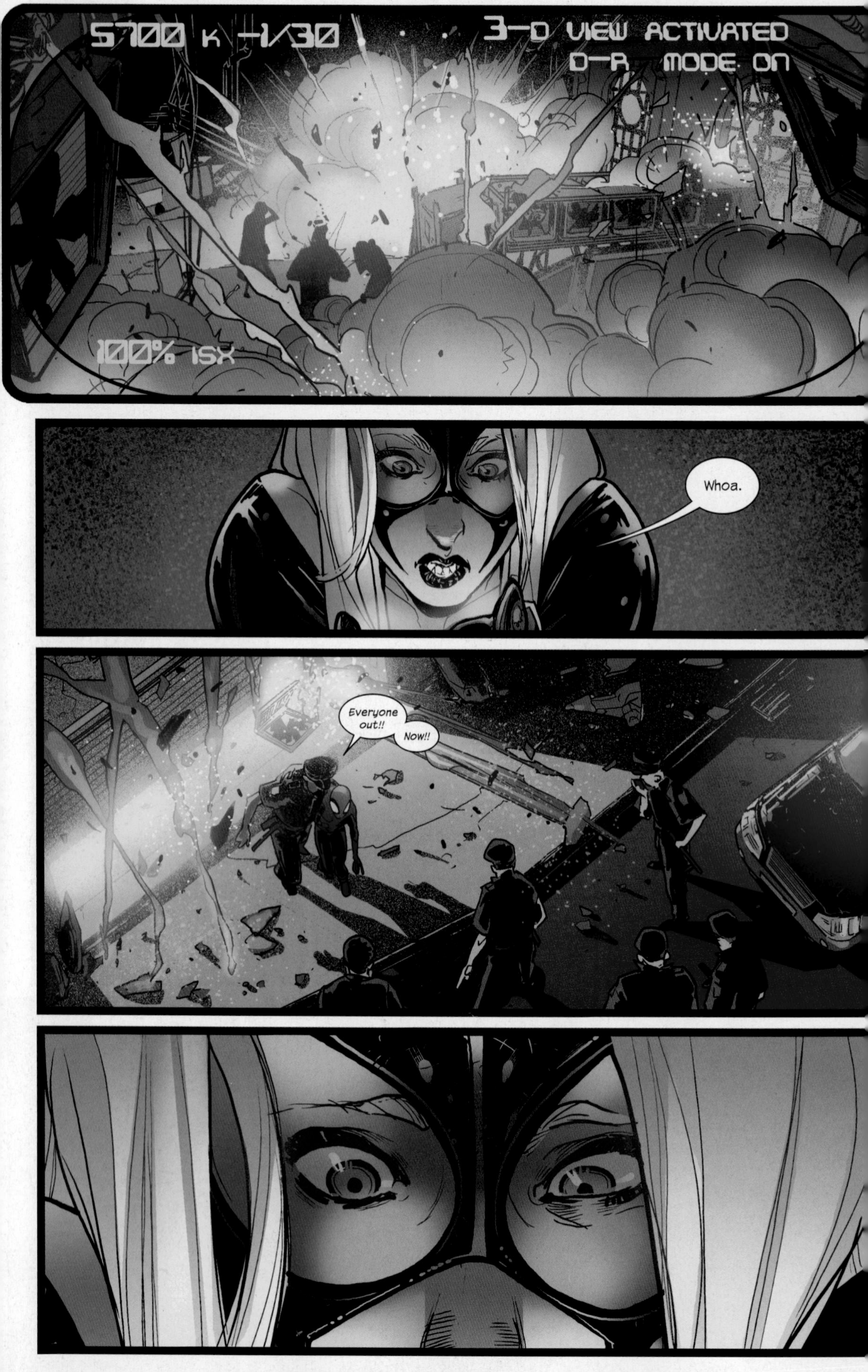
5700 K -1/30
3-D VIEW ACTIVATED
D-R MODE ON
100% ISX
Whoa.
Everyone out!!
Now!!

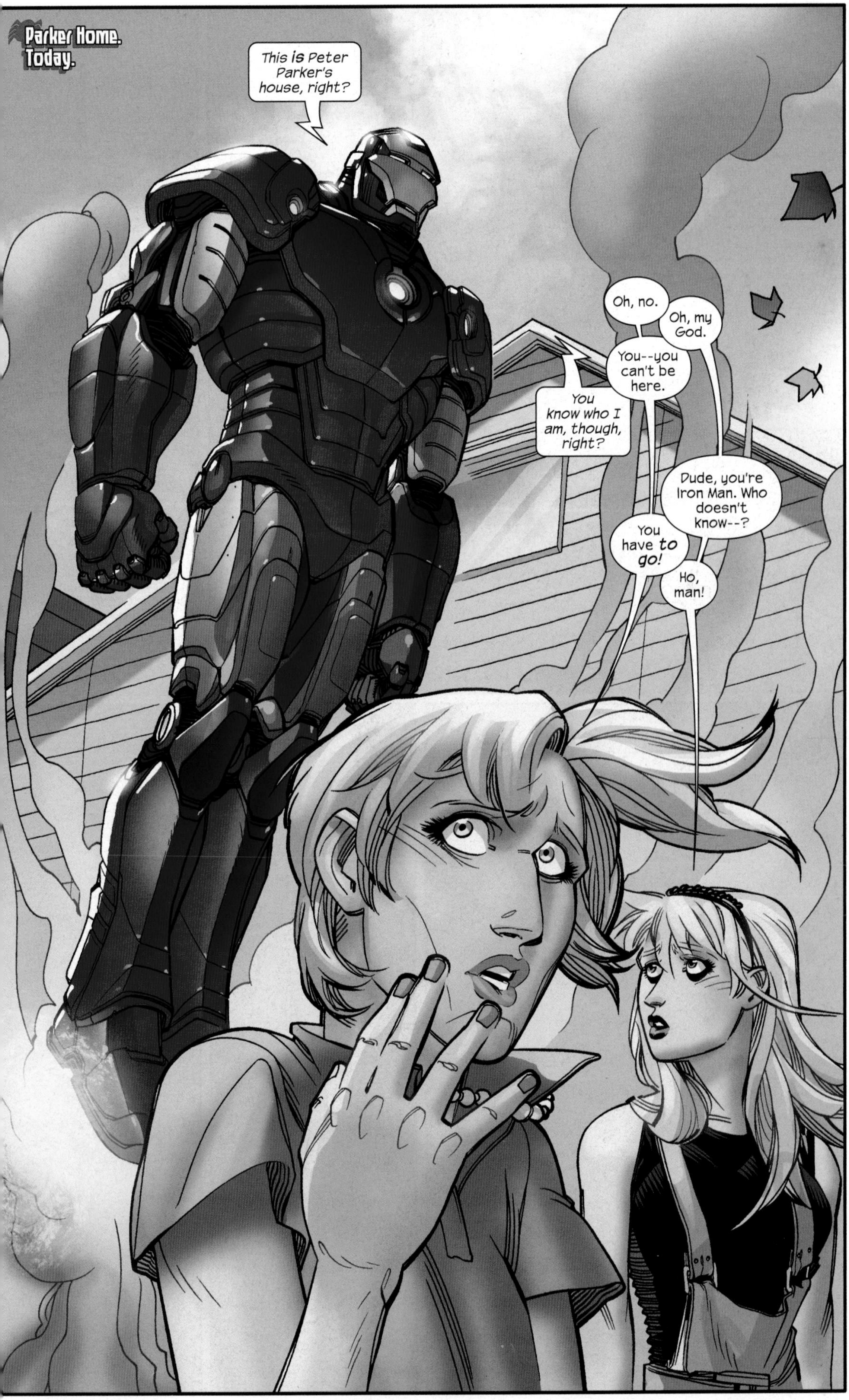
Parker Home.
Today.
This is Peter Parker's house, right?
Oh, no.
Oh, my God.
You--you can't be here.
You know who I am, though, right?
Dude, you're Iron Man. Who doesn't know--?
You have to go!
Ho, man!

Wow.

You can't *be* here!! You-you are ruining our lives!!

I'm confused. I was told to come here. Carol *Danvers* sent me. I was told that the kid needed some--

Not like *this.*

People don't *know.* People don't know who he is. You are blowing our-- you're blowing his *cover.*

You're ruining our lives.

Hmmm... Thank you for *the* directions, kind citizen!! You were a *huge help!!*

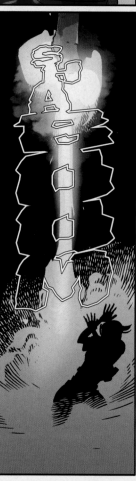

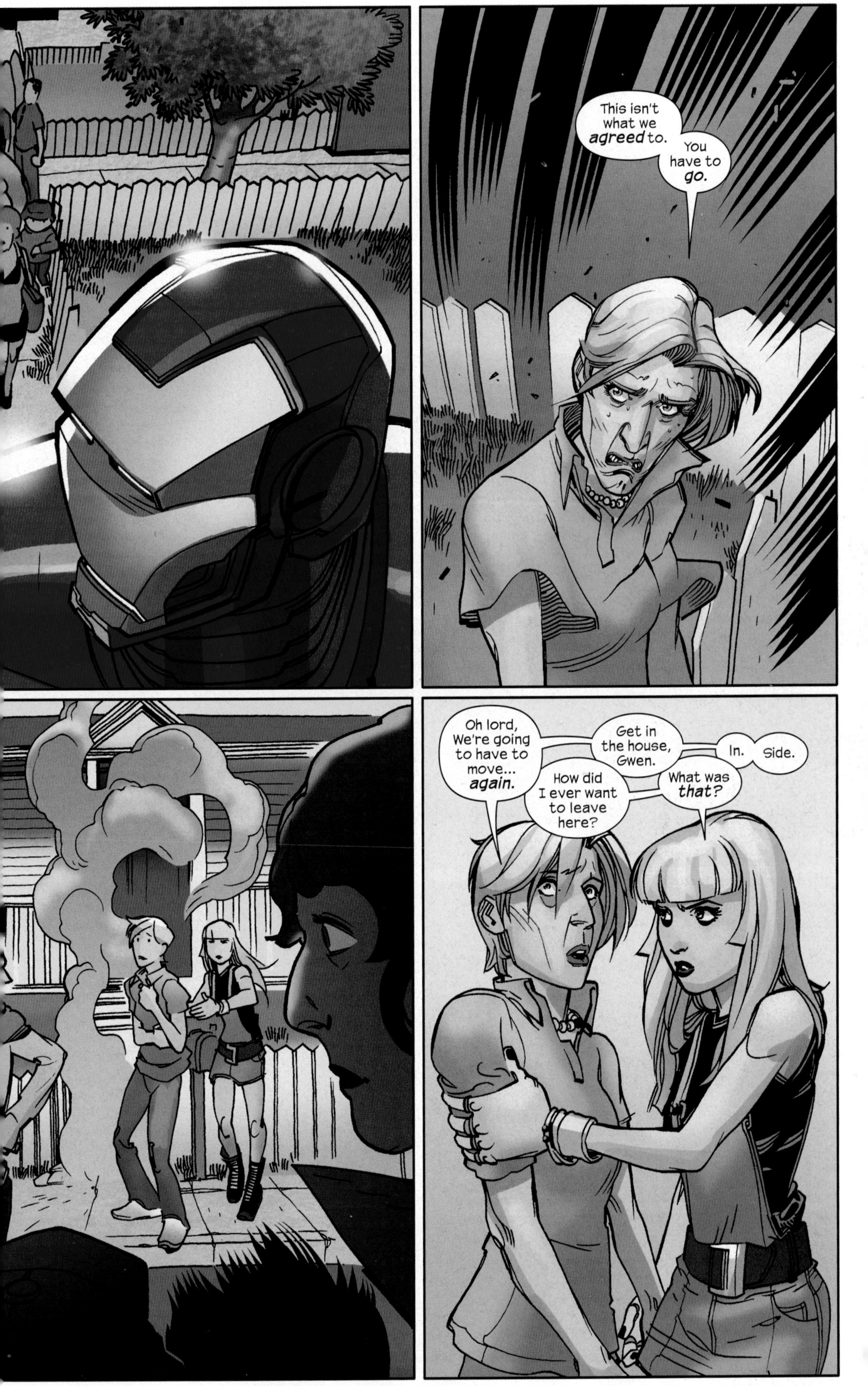
This isn't what we agreed to.
You have to go.
Oh lord, We're going to have to move... again.
Get in the house, Gwen.
How did I ever want to leave here?
What was that?
In.
Side.

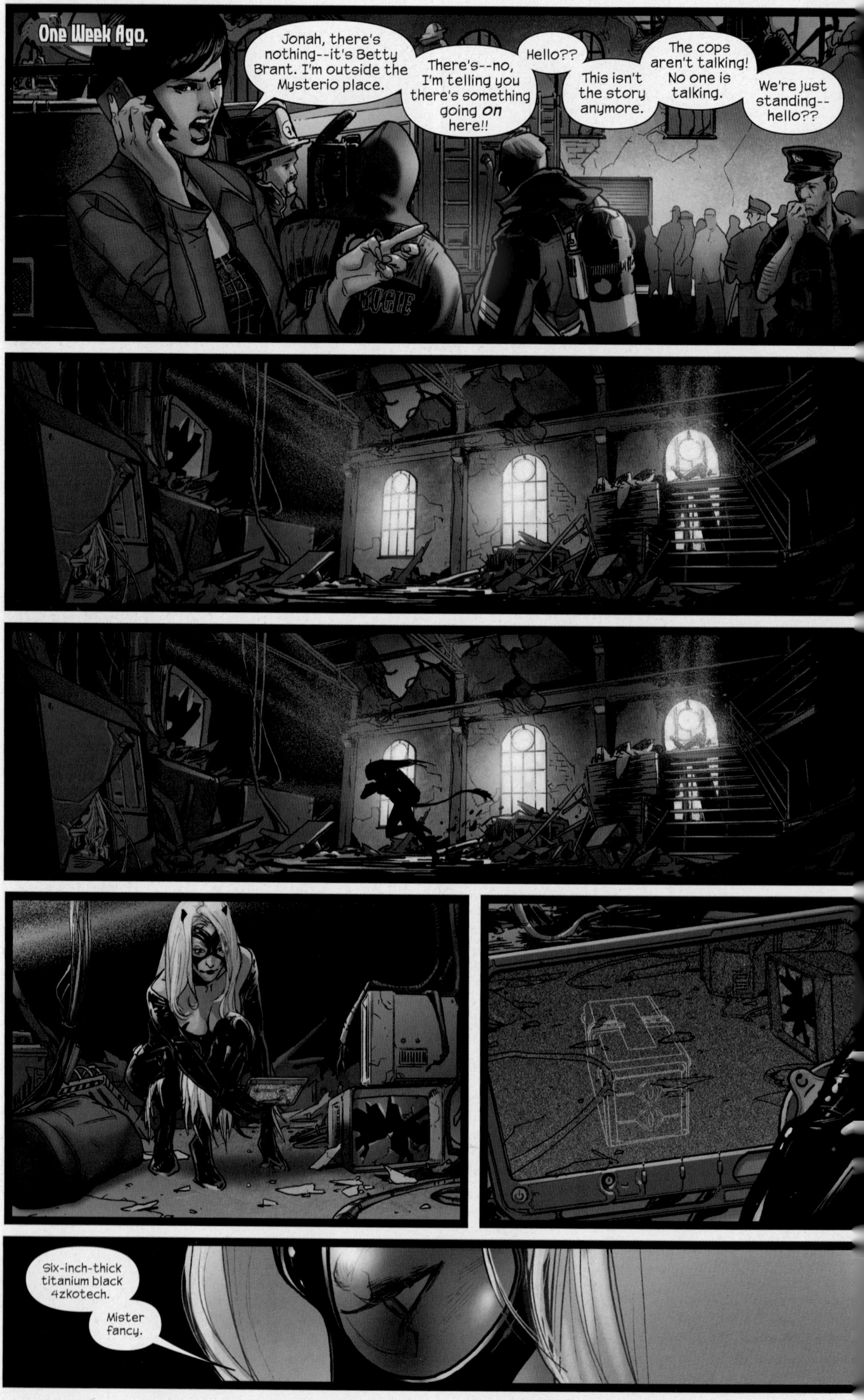
One Week Ago.
Jonah, there's nothing--it's Betty Brant. I'm outside the Mysterio place.
There's--no, I'm telling you there's something going *on* here!!
Hello??
This isn't the story anymore.
The cops aren't talking! No one is talking.
We're just standing--hello??
Six-inch-thick titanium black 4zkotech.
Mister fancy.

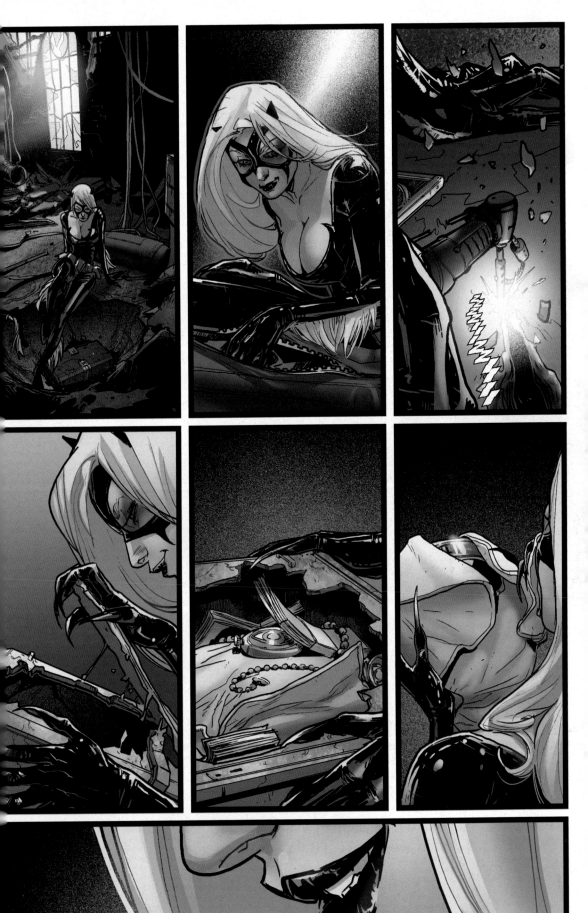

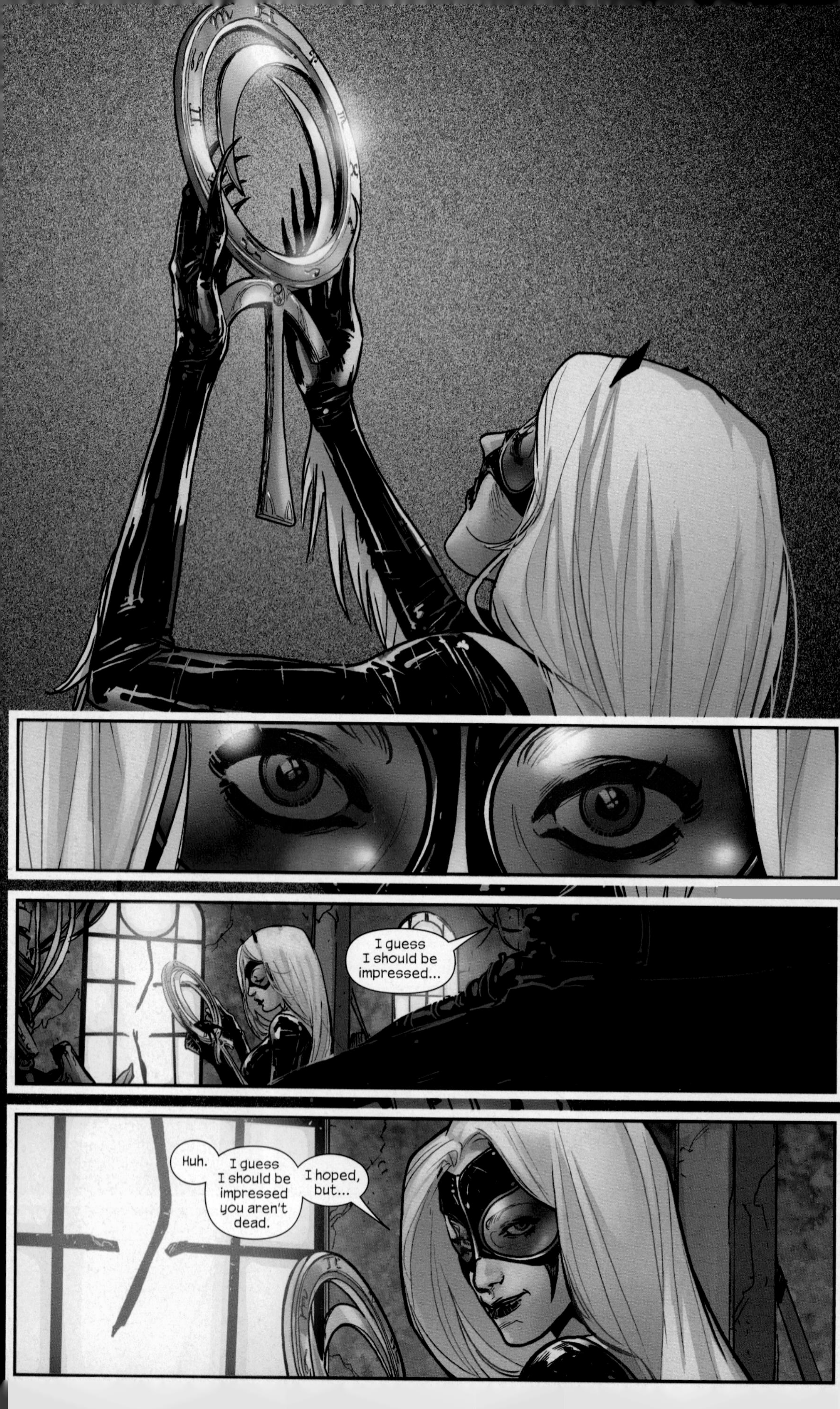
I guess
I should be
impressed...
Huh.
I guess
I should be
impressed
you aren't
dead.
I hoped,
but...

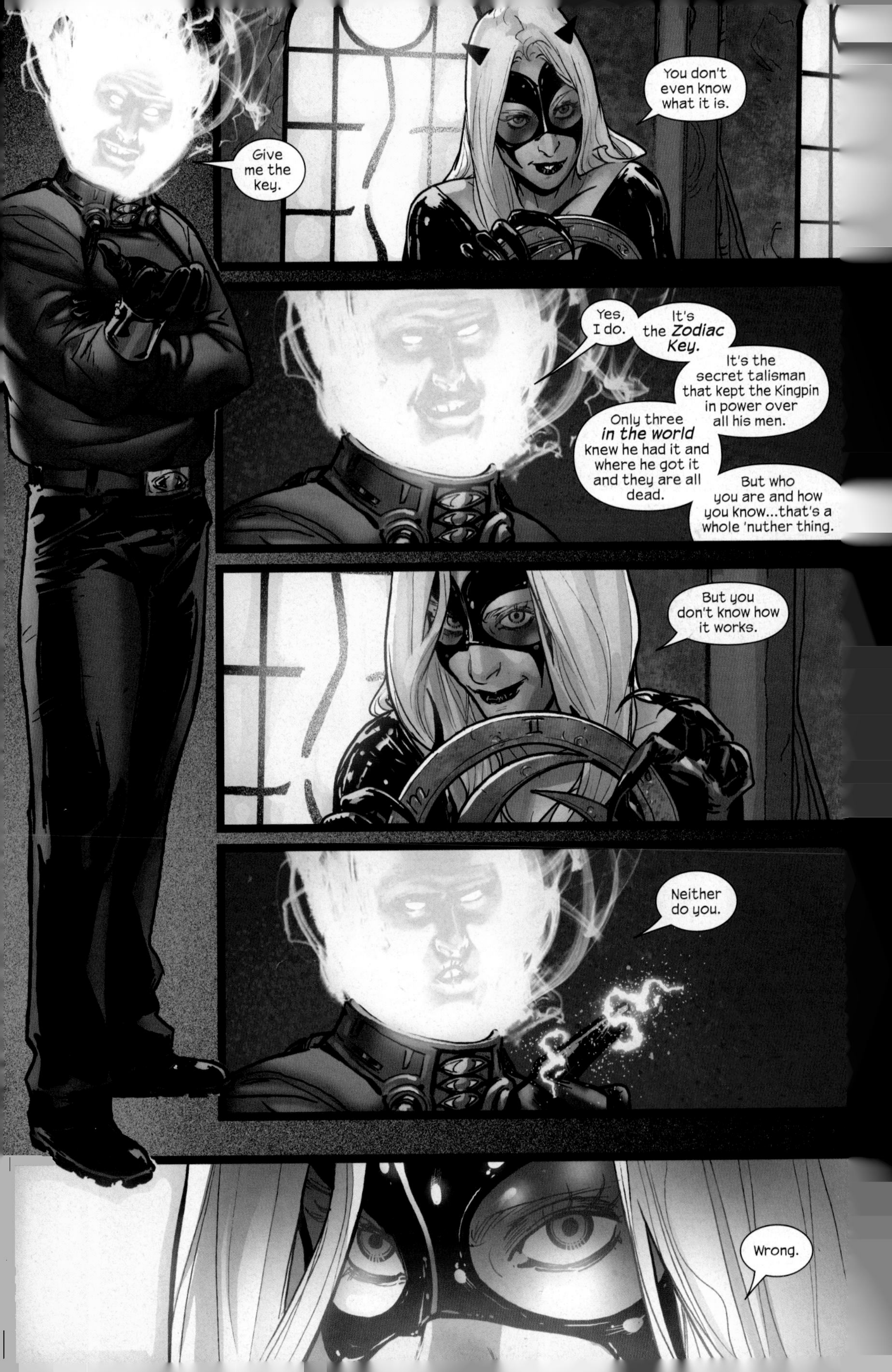

Give me the key.
You don't even know what it is.
Yes, I do.
It's the *Zodiac Key.*
It's the secret talisman that kept the Kingpin in power over all his men.
Only three *in the world* knew he had it and where he got it and they are all dead.
But who you are and how you know...that's a whole 'nuther thing.
But you don't know how it works.
Neither do you.
Wrong.

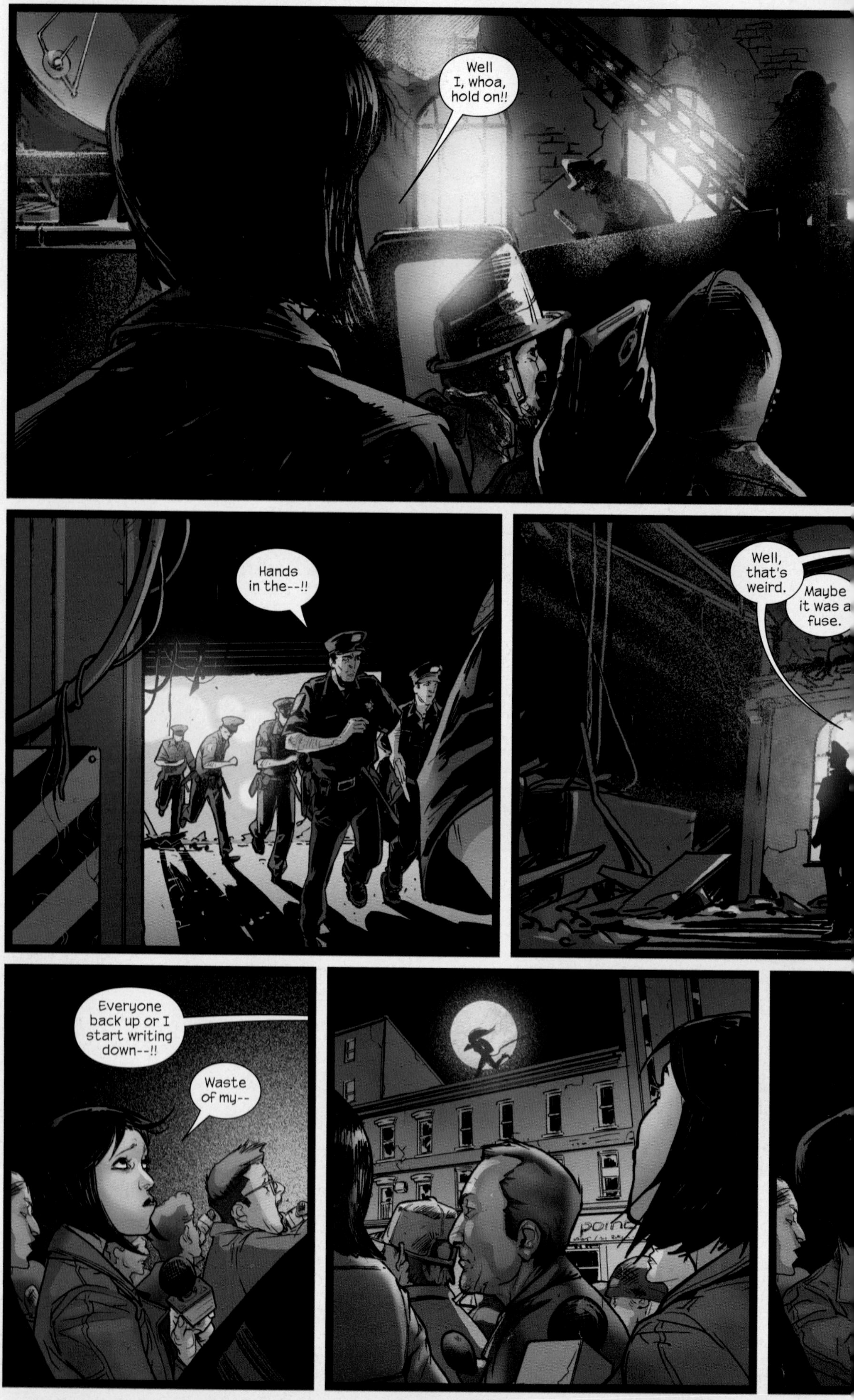
Well I, whoa, hold on!!
Hands in the--!!
Well, that's weird.
Maybe it was a fuse.
Everyone back up or I start writing down--!!
Waste of my--

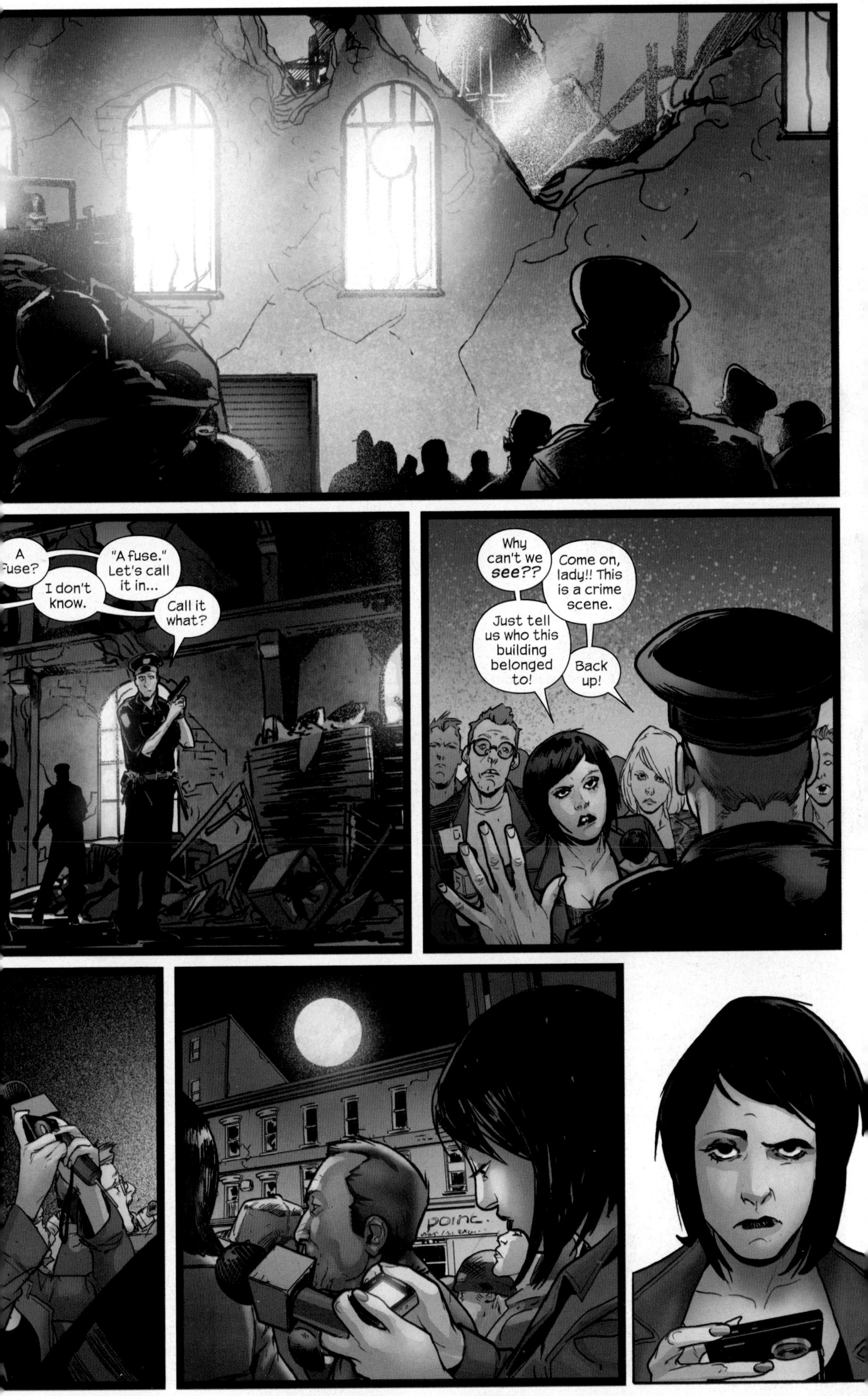
A Fuse?
I don't know.
"A fuse." Let's call it in...
Call it what?
Why can't we *see??*
Just tell us who this building belonged to!
Come on, lady!! This is a crime scene.
Back up!
point.

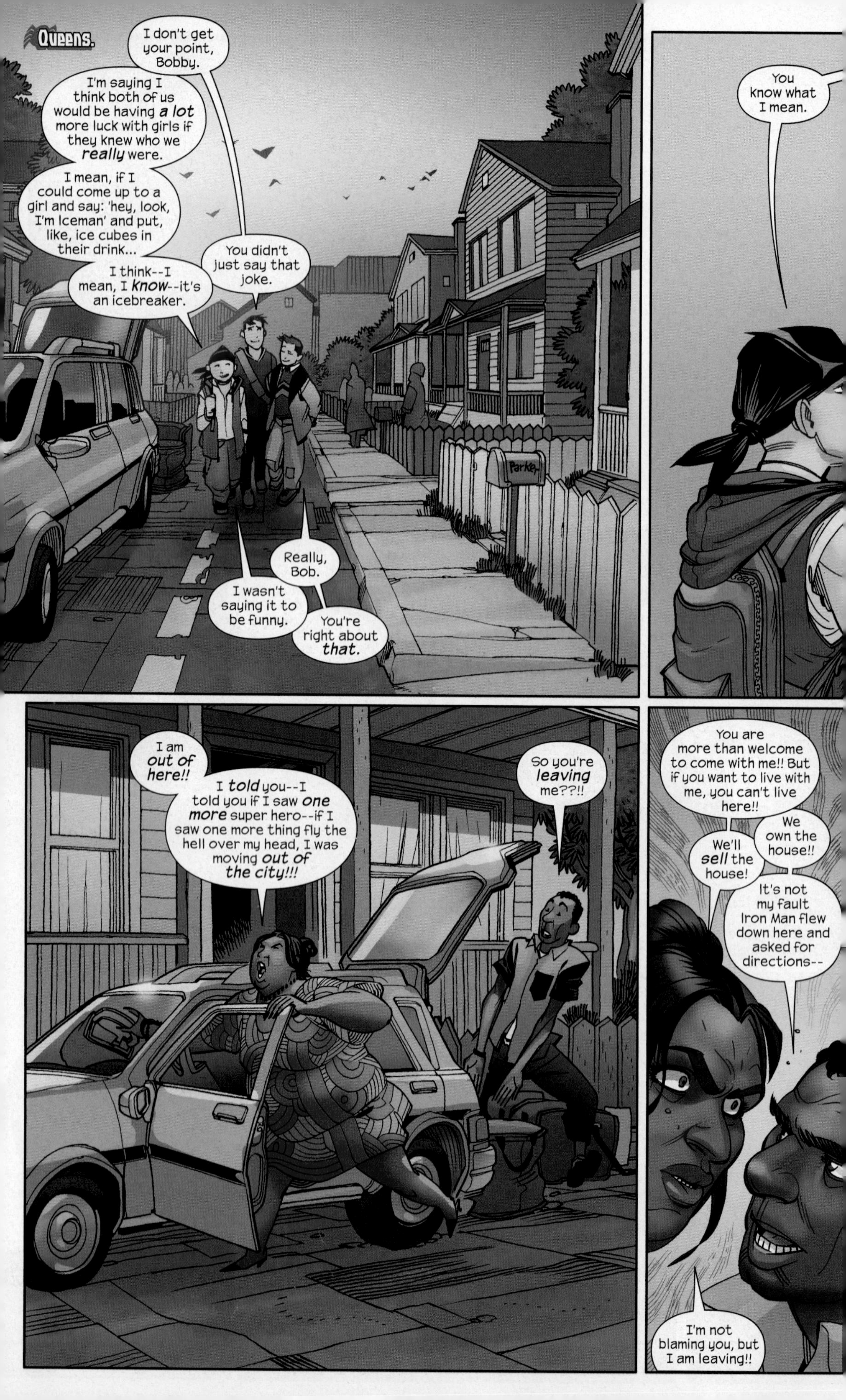
Queens.
I don't get your point, Bobby.
I'm saying I think both of us would be having a lot more luck with girls if they knew who we really were.
I mean, if I could come up to a girl and say: 'hey, look, I'm Iceman' and put, like, ice cubes in their drink...
I think--I mean, I know--it's an icebreaker.
You didn't just say that joke.
Really, Bob.
I wasn't saying it to be funny.
You're right about that.
Parker
You know what I mean.
I am out of here!!
I told you--I told you if I saw one more super hero--if I saw one more thing fly the hell over my head, I was moving out of the city!!!
So you're leaving me??!!
You are more than welcome to come with me!! But if you want to live with me, you can't live here!!
We own the house!!
We'll sell the house!
It's not my fault Iron Man flew down here and asked for directions--
I'm not blaming you, but I am leaving!!

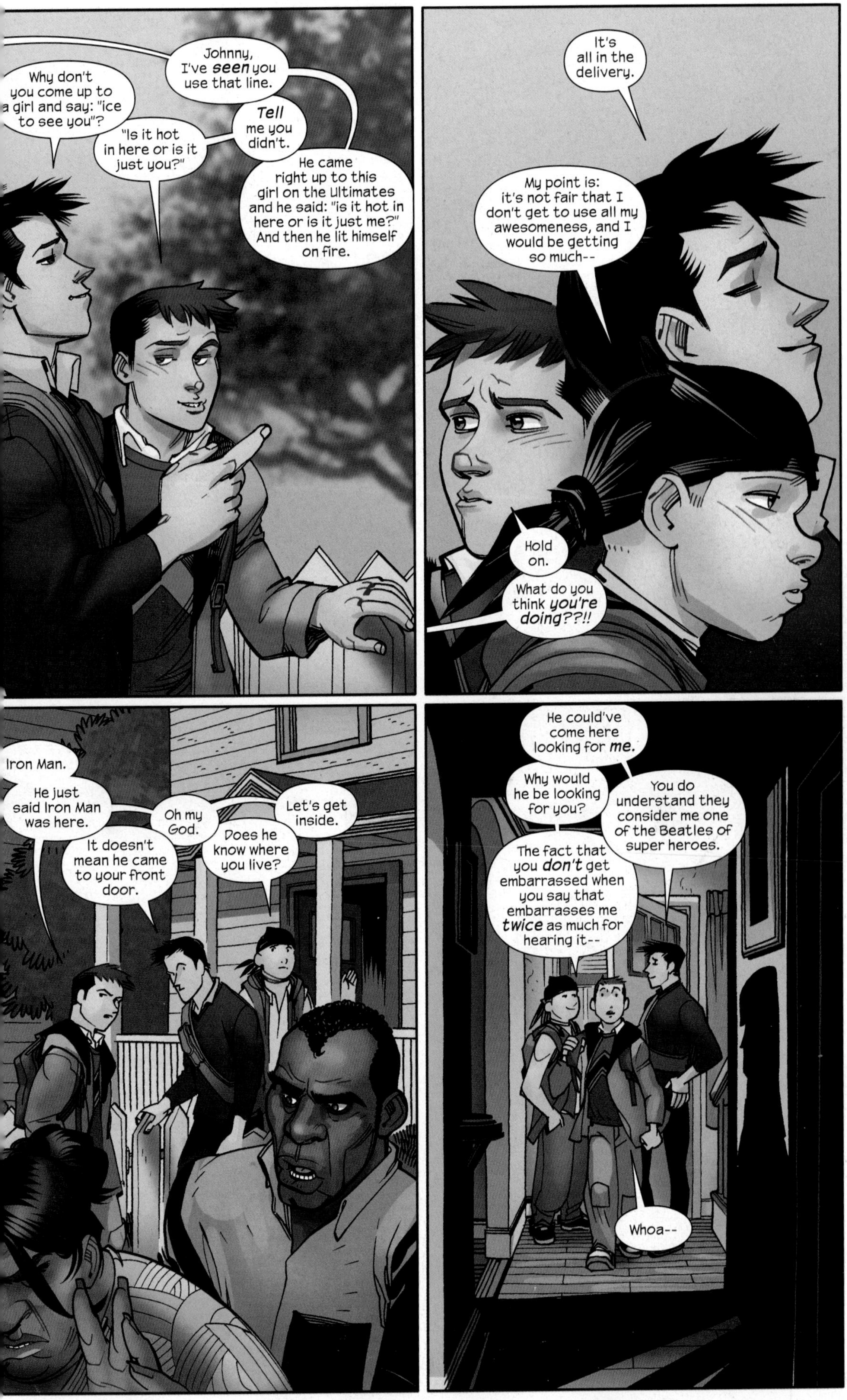
Why don't you come up to a girl and say: "ice to see you"?
Johnny, I've seen you use that line.
"Is it hot in here or is it just you?"
Tell me you didn't.
He came right up to this girl on the Ultimates and he said: "is it hot in here or is it just me?" And then he lit himself on fire.
It's all in the delivery.
My point is: it's not fair that I don't get to use all my awesomeness, and I would be getting so much--
Hold on.
What do you think you're doing??!!
Iron Man.
He just said Iron Man was here.
Oh my God.
Let's get inside.
It doesn't mean he came to your front door.
Does he know where you live?
He could've come here looking for me.
Why would he be looking for you?
You do understand they consider me one of the Beatles of super heroes.
The fact that you don't get embarrassed when you say that embarrasses me twice as much for hearing it--
Whoa--

Ta daa!!

Gwen Stacy is *back*!

I'm okay. Everything is okay.

Good for you!!

Okay, okay!!

I mean it! Good for you for coming back.

I know living with someone like me can get to be too much.

Like you what?

Oh, God.

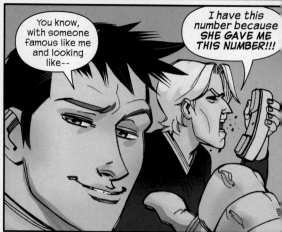

You know, with someone famous like me and looking like--

I have this number because SHE GAVE ME THIS NUMBER!!!

RRRR!!

Those S.H.I.E.L.D. people are really thick!!!

THICK!!

Thick thick thick!!!

Aunt May, please, calm down...

Your-- your heart.

Idiots!!

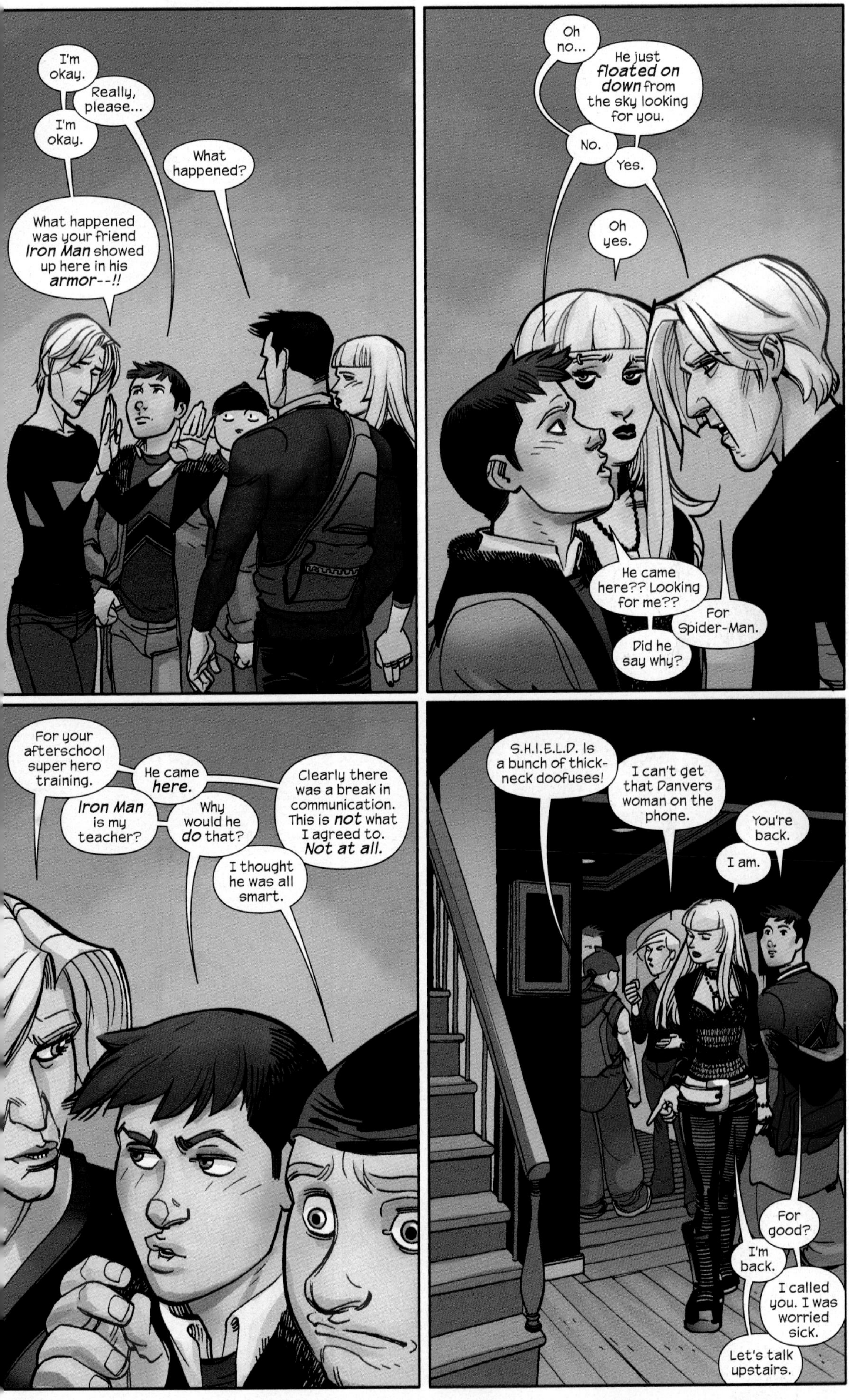
I'm okay.
Really, please...
I'm okay.
What happened?
What happened was your friend *Iron Man* showed up here in his *armor*--!!
Oh no...
He just *floated on down* from the sky looking for you.
No.
Yes.
Oh yes.
He came here?? Looking for me??
For Spider-Man.
Did he say why?
For your afterschool super hero training.
He came *here.*
Clearly there was a break in communication. This is *not* what I agreed to. *Not at all.*
Iron Man is my teacher?
Why would he *do* that?
I thought he was all smart.
S.H.I.E.L.D. Is a bunch of thick-neck doofuses!
I can't get that Danvers woman on the phone.
You're back.
I am.
For good?
I'm back.
I called you. I was worried sick.
Let's talk upstairs.

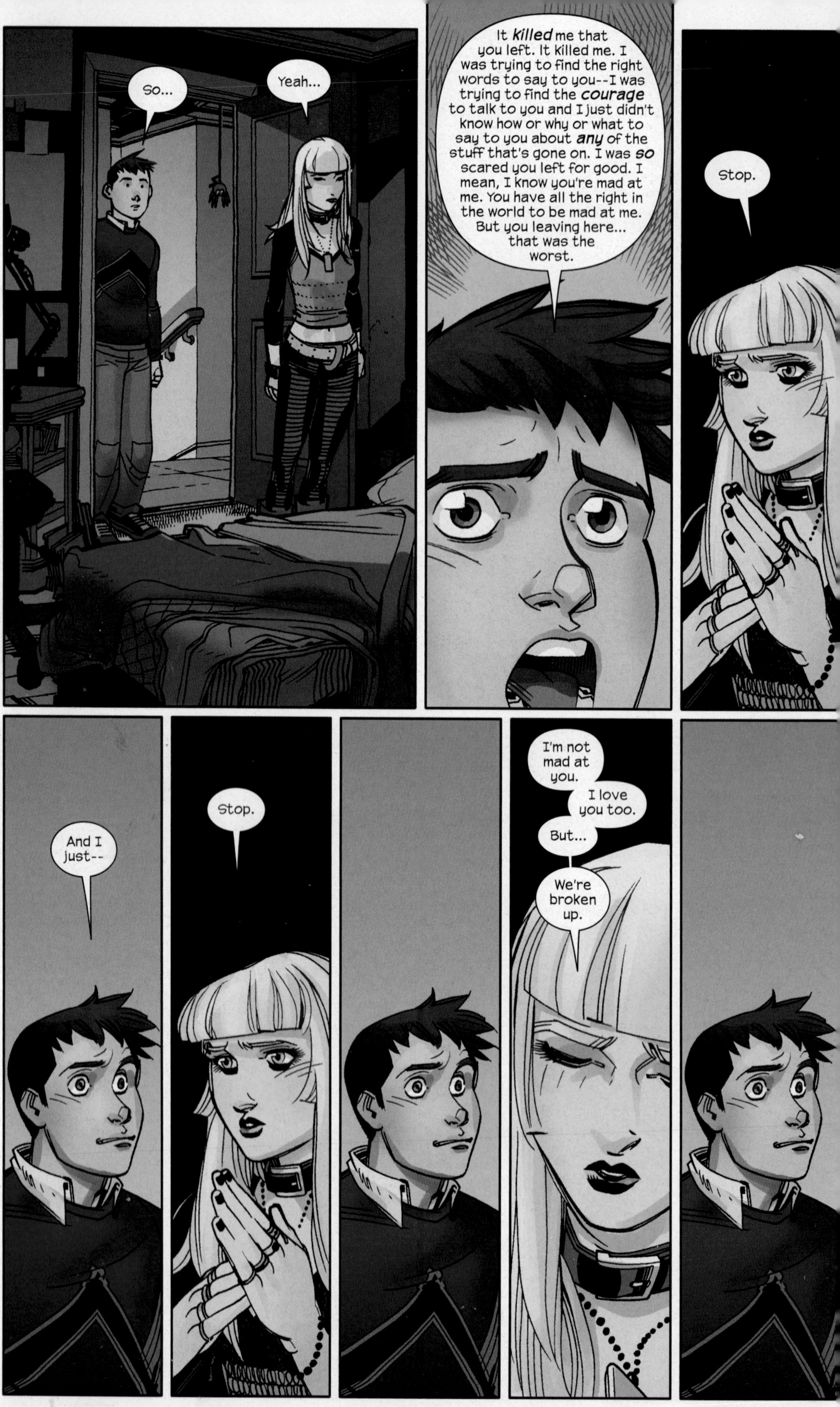
So...
Yeah...
It killed me that you left. It killed me. I was trying to find the right words to say to you--I was trying to find the courage to talk to you and I just didn't know how or why or what to say to you about any of the stuff that's gone on. I was so scared you left for good. I mean, I know you're mad at me. You have all the right in the world to be mad at me. But you leaving here... that was the worst.
Stop.
And I just--
Stop.
I'm not mad at you.
I love you too.
But...
We're broken up.

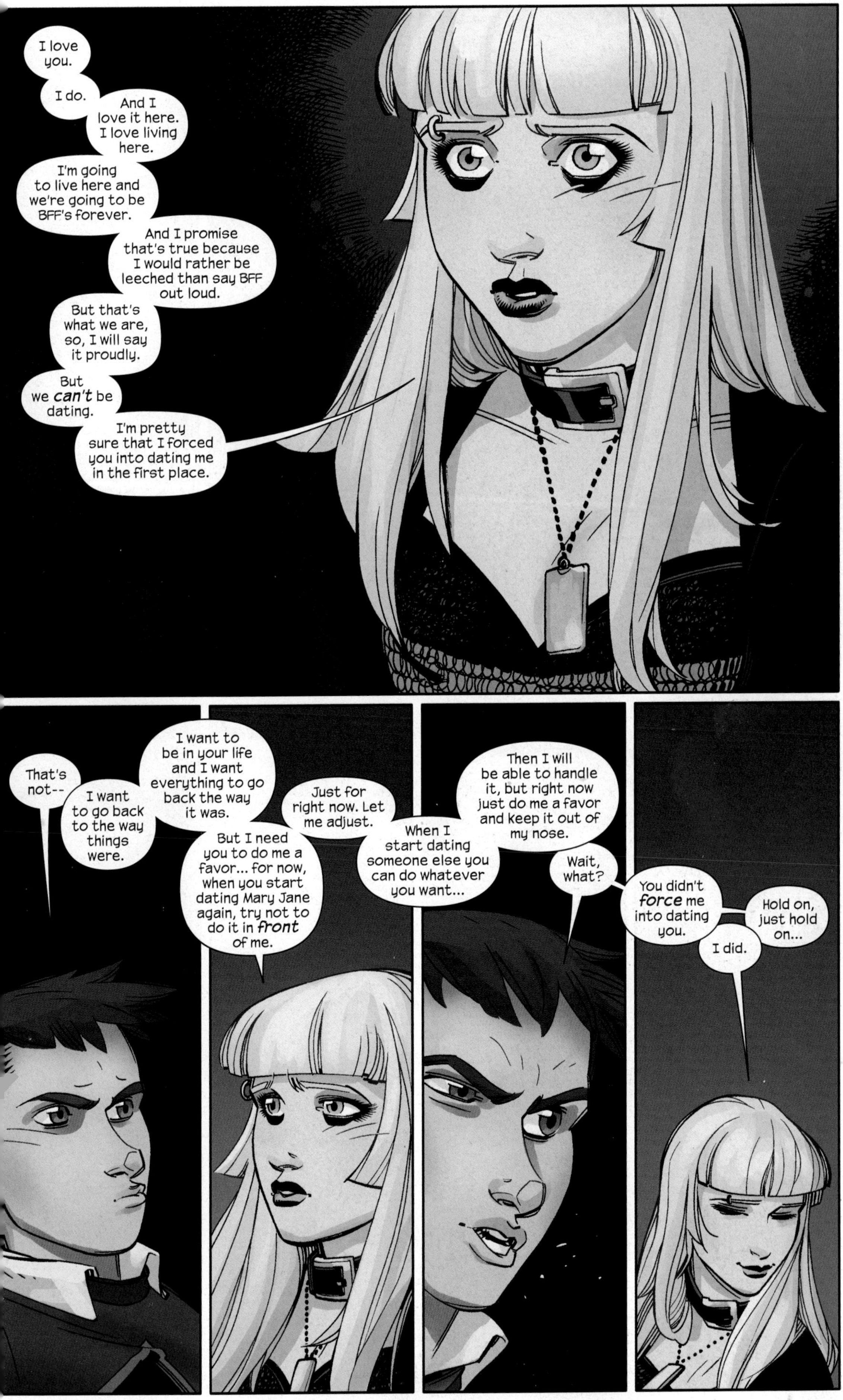

I love you.
I do.
And I love it here. I love living here.
I'm going to live here and we're going to be BFF's forever.
And I promise that's true because I would rather be leeched than say BFF out loud.
But that's what we are, so, I will say it proudly.
But we *can't* be dating.
I'm pretty sure that I forced you into dating me in the first place.
That's not--
I want to go back to the way things were.
I want to be in your life and I want everything to go back the way it was.
But I need you to do me a favor... for now, when you start dating Mary Jane again, try not to do it in *front* of me.
Just for right now. Let me adjust.
When I start dating someone else you can do whatever you want...
Then I will be able to handle it, but right now just do me a favor and keep it out of my nose.
Wait, what?
You didn't *force* me into dating you.
Hold on, just hold on...
I did.

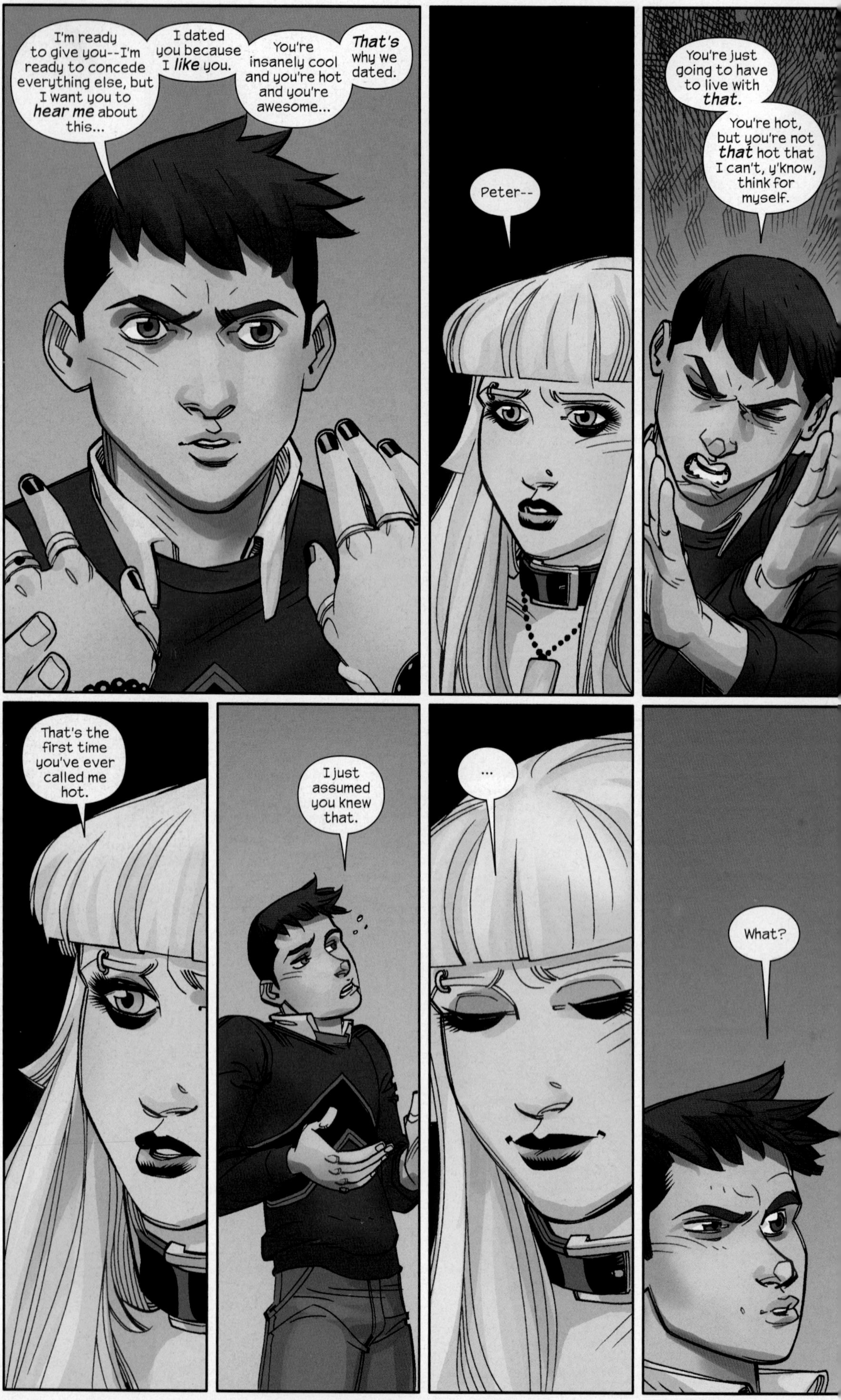

I'm ready to give you--I'm ready to concede everything else, but I want you to **hear me** about this...
I dated you because I *like* you.
You're insanely cool and you're hot and you're awesome...
That's why we dated.
Peter--
You're just going to have to live with ***that.***
You're hot, but you're not ***that*** hot that I can't, y'know, think for myself.
That's the first time you've ever called me hot.
I just assumed you knew that.
...
What?

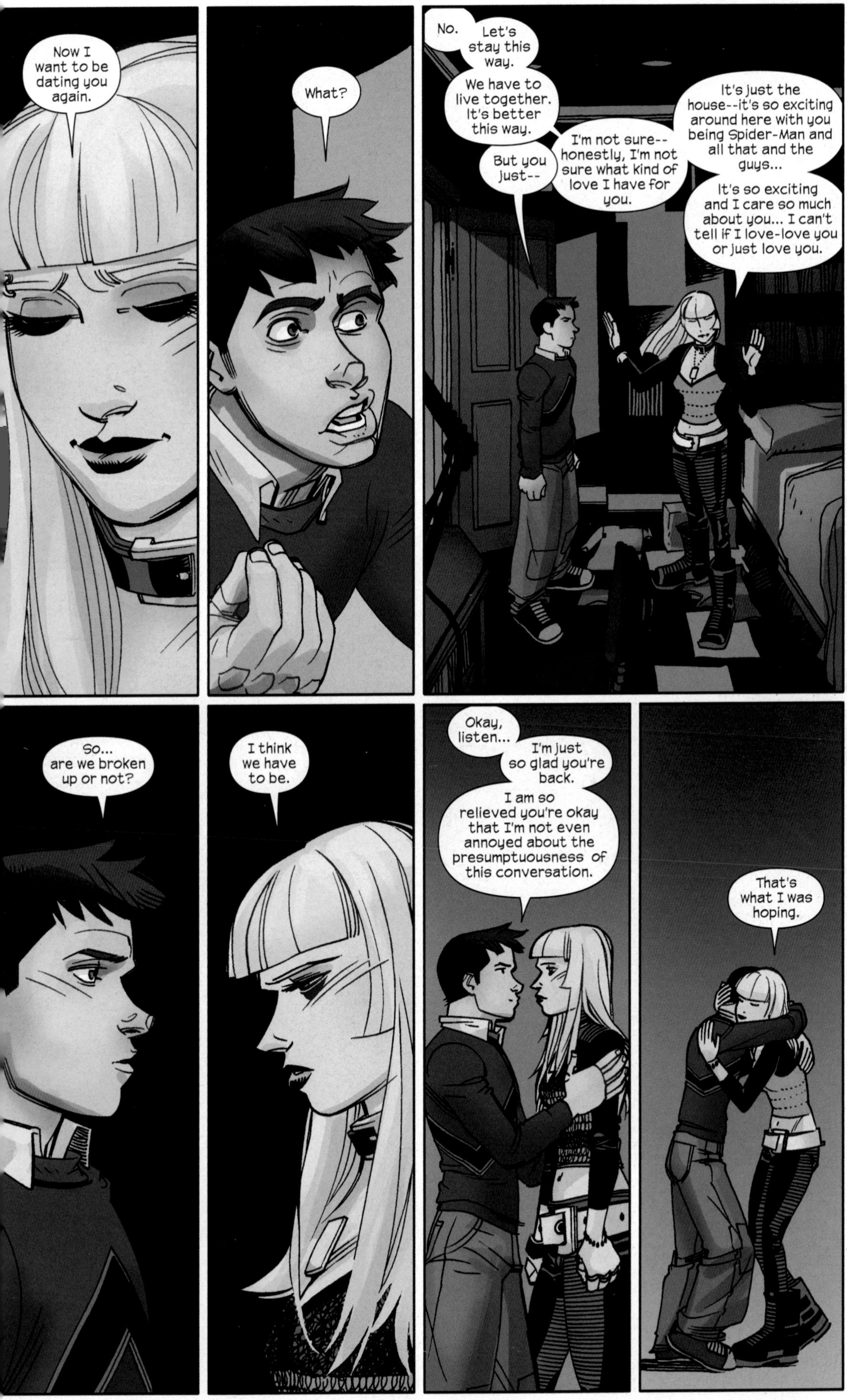
Now I want to be dating you again.
What?
No.
Let's stay this way.
We have to live together. It's better this way.
But you just--
I'm not sure--honestly, I'm not sure what kind of love I have for you.
It's just the house--it's so exciting around here with you being Spider-Man and all that and the guys...
It's so exciting and I care so much about you... I can't tell if I love-love you or just love you.
So... are we broken up or not?
I think we have to be.
Okay, listen...
I'm just so glad you're back.
I am so relieved you're okay that I'm not even annoyed about the presumptuousness of this conversation.
That's what I was hoping.

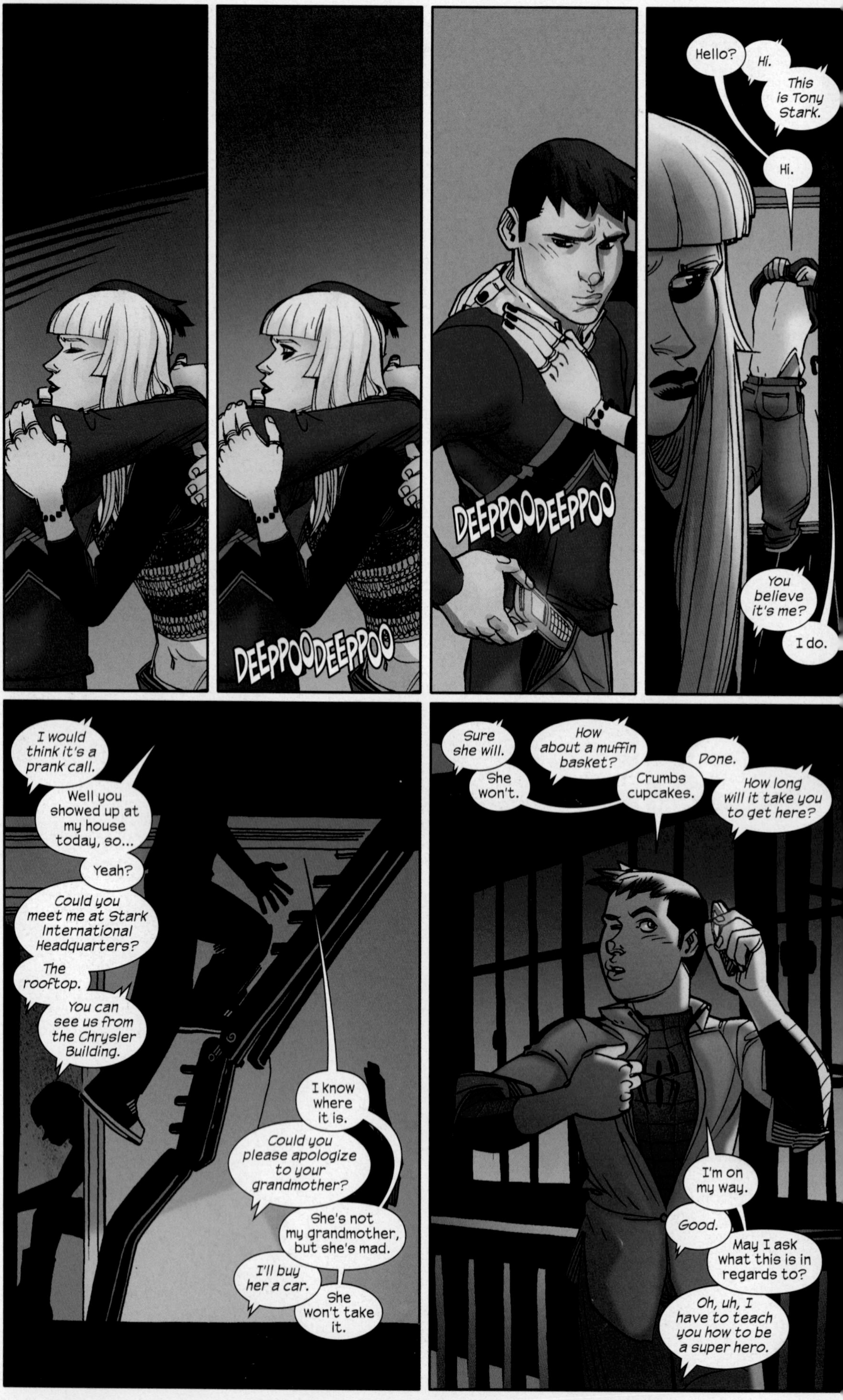

DEEPPOODEEPPOO
DEEPPOODEEPPOO
Hello?
Hi.
This is Tony Stark.
Hi.
You believe it's me?
I do.
I would think it's a prank call.
Well you showed up at my house today, so...
Yeah?
Could you meet me at Stark International Headquarters?
The rooftop.
You can see us from the Chrysler Building.
I know where it is.
Could you please apologize to your grandmother?
She's not my grandmother, but she's mad.
I'll buy her a car.
She won't take it.
Sure she will.
She won't.
How about a muffin basket?
Crumbs cupcakes.
Done.
How long will it take you to get here?
I'm on my way.
Good.
May I ask what this is in regards to?
Oh, uh, I have to teach you how to be a super hero.

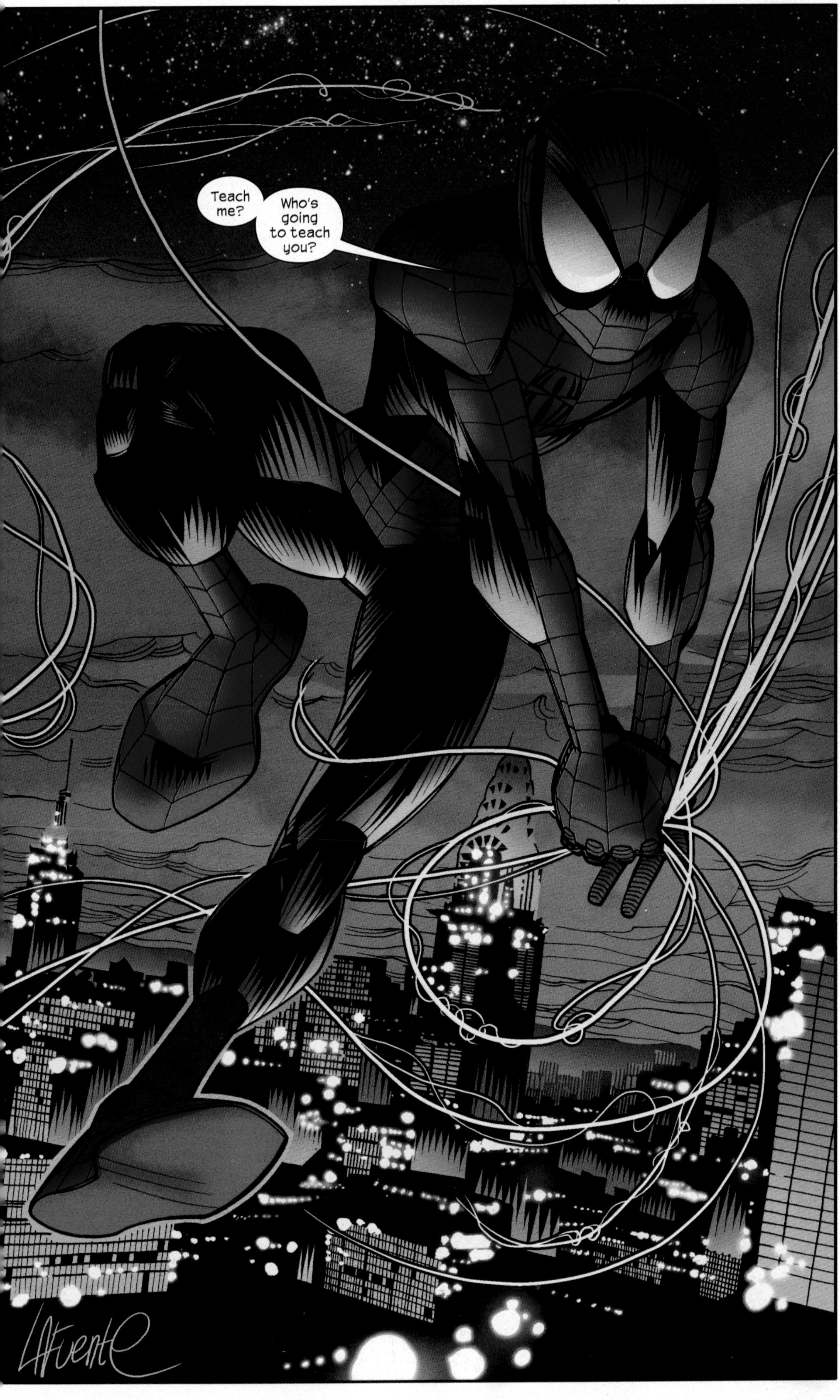
Teach me?
Who's going to teach you?
LaFuente

#153 VARIANT
BY SARA PICHELLI & MATTHEW WILSON

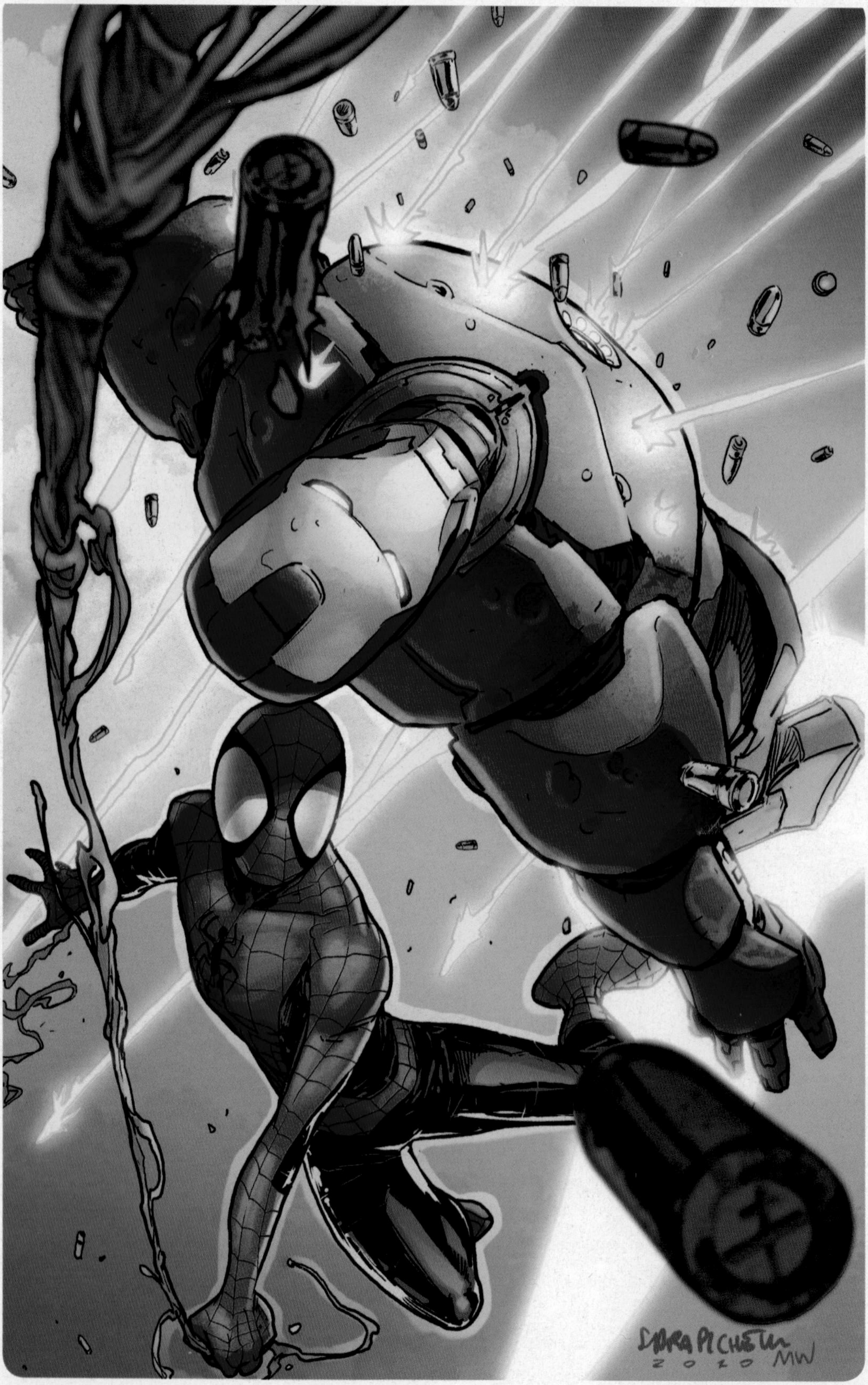

153

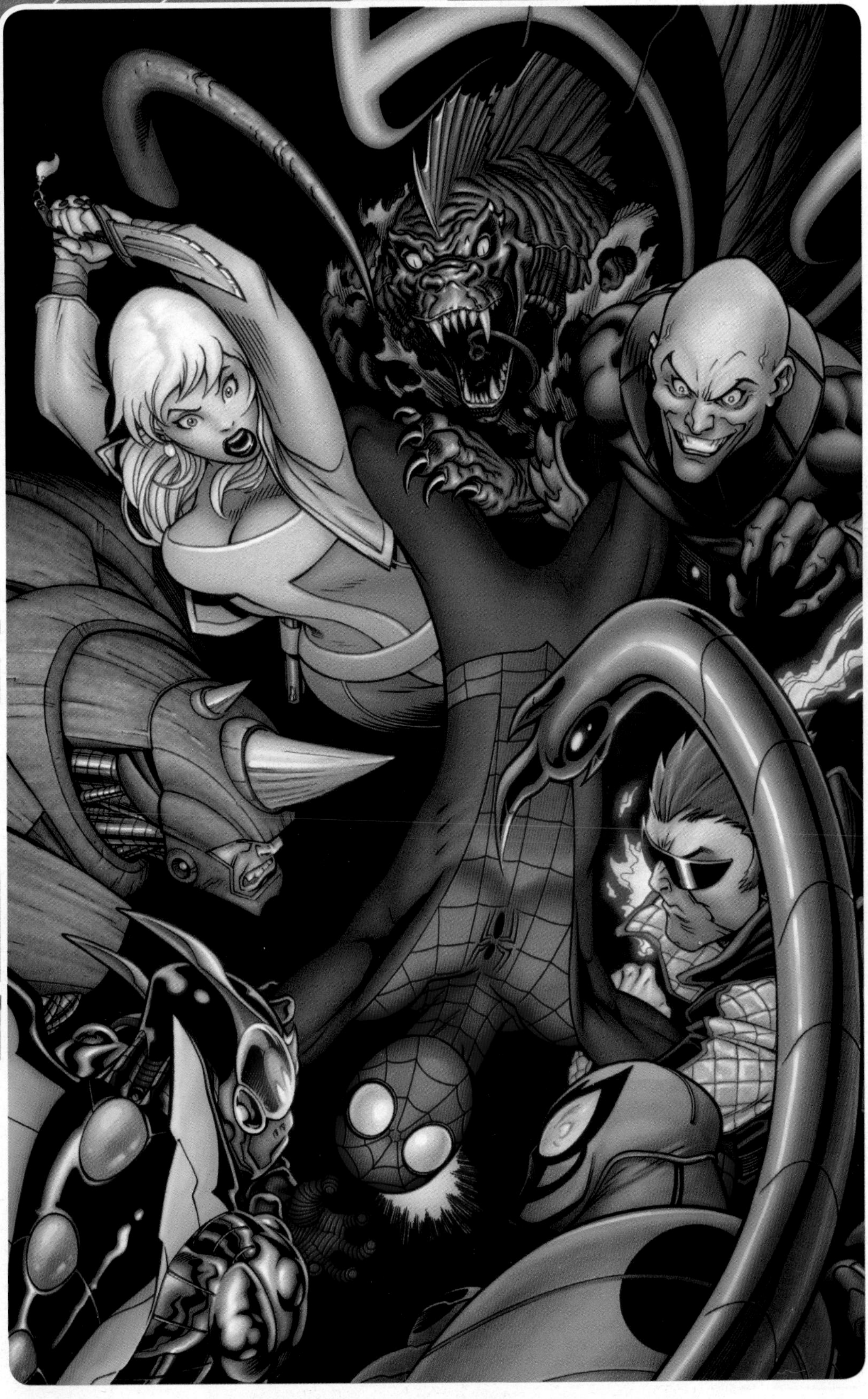

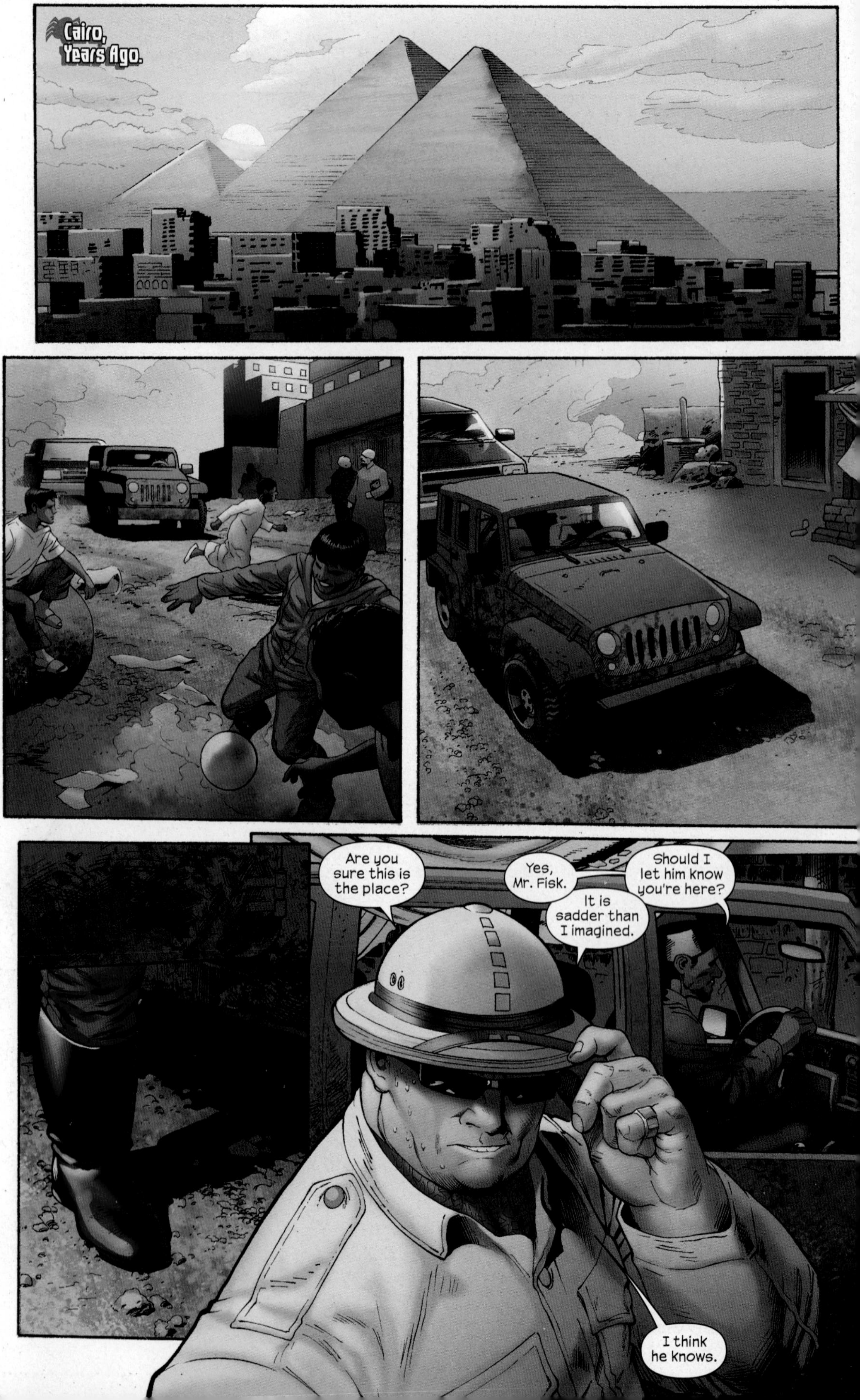
Cairo, Years Ago.
Are you sure this is the place?
Yes, Mr. Fisk.
Should I let him know you're here?
It is sadder than I imagined.
I think he knows.

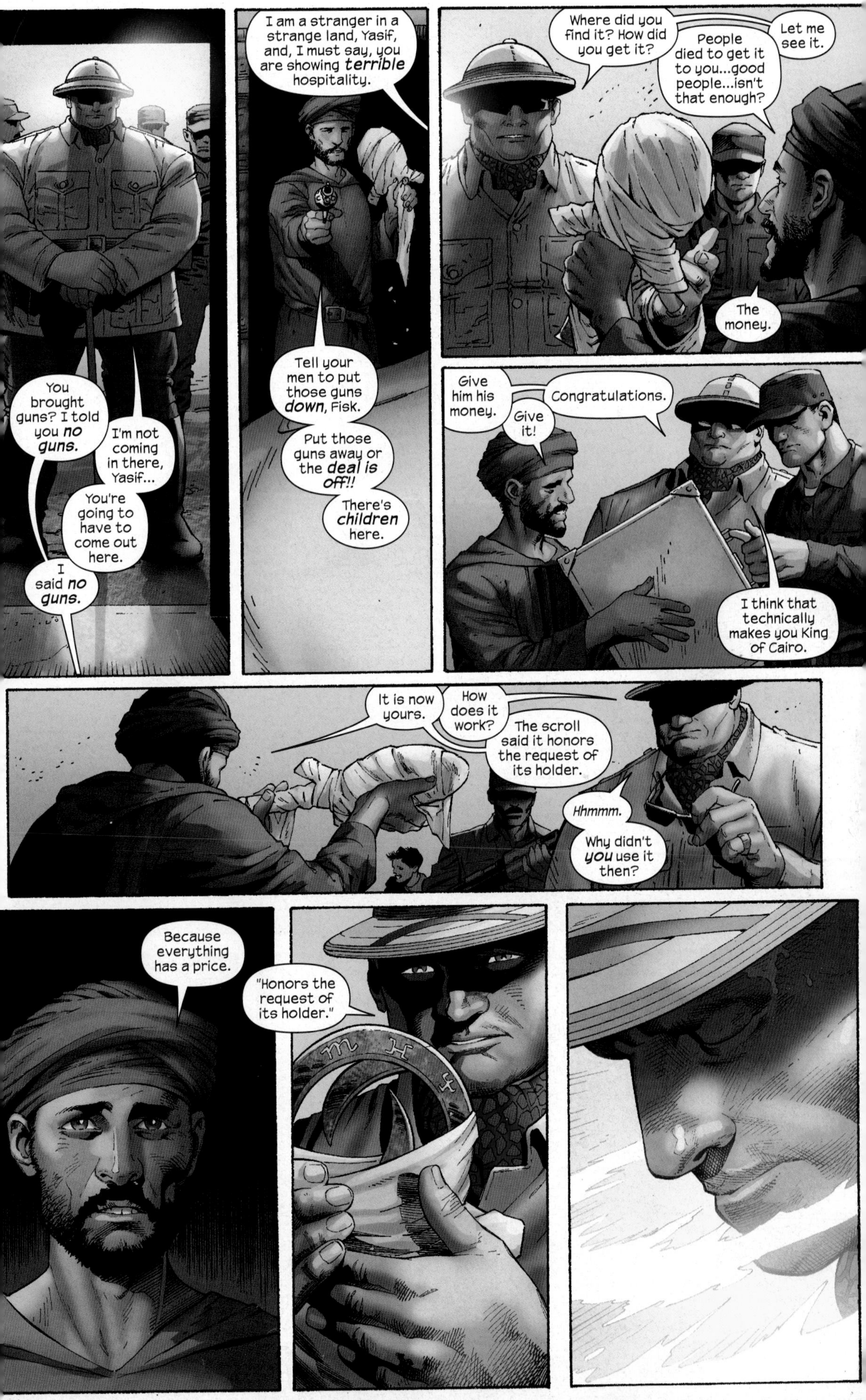
You brought guns? I told you *no guns.*
I'm not coming in there, Yasif...
You're going to have to come out here.
I said *no guns.*
I am a stranger in a strange land, Yasif, and, I must say, you are showing *terrible* hospitality.
Tell your men to put those guns *down*, Fisk.
Put those guns away or the *deal is off!!*
There's *children* here.
Where did you find it? How did you get it?
Let me see it.
People died to get it to you...good people...isn't that enough?
The money.
Give him his money.
Congratulations.
Give it!
I think that technically makes you King of Cairo.
It is now yours.
How does it work?
The scroll said it honors the request of its holder.
Hhmmm.
Why didn't *you* use it then?
Because everything has a price.
"Honors the request of its holder."

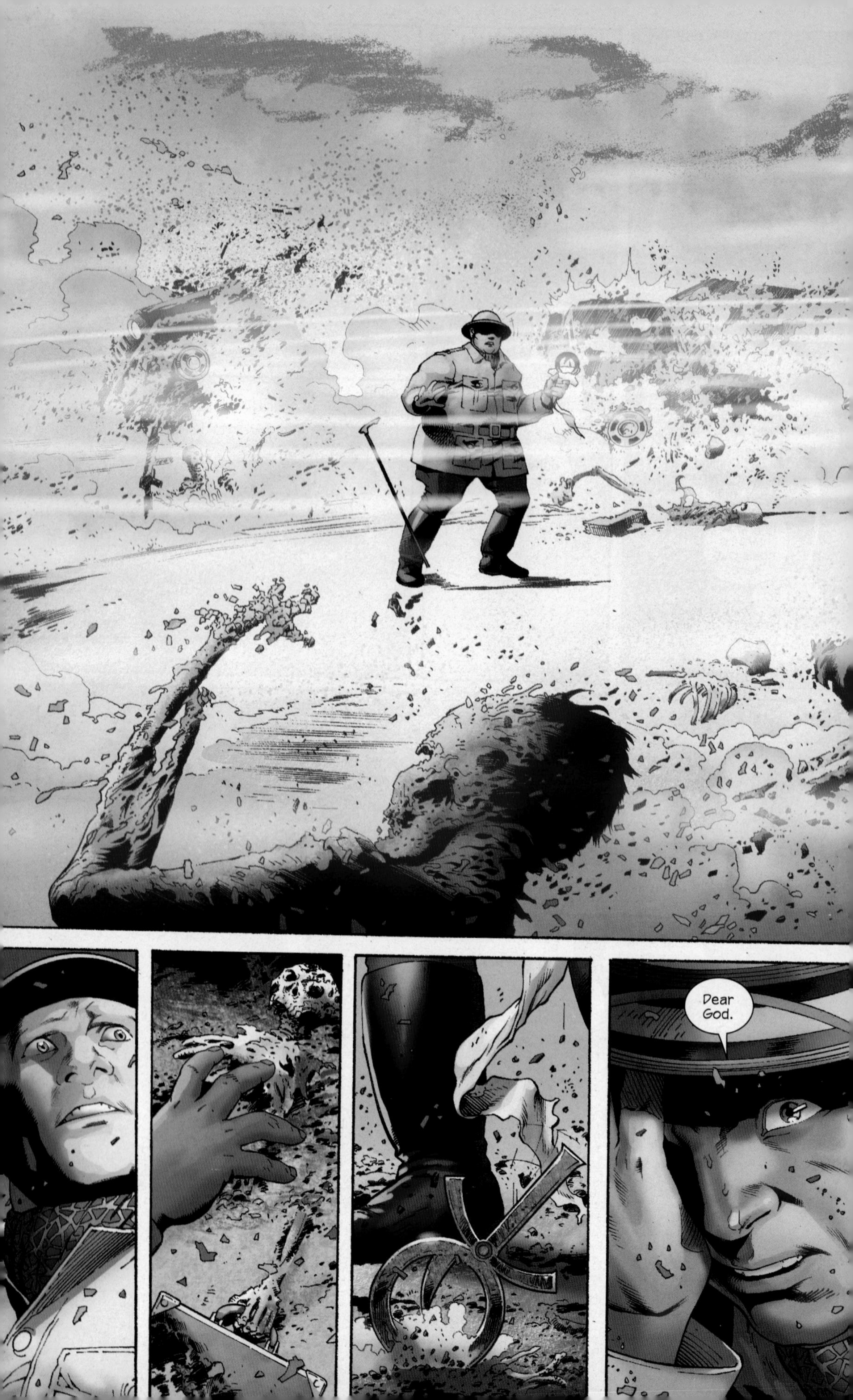
Dear
God.

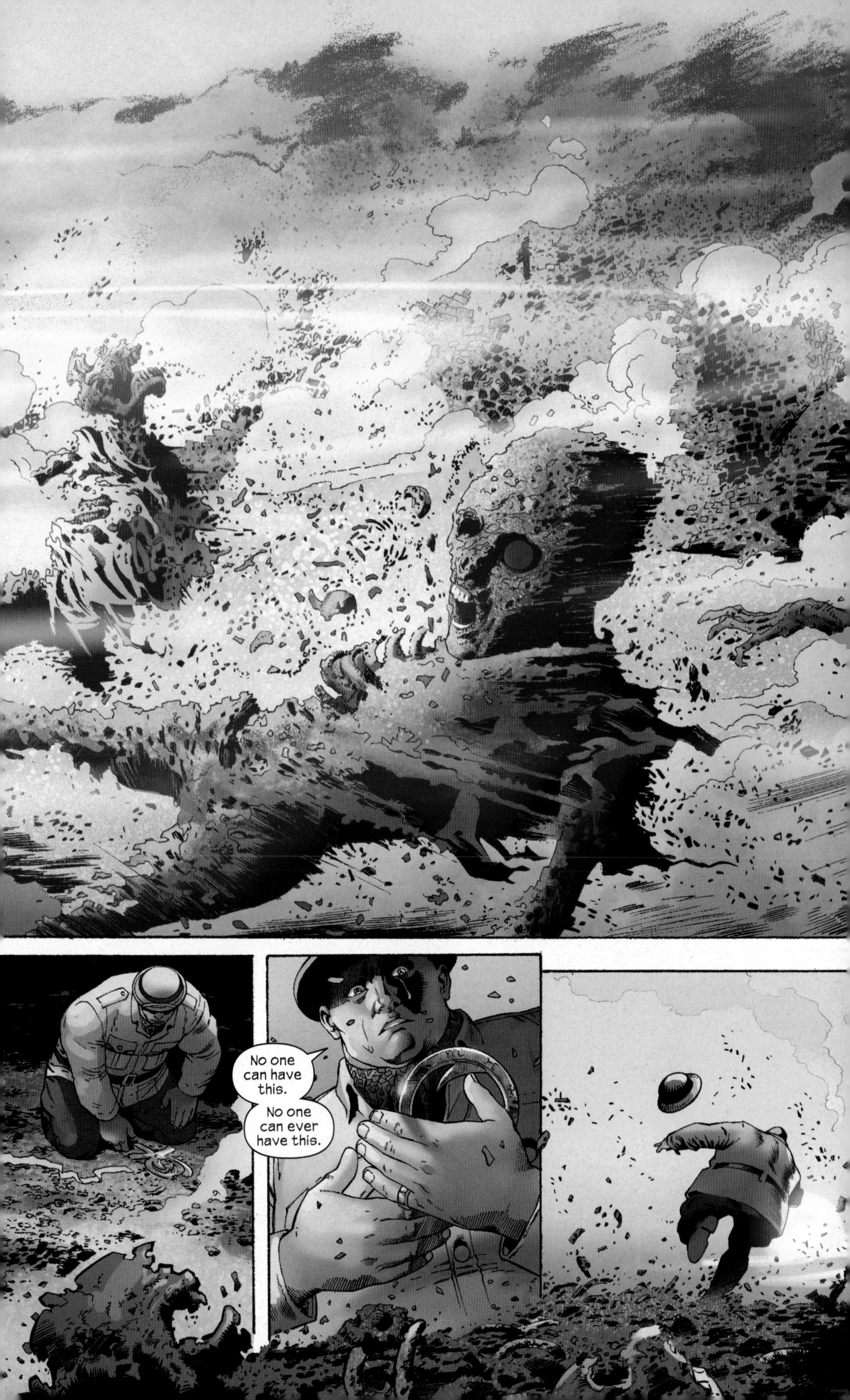
No one can have this.
No one can ever have this.

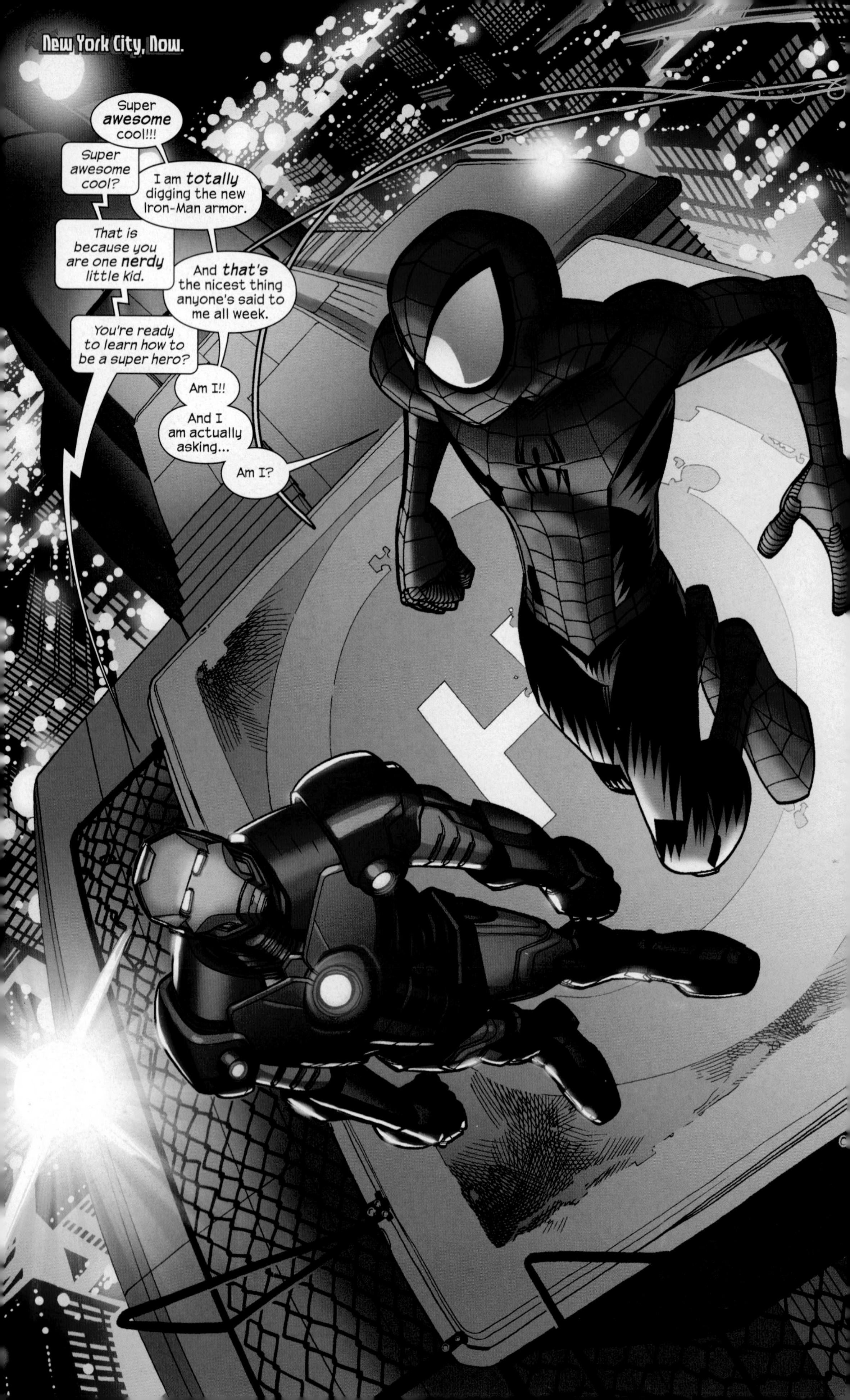

New York City, Now.
Super awesome cool!!!
Super awesome cool?
I am totally digging the new Iron-Man armor.
That is because you are one nerdy little kid.
And that's the nicest thing anyone's said to me all week.
You're ready to learn how to be a super hero?
Am I!!
And I am actually asking...
Am I?

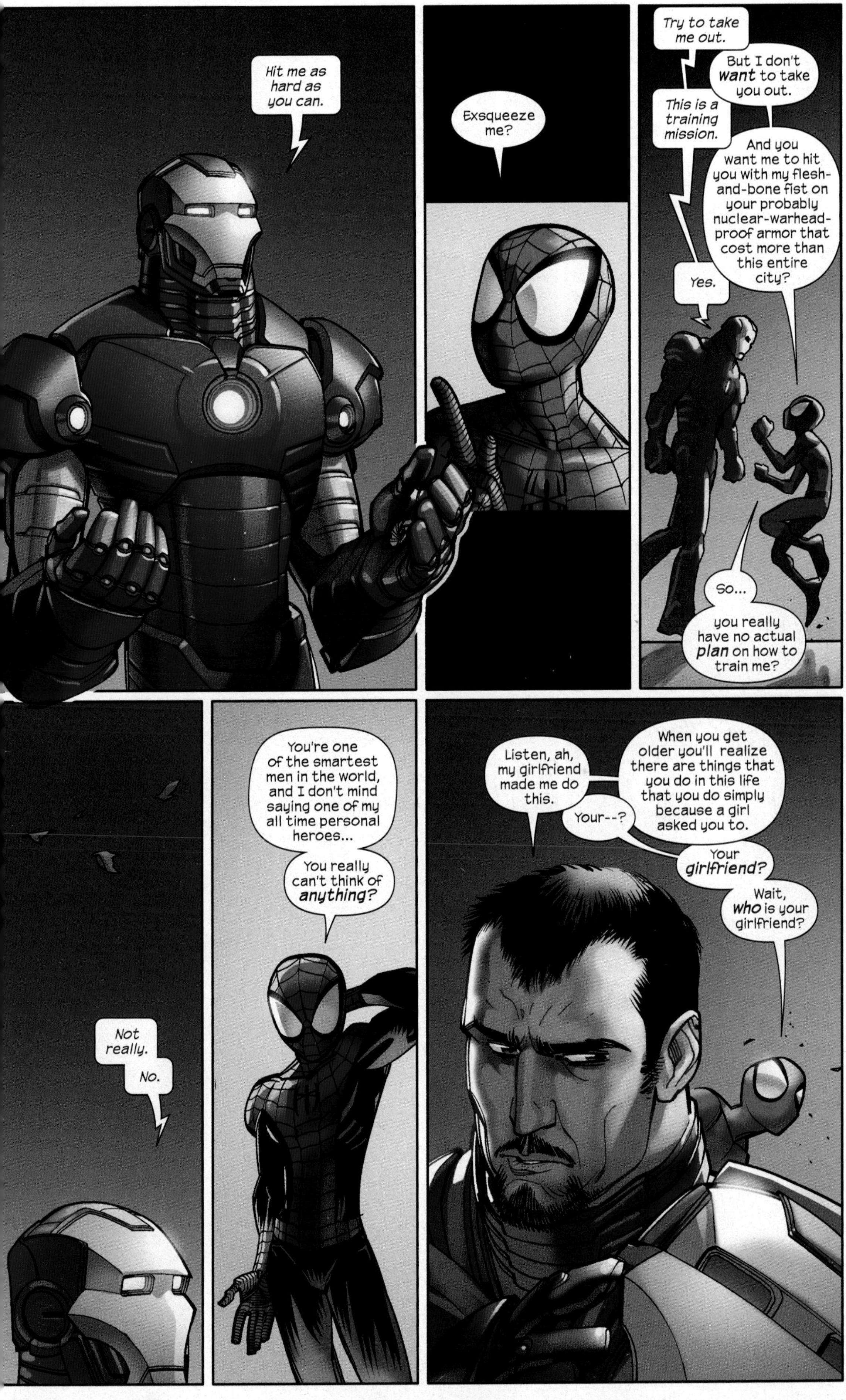

Hit me as hard as you can.
Exsqueeze me?
Try to take me out.
But I don't *want* to take you out.
This is a training mission.
And you want me to hit you with my flesh-and-bone fist on your probably nuclear-warhead-proof armor that cost more than this entire city?
Yes.
So...
you really have no actual *plan* on how to train me?
Not really.
No.
You're one of the smartest men in the world, and I don't mind saying one of my all time personal heroes...
You really can't think of *anything?*
Listen, ah, my girlfriend made me do this.
When you get older you'll realize there are things that you do in this life that you do simply because a girl asked you to.
Your--?
Your *girlfriend?*
Wait, *who* is your girlfriend?

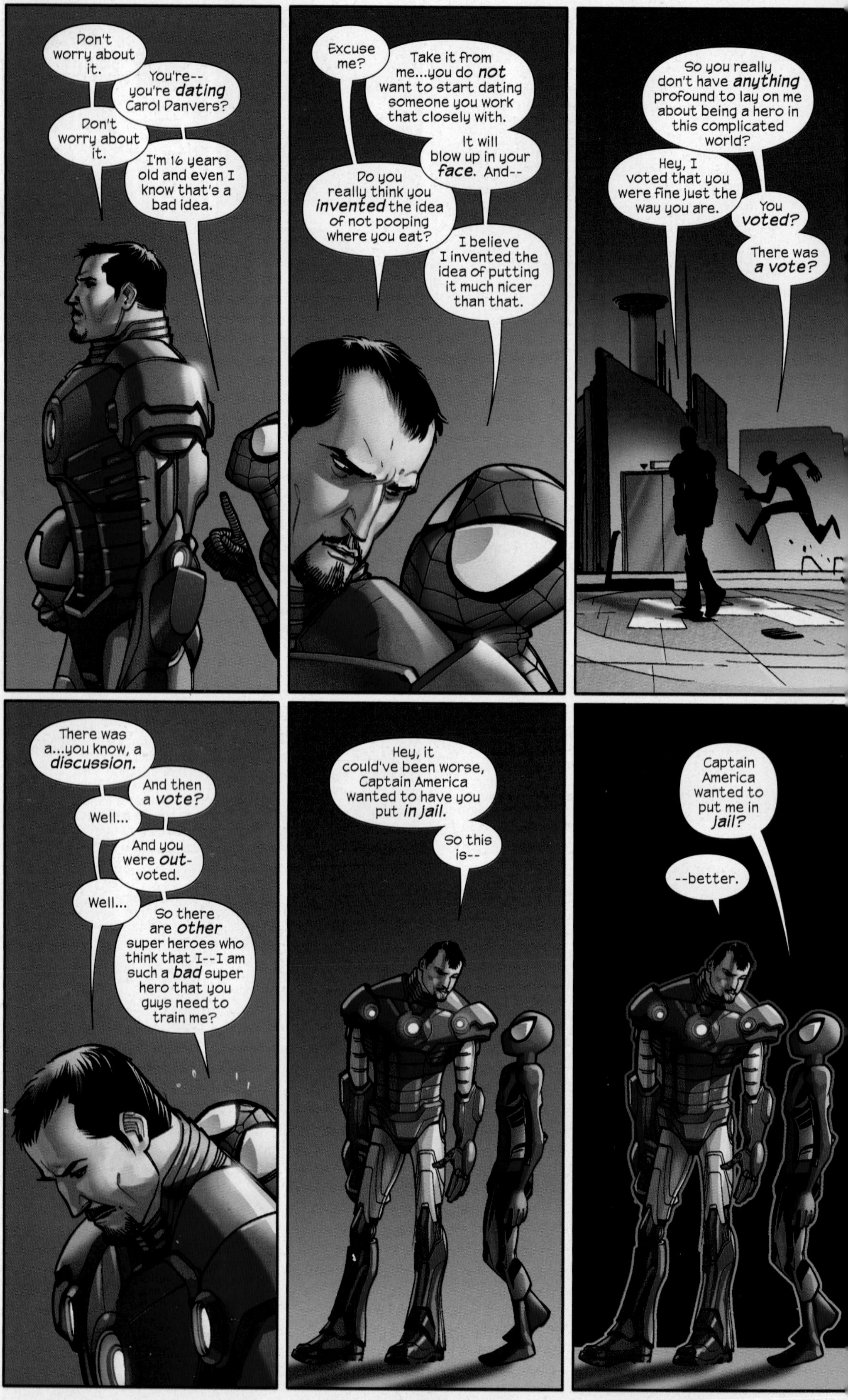

Don't worry about it.
You're-- you're dating Carol Danvers?
Don't worry about it.
I'm 16 years old and even I know that's a bad idea.
Excuse me?
Take it from me...you do not want to start dating someone you work that closely with.
It will blow up in your face. And--
Do you really think you invented the idea of not pooping where you eat?
I believe I invented the idea of putting it much nicer than that.
So you really don't have anything profound to lay on me about being a hero in this complicated world?
Hey, I voted that you were fine just the way you are.
You voted?
There was a vote?
There was a...you know, a discussion.
And then a vote?
Well...
And you were out-voted.
Well...
So there are other super heroes who think that I--I am such a bad super hero that you guys need to train me?
Hey, it could've been worse, Captain America wanted to have you put in jail.
So this is--
Captain America wanted to put me in jail?
--better.

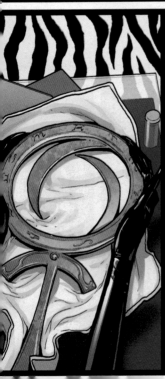

How much do you want for it, Felicia?

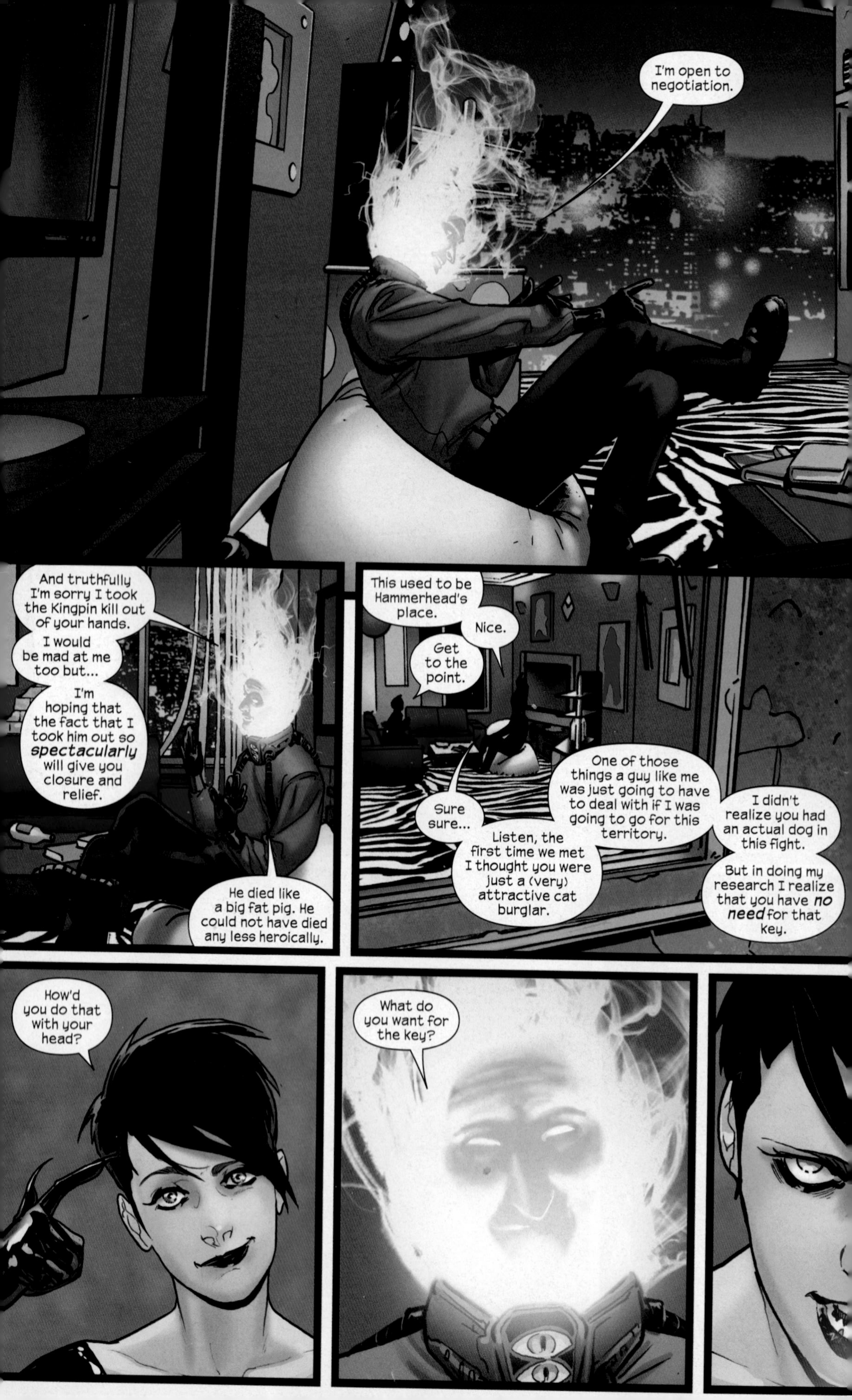
I'm open to negotiation.
And truthfully I'm sorry I took the Kingpin kill out of your hands.
I would be mad at me too but...
I'm hoping that the fact that I took him out so *spectacularly* will give you closure and relief.
He died like a big fat pig. He could not have died any less heroically.
This used to be Hammerhead's place.
Nice.
Get to the point.
Sure sure...
Listen, the first time we met I thought you were just a (very) attractive cat burglar.
One of those things a guy like me was just going to have to deal with if I was going to go for this territory.
I didn't realize you had an actual dog in this fight.
But in doing my research I realize that you have *no need* for that key.
How'd you do that with your head?
What do you want for the key?

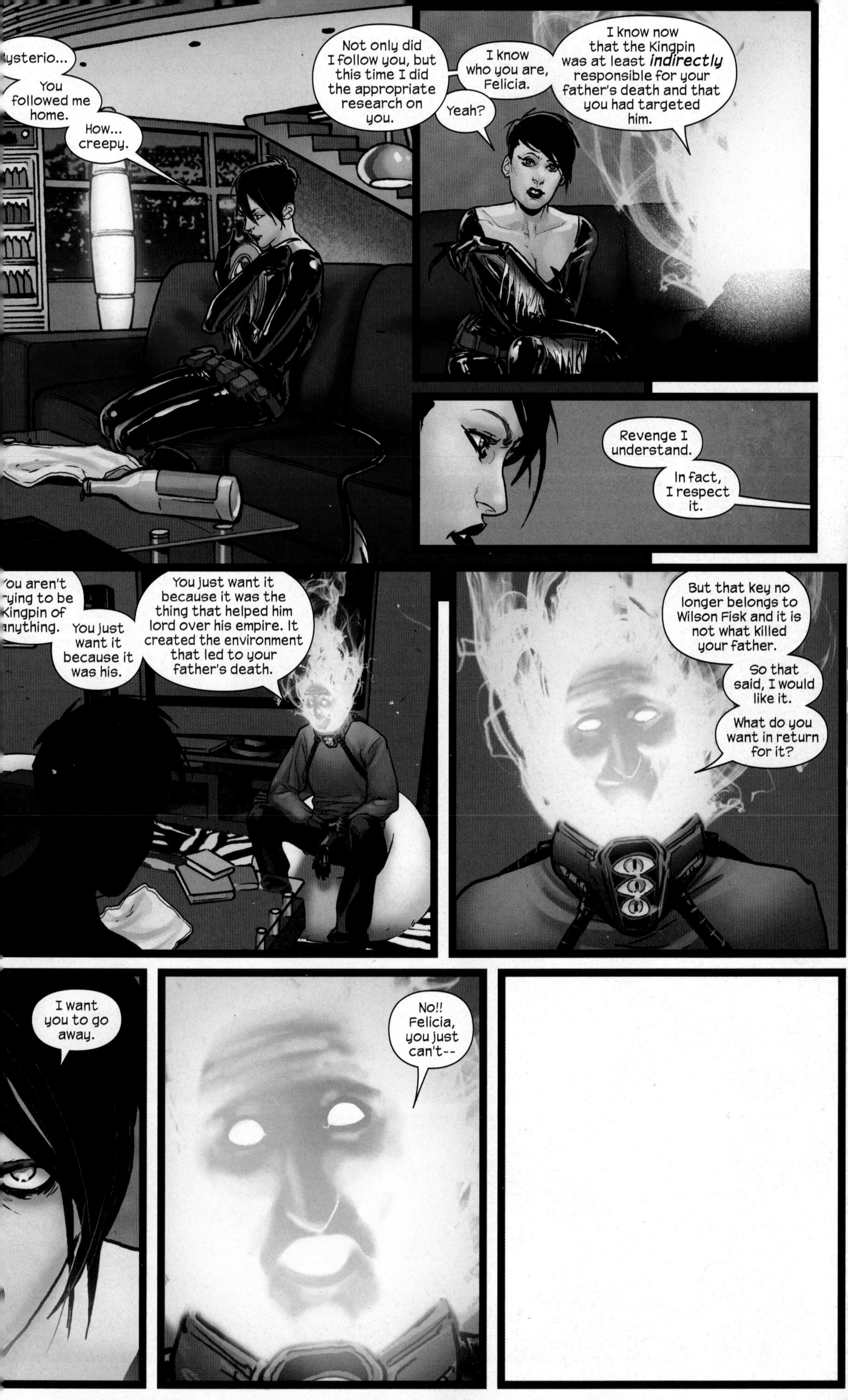
ysterio...
You followed me home.
How... creepy.
Not only did I follow you, but this time I did the appropriate research on you.
Yeah?
I know who you are, Felicia.
I know now that the Kingpin was at least *indirectly* responsible for your father's death and that you had targeted him.
Revenge I understand.
In fact, I respect it.
ou aren't rying to be Kingpin of anything.
You just want it because it was his.
You just want it because it was the thing that helped him lord over his empire. It created the environment that led to your father's death.
But that key no longer belongs to Wilson Fisk and it is not what killed your father.
So that said, I would like it.
What do you want in return for it?
I want you to go away.
No!! Felicia, you just can't--

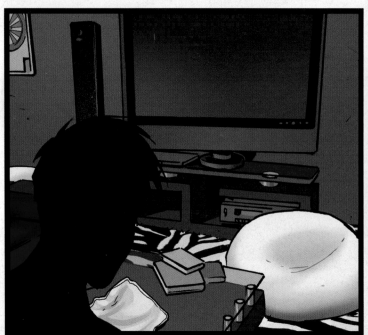

Listen to me, Felicia...

Oh my--!

You just can't activate the key like that.

You don't--you don't understand what kind of *power* you are holding.

I-I-I didn't mean to do that.

I know.

You need to keep your mind *clear.*

You could have *killed* me and you could've killed *yourself.*

Clear.

You need to understand your connection to it as long as you're holding it.

What is this?

What *is* this?

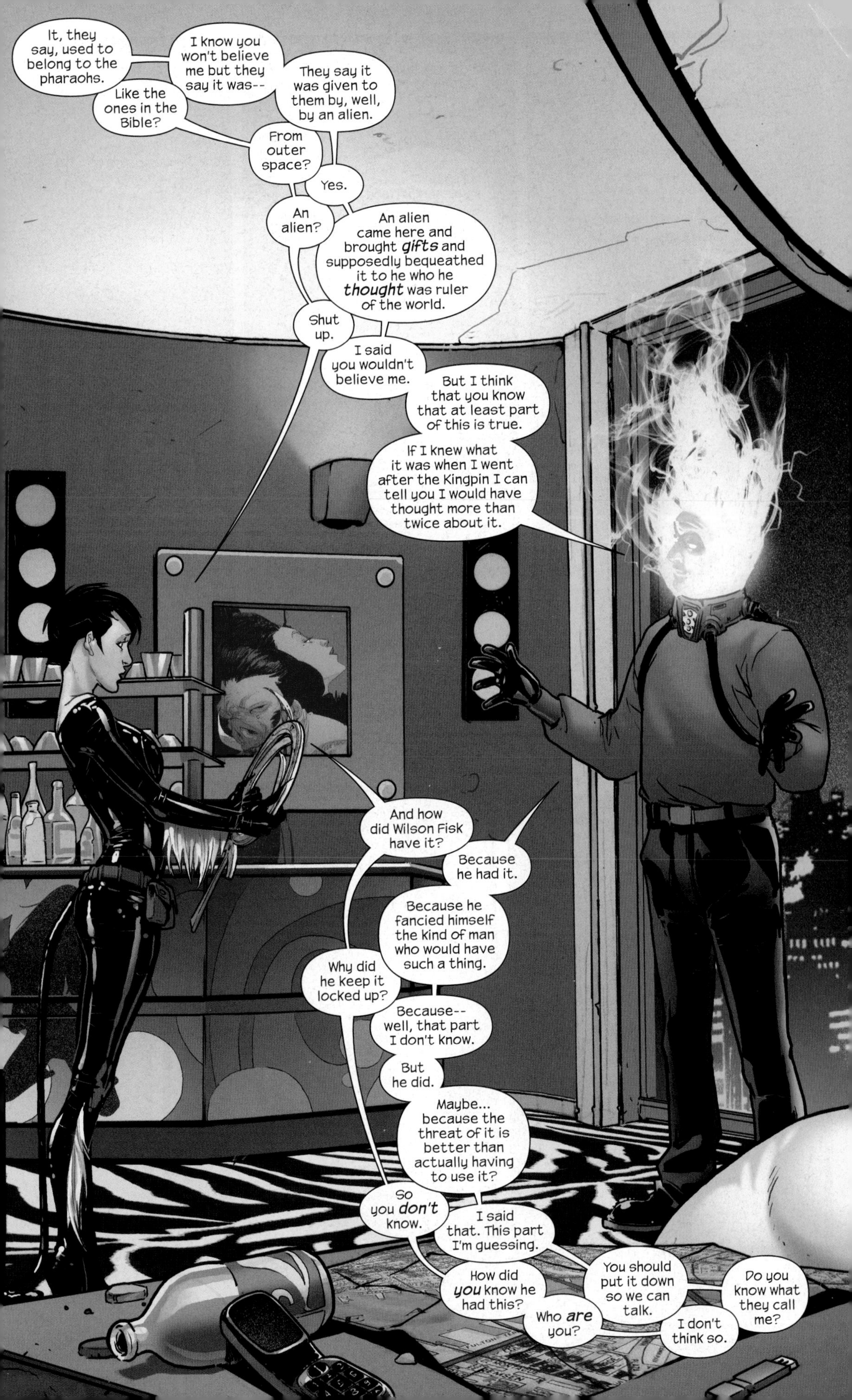
It, they say, used to belong to the pharaohs.
Like the ones in the Bible?
I know you won't believe me but they say it was--
They say it was given to them by, well, by an alien.
From outer space?
Yes.
An alien?
An alien came here and brought *gifts* and supposedly bequeathed it to he who he *thought* was ruler of the world.
Shut up.
I said you wouldn't believe me.
But I think that you know that at least part of this is true.
If I knew what it was when I went after the Kingpin I can tell you I would have thought more than twice about it.
And how did Wilson Fisk have it?
Because he had it.
Because he fancied himself the kind of man who would have such a thing.
Why did he keep it locked up?
Because-- well, that part I don't know.
But he did.
Maybe... because the threat of it is better than actually having to use it?
So you *don't* know.
I said that. This part I'm guessing.
How did *you* know he had this?
Who *are* you?
You should put it down so we can talk.
I don't think so.
Do you know what they call me?

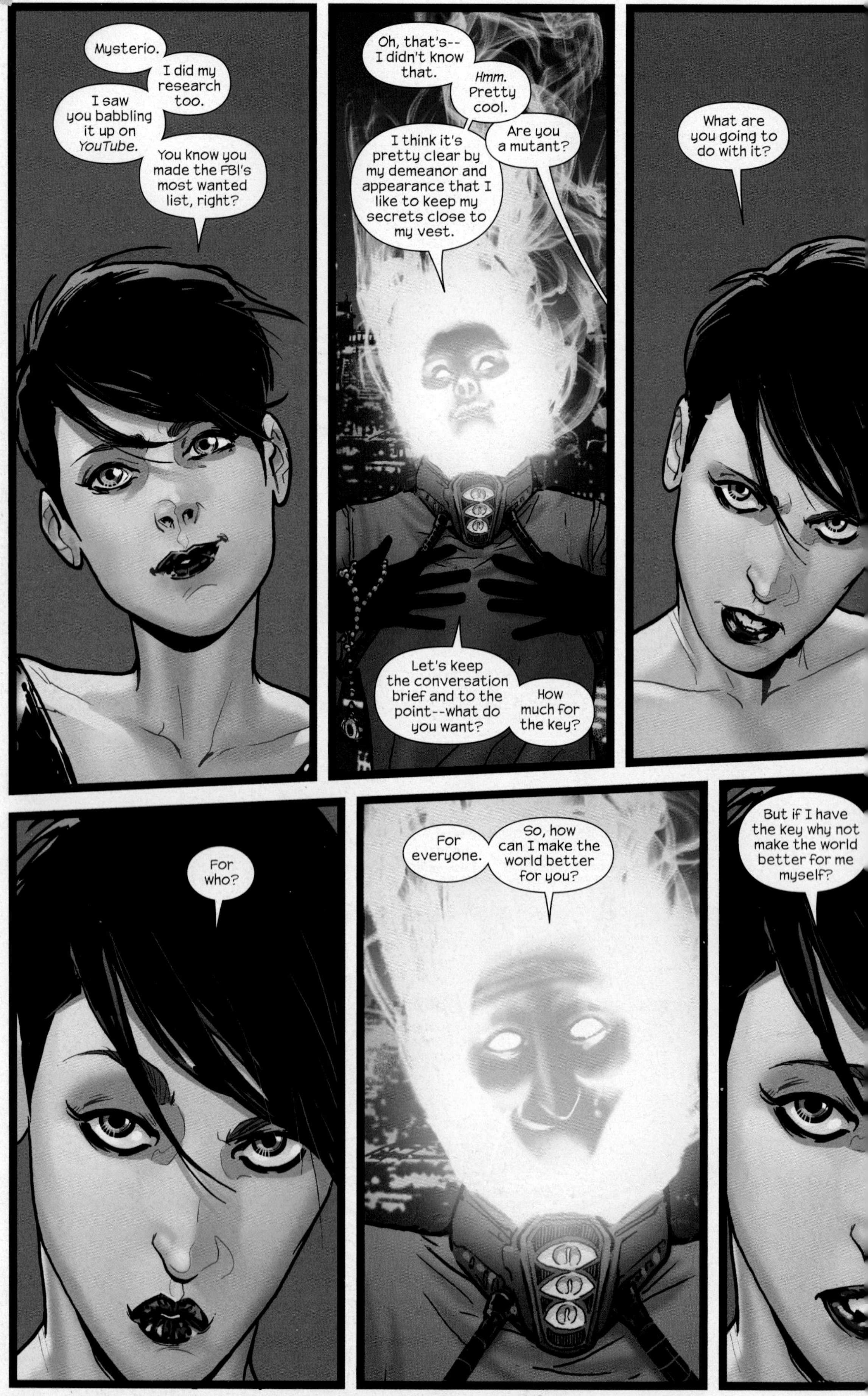
Mysterio.
I did my research too.
I saw you babbling it up on YouTube.
You know you made the FBI's most wanted list, right?
Oh, that's-- I didn't know that.
Hmm. Pretty cool.
Are you a mutant?
I think it's pretty clear by my demeanor and appearance that I like to keep my secrets close to my vest.
Let's keep the conversation brief and to the point--what do you want?
How much for the key?
What are you going to do with it?
For who?
For everyone.
So, how can I make the world better for you?
But if I have the key why not make the world better for me myself?

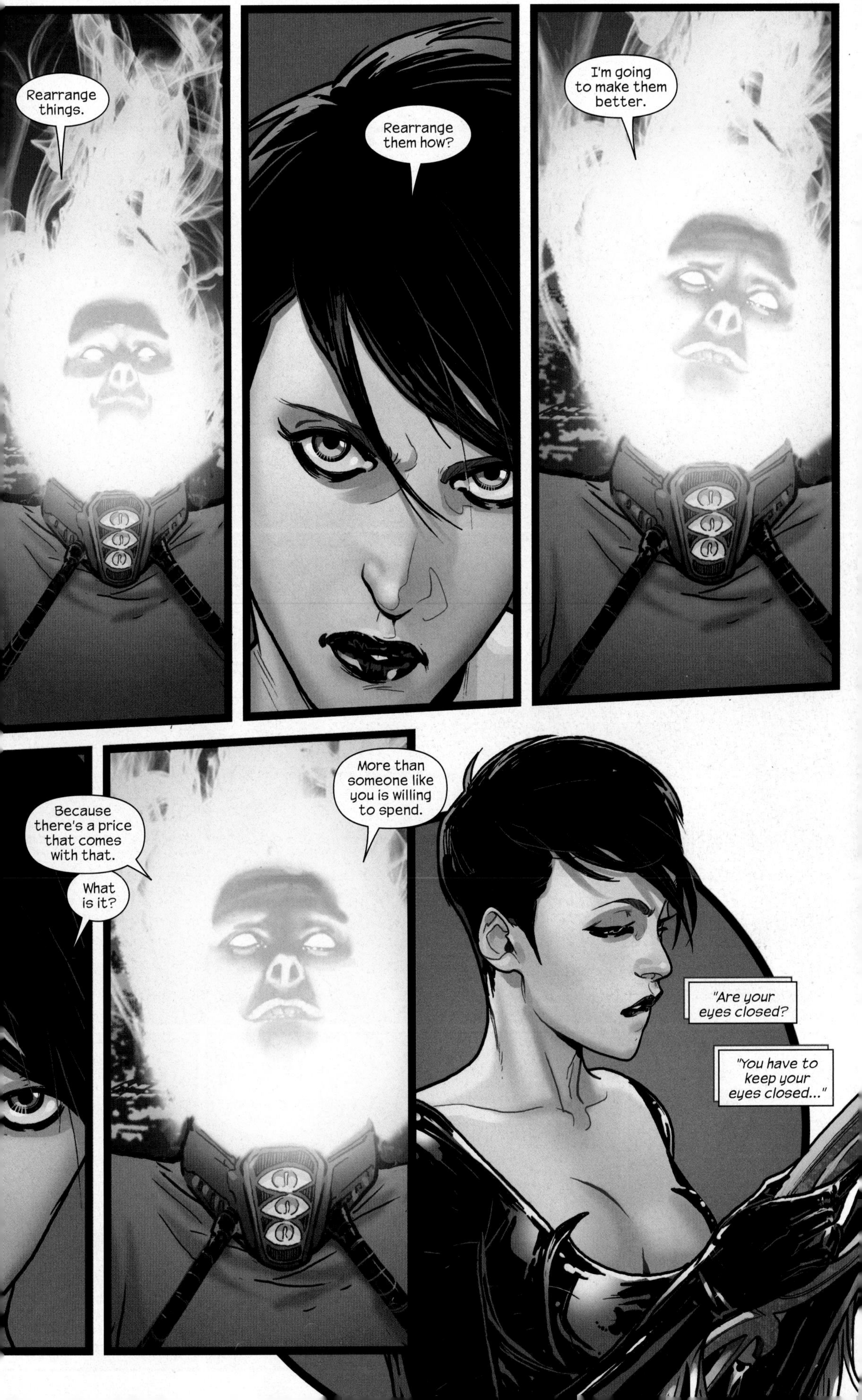

Rearrange things.
Rearrange them how?
I'm going to make them better.
Because there's a price that comes with that.
What is it?
More than someone like you is willing to spend.
"Are your eyes closed?
"You have to keep your eyes closed..."

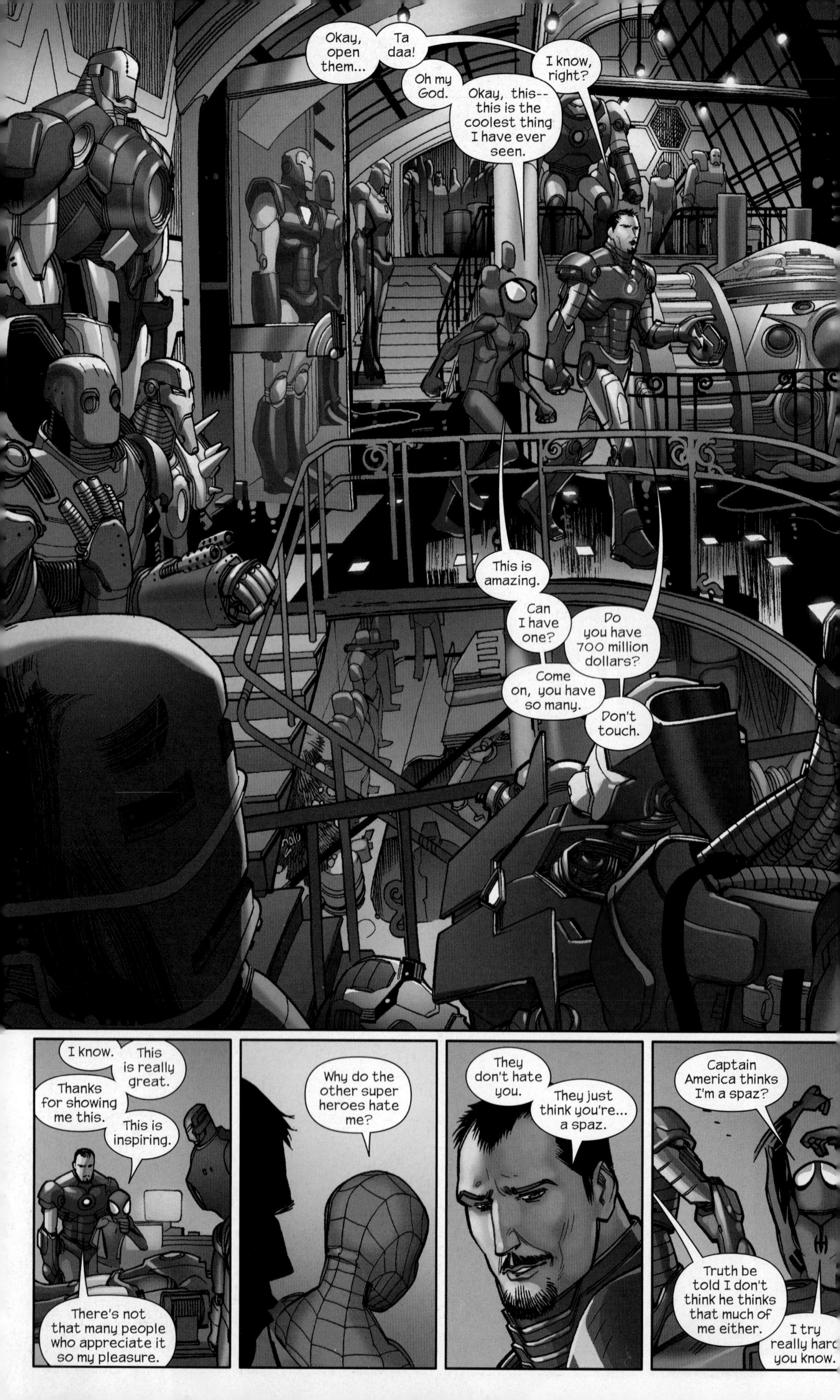
Okay, open them...
Ta daa!
Oh my God.
Okay, this-- this is the coolest thing I have ever seen.
I know, right?
This is amazing.
Can I have one?
Do you have 700 million dollars?
Come on, you have so many.
Don't touch.
I know.
This is really great.
Thanks for showing me this.
This is inspiring.
There's not that many people who appreciate it so my pleasure.
Why do the other super heroes hate me?
They don't hate you.
They just think you're... a spaz.
Captain America thinks I'm a spaz?
Truth be told I don't think he thinks that much of me either.
I try really hard you know.

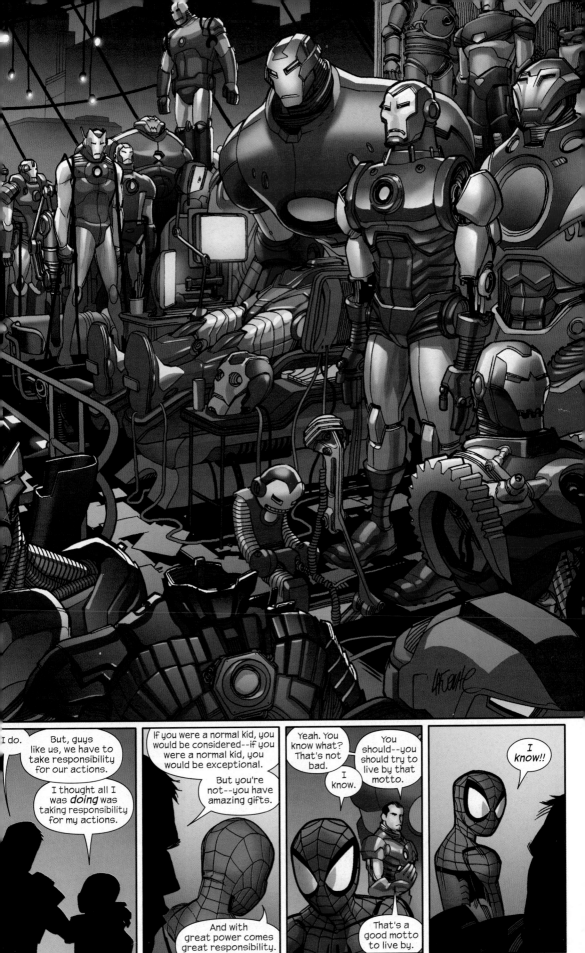

I do.

But, guys like us, we have to take responsibility for our actions.

I thought all I was *doing* was taking responsibility for my actions.

If you were a normal kid, you would be considered--if you were a normal kid, you would be exceptional.

But you're not--you have amazing gifts.

And with great power comes great responsibility.

Yeah. You know what? That's not bad.

I know.

You should--you should try to live by that motto.

That's a good motto to live by.

I know!!

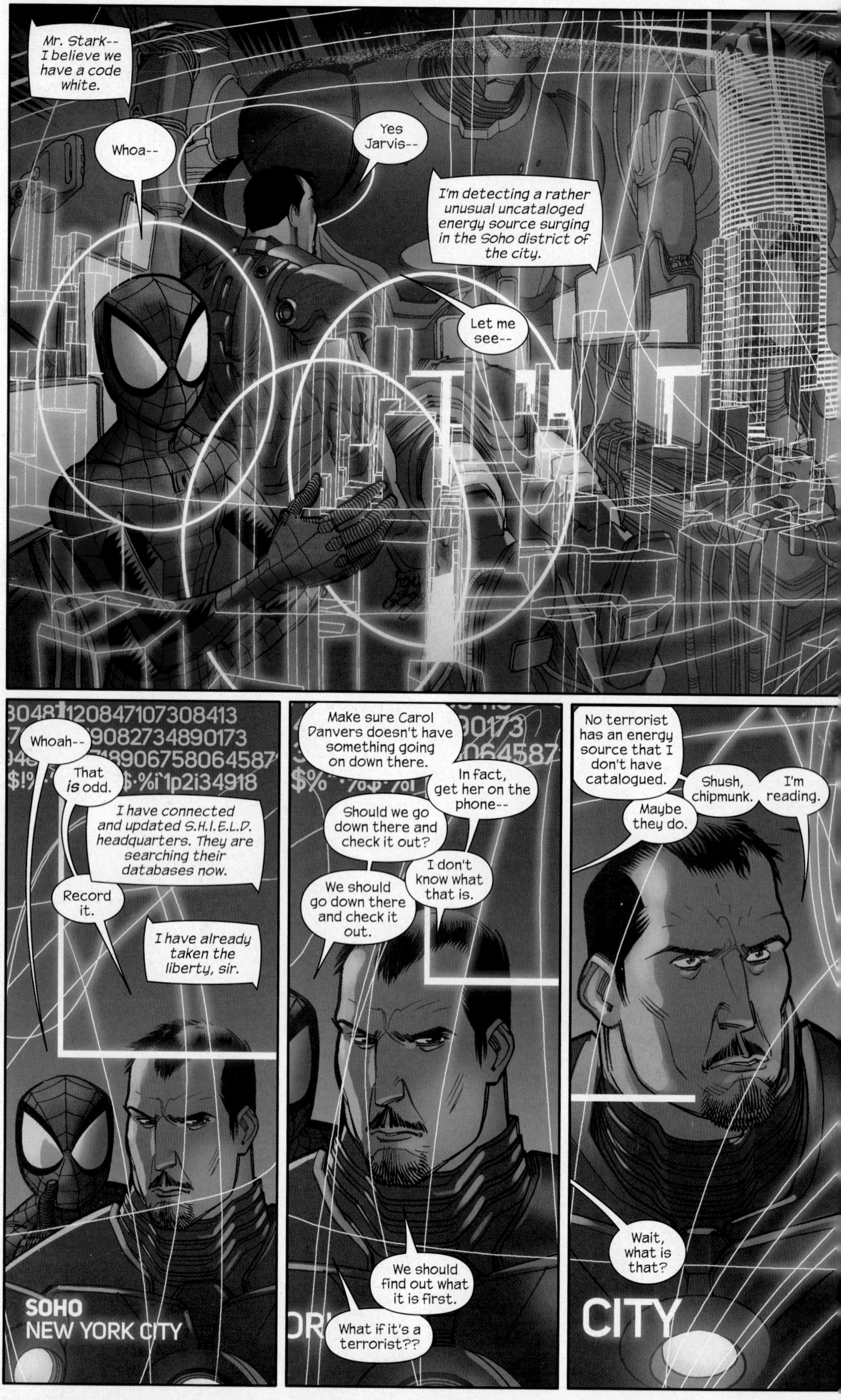

Mr. Stark-- I believe we have a code white.
Whoa--
Yes Jarvis--
I'm detecting a rather unusual uncataloged energy source surging in the Soho district of the city.
Let me see--
Whoah--
That *is* odd.
I have connected and updated S.H.I.E.L.D. headquarters. They are searching their databases now.
Record it.
I have already taken the liberty, sir.
SOHO
NEW YORK CITY
Make sure Carol Danvers doesn't have something going on down there.
In fact, get her on the phone--
Should we go down there and check it out?
I don't know what that is.
We should go down there and check it out.
We should find out what it is first.
What if it's a terrorist??
No terrorist has an energy source that I don't have catalogued.
Maybe they do.
Shush, chipmunk.
I'm reading.
Wait, what is that?
CITY

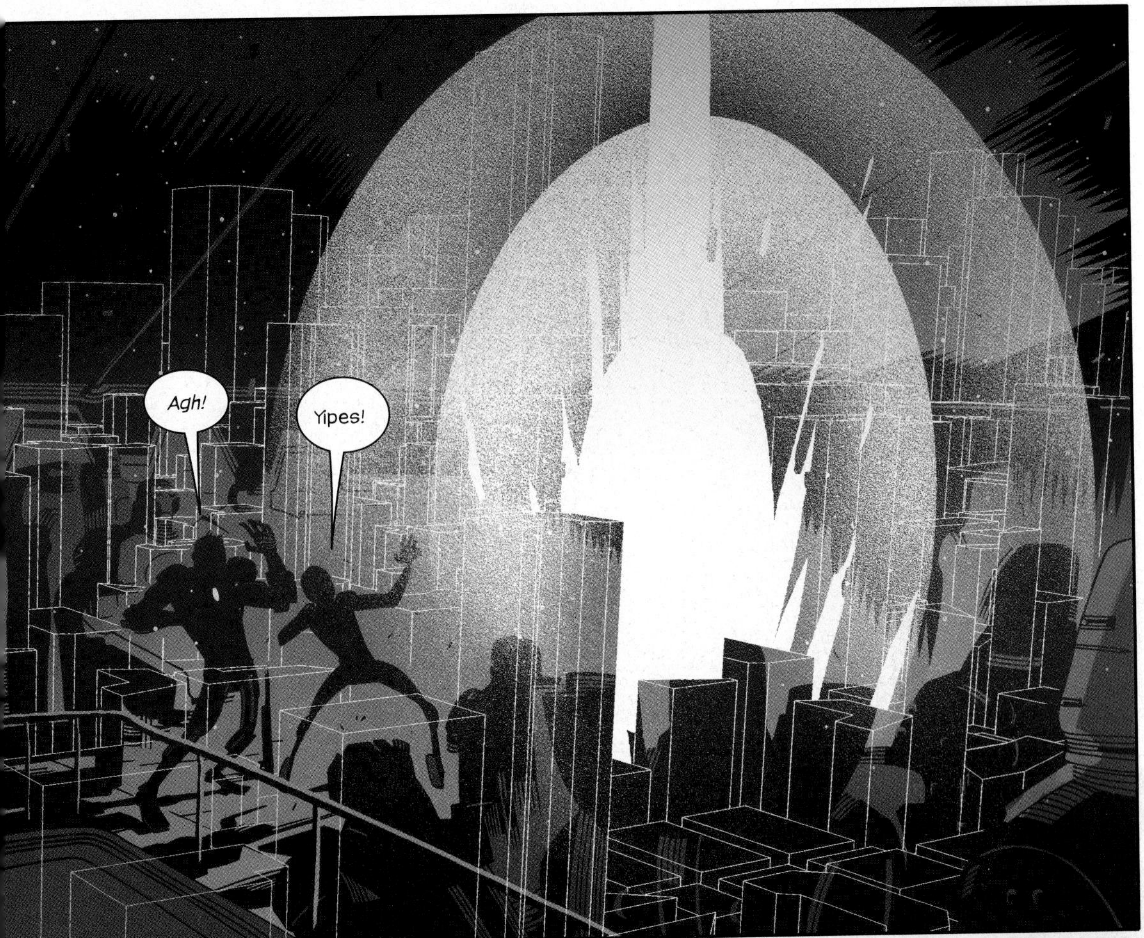
Agh!
Yipes!
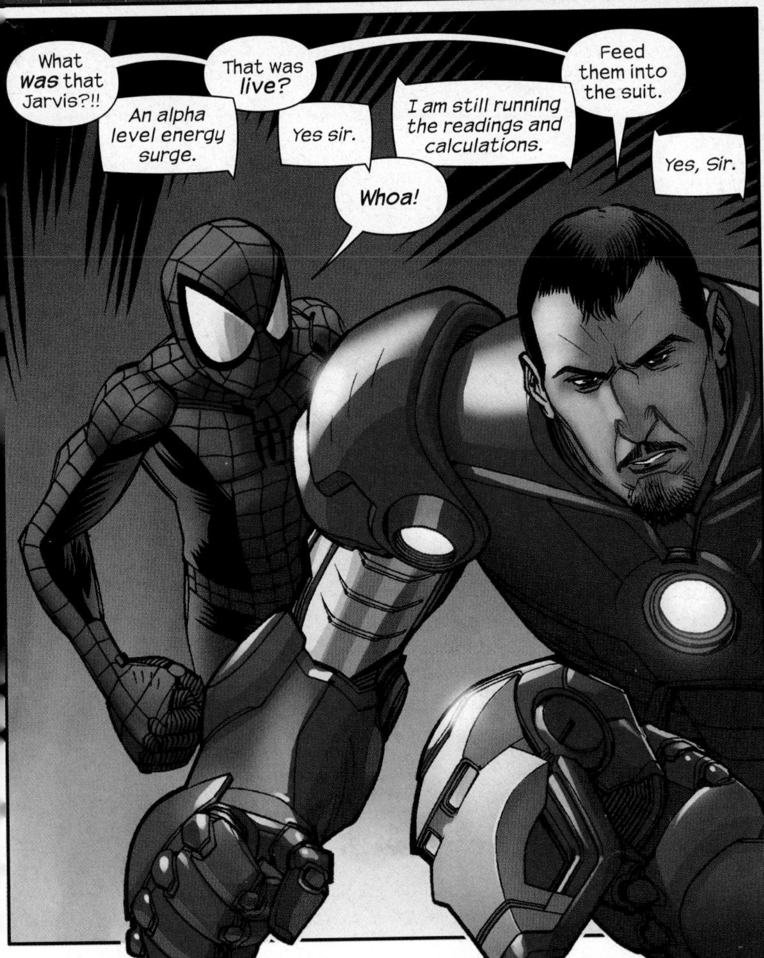
What was that Jarvis?!!
An alpha level energy surge.
That was live?
Yes sir.
Whoa!
I am still running the readings and calculations.
Feed them into the suit.
Yes, Sir.
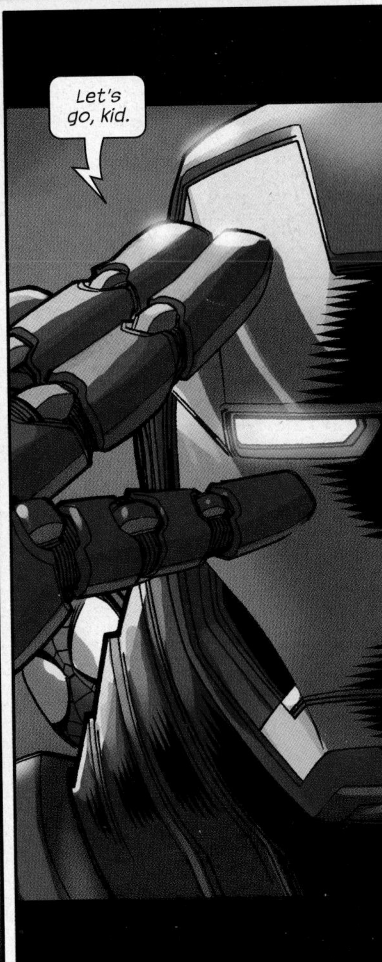
Let's go, kid.

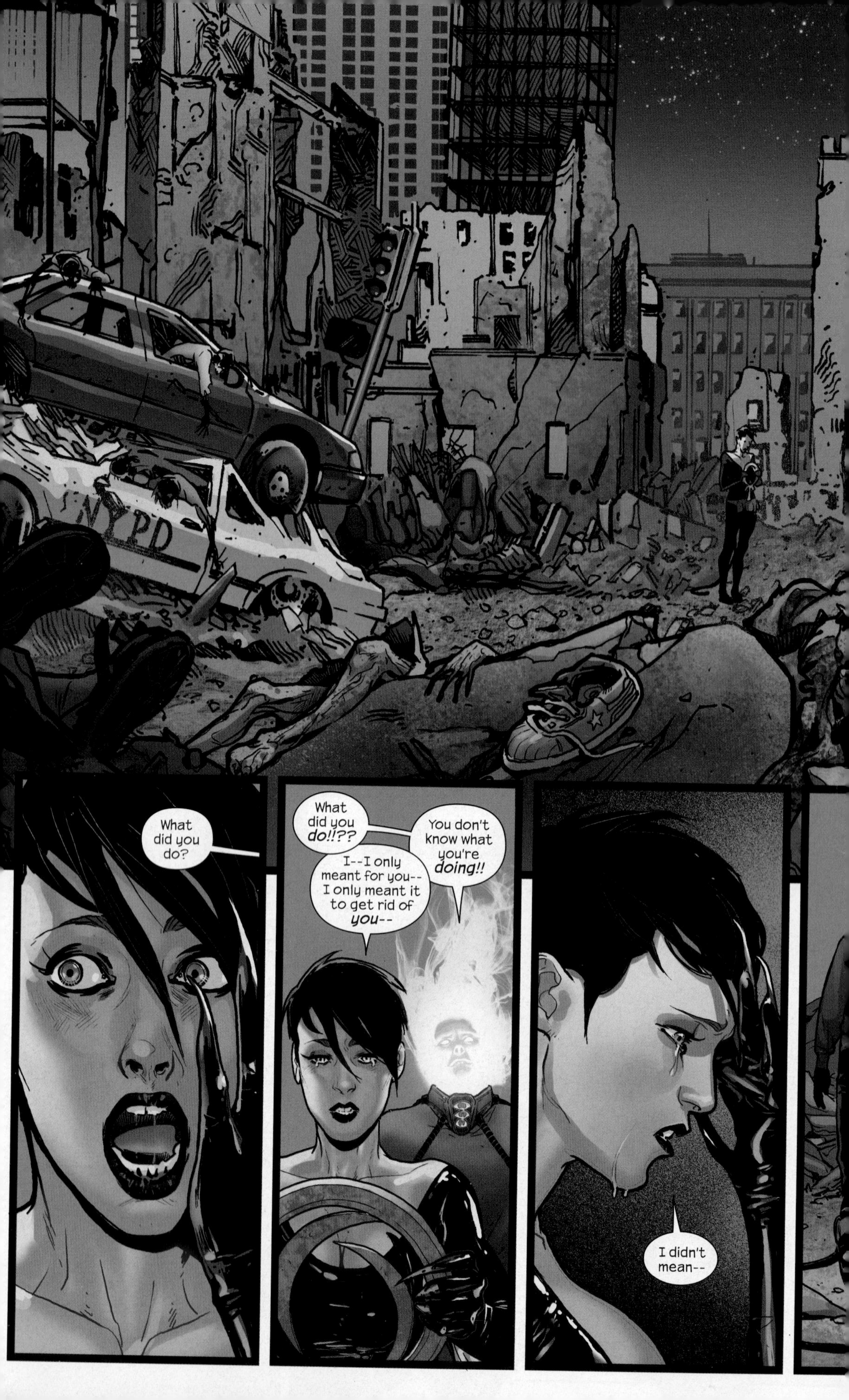

NYPD
What did you do?
What did you do!!??
You don't know what you're doing!!
I--I only meant for you-- I only meant it to get rid of you--
I didn't mean--

GIVE IT TO ME!!
You are going to kill us all!!
I--
I didn't mean--
Don't do it!!

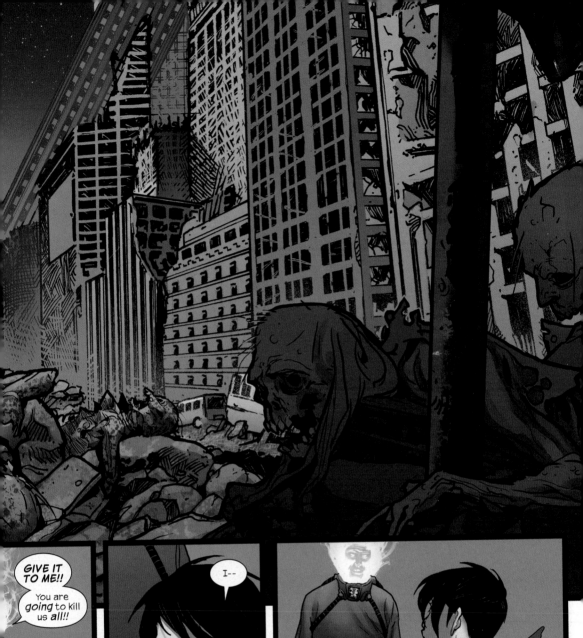

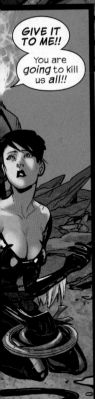

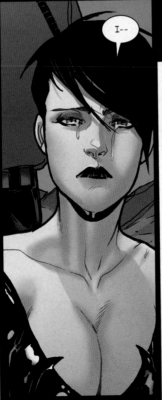

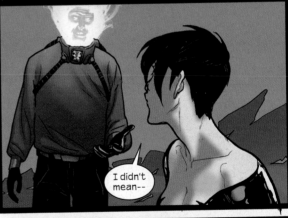

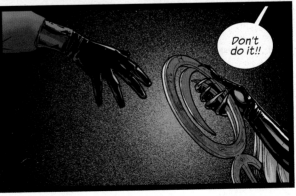

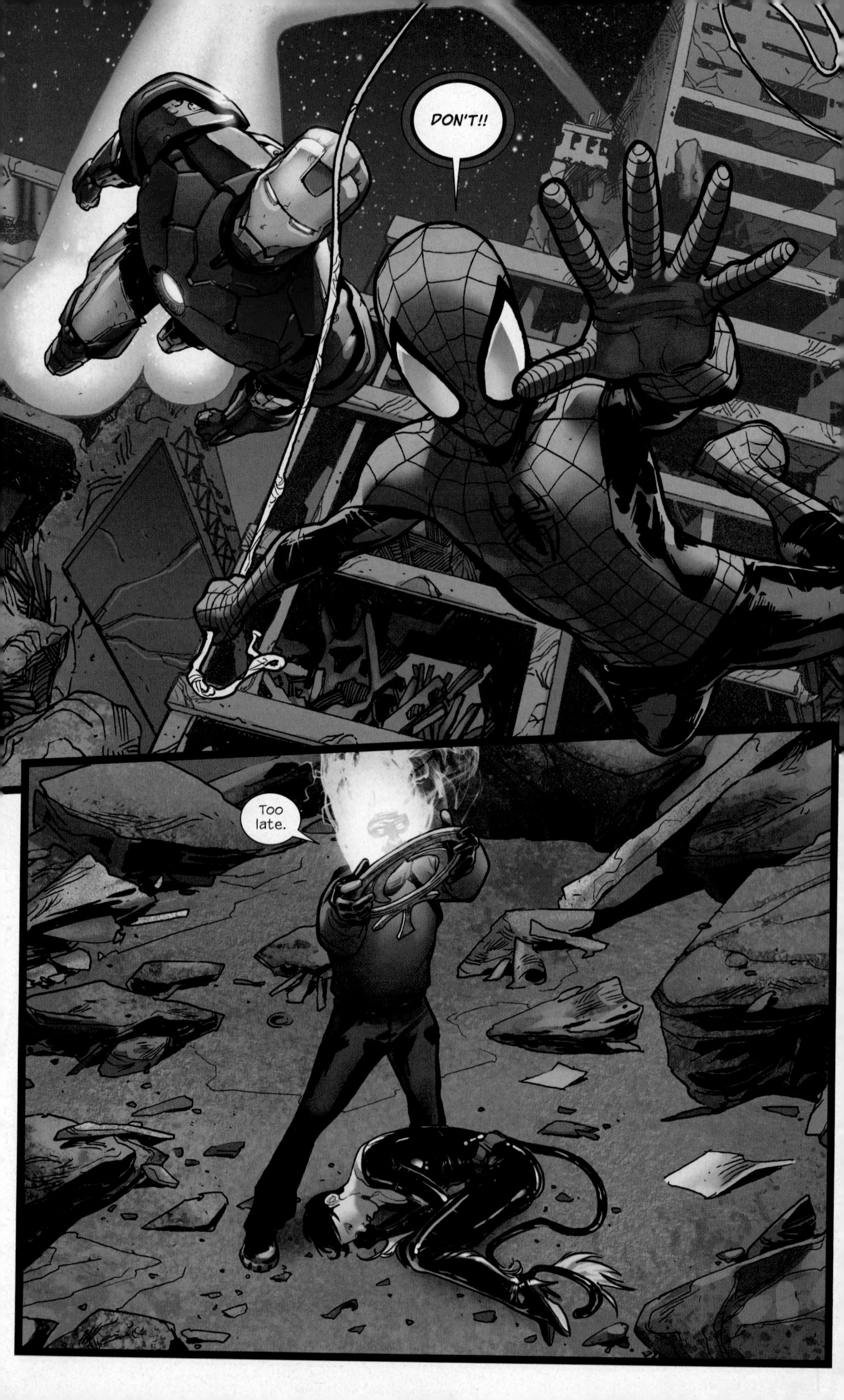
DON'T!!
Too late.

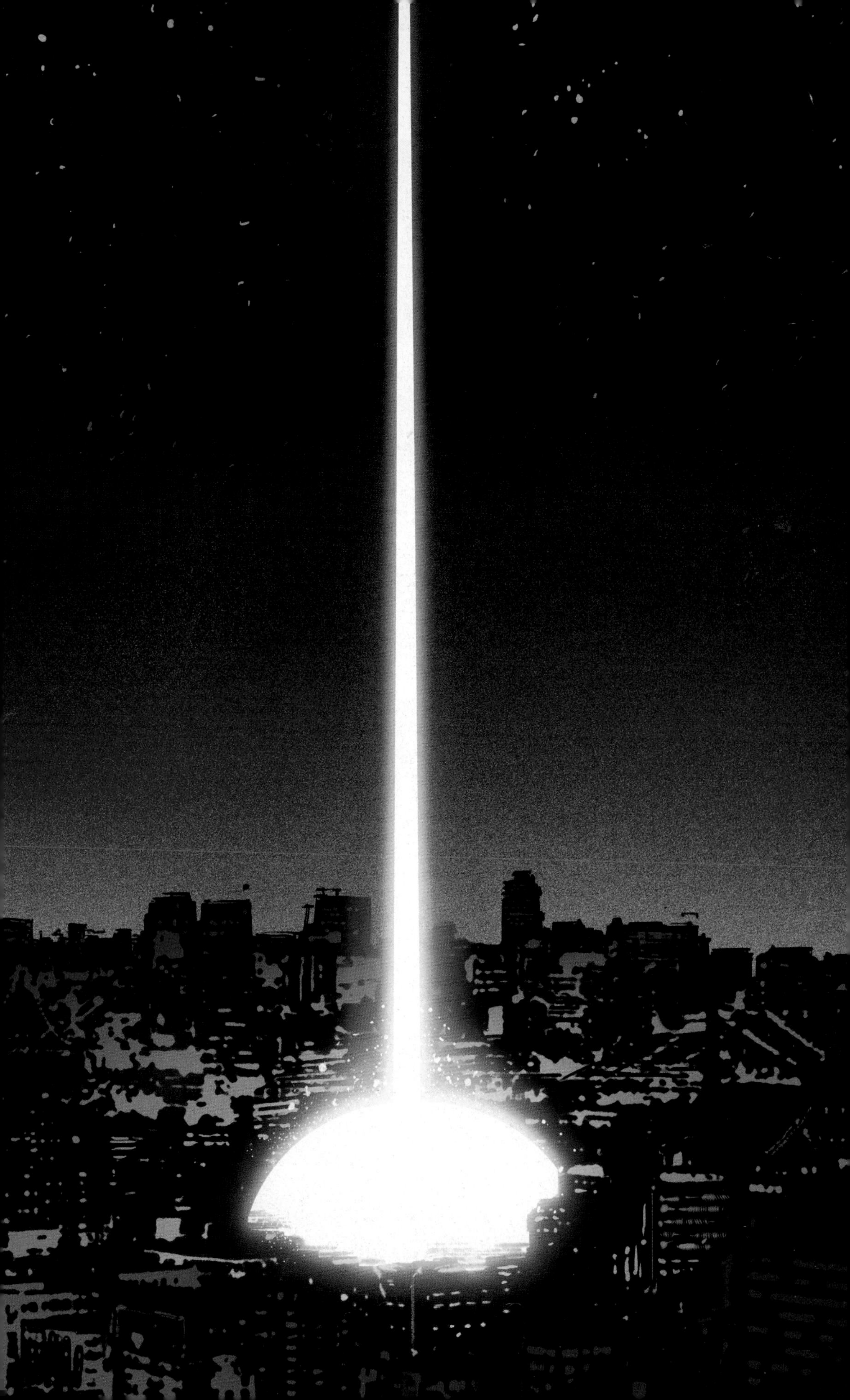

#154 VARIANT
BY SARA PICHELLI & JUSTIN PONSOR

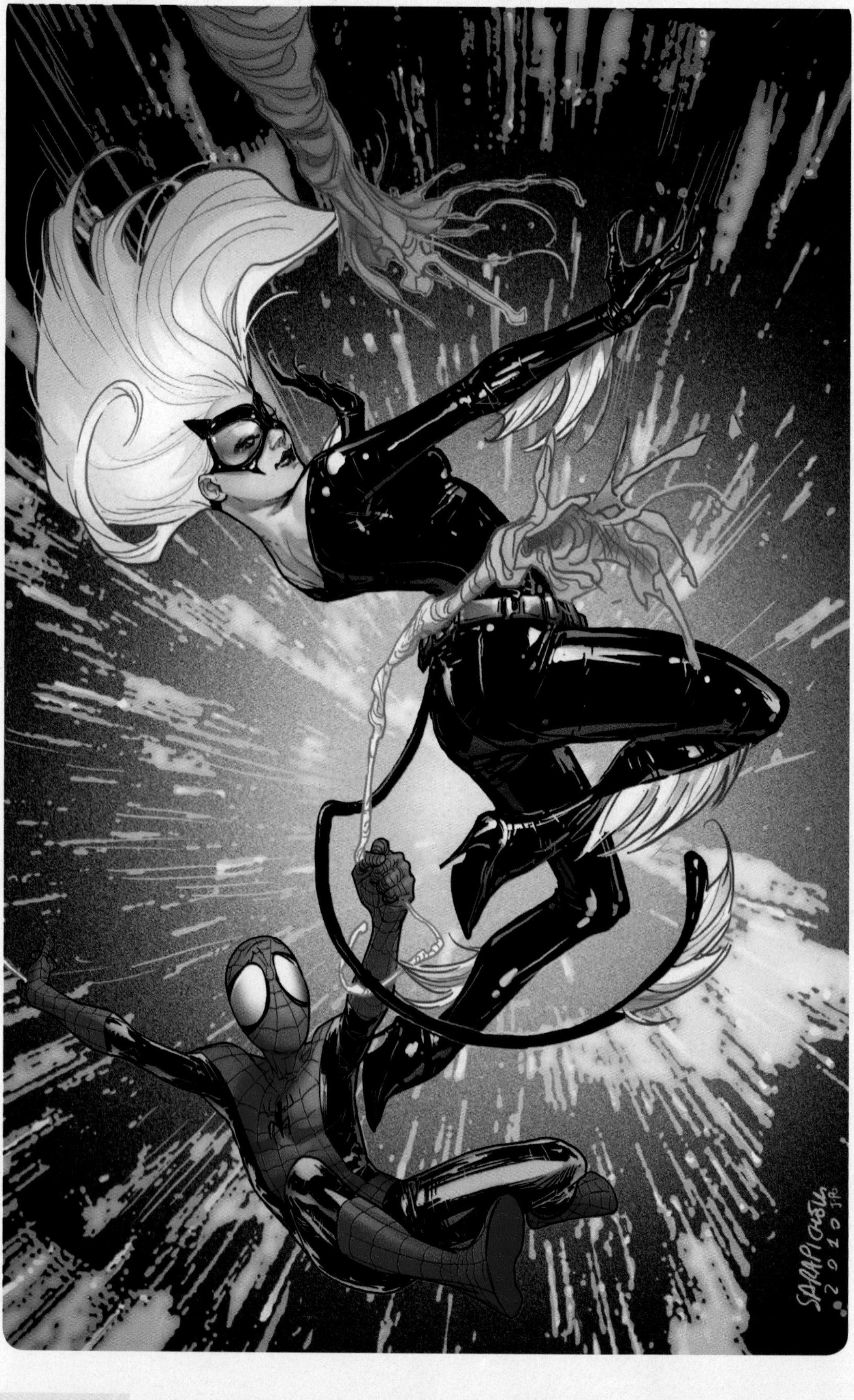

154

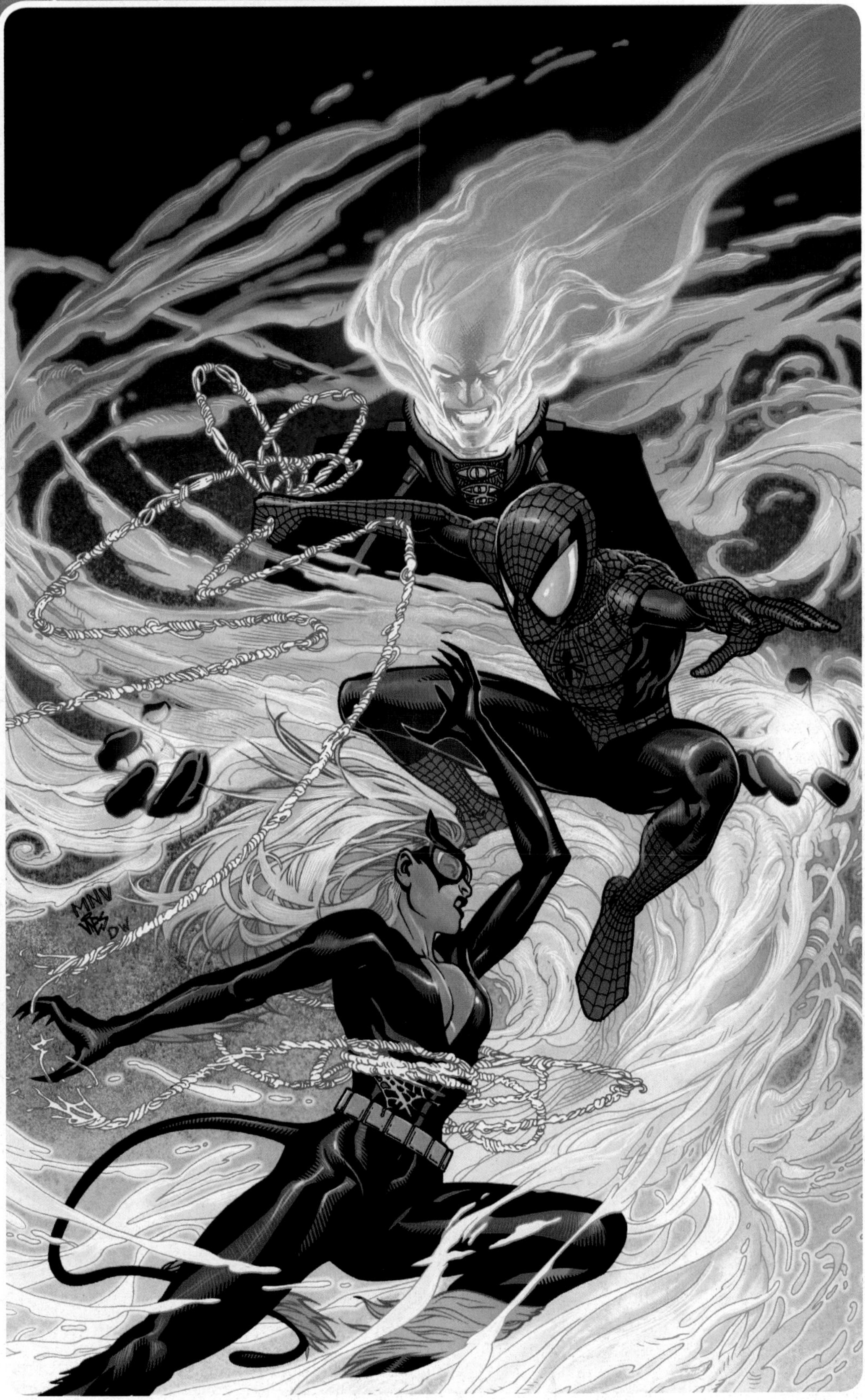

MNV
WBS
DW

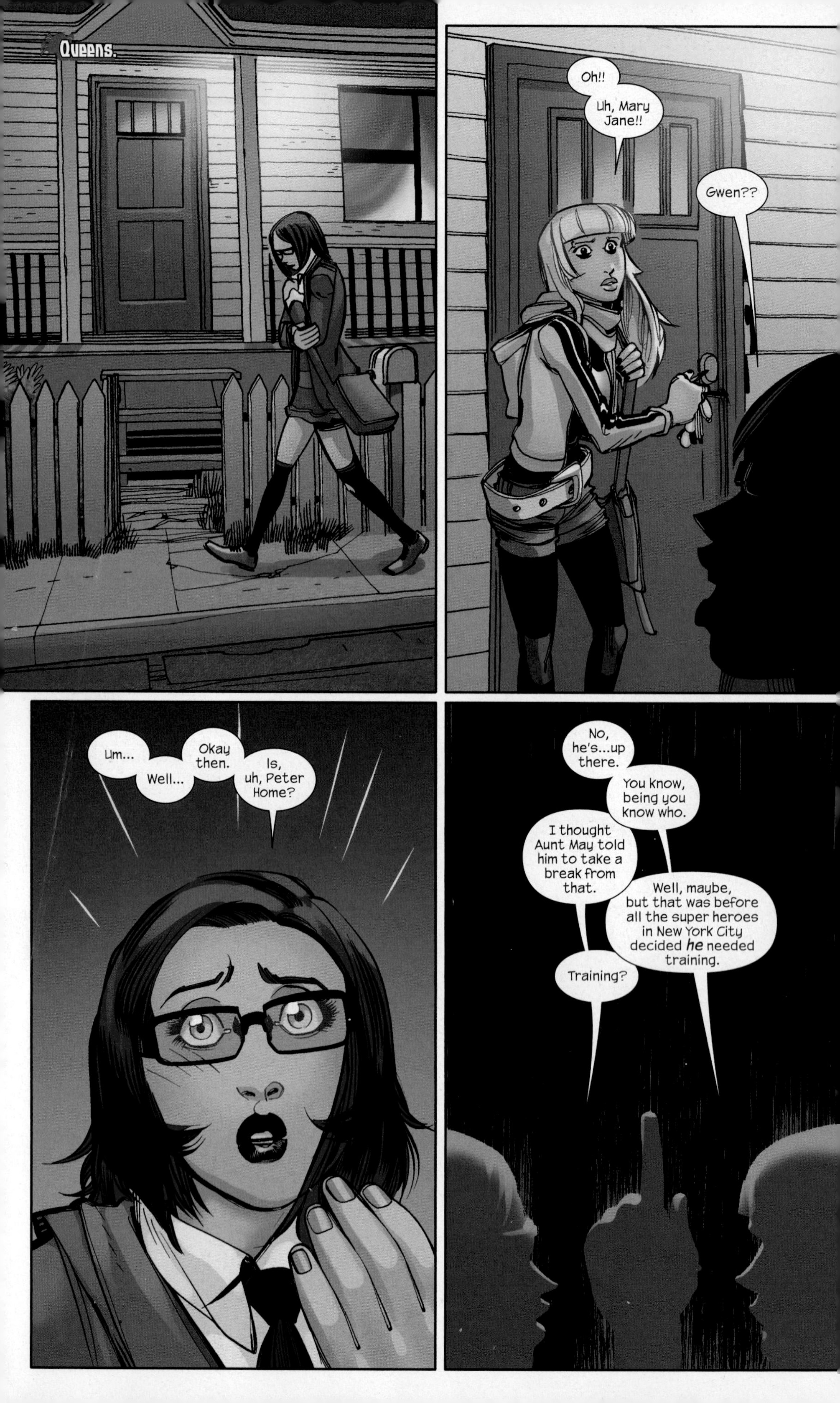
Queens.
Oh!!
Uh, Mary Jane!!
Gwen??
Um...
Well...
Okay then.
Is, uh, Peter Home?
No, he's...up there.
You know, being you know who.
I thought Aunt May told him to take a break from that.
Well, maybe, but that was before all the super heroes in New York City decided he needed training.
Training?

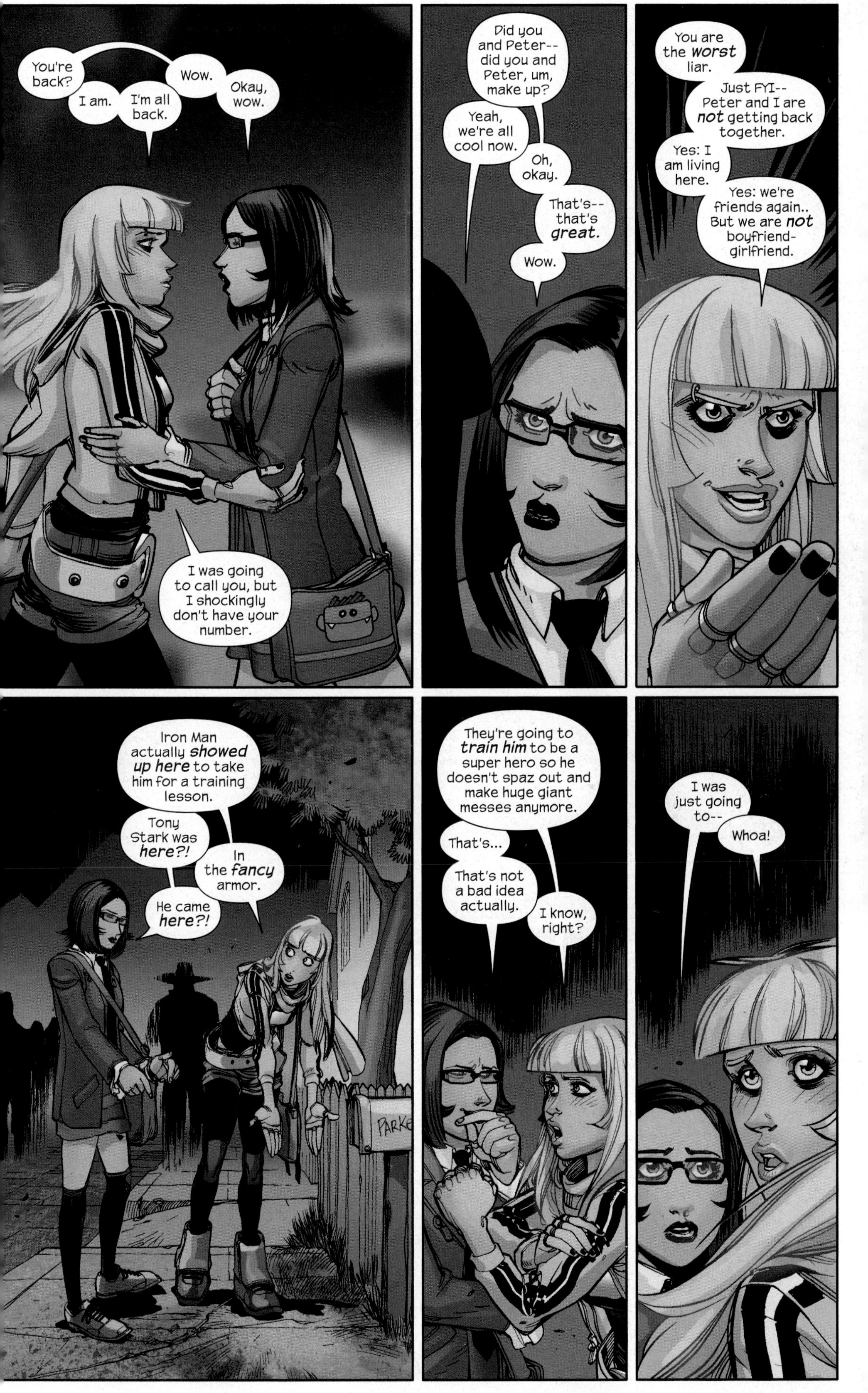
You're back?
I am.
I'm all back.
Wow.
Okay, wow.
I was going to call you, but I shockingly don't have your number.
Did you and Peter-- did you and Peter, um, make up?
Yeah, we're all cool now.
Oh, okay.
That's-- that's great.
Wow.
You are the worst liar.
Just FYI-- Peter and I are not getting back together.
Yes: I am living here.
Yes: we're friends again.. But we are not boyfriend-girlfriend.
Iron Man actually showed up here to take him for a training lesson.
Tony Stark was here?!
In the fancy armor.
He came here?!
PARKE
They're going to train him to be a super hero so he doesn't spaz out and make huge giant messes anymore.
That's...
That's not a bad idea actually.
I know, right?
I was just going to--
Whoa!

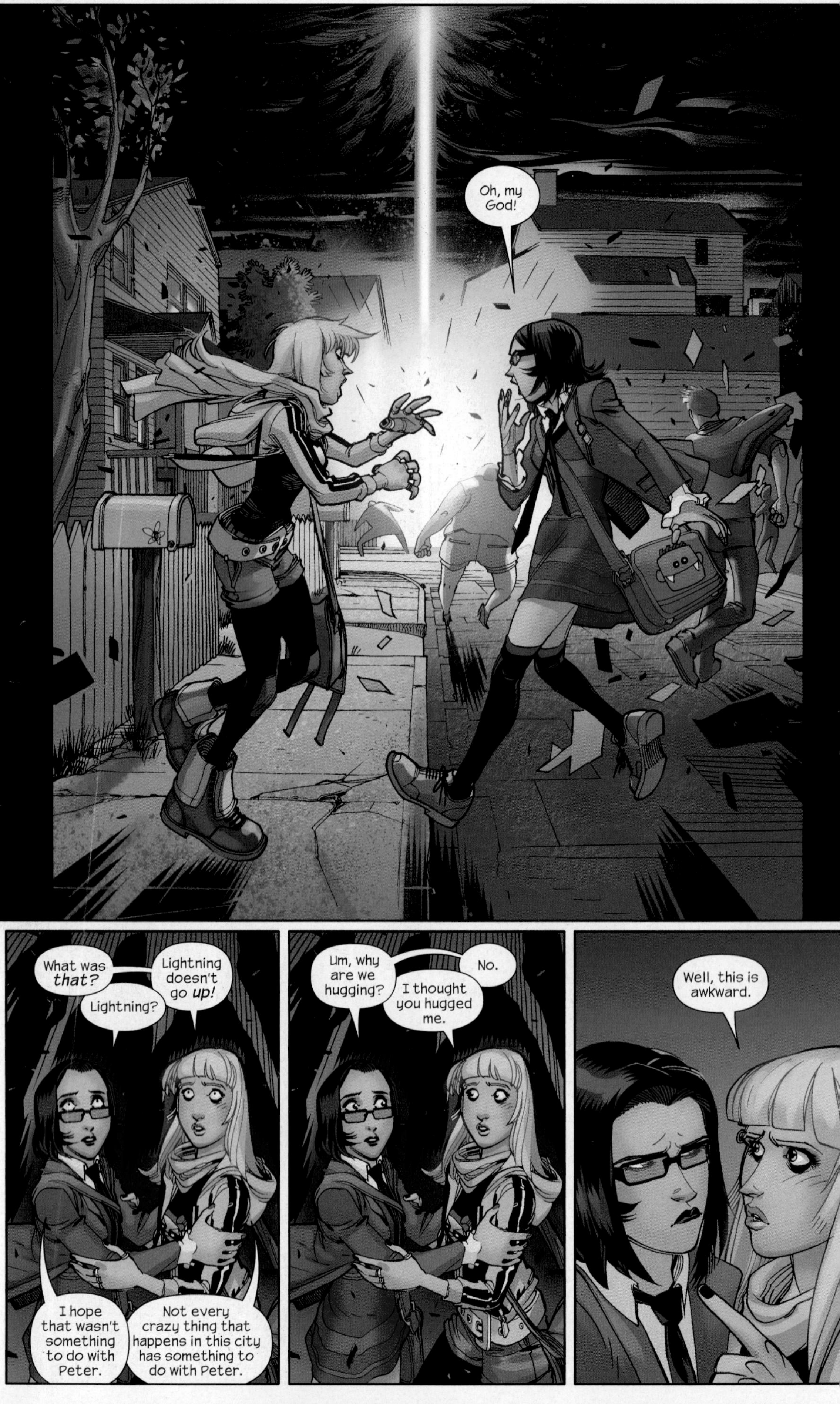
Oh, my God!
What was *that?*
Lightning?
Lightning doesn't go *up!*
I hope that wasn't something to do with Peter.
Not every crazy thing that happens in this city has something to do with Peter.
Um, why are we hugging?
No.
I thought you hugged me.
Well, this is awkward.

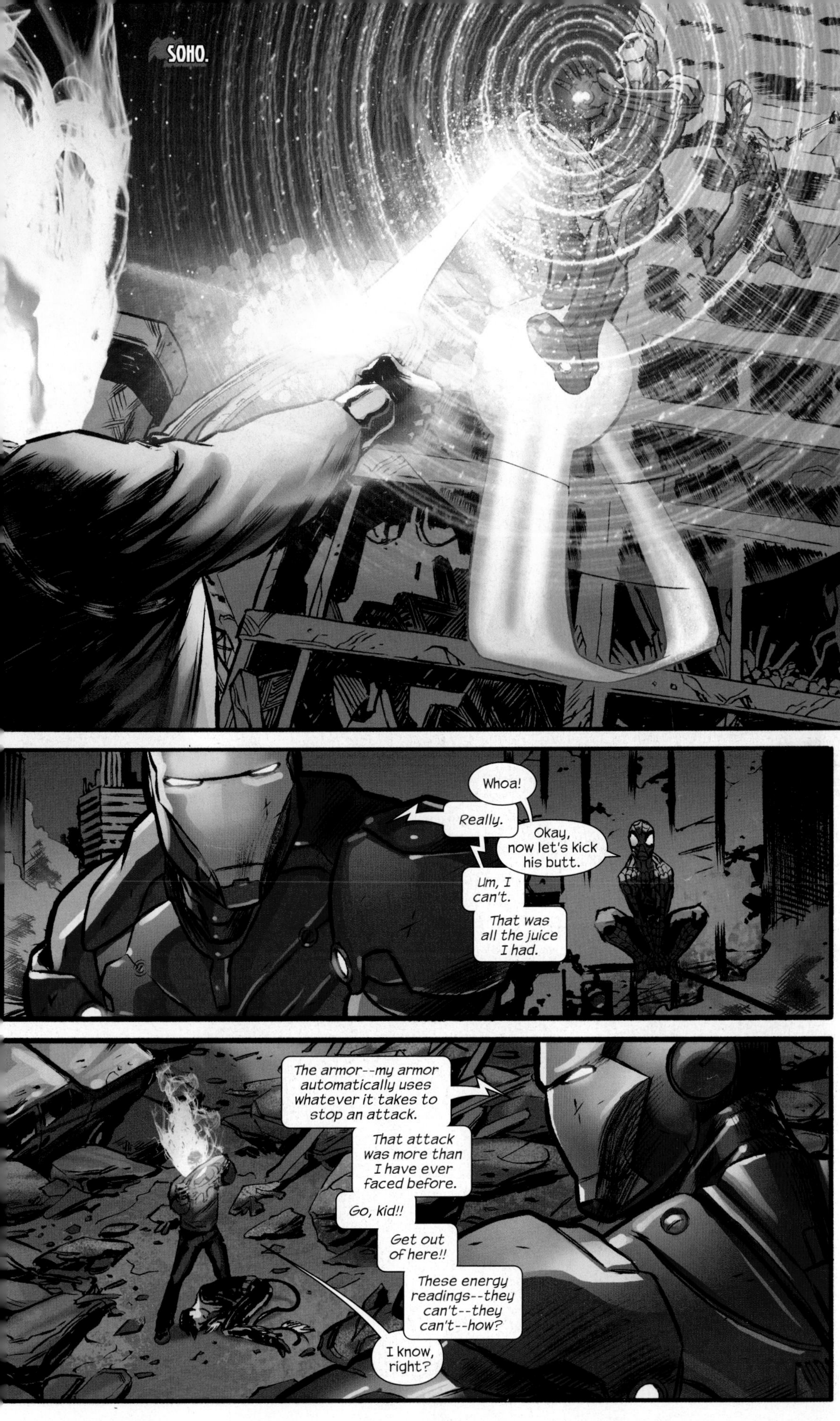
SOHO.
Whoa!
Really.
Okay, now let's kick his butt.
Um, I can't.
That was all the juice I had.
The armor--my armor automatically uses whatever it takes to stop an attack.
That attack was more than I have ever faced before.
Go, kid!!
Get out of here!!
These energy readings--they can't--they can't--how?
I know, right?

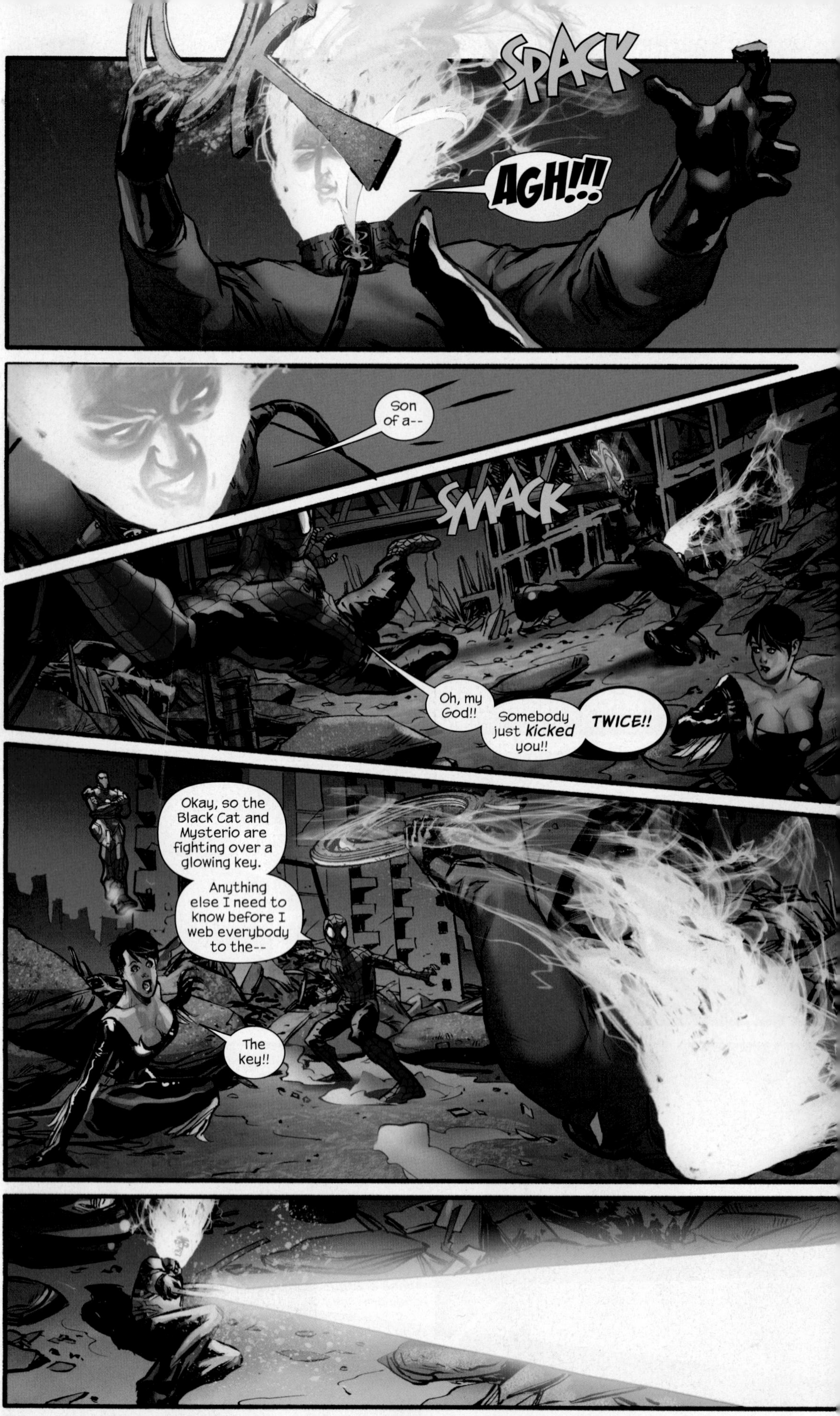
SPACK
AGH!!!
Son of a--
SMACK
Oh, my God!!
Somebody just *kicked* you!!
TWICE!!
Okay, so the Black Cat and Mysterio are fighting over a glowing key.
Anything else I need to know before I web everybody to the--
The key!!

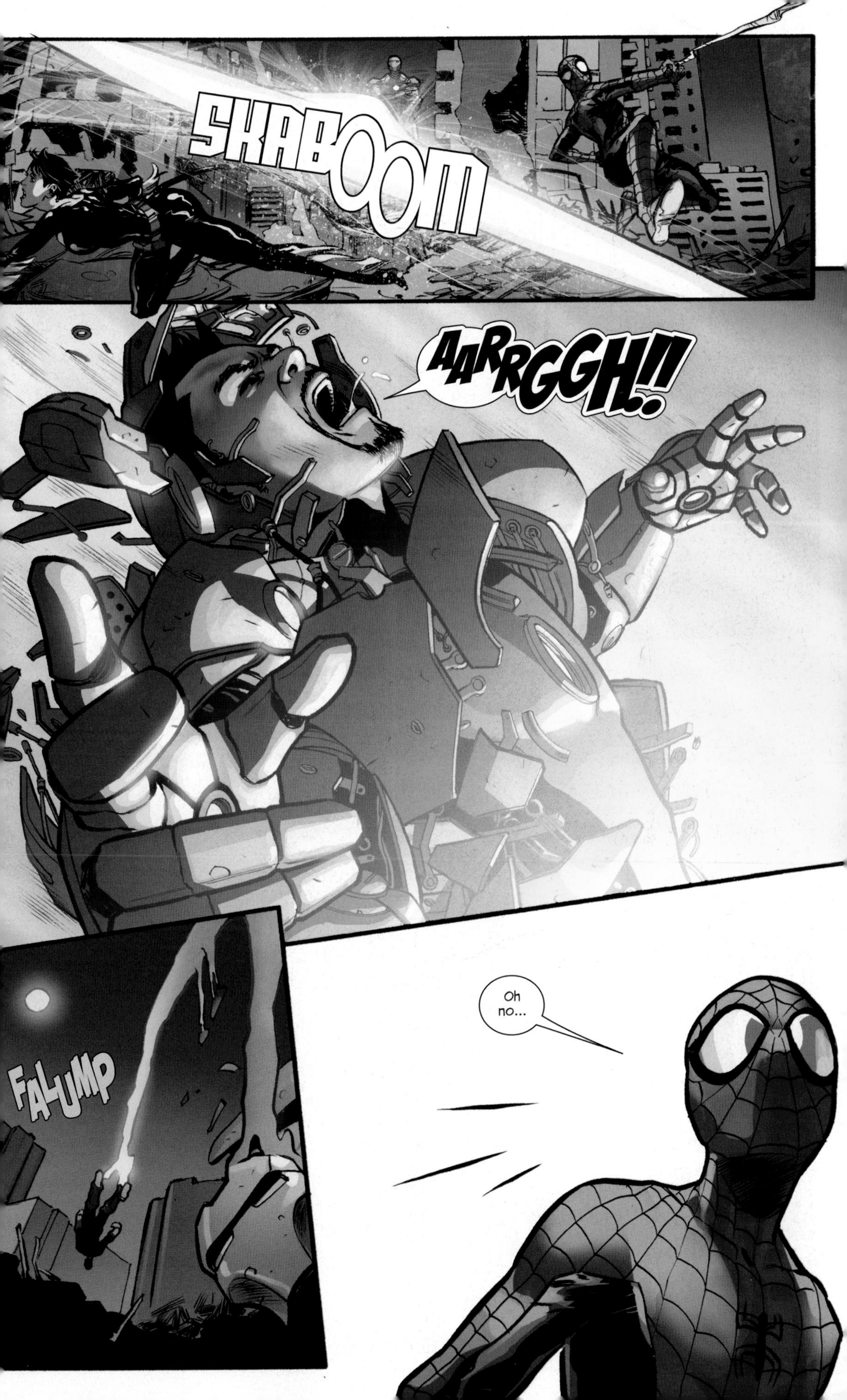
SKABOOM
AARRGGH!!
FALUMP
Oh no...

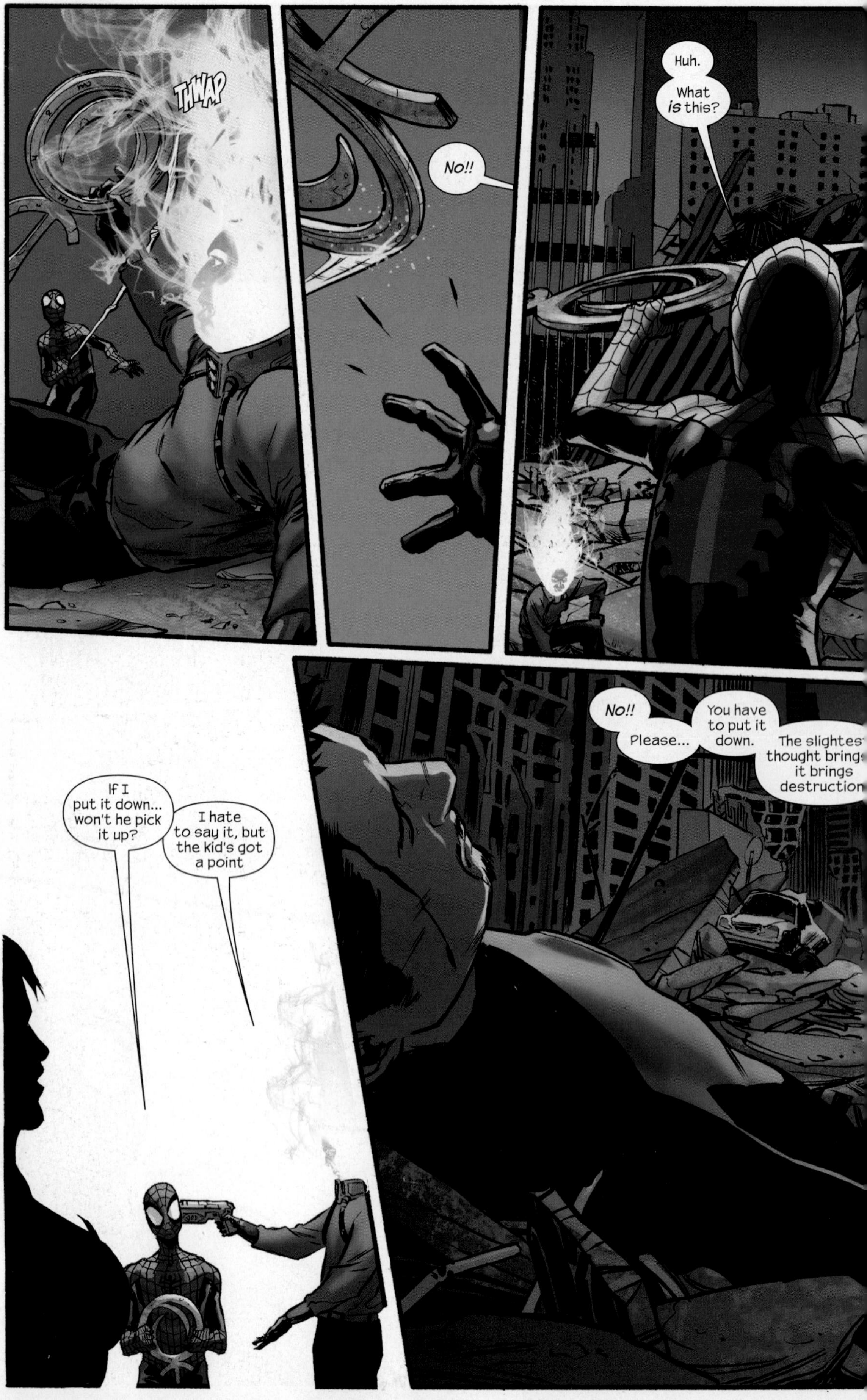
THWAP
No!!
Huh.
What *is* this?
No!!
Please...
You have to put it down.
The slightest thought brings it brings destruction
If I put it down... won't he pick it up?
I hate to say it, but the kid's got a point

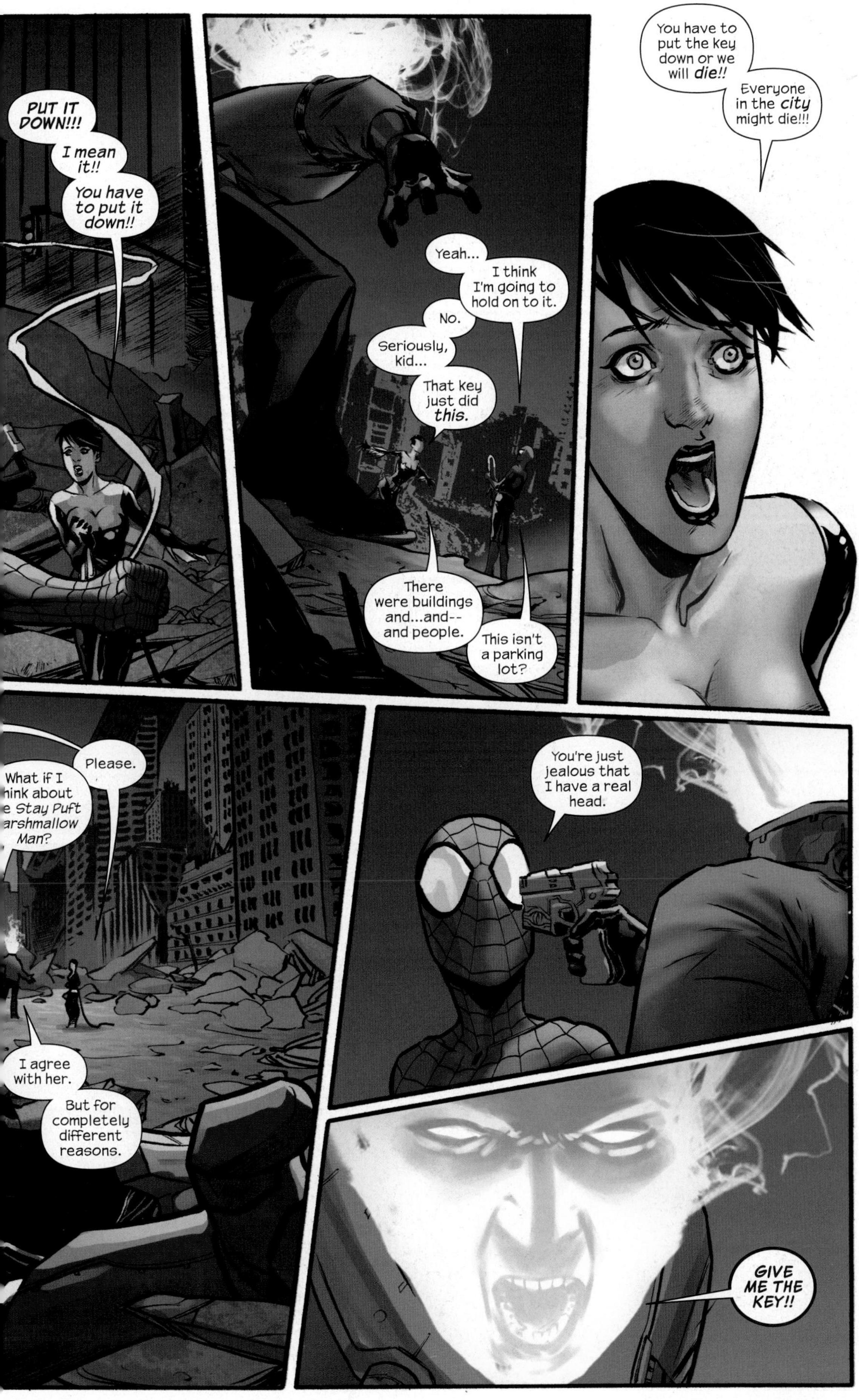
PUT IT DOWN!!!
I mean it!!
You have to put it down!!
Yeah...
I think I'm going to hold on to it.
No.
Seriously, kid...
That key just did this.
There were buildings and...and-- and people.
This isn't a parking lot?
You have to put the key down or we will die!!
Everyone in the city might die!!!
Please.
What if I hink about e Stay Puft arshmallow Man?
I agree with her.
But for completely different reasons.
You're just jealous that I have a real head.
GIVE ME THE KEY!!

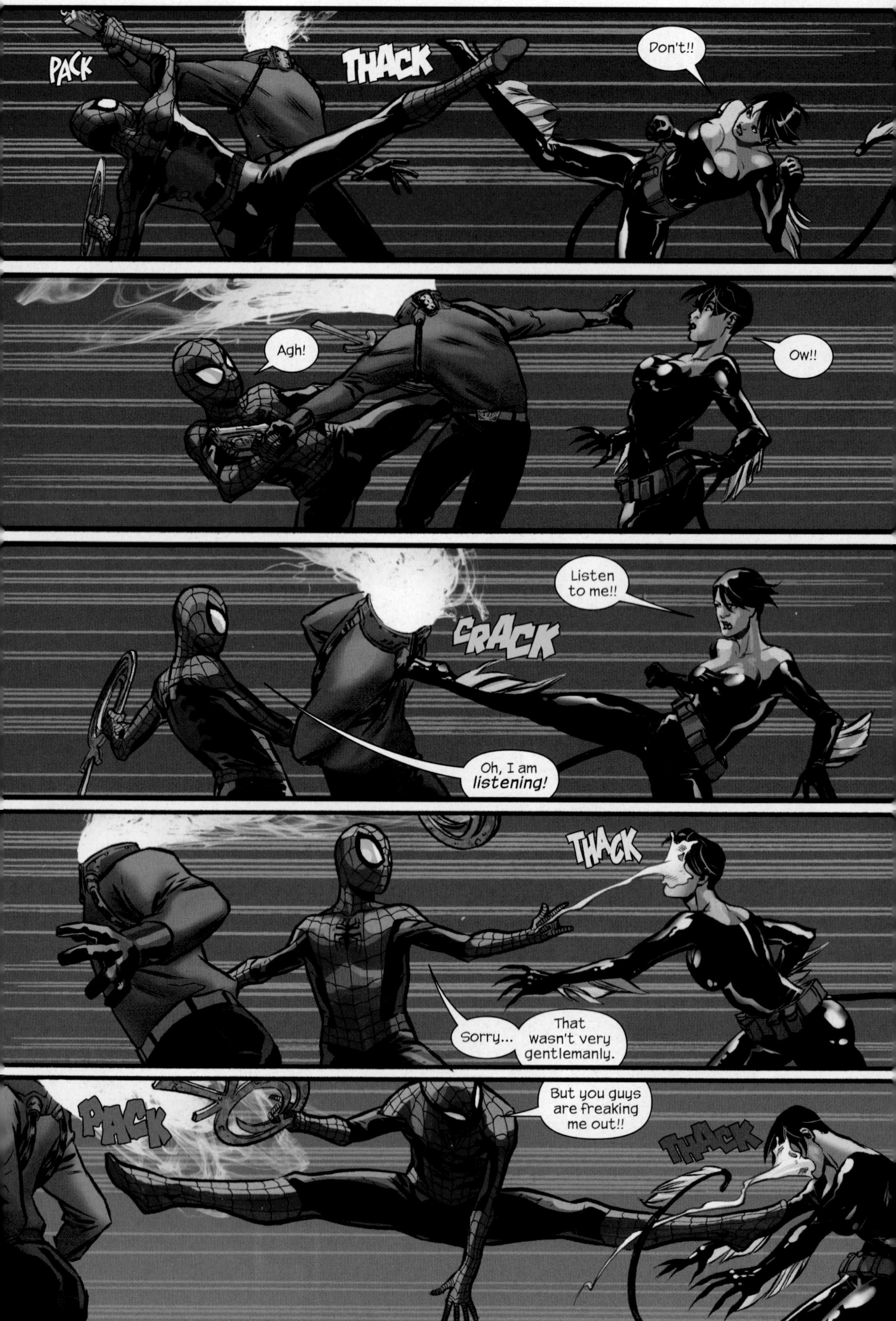
PACK
THACK
Don't!!
Agh!
Ow!!
Listen to me!!
CRACK
Oh, I am *listening!*
THACK
Sorry...
That wasn't very gentlemanly.
PACK
But you guys are freaking me out!!
THACK

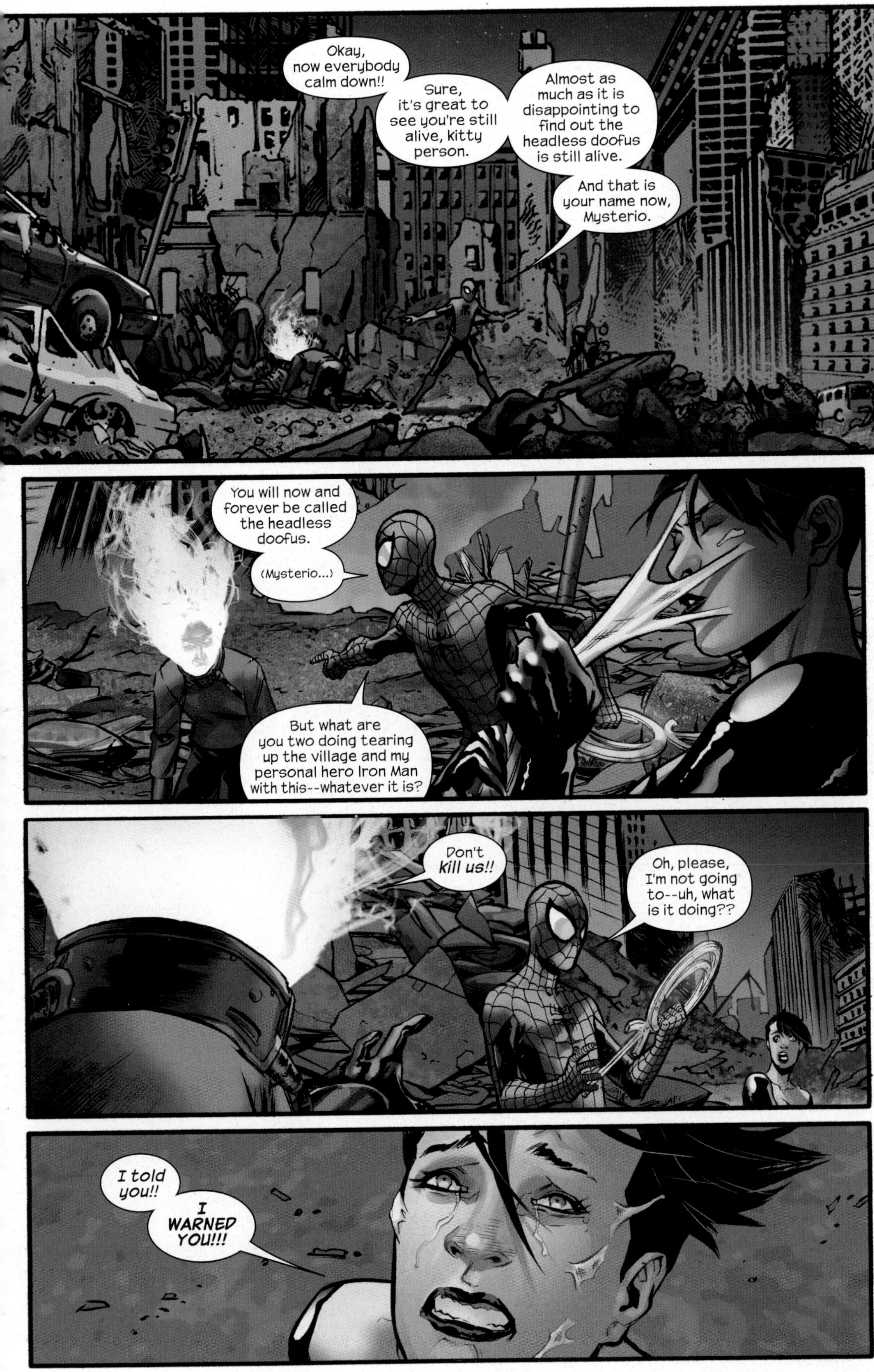
Okay, now everybody calm down!!
Sure, it's great to see you're still alive, kitty person.
Almost as much as it is disappointing to find out the headless doofus is still alive.
And that is your name now, Mysterio.
You will now and forever be called the headless doofus.
(Mysterio...)
But what are you two doing tearing up the village and my personal hero Iron Man with this--whatever it is?
Don't *kill us!!*
Oh, please, I'm not going to--uh, what is it doing??
I told you!!
I WARNED YOU!!!

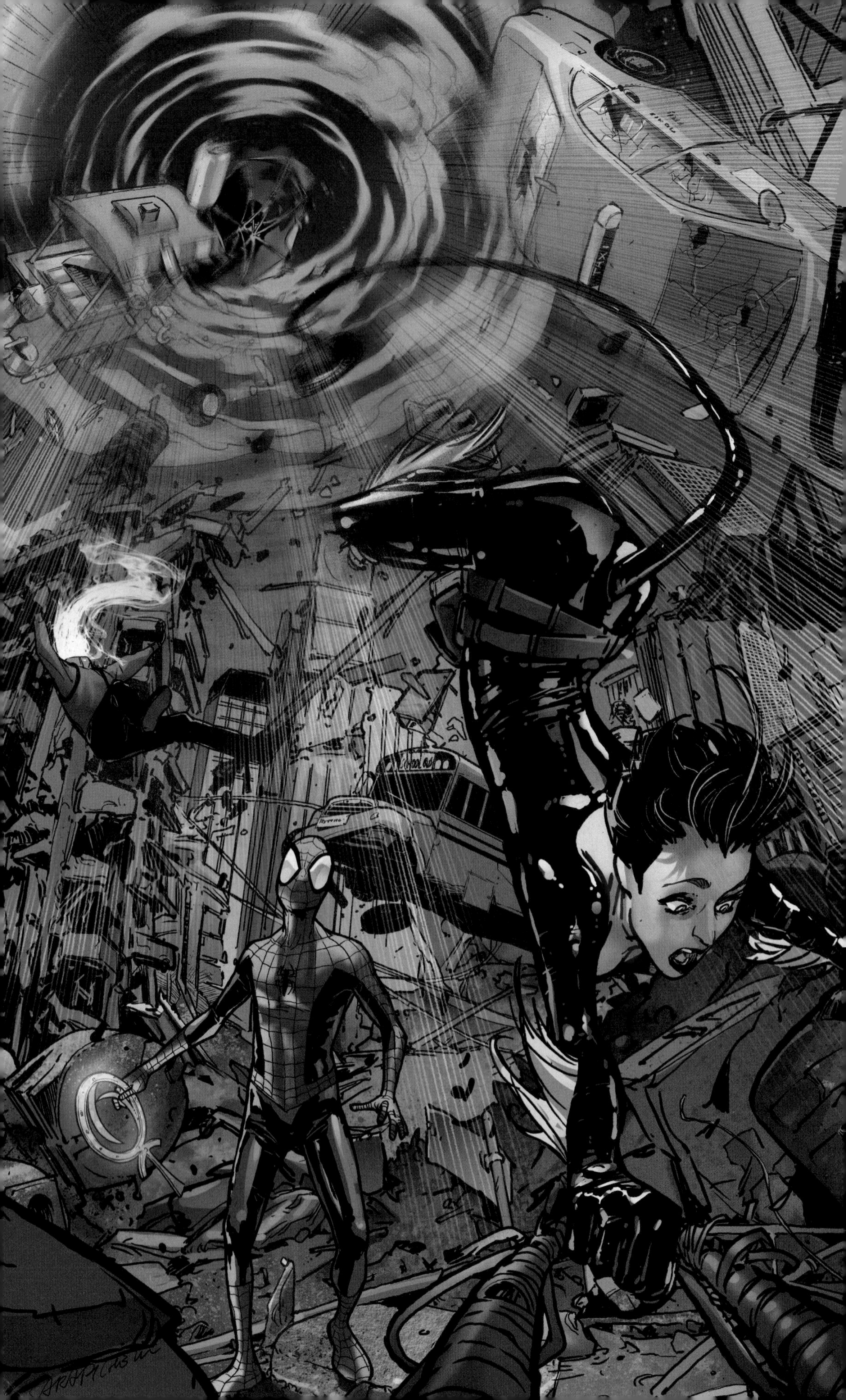

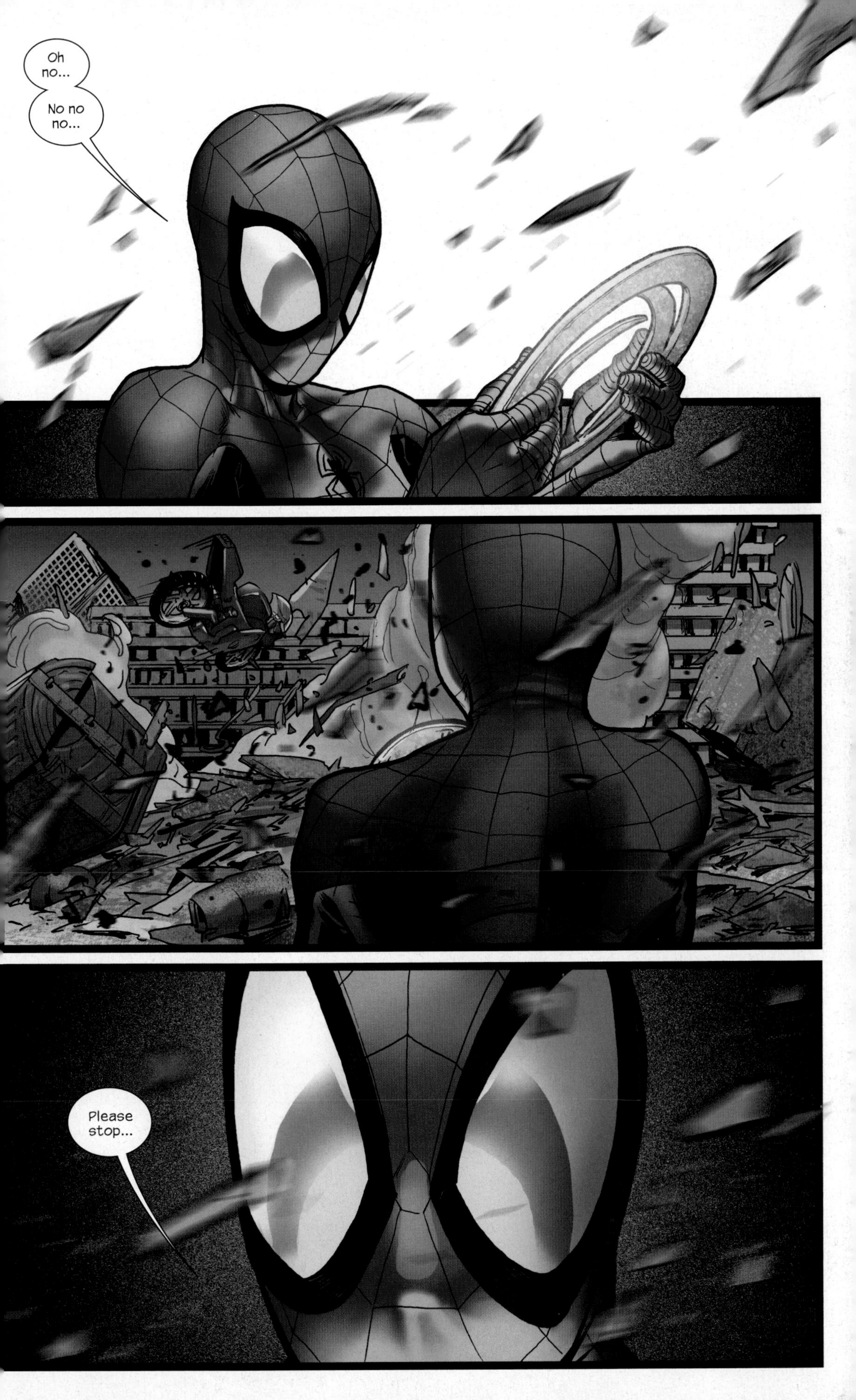
Oh no...
No no no...
Please stop...

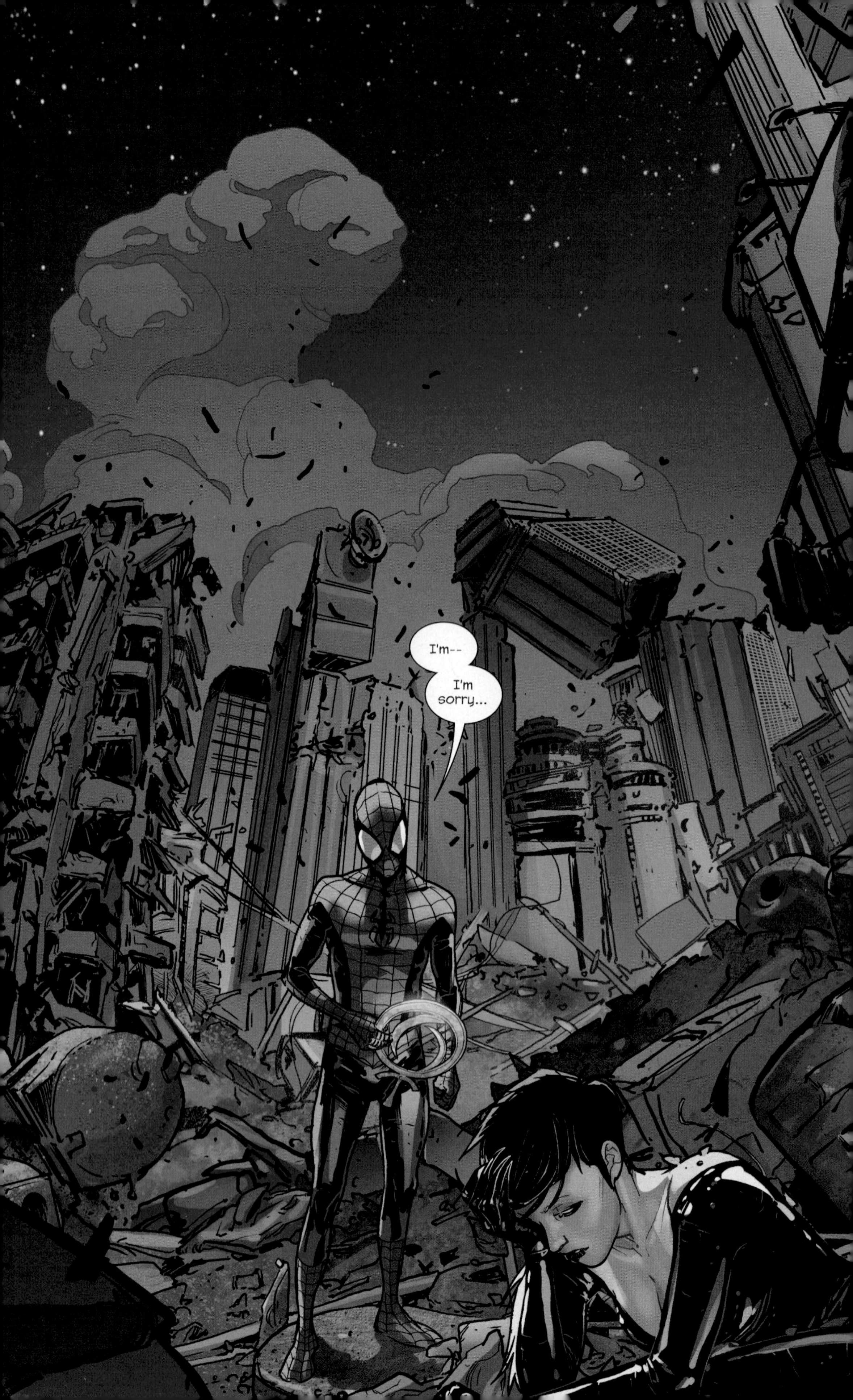
I'm--
I'm sorry...

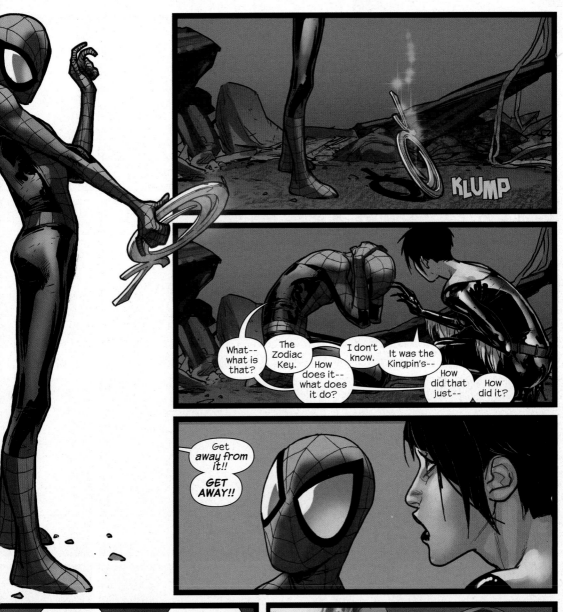

KLUMP

What-- what is that?

The Zodiac Key.

How does it-- what does it do?

I don't know.

It was the Kingpin's--

How did that just--

How did it?

Get away from it!!

GET AWAY!!

I'll kill you if you come near it!!

If your weapon worked, you would have fired it.

I'll melt your head!!

Back off.

Count of three.

You have till the count of three.

One!

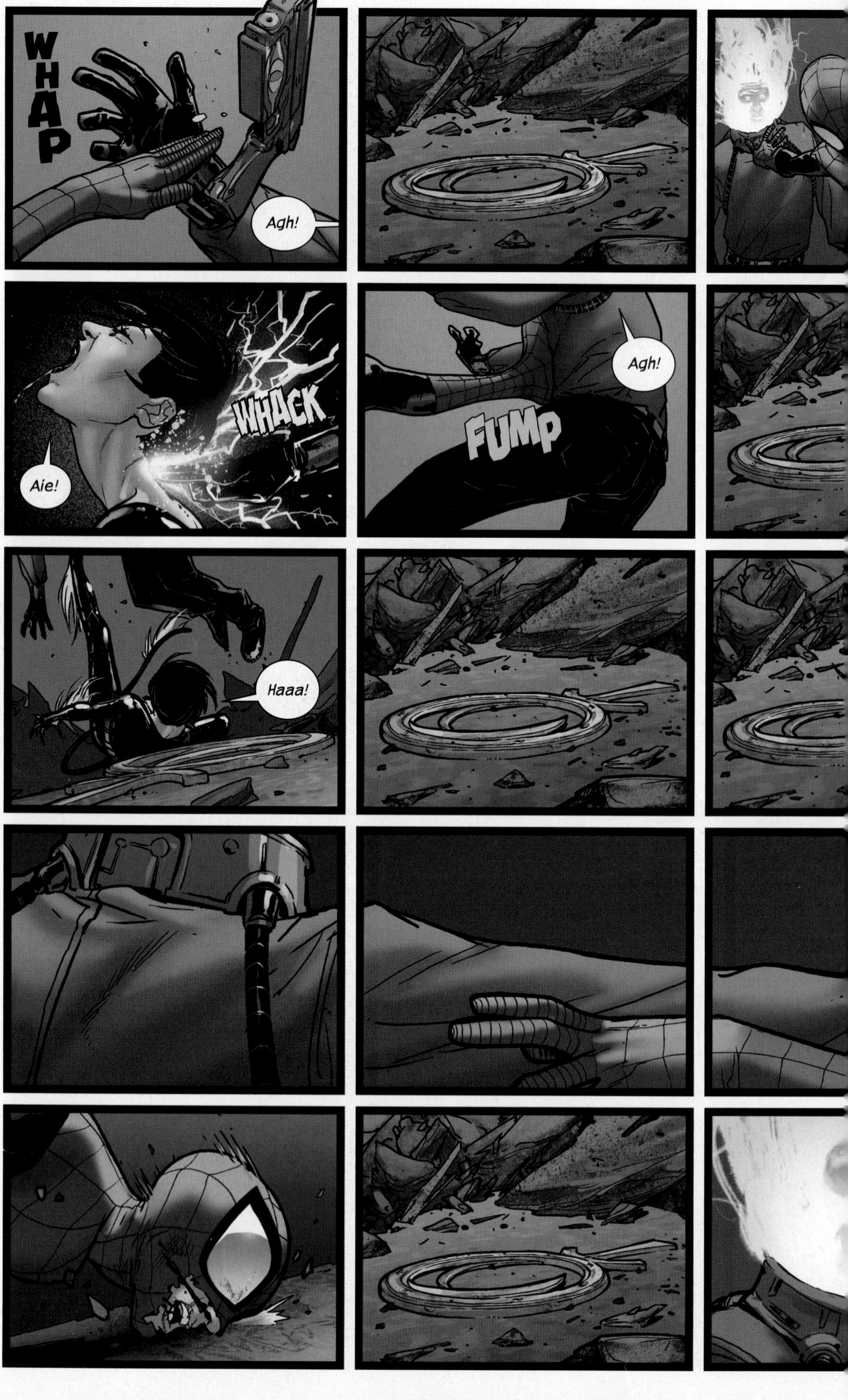

WHAP
Agh!
Aie!
WHACK
Agh!
FUMP
Haaa!

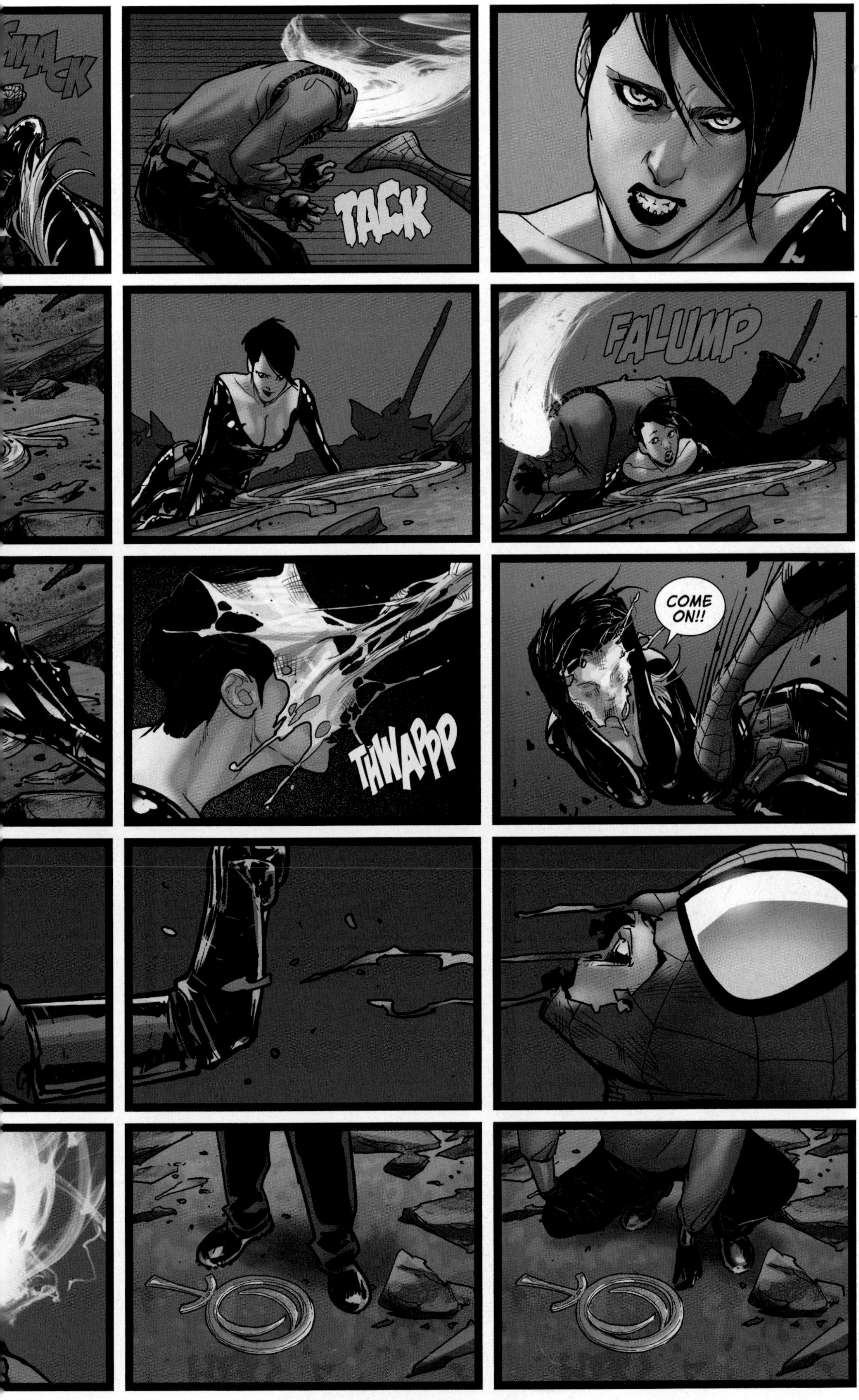
TACK
FALUMP
THWAPPP
COME ON!!

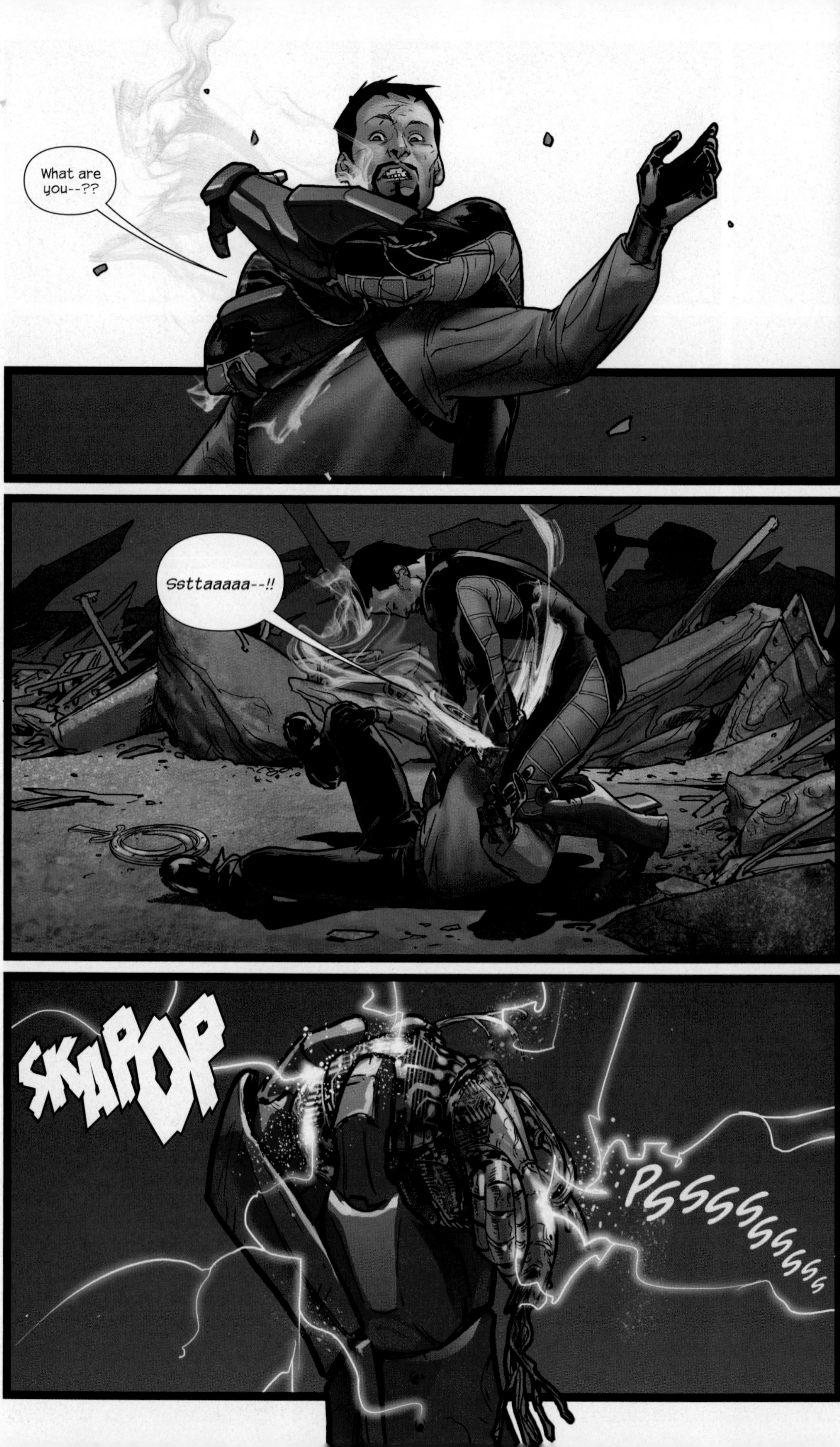
What are you--??
Ssttaaaaa--!!
SKAPOP
PSSSSSSSSSS

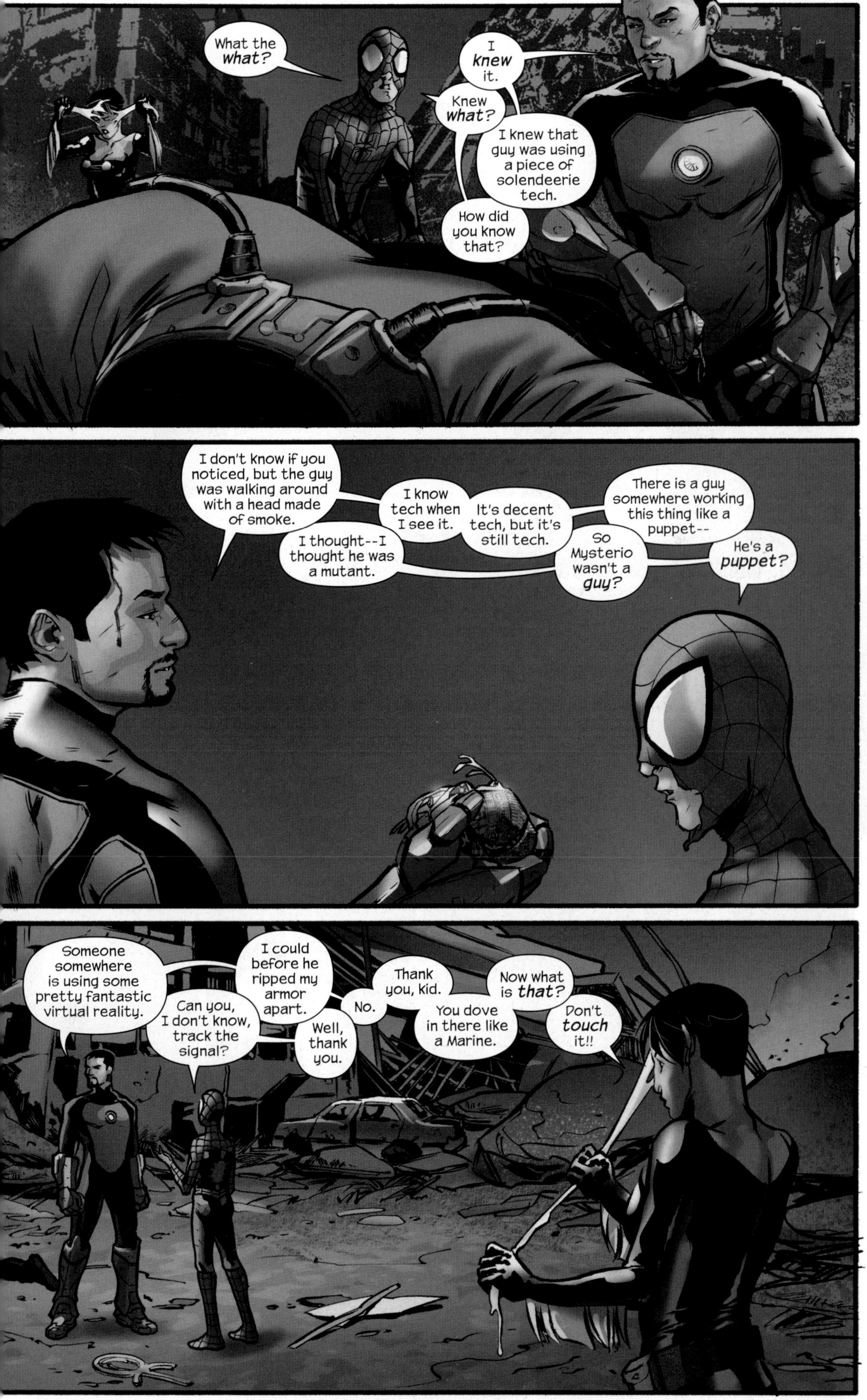
What the *what?*
I *knew* it.
Knew *what?*
I knew that guy was using a piece of solendeerie tech.
How did you know that?
I don't know if you noticed, but the guy was walking around with a head made of smoke.
I thought--I thought he was a mutant.
I know tech when I see it.
It's decent tech, but it's still tech.
So Mysterio wasn't a *guy?*
There is a guy somewhere working this thing like a puppet--
He's a *puppet?*
Someone somewhere is using some pretty fantastic virtual reality.
Can you, I don't know, track the signal?
I could before he ripped my armor apart.
Well, thank you.
No.
Thank you, kid.
You dove in there like a Marine.
Now what is *that?*
Don't *touch* it!!

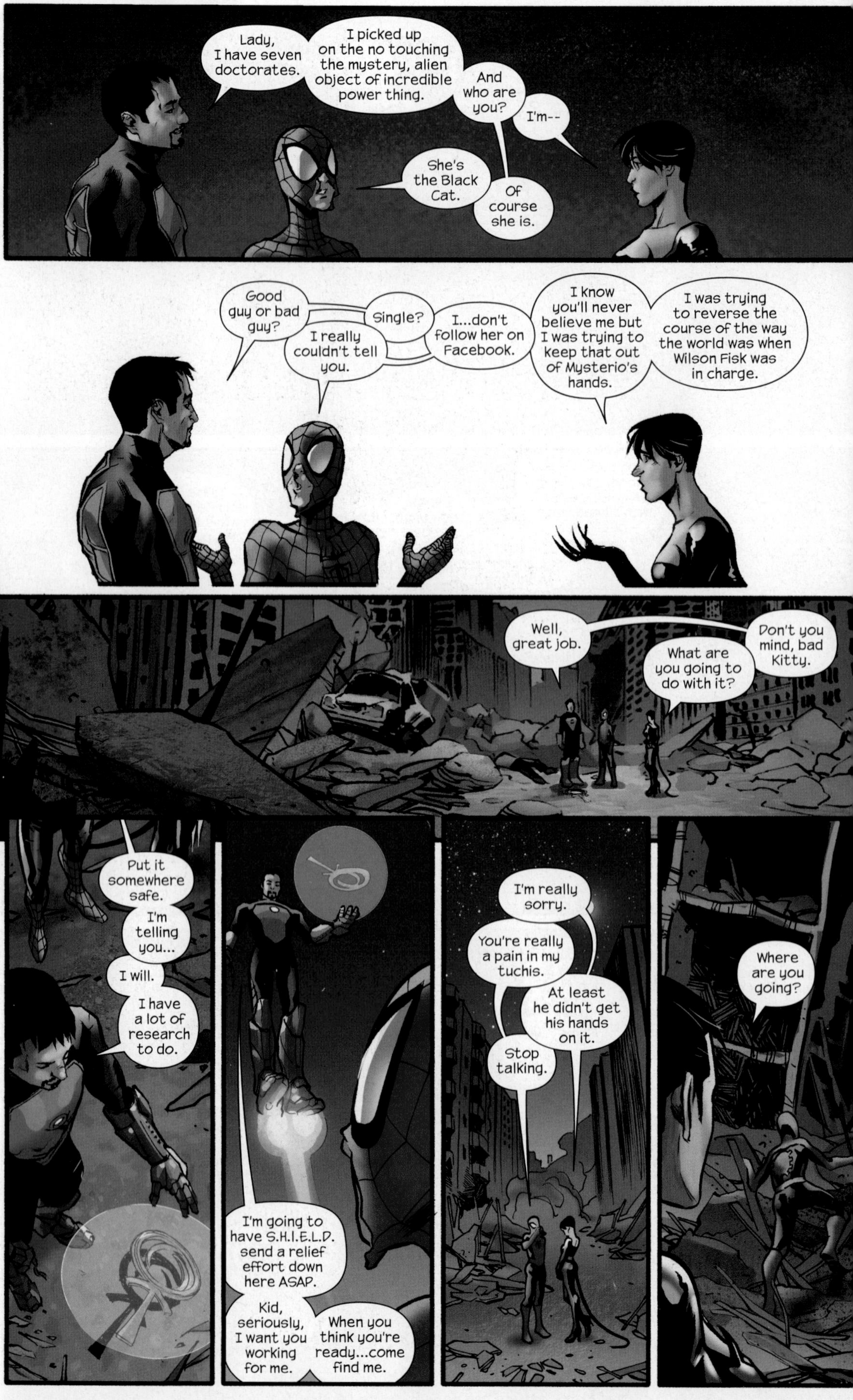

Lady, I have seven doctorates.
I picked up on the no touching the mystery, alien object of incredible power thing.
And who are you?
I'm--
She's the Black Cat.
Of course she is.
Good guy or bad guy?
Single?
I really couldn't tell you.
I...don't follow her on Facebook.
I know you'll never believe me but I was trying to keep that out of Mysterio's hands.
I was trying to reverse the course of the way the world was when Wilson Fisk was in charge.
Well, great job.
Don't you mind, bad Kitty.
What are you going to do with it?
Put it somewhere safe.
I'm telling you...
I will.
I have a lot of research to do.
I'm going to have S.H.I.E.L.D. send a relief effort down here ASAP.
Kid, seriously, I want you working for me.
When you think you're ready...come find me.
I'm really sorry.
You're really a pain in my tuchis.
At least he didn't get his hands on it.
Stop talking.
Where are you going?

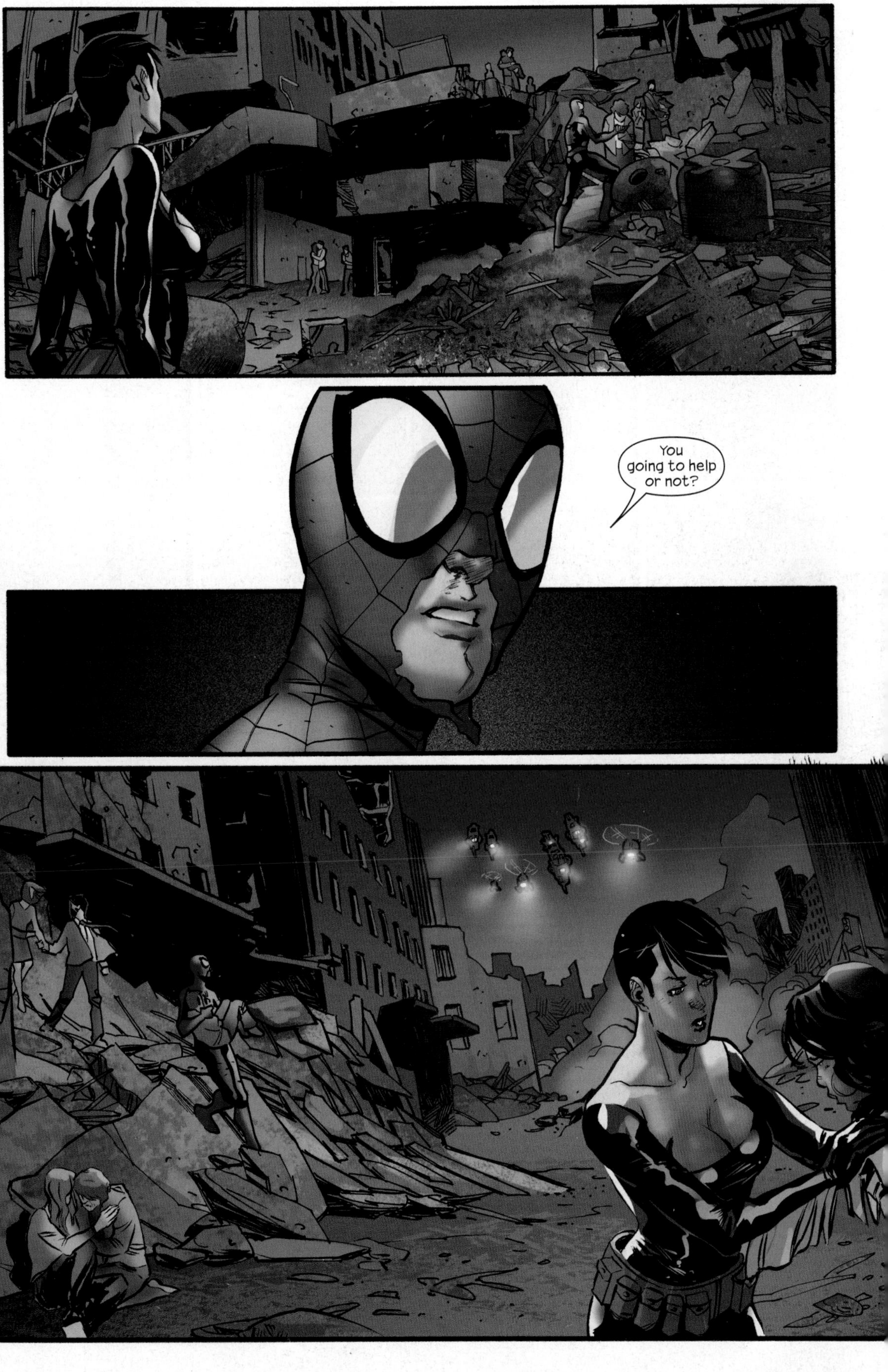
You going to help or not?

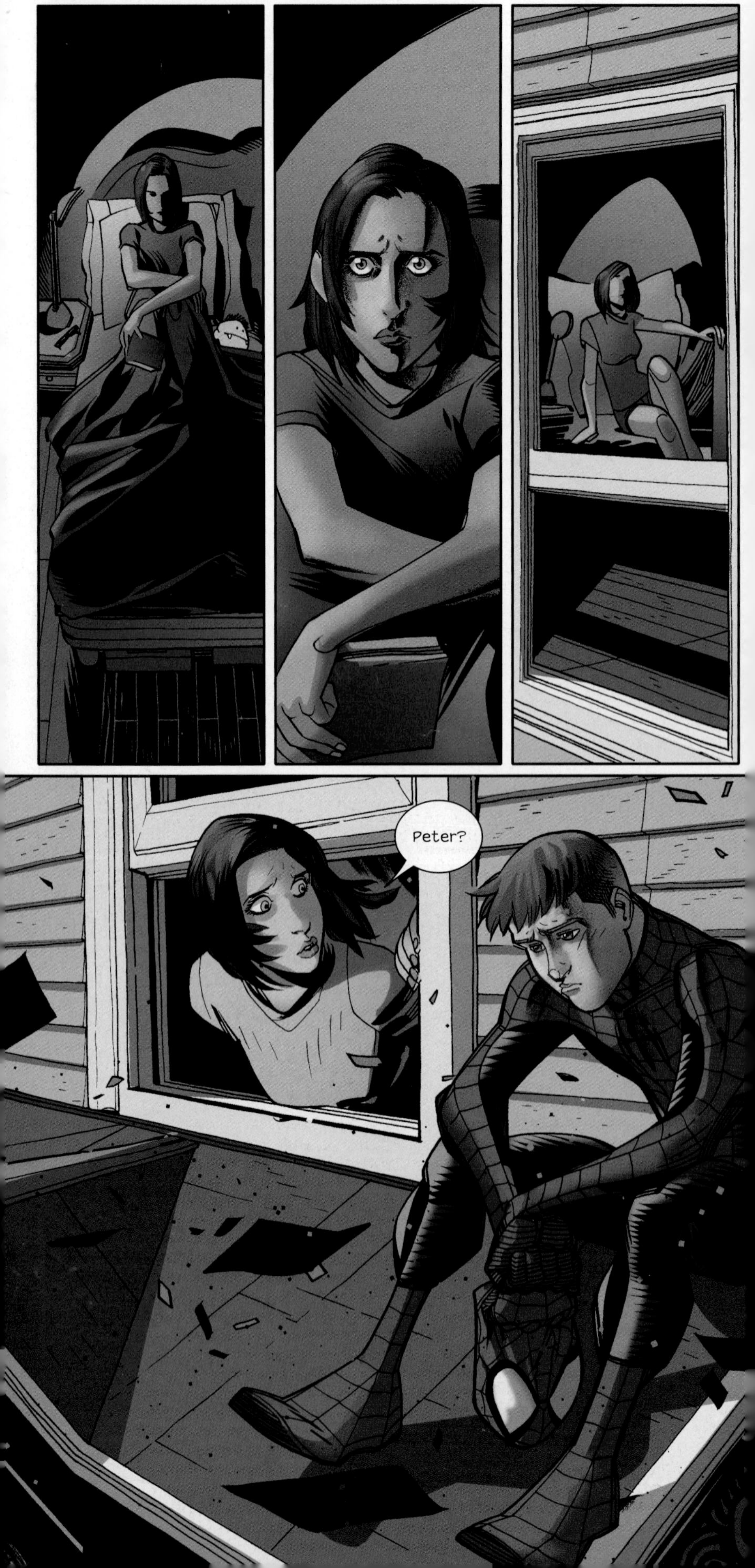
Peter?

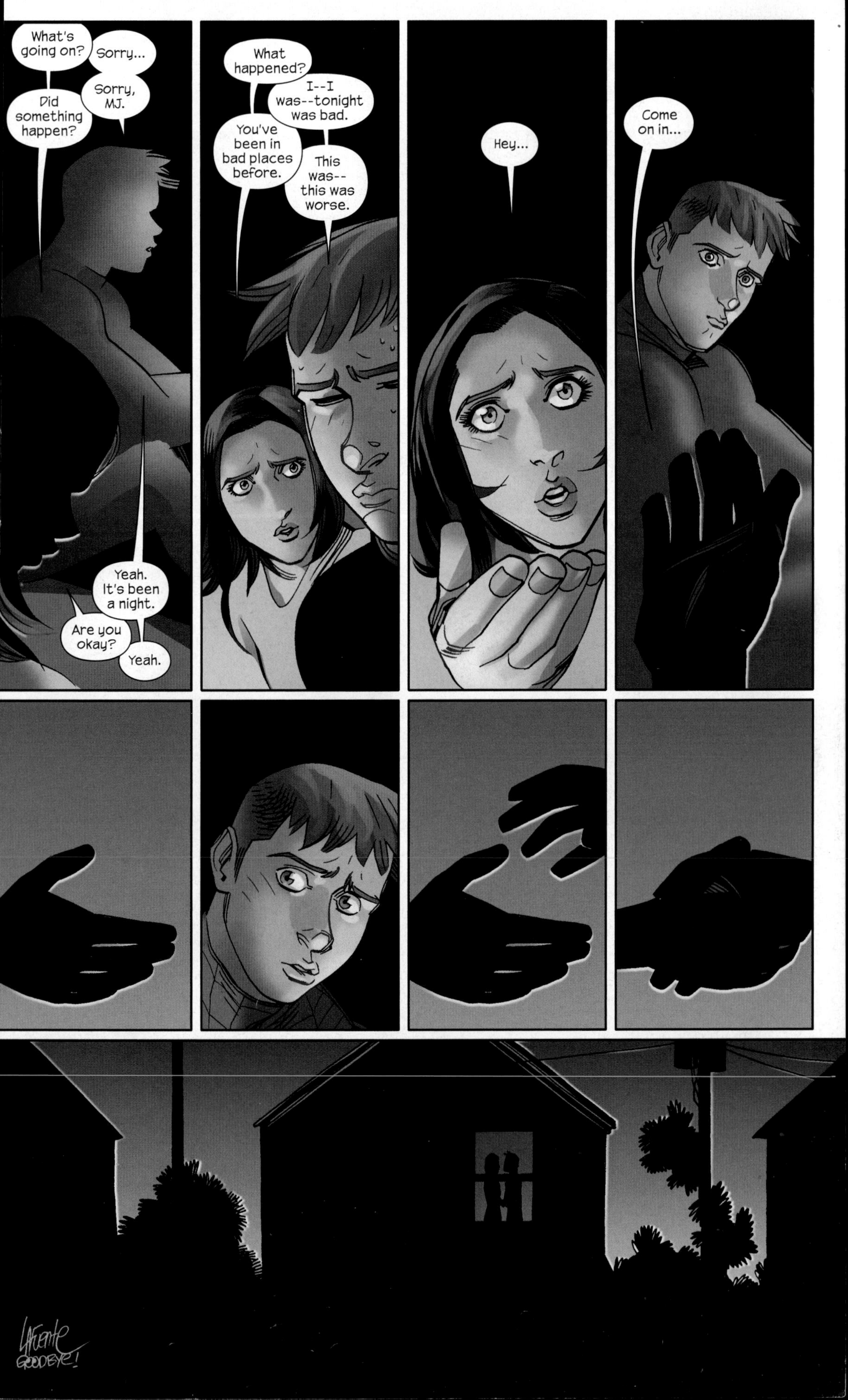
What's going on?
Sorry...
Sorry, MJ.
Did something happen?
Yeah. It's been a night.
Are you okay?
Yeah.
What happened?
I--I was--tonight was bad.
You've been in bad places before.
This was--this was worse.
Hey...
Come on in...
LaFuente
GOODBYE!

#155 VARIANT
BY SARA PICHELLI & JUSTIN PONSOR

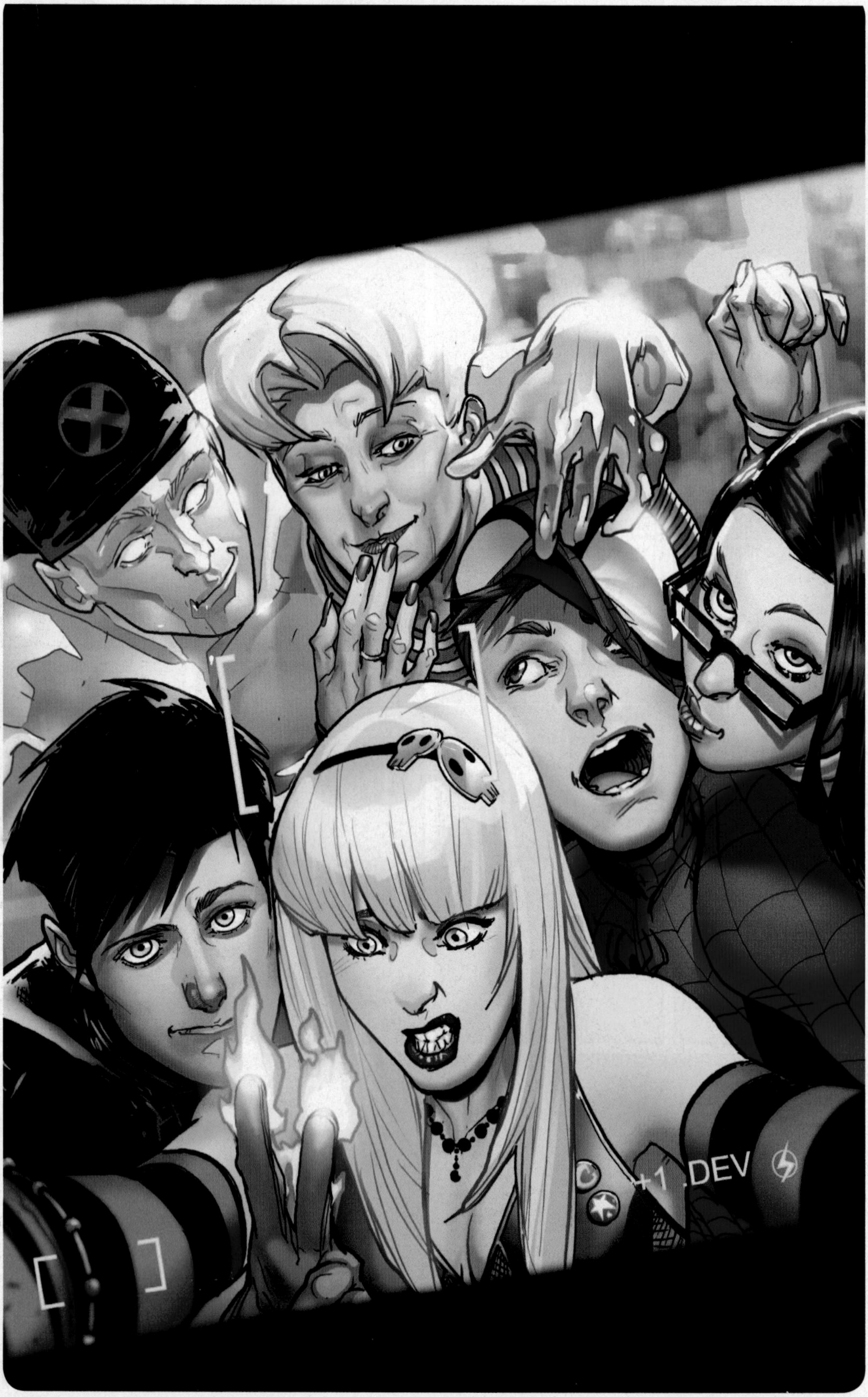
+1 .DEV

155

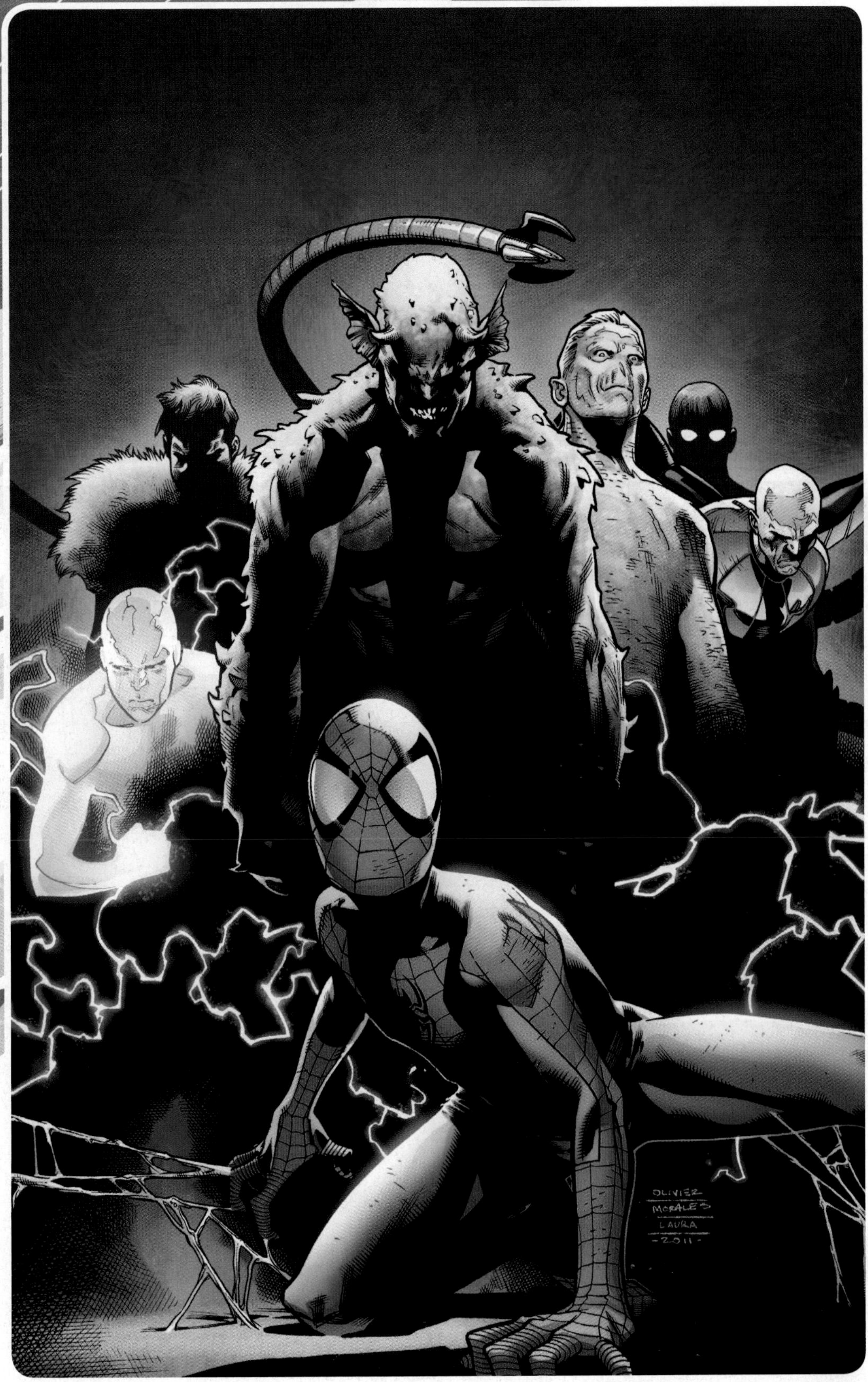
OLIVIER
MORALES
LAURA
-2011-

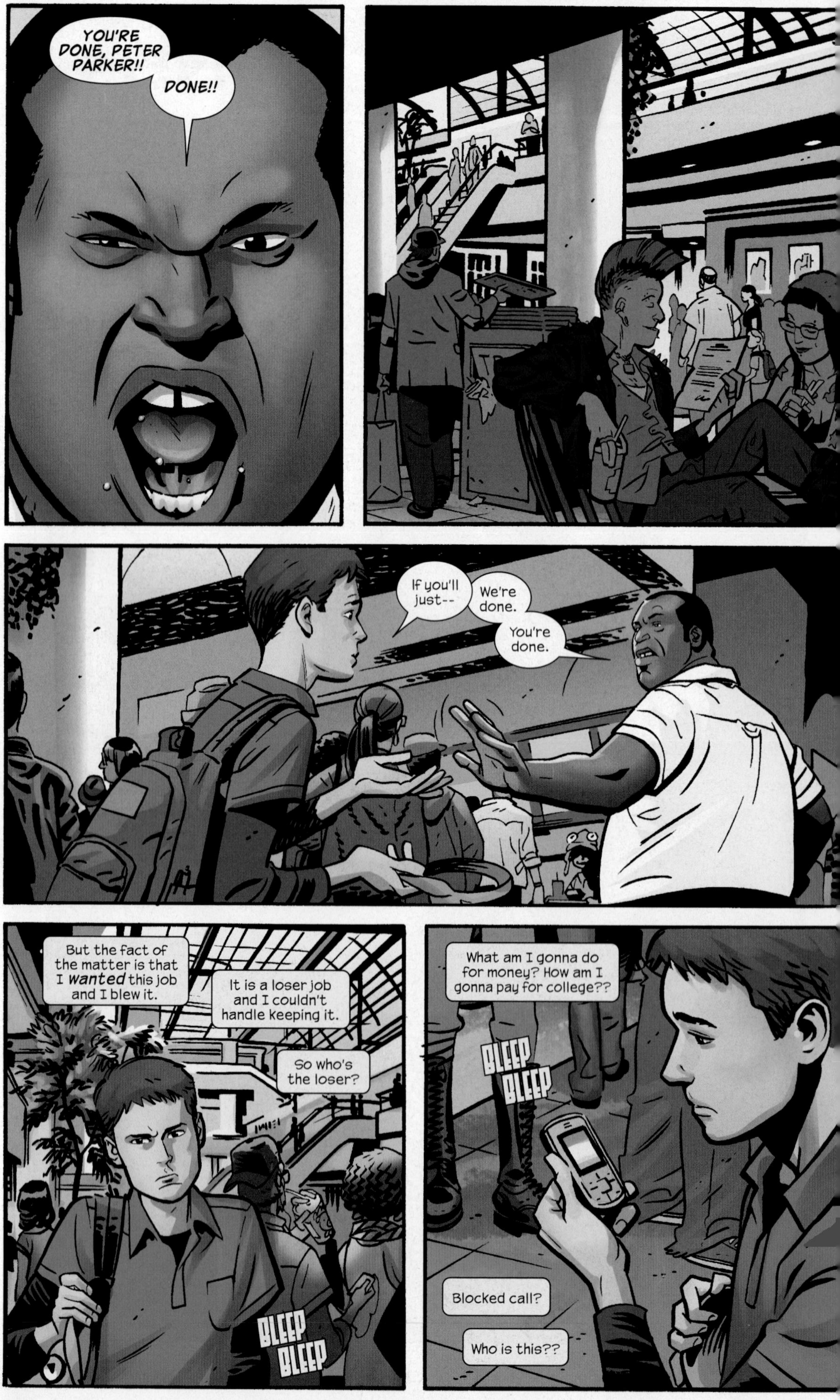
YOU'RE DONE, PETER PARKER!!
DONE!!
If you'll just--
We're done.
You're done.
But the fact of the matter is that I *wanted* this job and I blew it.
It is a loser job and I couldn't handle keeping it.
So who's the loser?
BLEEP BLEEP
What am I gonna do for money? How am I gonna pay for college??
BLEEP BLEEP
Blocked call?
Who is this??

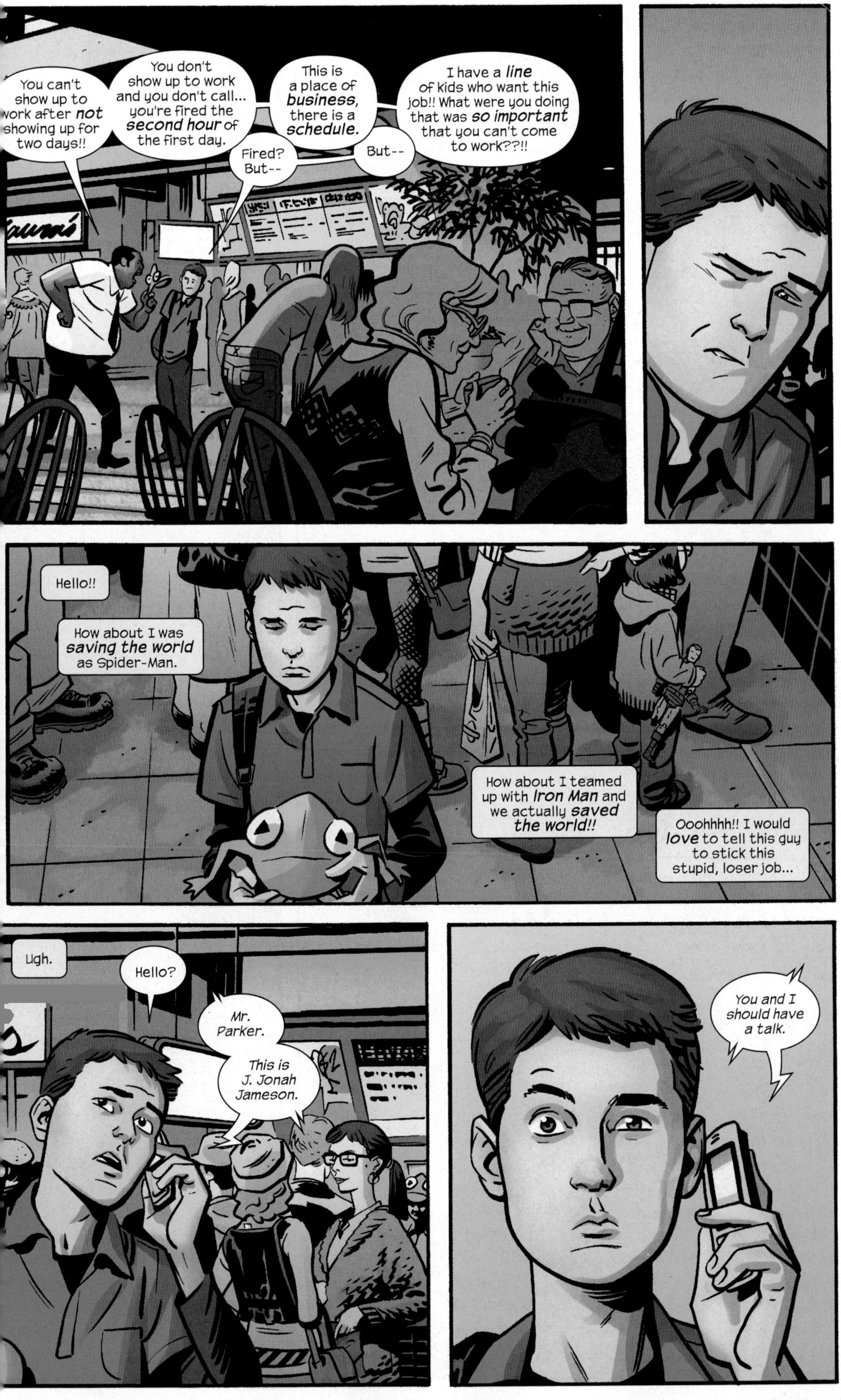
You can't show up to work after *not* showing up for two days!!
You don't show up to work and you don't call... you're fired the *second hour* of the first day.
Fired? But--
This is a place of *business*, there is a *schedule.*
But--
I have a *line* of kids who want this job!! What were you doing that was *so important* that you can't come to work??!!
Hello!!
How about I was *saving the world* as Spider-Man.
How about I teamed up with *Iron Man* and we actually *saved the world!!*
Ooohhhh!! I would *love* to tell this guy to stick this stupid, loser job...
Ugh.
Hello?
Mr. Parker.
This is J. Jonah Jameson.
You and I should have a talk.

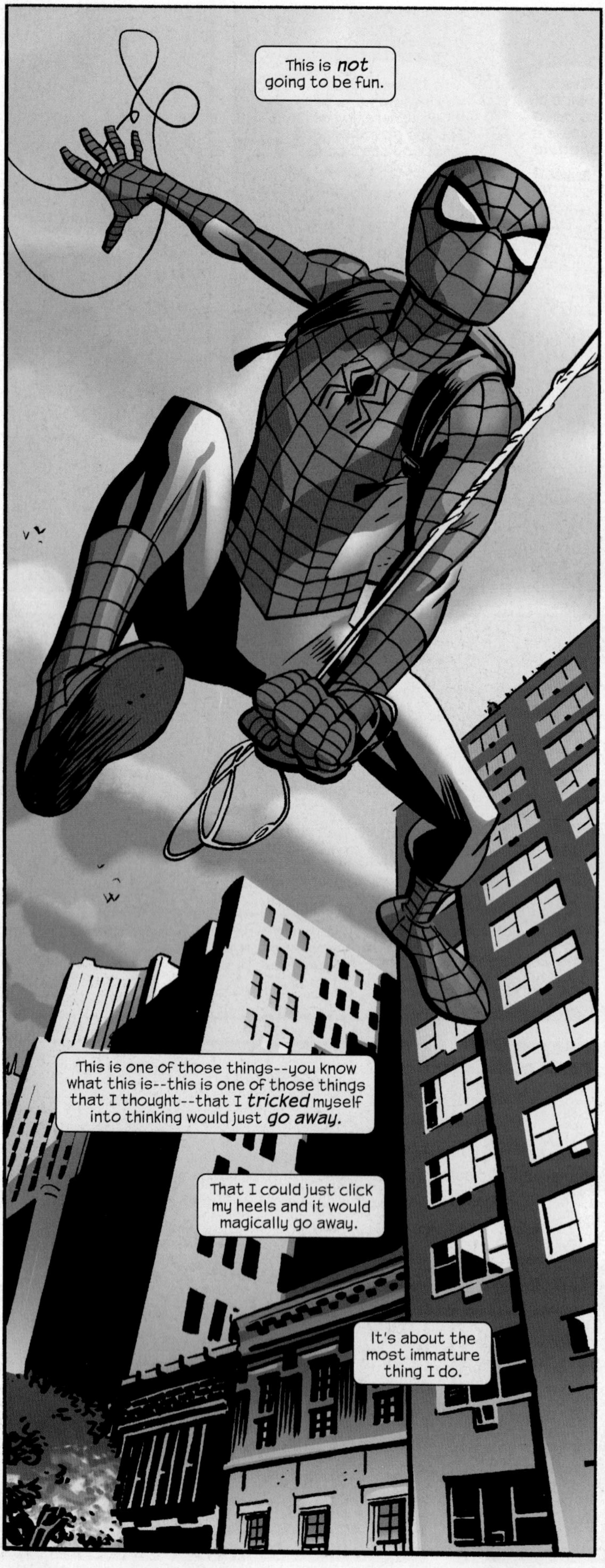
This is not going to be fun.
This is one of those things--you know what this is--this is one of those things that I thought--that I tricked myself into thinking would just go away.
That I could just click my heels and it would magically go away.
It's about the most immature thing I do.

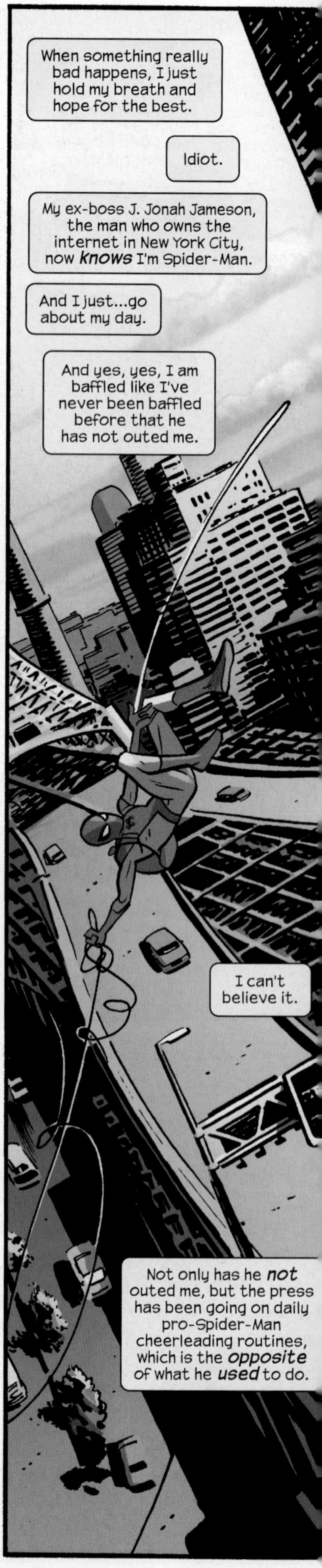
When something really bad happens, I just hold my breath and hope for the best.
Idiot.
My ex-boss J. Jonah Jameson, the man who owns the internet in New York City, now knows I'm Spider-Man.
And I just...go about my day.
And yes, yes, I am baffled like I've never been baffled before that he has not outed me.
I can't believe it.
Not only has he not outed me, but the press has been going on daily pro-Spider-Man cheerleading routines, which is the opposite of what he used to do.

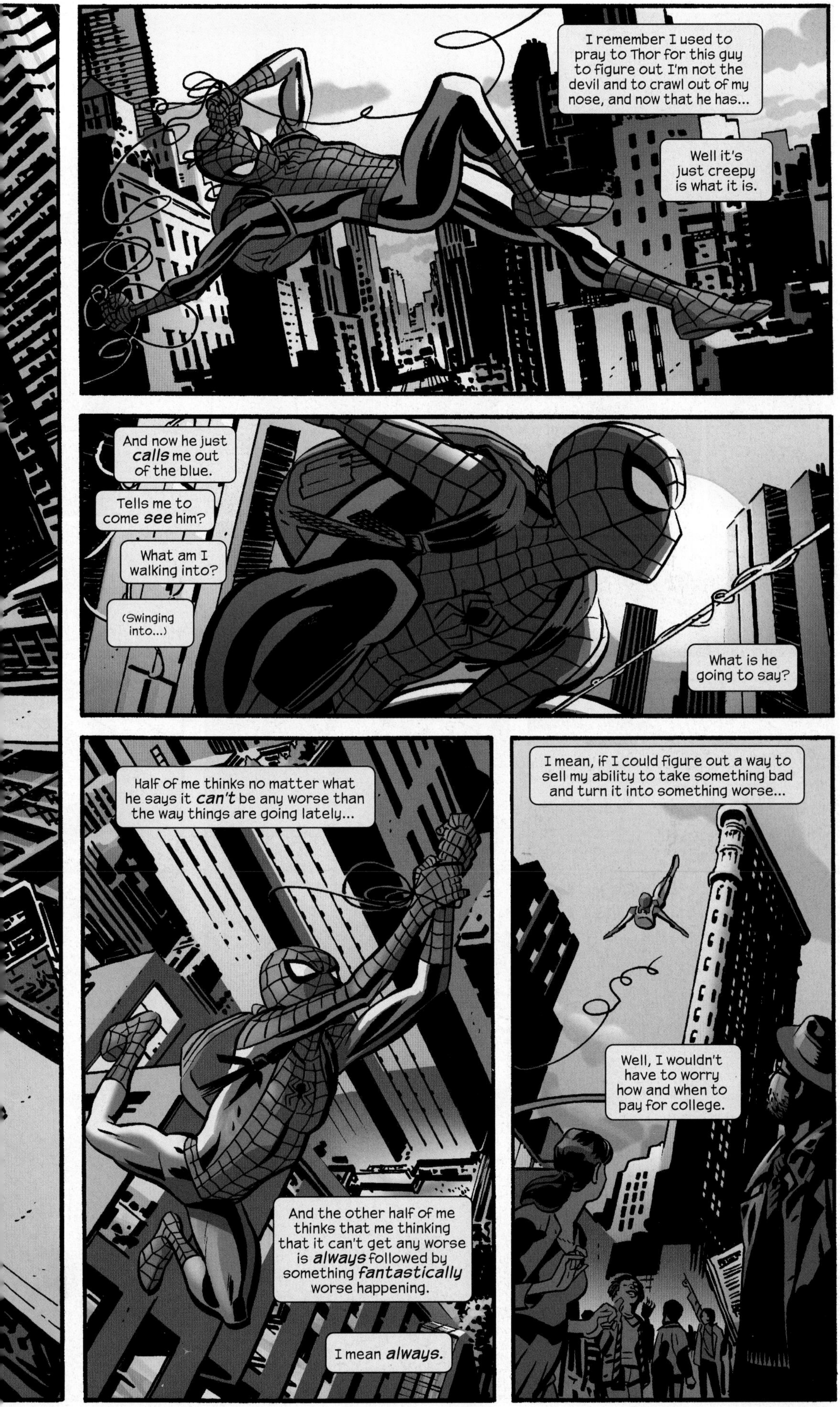
I remember I used to pray to Thor for this guy to figure out I'm not the devil and to crawl out of my nose, and now that he has...
Well it's just creepy is what it is.
And now he just *calls* me out of the blue.
Tells me to come *see* him?
What am I walking into?
(Swinging into...)
What is he going to say?
Half of me thinks no matter what he says it *can't* be any worse than the way things are going lately...
And the other half of me thinks that me thinking that it can't get any worse is *always* followed by something *fantastically* worse happening.
I mean *always*.
I mean, if I could figure out a way to sell my ability to take something bad and turn it into something worse...
Well, I wouldn't have to worry how and when to pay for college.

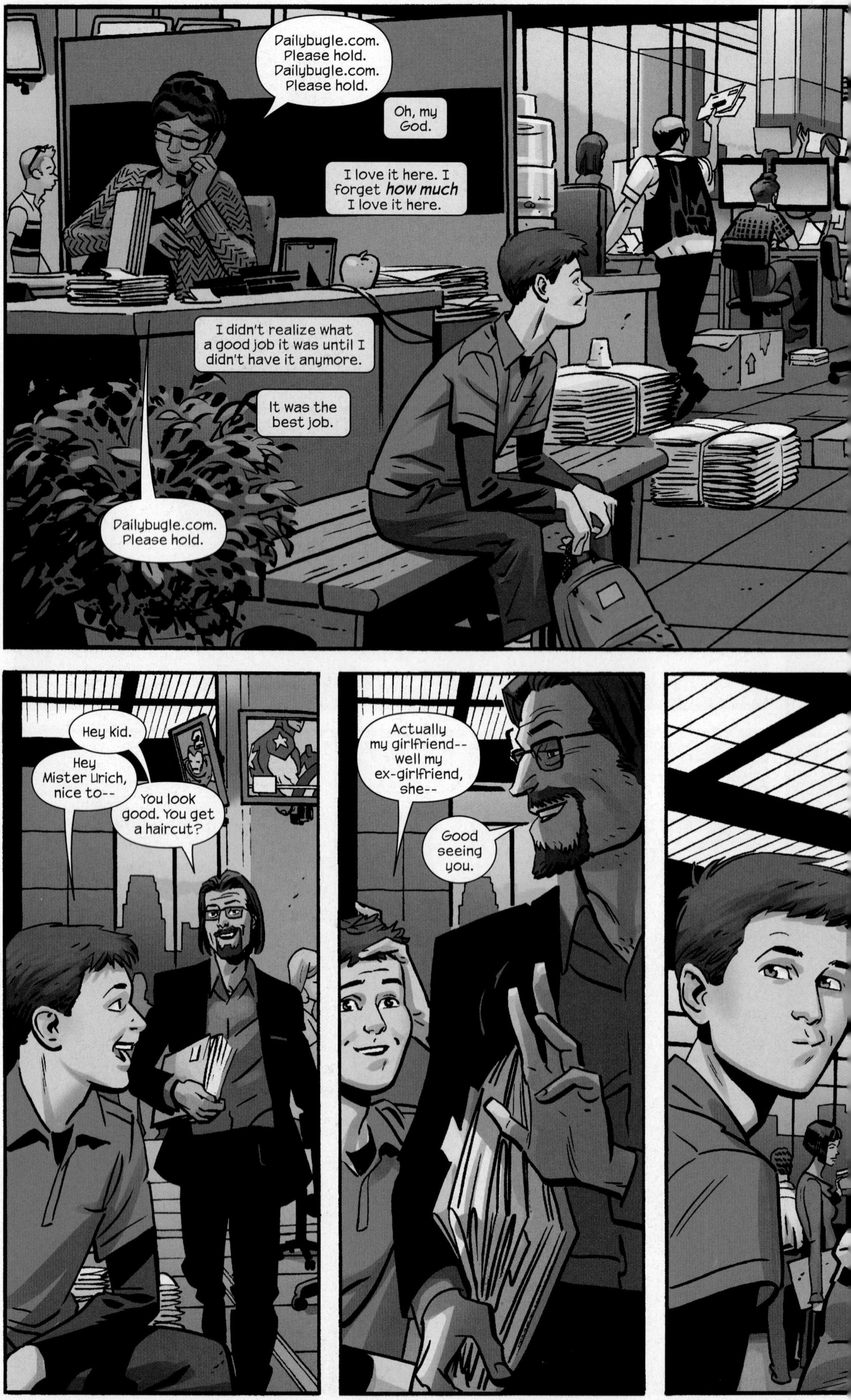
Dailybugle.com.
Please hold.
Dailybugle.com.
Please hold.
Oh, my God.
I love it here. I forget *how much* I love it here.
I didn't realize what a good job it was until I didn't have it anymore.
It was the best job.
Dailybugle.com.
Please hold.
Hey kid.
Hey Mister Urich, nice to--
You look good. You get a haircut?
Actually my girlfriend-- well my ex-girlfriend, she--
Good seeing you.

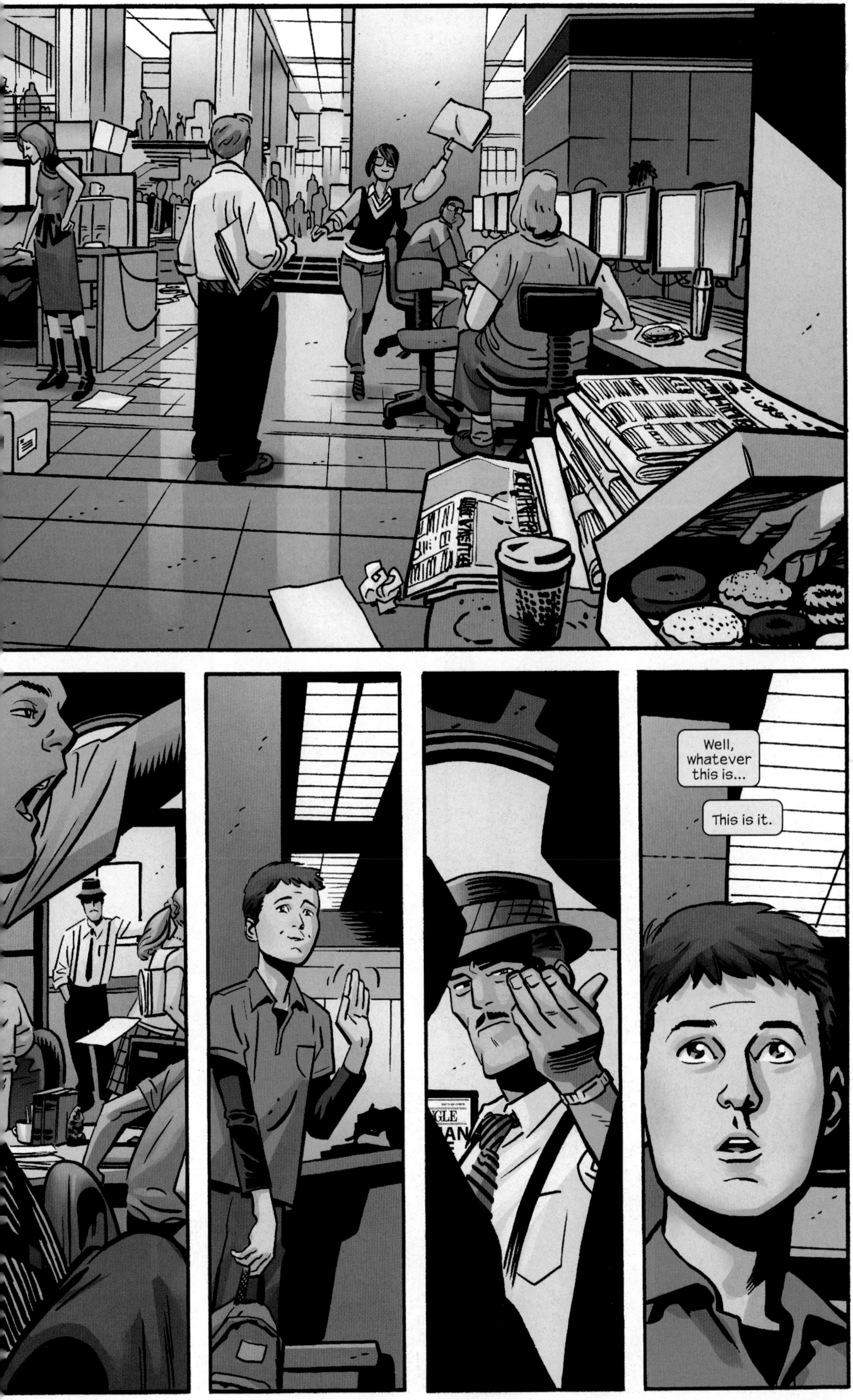
Well, whatever this is...
This is it.

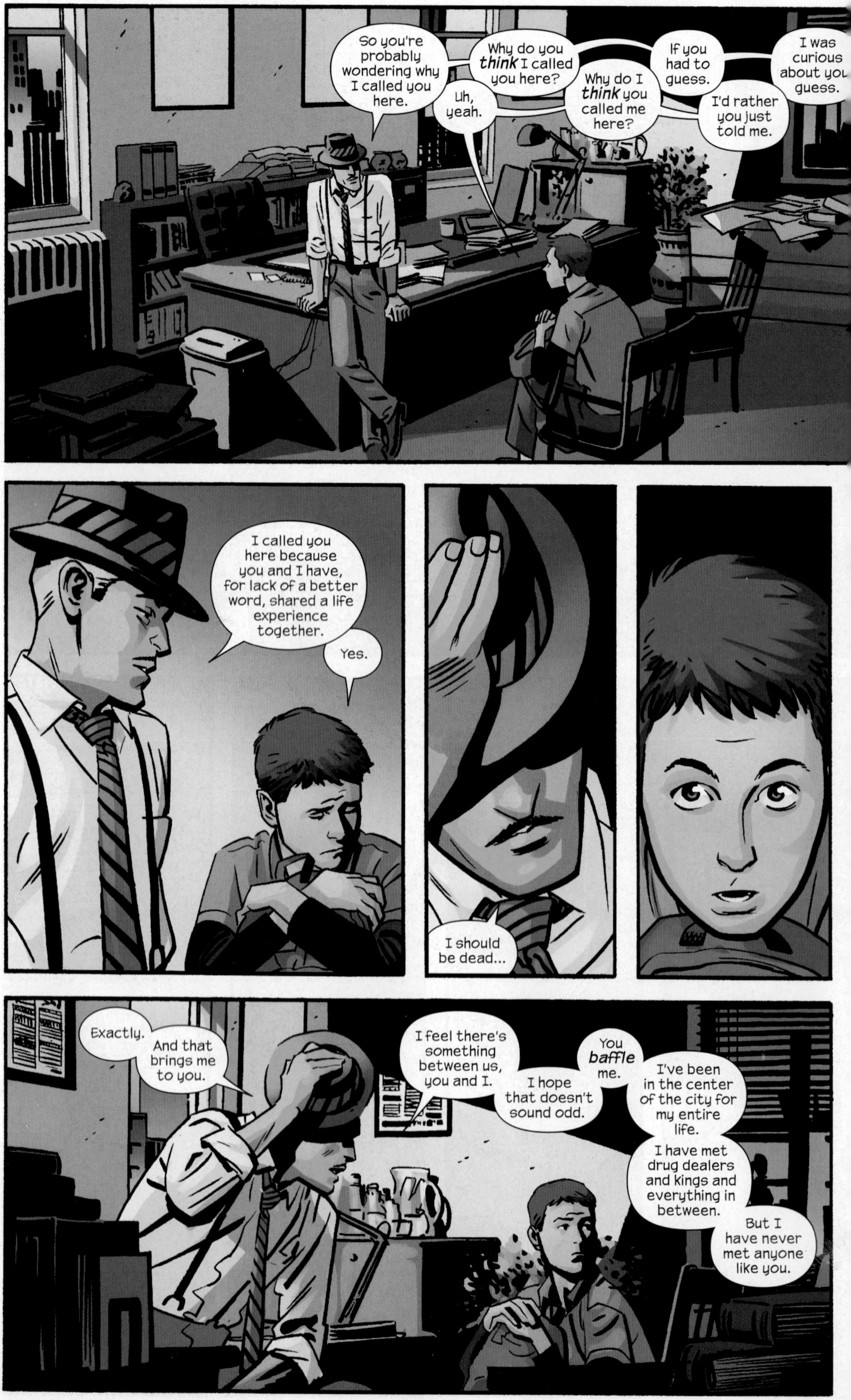
So you're probably wondering why I called you here.
Uh, yeah.
Why do you *think* I called you here?
Why do I *think* you called me here?
If you had to guess.
I'd rather you just told me.
I was curious about you guess.
I called you here because you and I have, for lack of a better word, shared a life experience together.
Yes.
I should be dead...
Exactly.
And that brings me to you.
I feel there's something between us, you and I.
I hope that doesn't sound odd.
You *baffle* me.
I've been in the center of the city for my entire life.
I have met drug dealers and kings and everything in between.
But I have never met anyone like you.

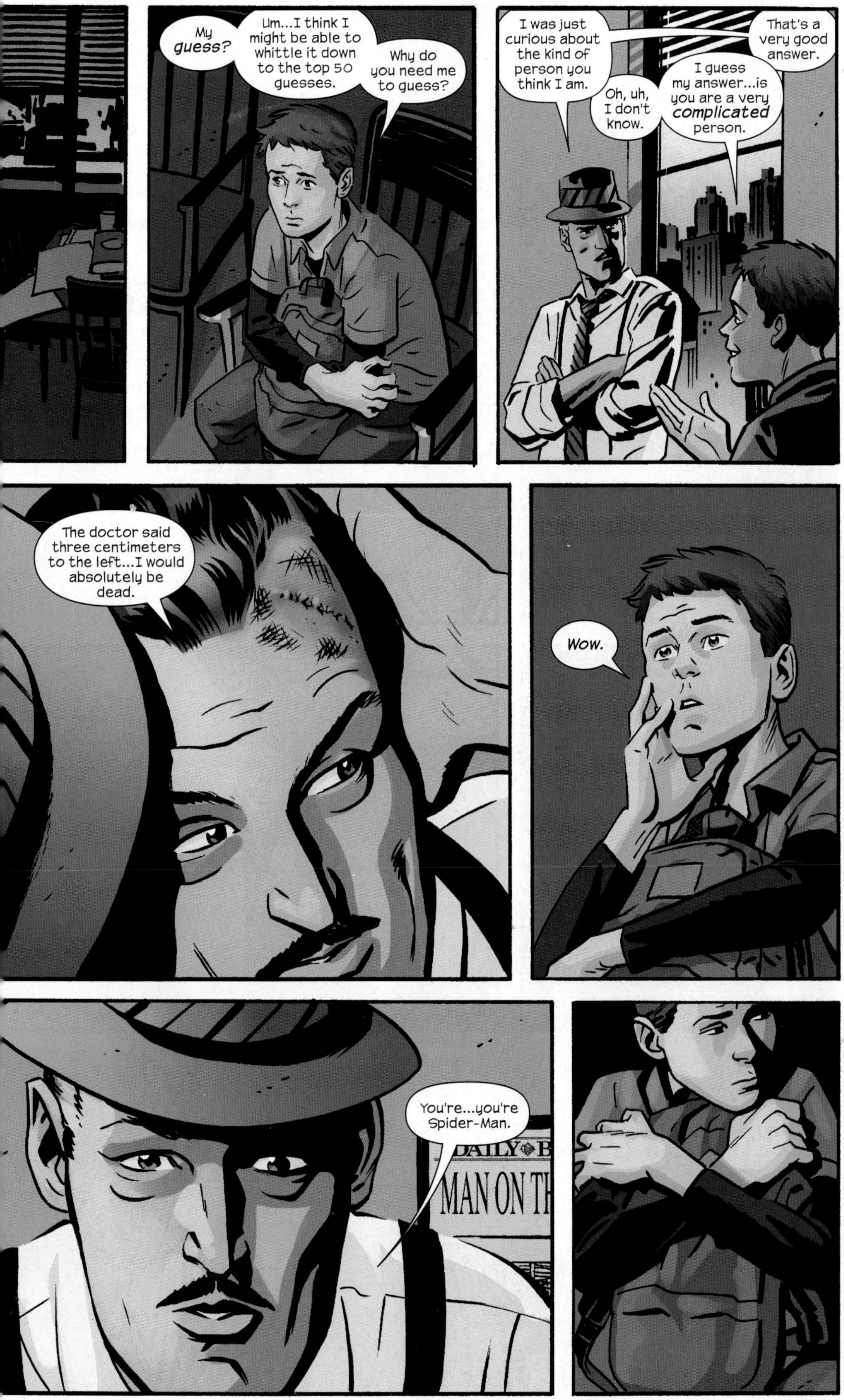
My *guess?*
Um...I think I might be able to whittle it down to the top 50 guesses.
Why do you need me to guess?
I was just curious about the kind of person you think I am.
Oh, uh, I don't know.
That's a very good answer.
I guess my answer...is you are a very *complicated* person.
The doctor said three centimeters to the left...I would absolutely be dead.
Wow.
You're...you're Spider-Man.
DAILY B
MAN ON TH

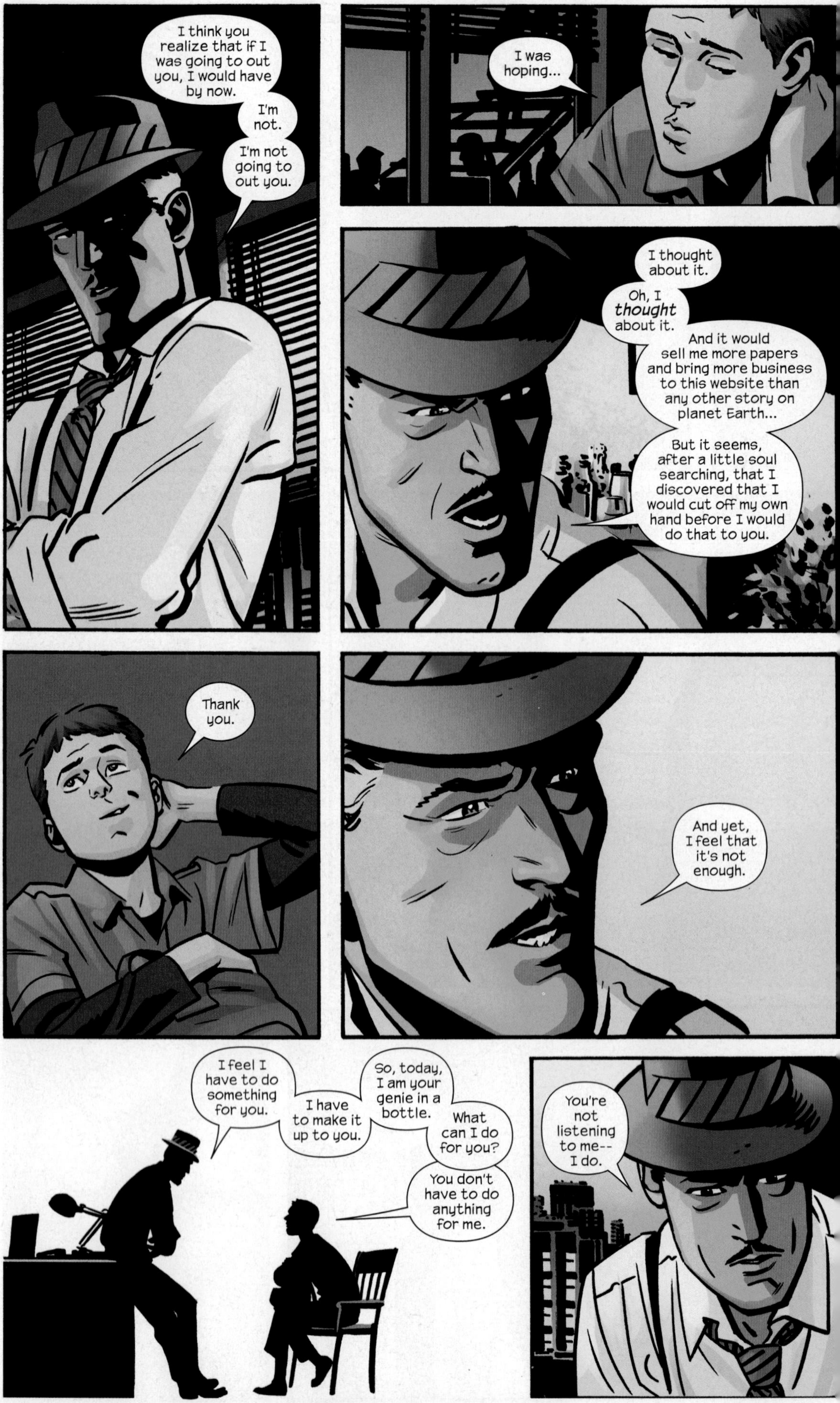

I think you realize that if I was going to out you, I would have by now.
I'm not.
I'm not going to out you.
I was hoping...
I thought about it.
Oh, I *thought* about it.
And it would sell me more papers and bring more business to this website than any other story on planet Earth...
But it seems, after a little soul searching, that I discovered that I would cut off my own hand before I would do that to you.
Thank you.
And yet, I feel that it's not enough.
I feel I have to do something for you.
I have to make it up to you.
So, today, I am your genie in a bottle.
What can I do for you?
You don't have to do anything for me.
You're not listening to me-- I do.

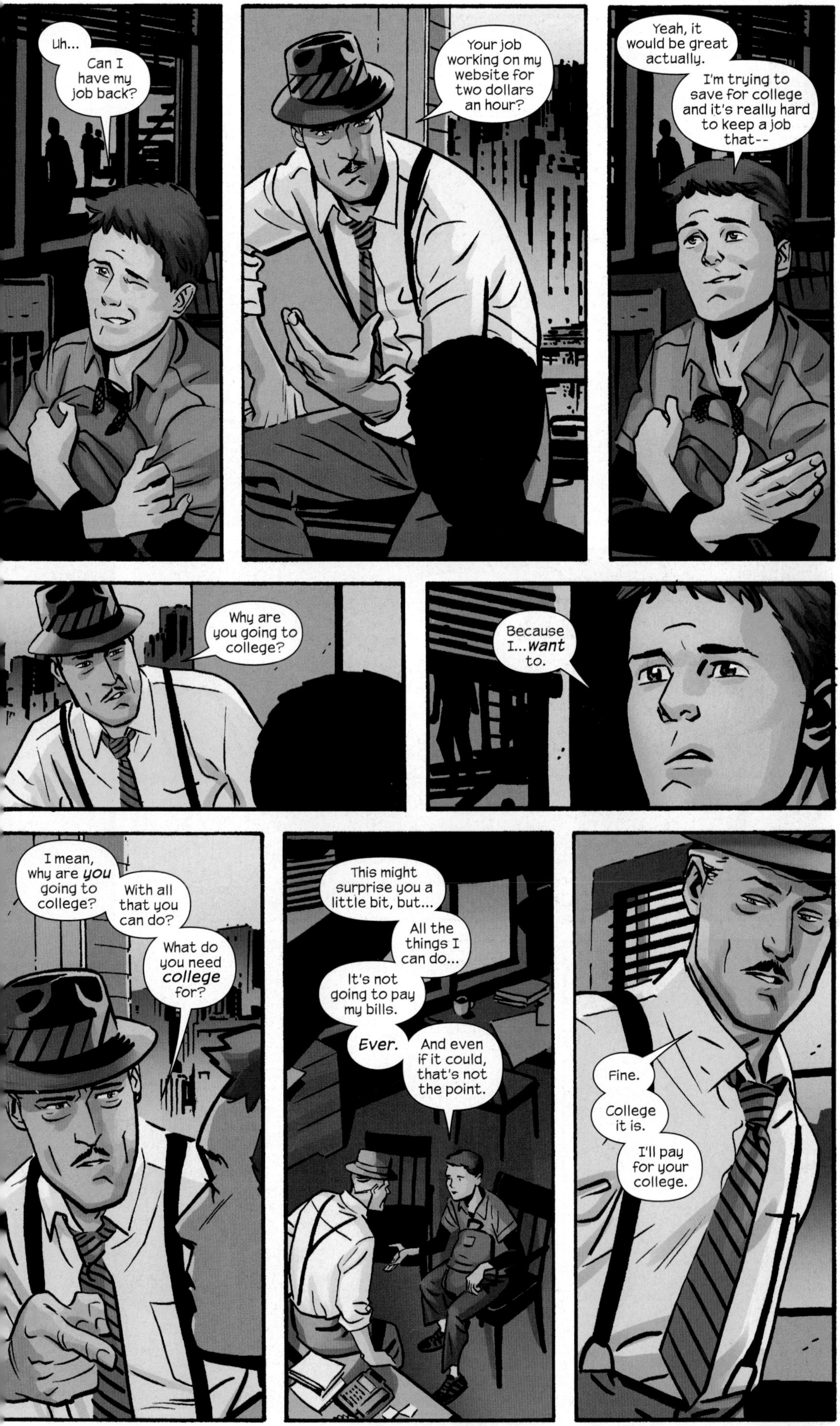

Uh...
Can I have my job back?
Your job working on my website for two dollars an hour?
Yeah, it would be great actually.
I'm trying to save for college and it's really hard to keep a job that--
Why are you going to college?
Because I...*want* to.
I mean, why are *you* going to college?
With all that you can do?
What do you need *college* for?
This might surprise you a little bit, but...
All the things I can do...
It's not going to pay my bills.
Ever.
And even if it could, that's not the point.
Fine.
College it is.
I'll pay for your college.

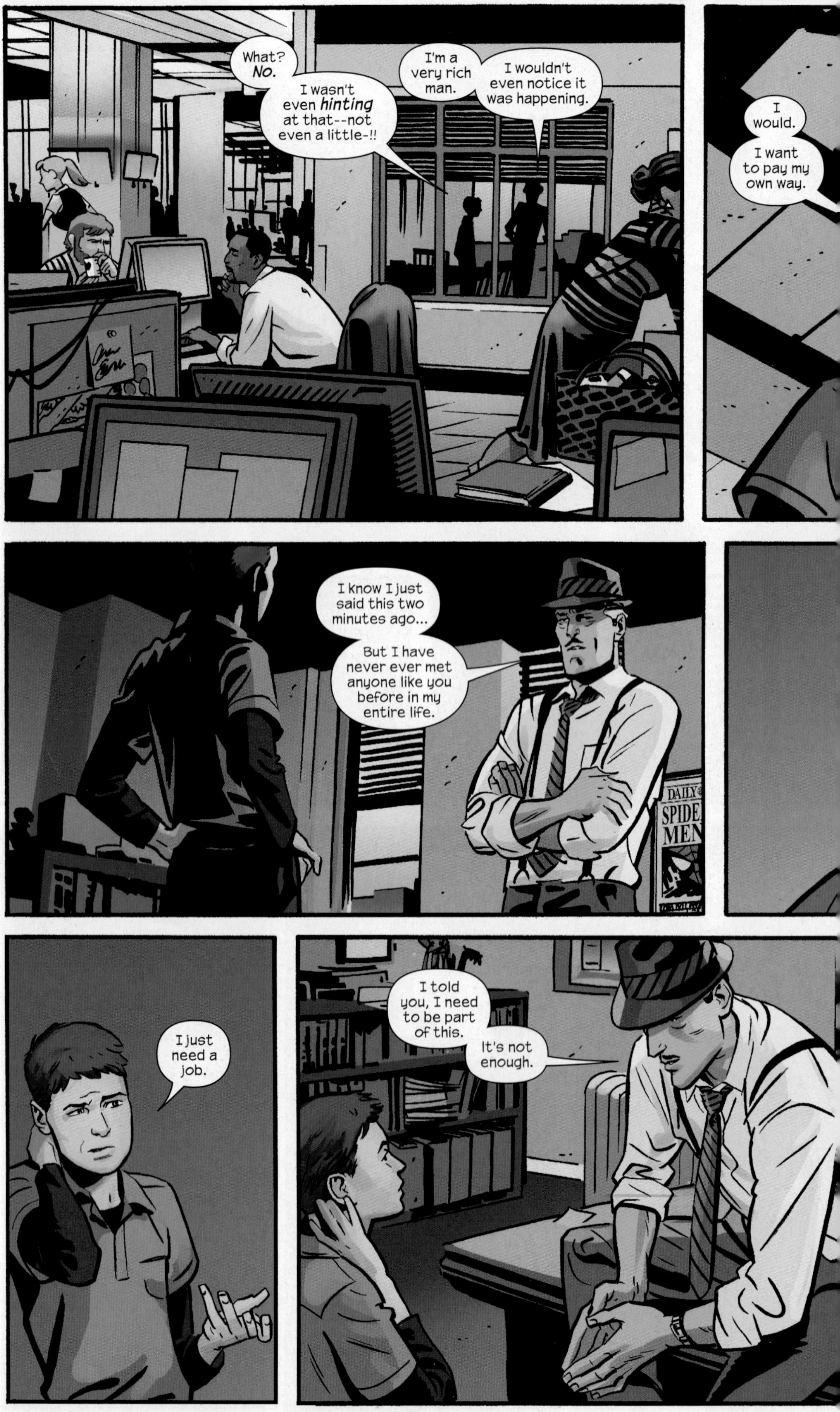
What? No.
I wasn't even hinting at that--not even a little-!!
I'm a very rich man.
I wouldn't even notice it was happening.
I would.
I want to pay my own way.
I know I just said this two minutes ago...
But I have never ever met anyone like you before in my entire life.
DAILY
SPIDER-MEN
I just need a job.
I told you, I need to be part of this.
It's not enough.

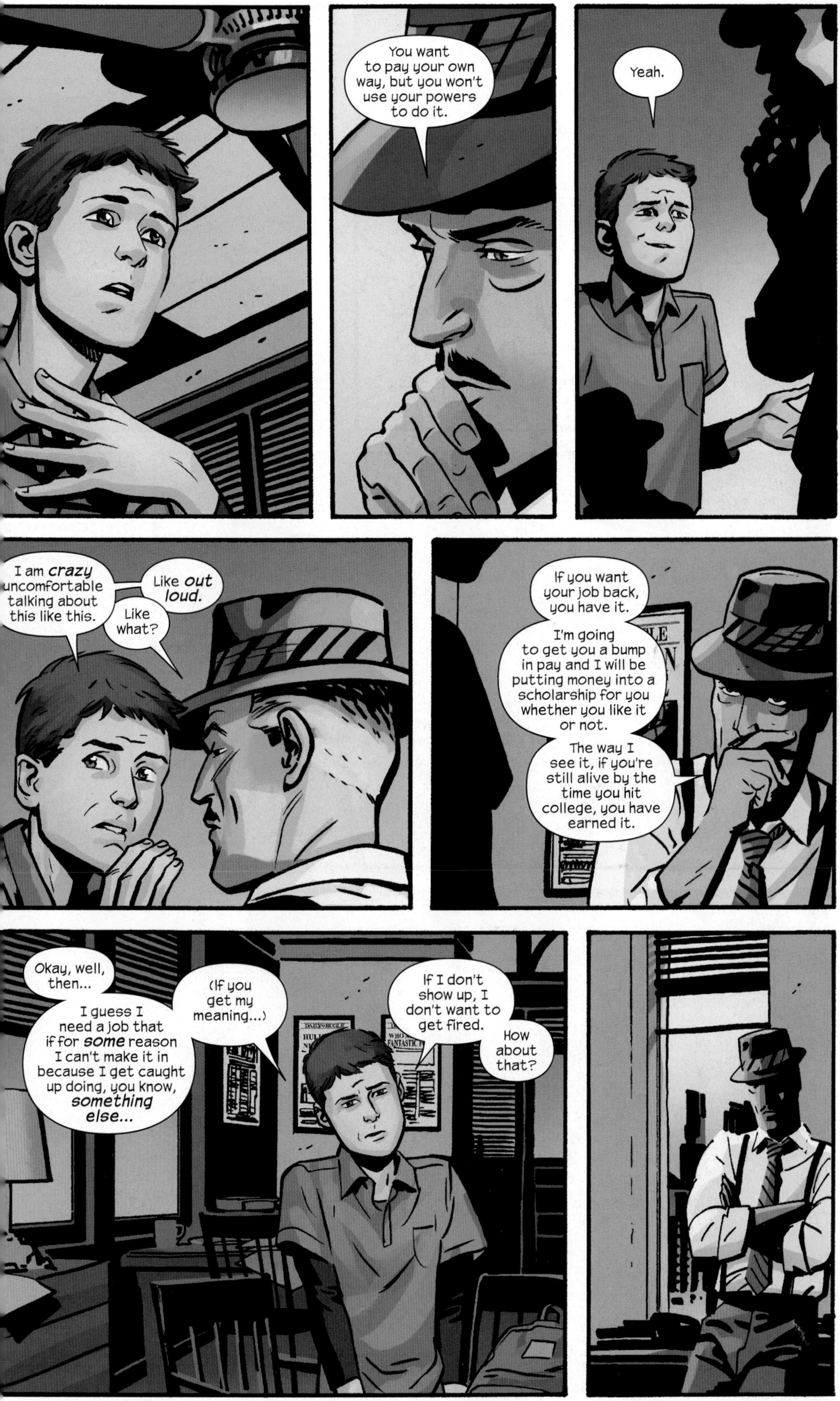
You want to pay your own way, but you won't use your powers to do it.
Yeah.
I am crazy uncomfortable talking about this like this.
Like what?
Like out loud.
If you want your job back, you have it.
I'm going to get you a bump in pay and I will be putting money into a scholarship for you whether you like it or not.
The way I see it, if you're still alive by the time you hit college, you have earned it.
Okay, well, then...
I guess I need a job that if for some reason I can't make it in because I get caught up doing, you know, something else...
(If you get my meaning...)
If I don't show up, I don't want to get fired.
How about that?

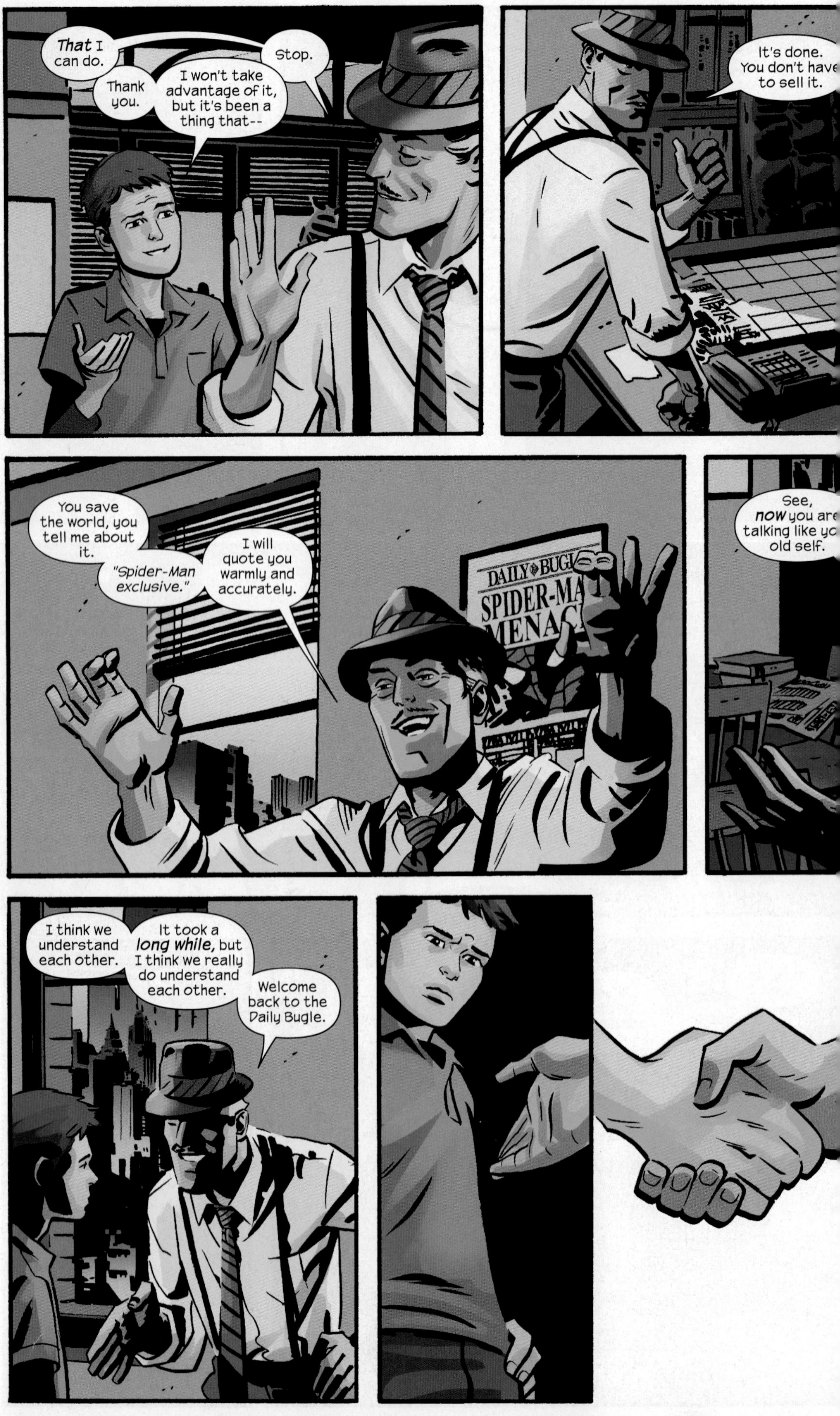
That I can do.
Thank you.
I won't take advantage of it, but it's been a thing that--
Stop.
It's done. You don't have to sell it.
You save the world, you tell me about it.
"Spider-Man exclusive."
I will quote you warmly and accurately.
DAILY BUGLE
SPIDER-MAN MENACE
See, NOW you are talking like your old self.
I think we understand each other.
It took a long while, but I think we really do understand each other.
Welcome back to the Daily Bugle.

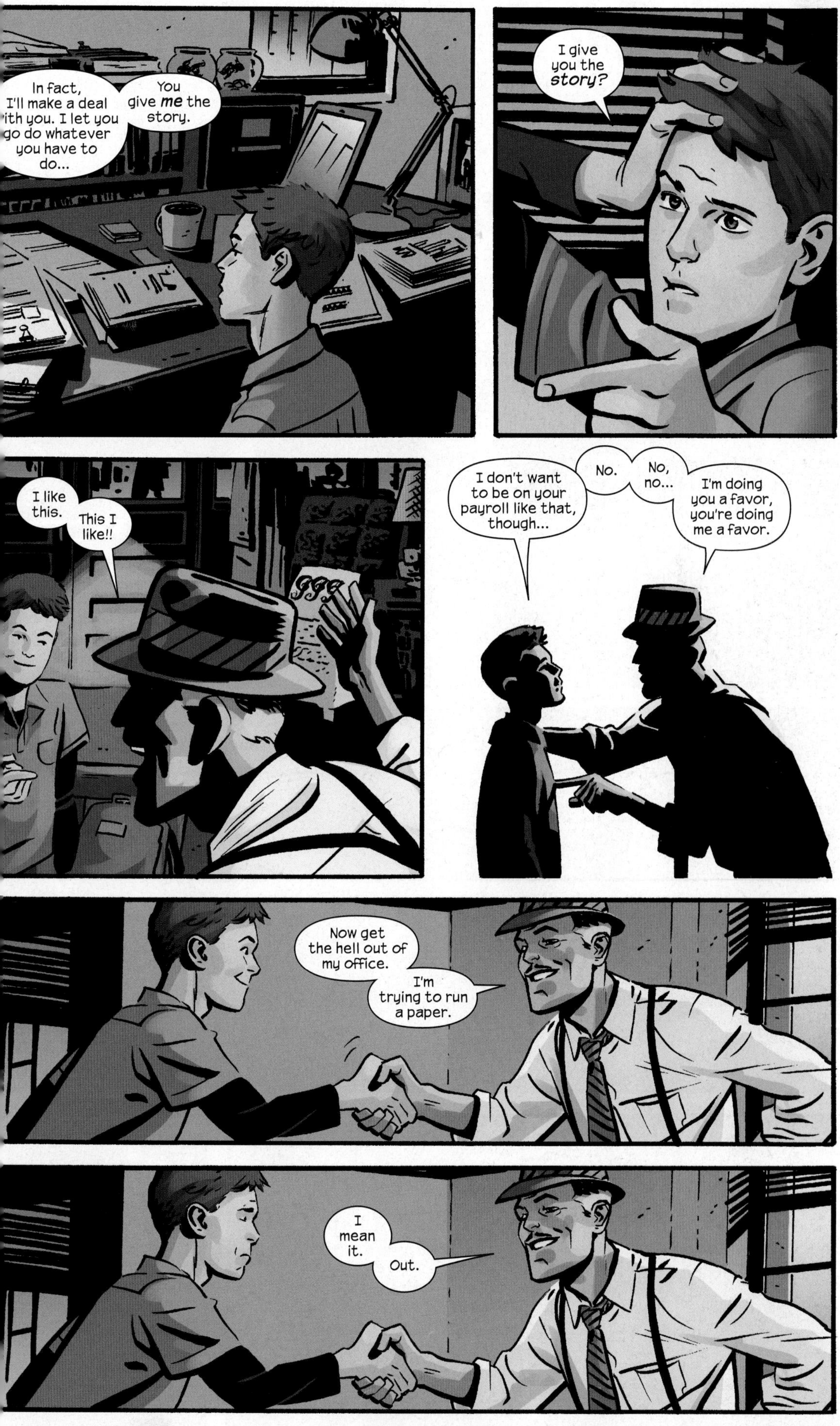
In fact, I'll make a deal ith you. I let you go do whatever you have to do...
You give *me* the story.
I give you the *story?*
I like this.
This I like!!
I don't want to be on your payroll like that, though...
No.
No, no...
I'm doing you a favor, you're doing me a favor.
Now get the hell out of my office.
I'm trying to run a paper.
I mean it.
Out.

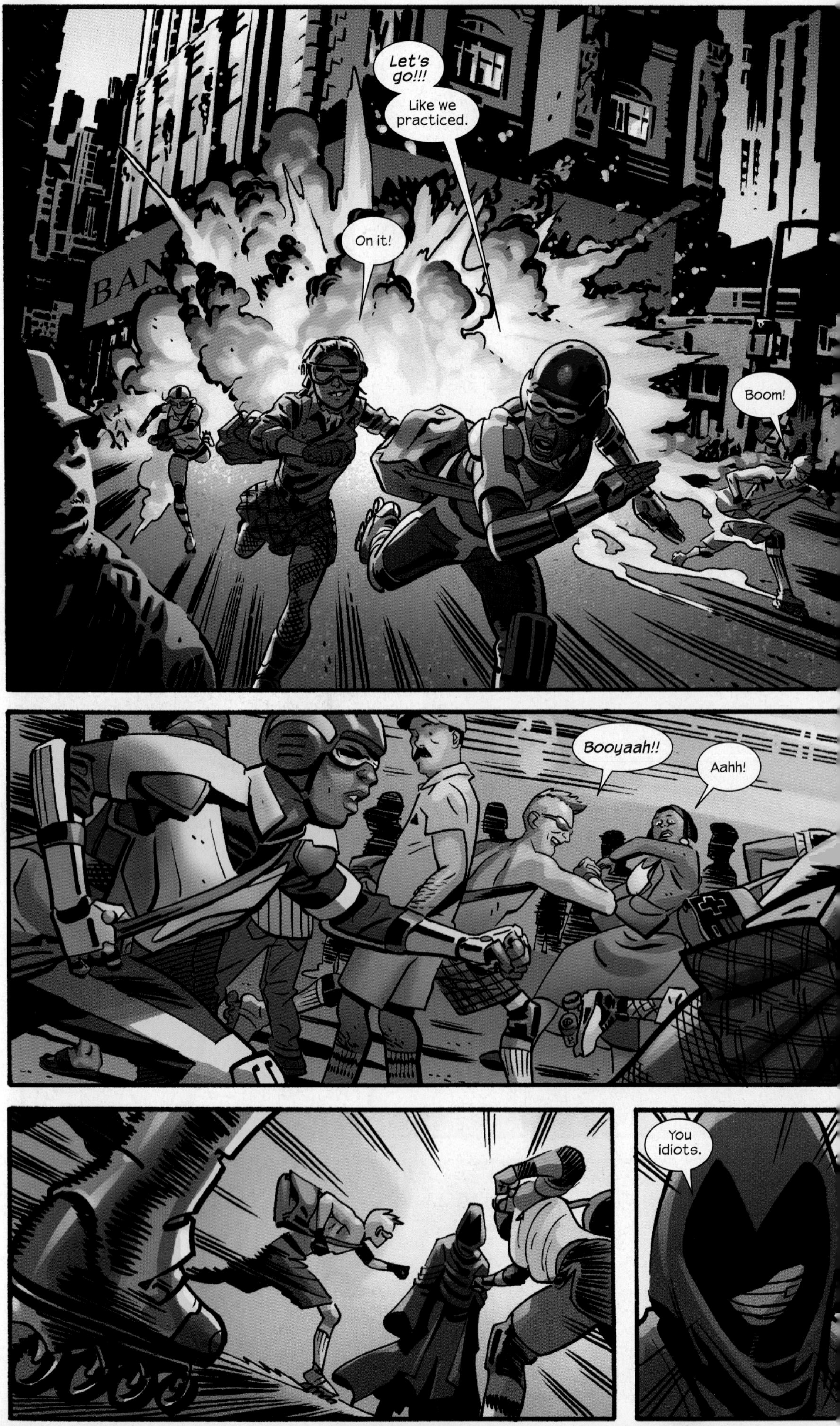
Let's go!!!
Like we practiced.
On it!
BAN
Boom!
Booyaah!!
Aahh!
You idiots.

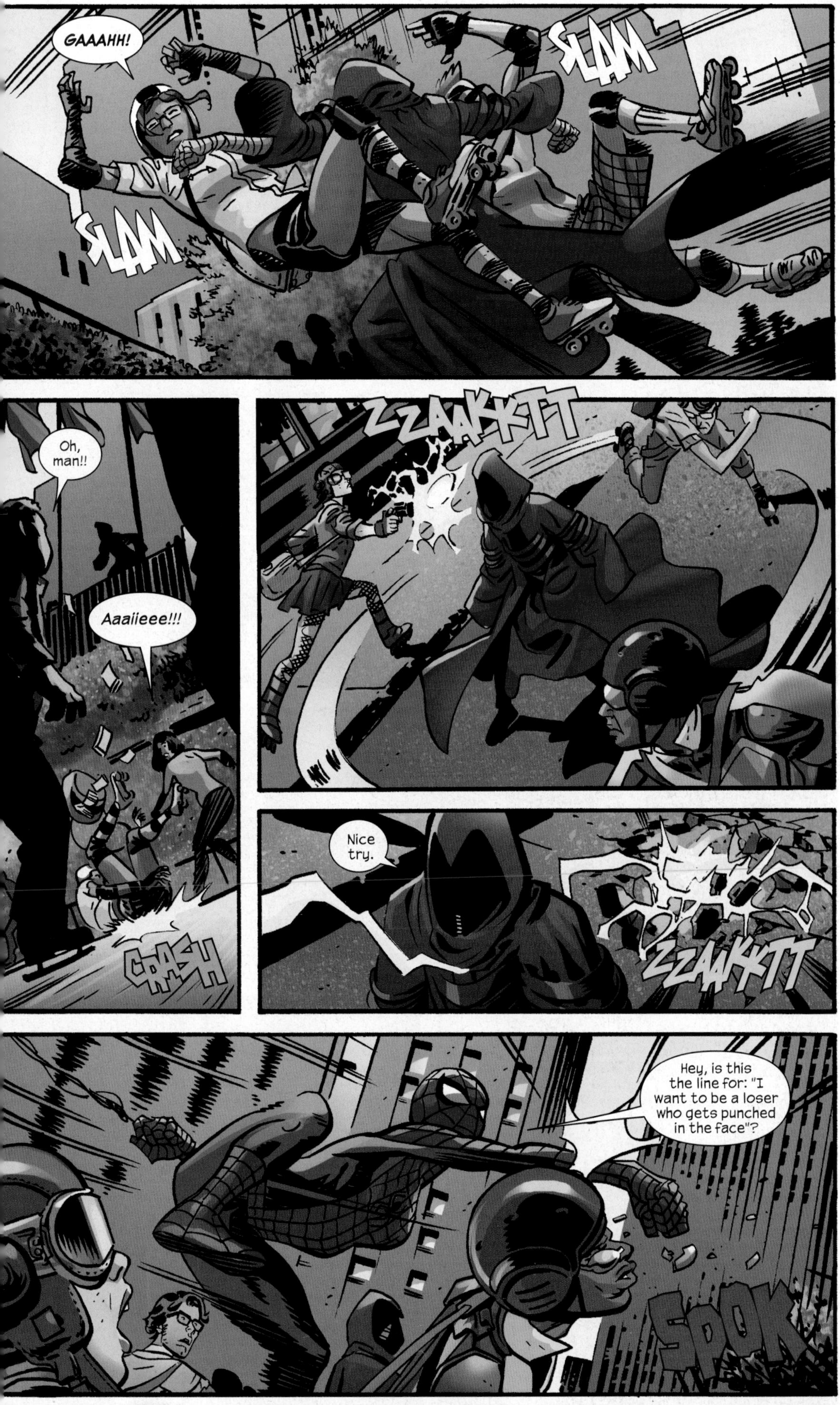
GAAAHH!
SLAM
SLAM
Oh, man!!
Aaaiieee!!!
CRASH
ZZAAKKTT
Nice try.
ZZAAKKTT
Hey, is this the line for: "I want to be a loser who gets punched in the face"?
SPOK

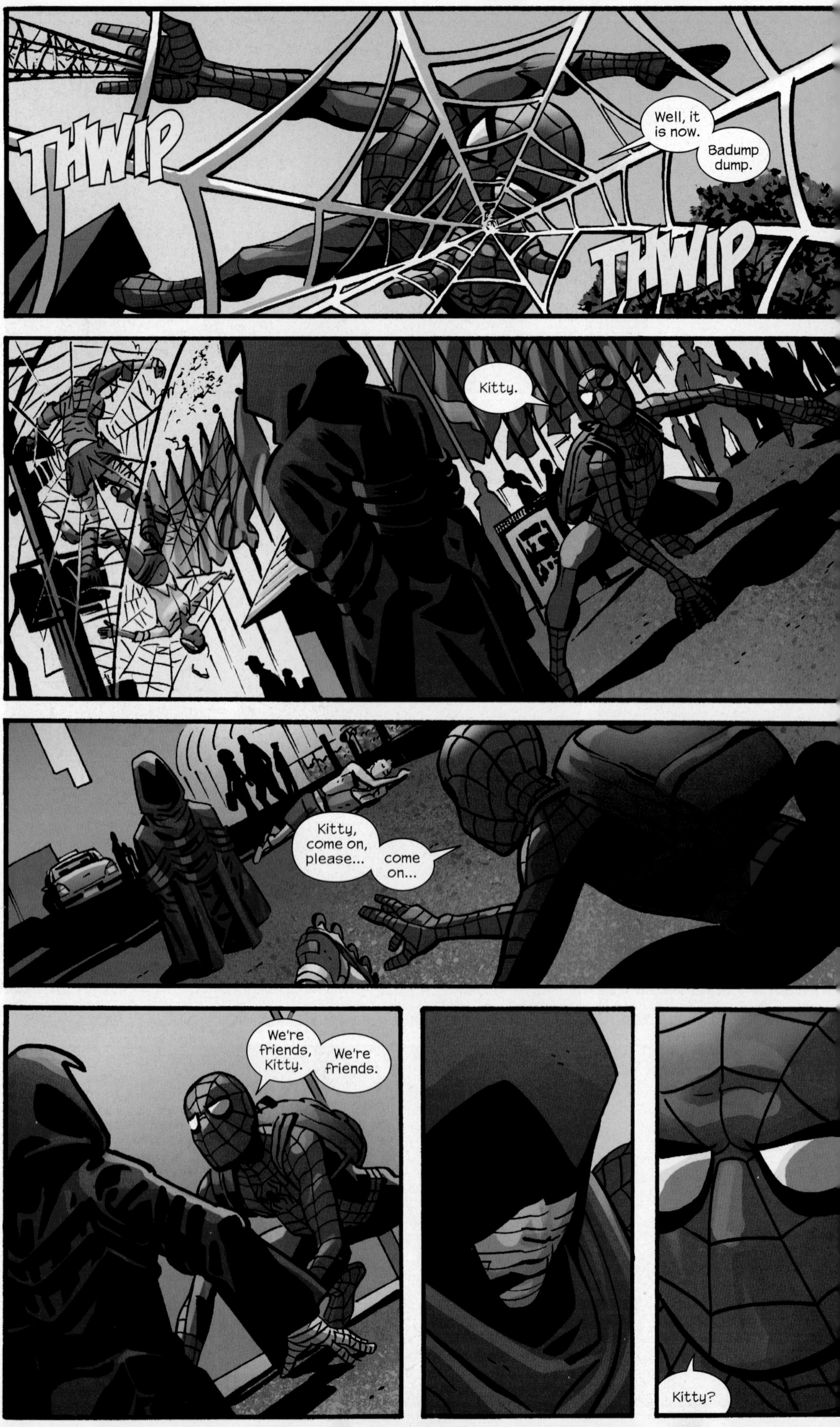
THWIP
Well, it is now.
Badump dump.
THWIP
Kitty.
Kitty, come on, please...
come on...
We're friends, Kitty.
We're friends.
Kitty?

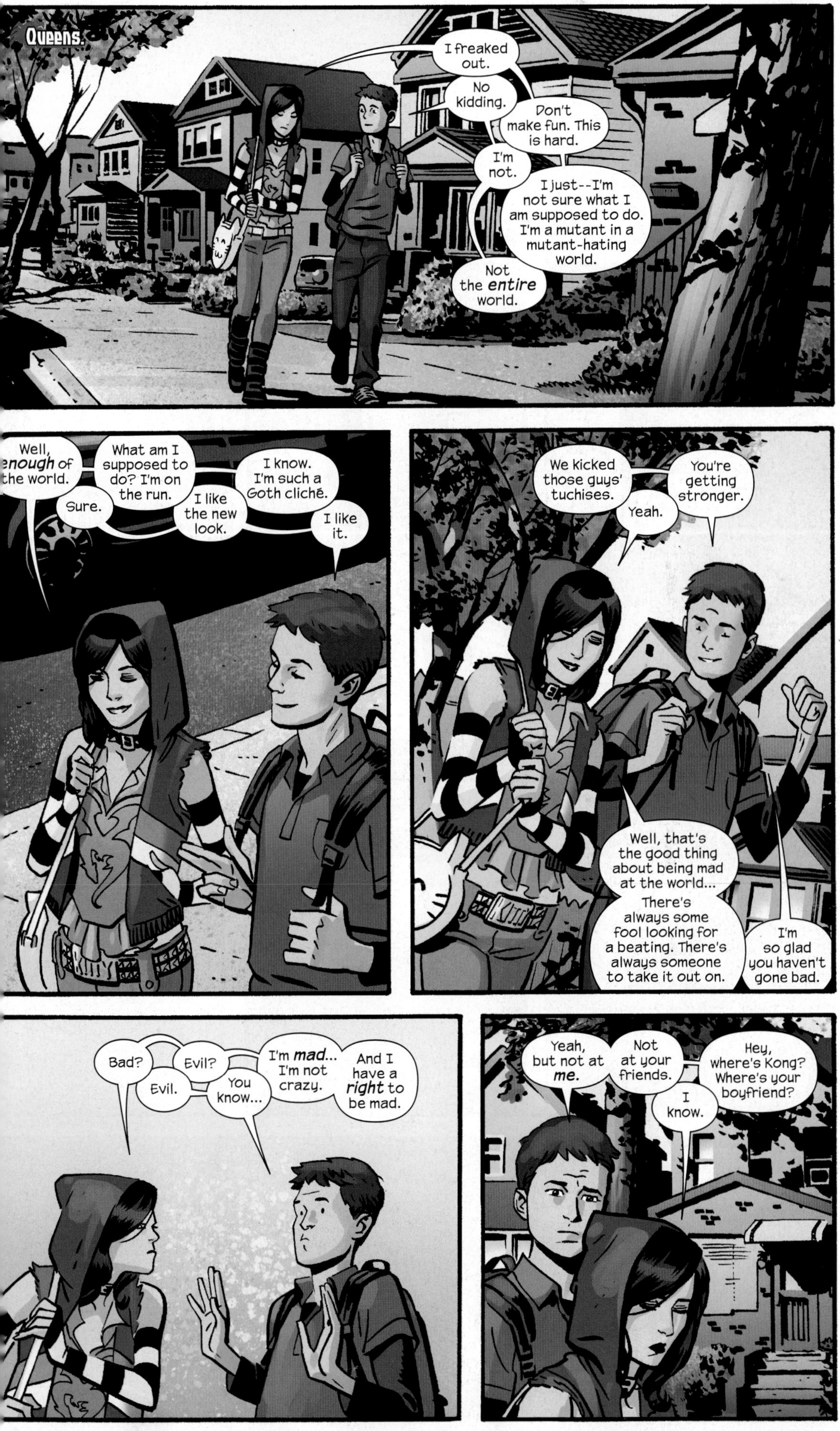
Queens.
I freaked out.
No kidding.
Don't make fun. This is hard.
I'm not.
I just--I'm not sure what I am supposed to do. I'm a mutant in a mutant-hating world.
Not the *entire* world.
Well, *enough* of the world.
Sure.
What am I supposed to do? I'm on the run.
I like the new look.
I know. I'm such a Goth cliché.
I like it.
We kicked those guys' tuchises.
Yeah.
You're getting stronger.
Well, that's the good thing about being mad at the world...
There's always some fool looking for a beating. There's always someone to take it out on.
I'm so glad you haven't gone bad.
Bad?
Evil?
Evil.
You know...
I'm *mad*... I'm not crazy.
And I have a *right* to be mad.
Yeah, but not at *me*.
Not at your friends.
I know.
Hey, where's Kong? Where's your boyfriend?

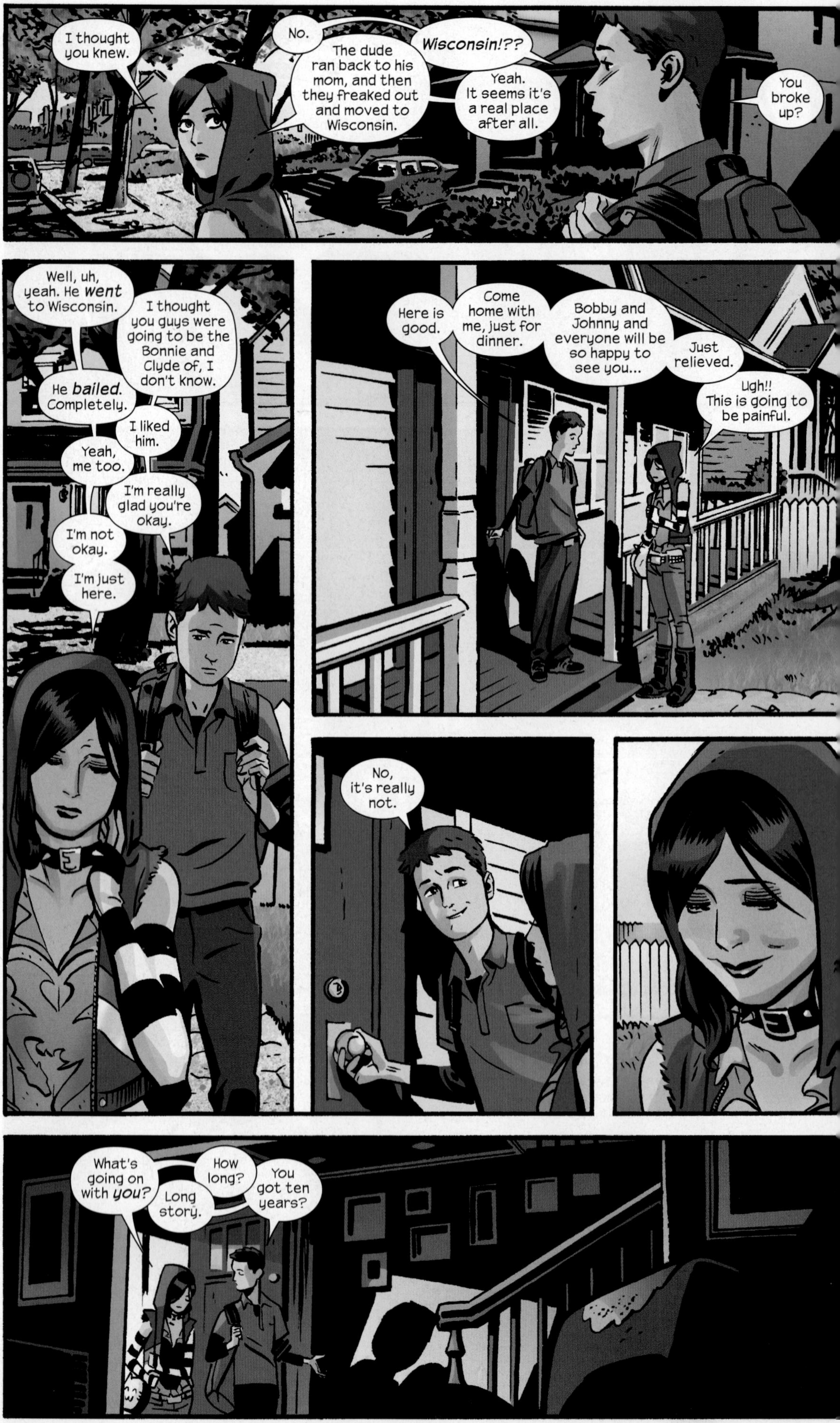
I thought you knew.
No.
Wisconsin!??
The dude ran back to his mom, and then they freaked out and moved to Wisconsin.
Yeah. It seems it's a real place after all.
You broke up?
Well, uh, yeah. He *went* to Wisconsin.
I thought you guys were going to be the Bonnie and Clyde of, I don't know.
He *bailed*. Completely.
I liked him.
Yeah, me too.
I'm really glad you're okay.
I'm not okay.
I'm just here.
Here is good.
Come home with me, just for dinner.
Bobby and Johnny and everyone will be so happy to see you...
Just relieved.
Ugh!! This is going to be painful.
No, it's really not.
What's going on with *you?*
Long story.
How long?
You got ten years?

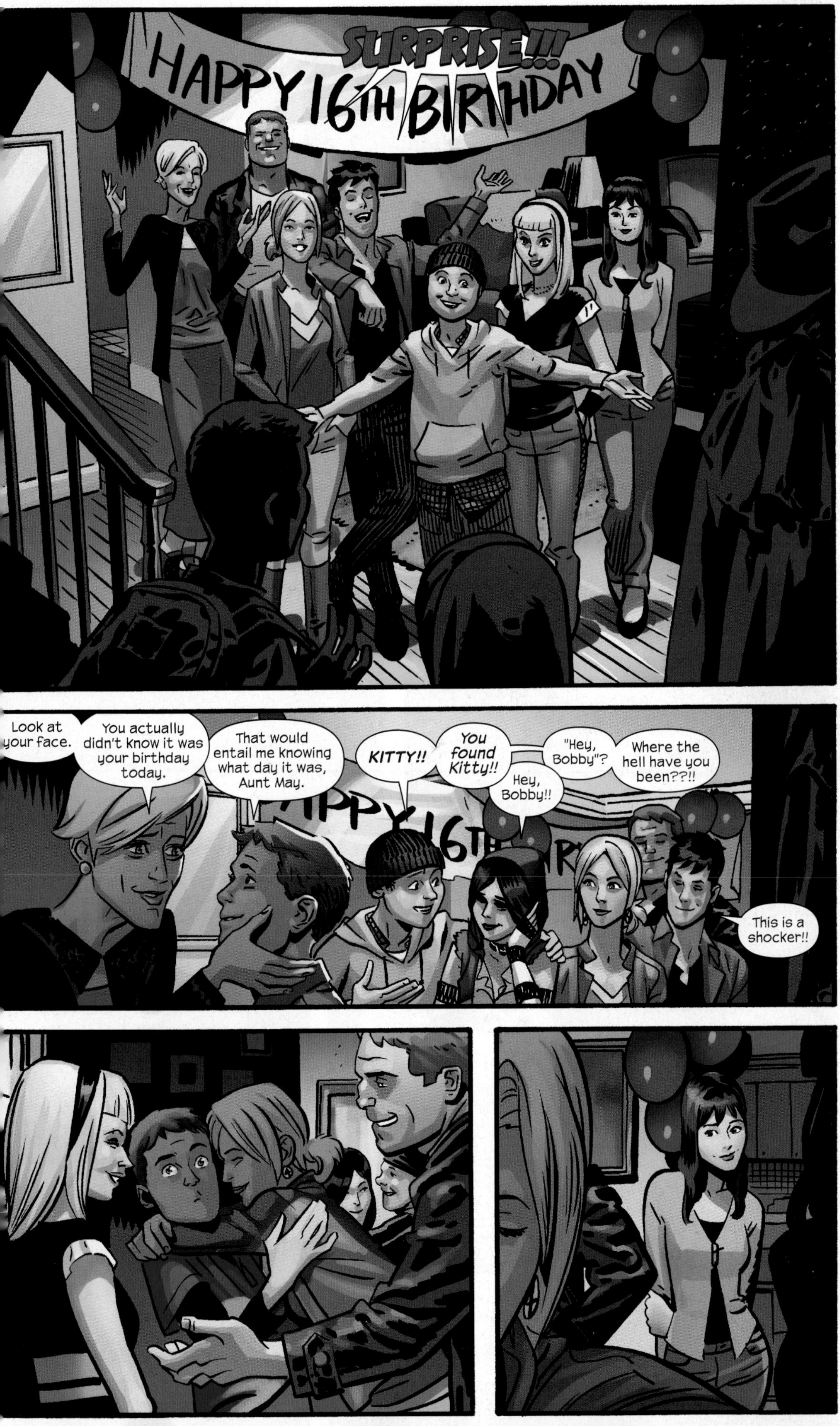
SURPRISE!!!
HAPPY 16TH BIRTHDAY
Look at your face.
You actually didn't know it was your birthday today.
That would entail me knowing what day it was, Aunt May.
KITTY!!
You found Kitty!!
Hey, Bobby!!
"Hey, Bobby"?
Where the hell have you been??!!
This is a shocker!!

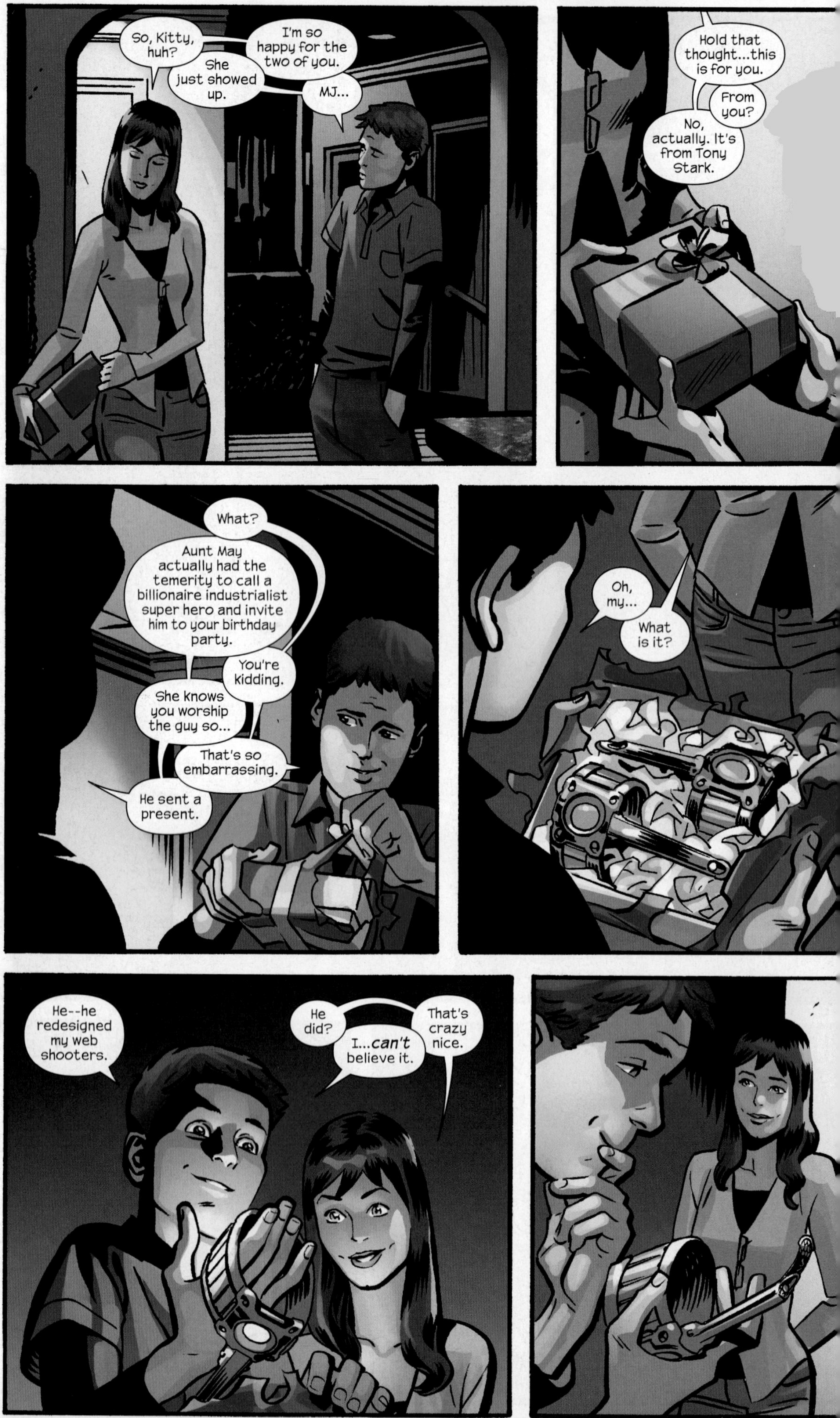
So, Kitty, huh?
I'm so happy for the two of you.
She just showed up.
MJ...
Hold that thought...this is for you.
From you?
No, actually. It's from Tony Stark.
What?
Aunt May actually had the temerity to call a billionaire industrialist super hero and invite him to your birthday party.
You're kidding.
She knows you worship the guy so...
That's so embarrassing.
He sent a present.
Oh, my...
What is it?
He--he redesigned my web shooters.
He did?
I...*can't* believe it.
That's crazy nice.

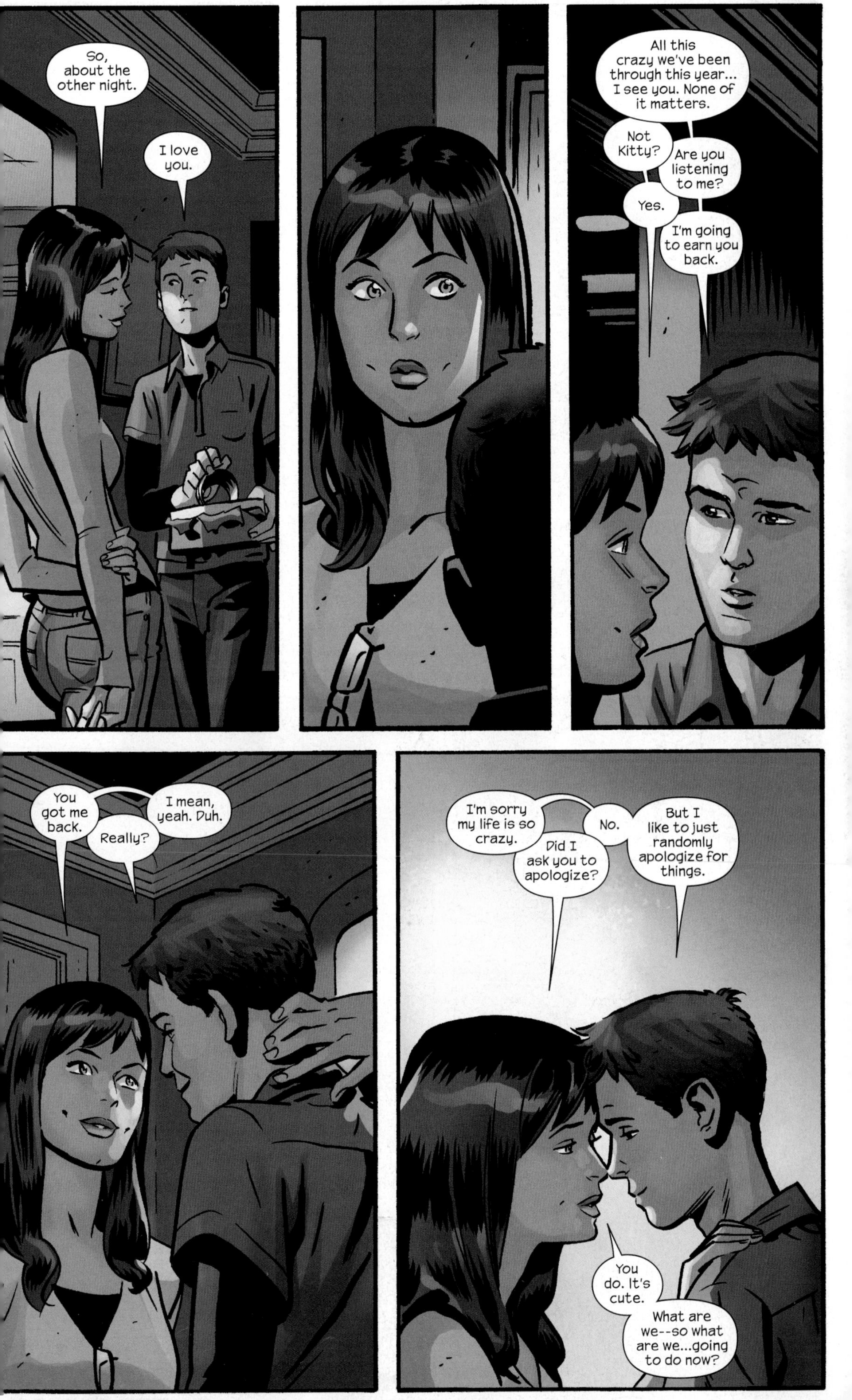
So, about the other night.
I love you.
All this crazy we've been through this year... I see you. None of it matters.
Not Kitty?
Are you listening to me?
Yes.
I'm going to earn you back.
You got me back.
Really?
I mean, yeah. Duh.
I'm sorry my life is so crazy.
Did I ask you to apologize?
No.
But I like to just randomly apologize for things.
You do. It's cute.
What are we--so what are we...going to do now?

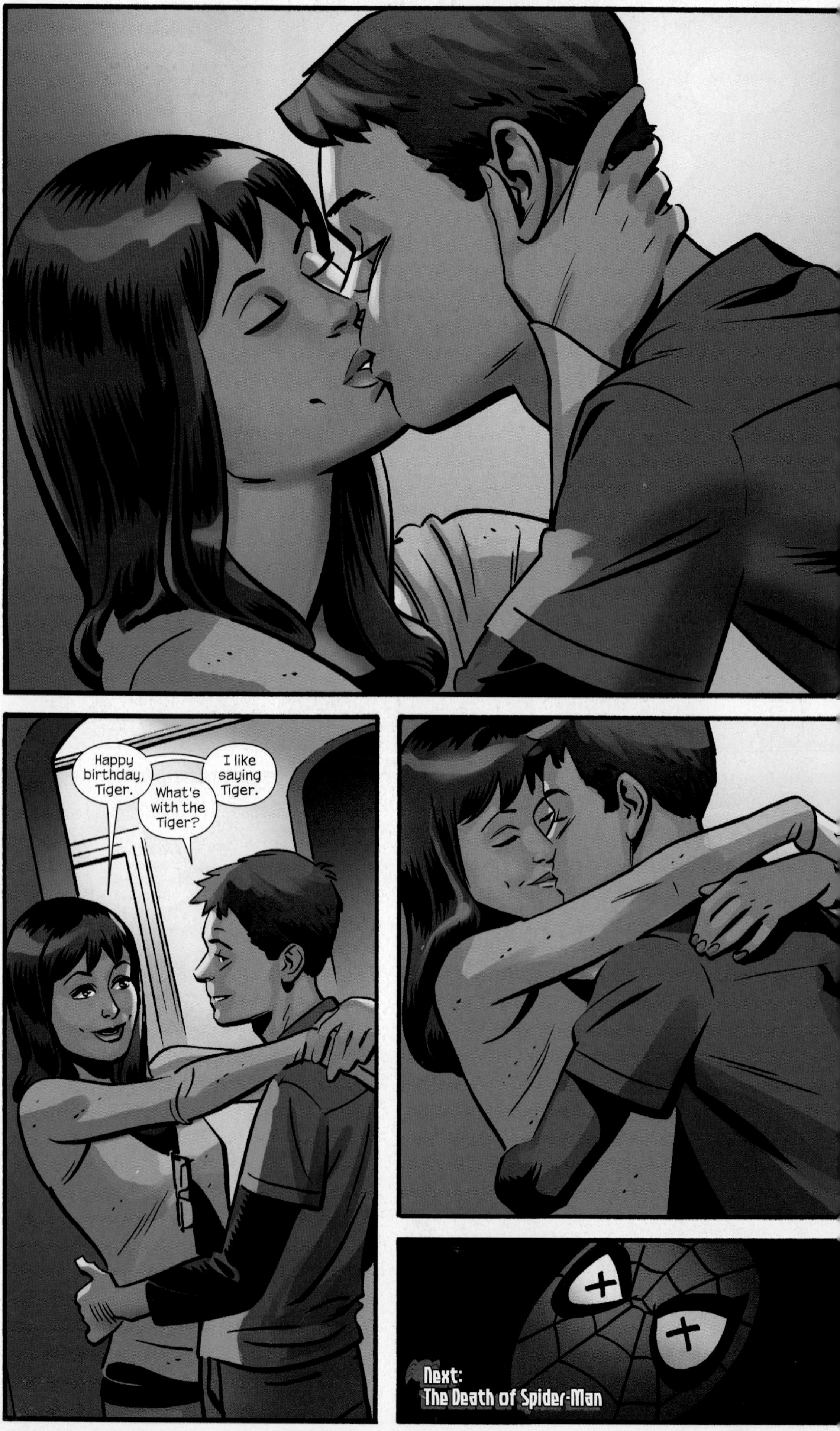
Happy birthday, Tiger.
What's with the Tiger?
I like saying Tiger.
Next:
The Death of Spider-Man

#150 VARIANT

BY J. SCOTT CAMPBELL & JUSTIN PONSOR

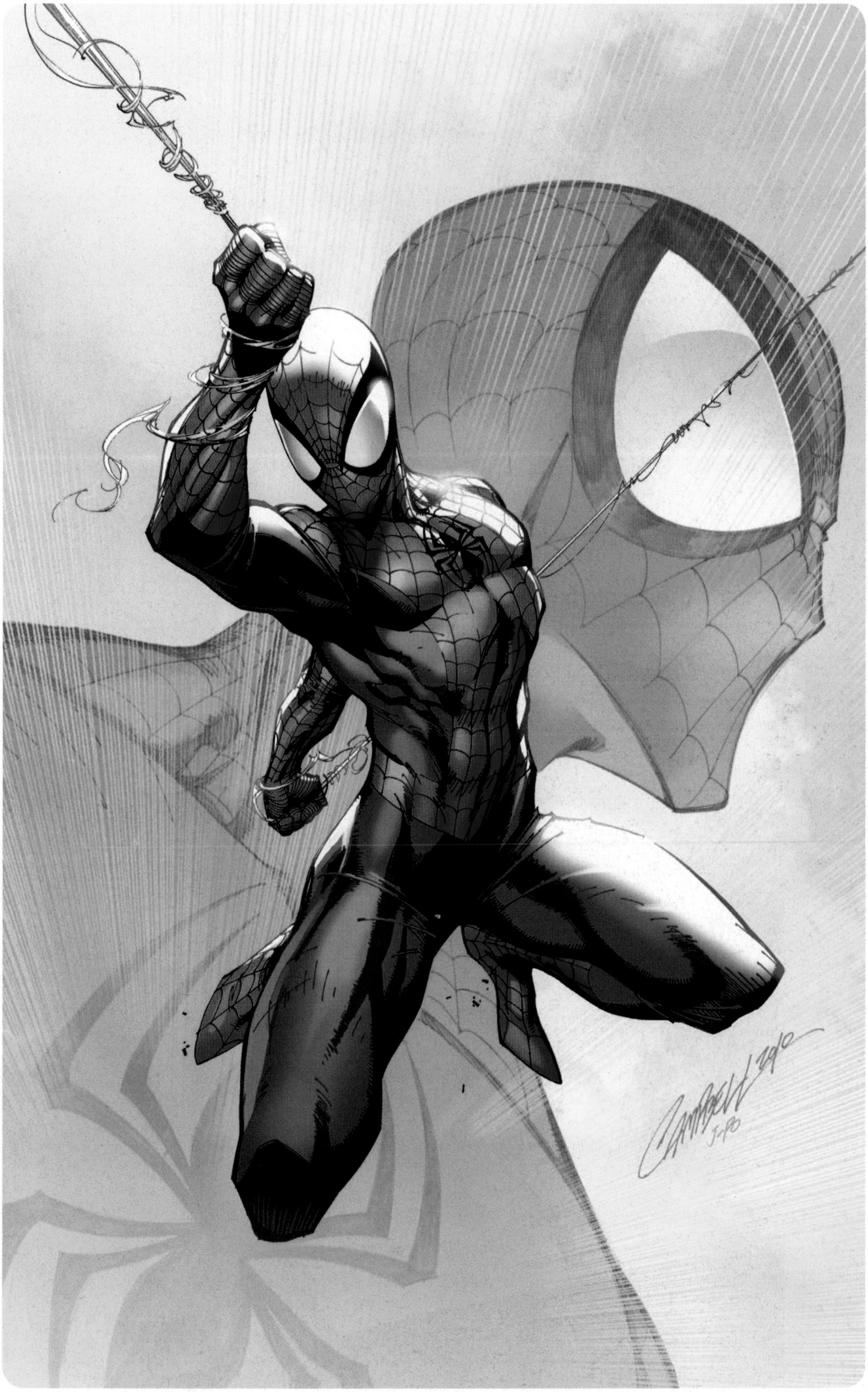

#150 VARIANT
BY MARK BAGLEY, SCOTT HANNA & PETE PANTAZIS

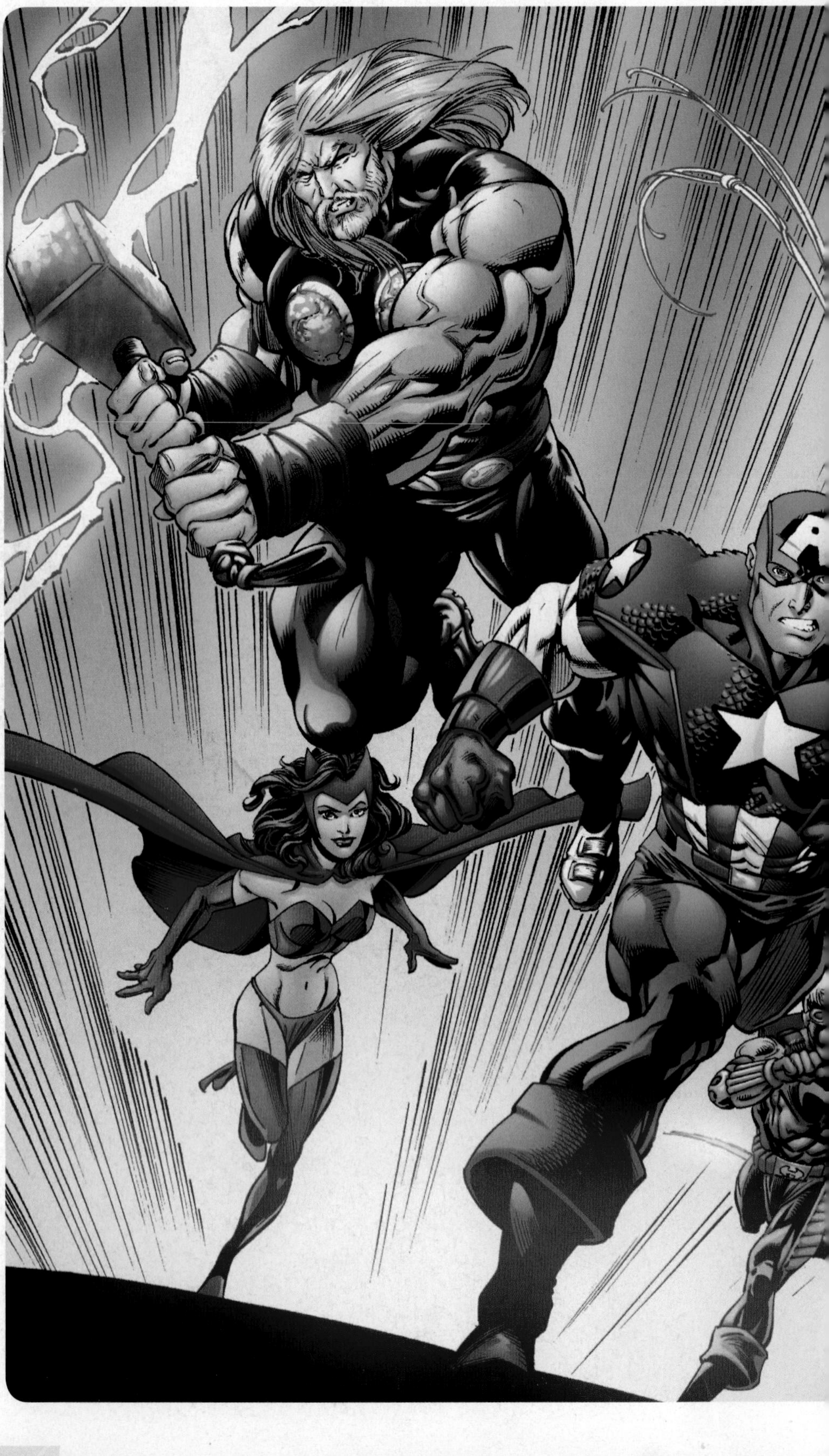

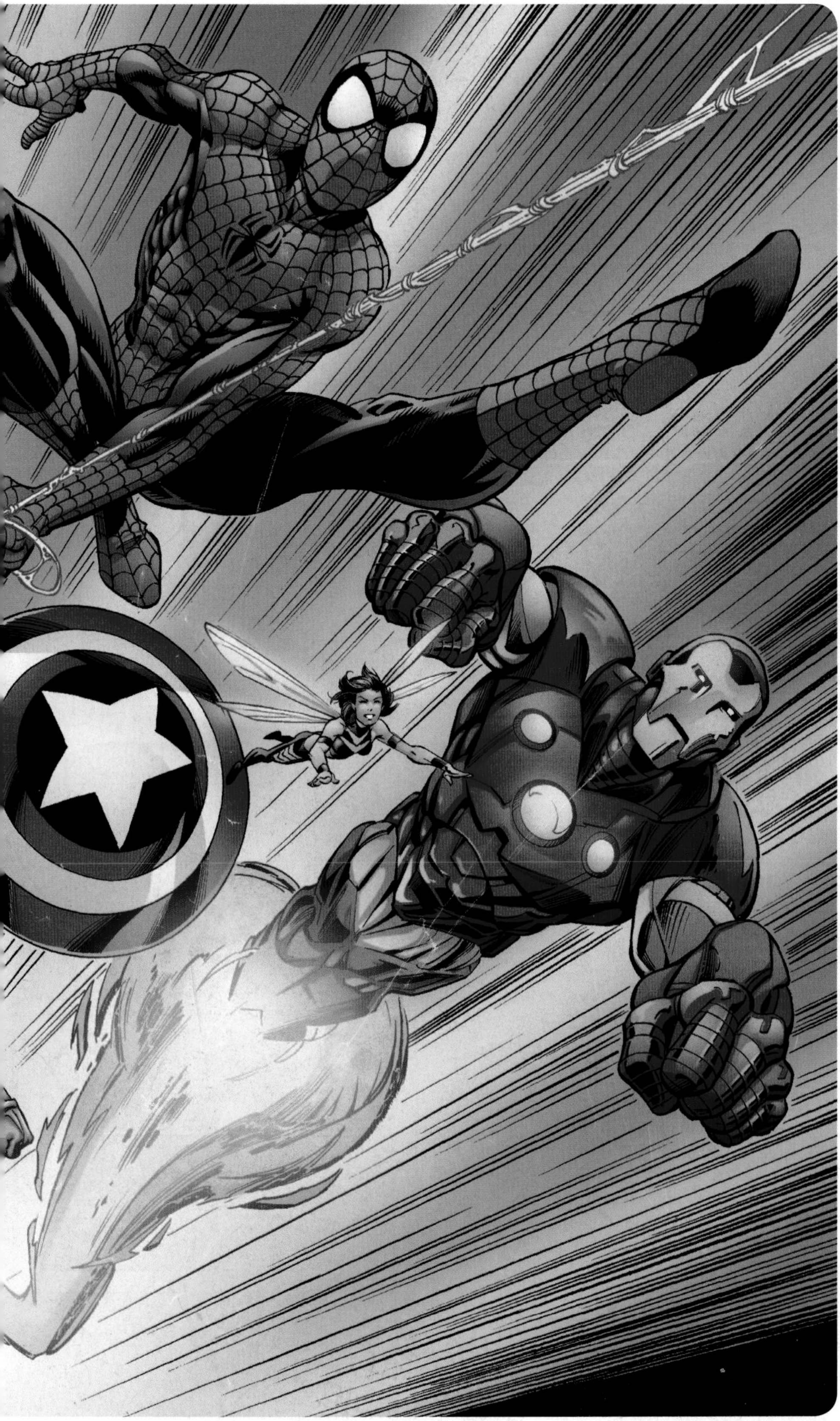

CELEBRATING THE WOMEN of MARVEL®

Throughout 2010, Marvel is proud to shine the spotlight on our rich cast of female super heroes as well as on the women working in comics today. Every month, look to this page for a new interview with one of the top women in comics today.

MARVEL: To kick things off, we need to know, who's your favorite Woman of Marvel?

SARA PICHELLI: Maybe a lot of people expect me to say something "womanly nice" like Pixie, Ms. Marvel, or Susan Storm, but sorry to disappoint because I'm in love with Moonstone. Especially the one from Warren Ellis' story arc of *Thunderbolts*.

MARVEL: How did you get your start in the comics industry?

SP: A small Italian publisher contacted me to do a short story for an anthology, and then I worked as an assistant for David Messina for some issues of *Star Trek*. After this "training," I decided to join the Chesterquest, hoping to be selected!

MARVEL: How did you break into Marvel?

SP: I won the Chesterquest! :)

MARVEL: Can you tell us a little bit about your art background? What made you get into drawing, and comics specifically?

SP: I used to work in the animation business as a storyboard artist and character designer before even thinking about a comic book career. I come from a very small town on the east coast of Italy where there aren't comic book stores. You can find some manga on the newsstand, but honestly, they aren't for me. So when I moved to Rome, my boyfriend showed me for the first time the marvels of the comic book world, and it was love at first sight! This job is amazing because when you get a script — you become a director and an actor all at the same time. You have the power to translate words into images, and that's awesome...but sooner or later, I would like to draw a story written by me! Who knows, we'll see...

MARVEL: Are there characters who you love to draw? Are there some who you haven't had the chance to draw but would love to take a stab at?

SP: Bad girls are my soft spot...Black Widow, Moonstone, Elektra, X-23, Domino...but I have a male character I love so much, and he's Daredevil (because I'm in love with Matt Murdock).

MARVEL: What's it like working on Ultimate Comics Spider-Man as opposed to some of your other work?

SP: That's a difficult question! The biggest difference is that I can feel the weight of the history of the character and all the great artists who drew him before me. So I'm studying a lot to understand the character and his complexity, looking for the best way to give my version of Peter Parker without being a copy of past artists or betraying the essence of the character.

MARVEL: More and more at cons, via e-mail, and even in local comic shops, we've seen an increased interest in females wanting to get involved in the industry. What is your advice for women who want to pursue a career in comics?

SP: My advice is, don't feel as if you are an exception or a stranger in this world, just think that you finally came home.

FEATURING: ARTIST SARA PICHELLI

ULTIMATE SPIDER-MAN